My Life
in the
Cleveland Zoo

A Memoir

maybe i should go to the hospital. When i lay down. I going to sleep. and then your downgrading don't help. So show some more shit on the plate, I'm fucking trying.

Adam A. Smith

My Life in the Cleveland Zoo

A Memoir

10-30. Good B/m

Edited and with an Epilogue by
Rob Smith

Drinian Press/
Huron, Ohio

My Life in the Cleveland Zoo: A Memoir
Smith, Adam A. (1949-2014)

The conversations included in this book are entirely from the author's recollections and do not represent word-for-word transcripts. This book has not been authorized or endorsed by the Cleveland Metroparks Zoo.

2014 Drinian Press Edition, edited and with an epilogue by Smith, Rob 1947-

Cover photo: *Masai Giraffe* by Drinian Press LLC.
Author photo from Adam Smith's archive. A similar photo was used in his article, "The Hippo that (Almost) Devoured Cleveland" which appeared in the September 1987 edition of *Cleveland Magazine.*

Drinian Press LLC
PO Box 63
Huron, Ohio 44839

Online at www.DrinianPress.com.

Library of Congress Control Number: 2014947590

ISBN-10: 0-9833069-9-0

ISBN-13: 978-0-9833069-9-3

Printed in the United States of America

My Life in the Cleveland Zoo
A Memoir

Contents

PROLOGUE

My first trip to the Cleveland Zoo was a family outing in the summer of 1960. The visit was great, but what I really wanted to do was ride on the tour trains which my Dad pronounced *too expensive* at a nickel a stop for each person. Since there were five of us in total, he evoked his usual mantra: "Besides, walking is the best exercise." We walked.

It seemed that we walked for hours. Of course, we went inside the Old Main Zoo Building, which contained the apes, monkeys, hyenas, wolves, and some big cats. I remember a large chimp who was really going berserk in his cage. He romped around like a wild man, swinging on a suspended tire, and crashing into the bars. I also remember the juvenile gorilla. That animal was in a cage in the far end of the building. He was just curled up in a ball in the back corner, and he was the only young gorilla in the zoo at that time.

Not far from the Old Main Building were the giant tortoises. My brother and I sat on the biggest one's back. The hard shell felt like a cool, massive rock. Back then, any kids who came to the Cleveland Zoo could sit on those big tortoises. That was the first time I ever touched a zoo animal. My sister took the photos that day on the family's Kodak Brownie Hawkeye camera. From my point of view, she did not have a steady enough hand to capture good images. I would have liked to take over the responsibility as the documentary photographer, but I was the youngest and my excitement became a bit of an irritation to a family group attempting to press on. Maybe it was the scale of the animals, but I could not get enough of looking at the elephants and giraffes. In a huge barren yard, three hungry elephants were begging peanuts from a crowd of onlookers. Two of those young elephants were named Simba and Tara. I watched for a long time, and would have stayed longer except my father said we needed to get going; there were other things to see.

The only pictures taken of the elephants that day were from a distance and appeared as two dark smudges in the black and white photos. I wanted to take charge of the camera, but that clearly was not going to happen. Later in life, I would shoot a lot of video for advertizing clients, but at eleven, my only option was to give direction to my older sister, who was not entirely open to my ideas of image filmmaking. To the side of the big Pachyderm Building, there were two ponderous hippopotamuses in a big yard. (I didn't know it at the time, but the names of those hippos were

Blackie and Red.) My suggestion to the camera operator was to steady the camera by resting it on the walled enclosure. The rebuff followed the same format as all the previous ones, and the handheld camera created the same blurry results as with the elephants.

That was my introduction to zoo life, and to some of the very animals who would become my business associates.

BOOK I: THE TOUR DRIVER YEARS

To Les Mertus,
who, like the poet Keats,
is forever young

CHAPTER ONE

I was in college in the late sixties and needed to find one of those dreaded *summer jobs*. They were dreaded because they didn't pay well and were pretty much unrelated to the dreams and aspirations of youth. My real goal was to get money, enough money to fund spending for the next school year and to reimburse some of my tuition costs to my father who had just finished putting my sister through college and was now saddled with two sons in school at the same time. My brother and I were both subject to the same contribution formula: eighty percent of our earnings were to go toward tuition, and twenty percent was for spending money during the school year.

The year before, I had worked in a men's shop called *The Captain's Corner*. It was owned by a neighbor and I remember those days as being itchy, mostly because it was my job to put price tags on woolen sweaters, vacuum up pins, and paint sidewalks. Even more distressing was that the job paid only minimum wage which, at that time, was a dollar an hour. This year, I would try to do better.

My job search began with the Cleveland Yellow Pages. I browsed through the categories of businesses and didn't see anything I liked until I got to the T's. There I saw an ad for a tire store. So I called them. A guy answered the phone. I said I was a college student home for the summer and I needed a job.

"Doing what?" the man asked.

"I was thinking, like, maybe, putting tires on cars."

"Have you ever taken tires off a rim or mounted tires on a rim before?"

"Well, sure, lots of times."

"How did you do that?"

"With big screwdrivers. By hand." I thought that would impress him. To break the old tire off the rim, I would lower the frame of our family's travel trailer onto the tire with a jack. I could take tires off a rim and put the new tire on with no equipment.

He asked, "Have you ever used a tire-changing machine?"

"No."

"Well, we'd rather have someone with experience."

The guy hung up.

I was thinking, *How hard can it be to use a machine?* On the positive side, however, is the fact that if the man had offered me a job, the name of this book would be *My Life as a Tire Puller.*

So I kept turning the pages in the phone book and didn't see anything that looked hopeful. On the last page, left hand side, were all the businesses that began with Z. There was only one. Under the heading *Zoological Parks* it said: *Cleveland Zoo/Brookside Park*. And there was a phone number. I would not have called if there had been another page to turn, but there wasn't. This was my last option, so I picked up the phone.

I spoke to the receptionist, I guess. "Hello, I'm a college student home on break. Is the zoo hiring anyone for the summer?"

"A college student, you say? Just a moment. I'll let you talk to our Comptroller, Mr. Huhtala."

After a minute, a no-nonsense man with a European accent came on the line. His name was Eugene Huhtala.

"Sir," I said, "I'm a college student home for the summer…"

"A college student, you say?" he blurted enthusiastically. "Do you have a driver's license?" When I said that I did, the interview went further. "Can you drive a stick shift?" Truth was that it had been a while, but that was part of my driver's education class n high school.

"What college do you go to?"

"Westminster College."

"Huh?"

"It's a small, liberal arts college in Pennsylvania."

"Ah. So you don't go to Ohio State?" He actually asked that question, and it took me by surprise. "That is good. Good. Well, you should come down to see me tomorrow at the zoo. Do you know where it is?"

"Yes, Sir. Brookside Park." (Actually, I had no idea where the zoo was. My childhood visit had been years earlier, and I didn't drive then.)

"I am in the Administration Building. That's on the Fulton Parkway side, upper level. Ten o'clock tomorrow, in the morning. Write this down: Gene Huhtala. Okay?" (I had not met this man, but he was a lot nicer to me than the guy with the tires.) "Now I am going to let you talk to my secretary. Okay? Stay on the line."

I thanked him and the woman who had first answered came back on the line. "Hello, this is Leona…" She confirmed the appointment for 10:00 a.m. the next day. I told her I would be there.

"Do you know where the zoo is?" Leona asked.

"Oh, sure. I've been there lots of times." (Part of my answer was actually true, but knowing where it was, that was a bit of a stretch. I didn't want to be any trouble.)

"You'll want to come to Entrance Number 3. That's in the upper level. Not the main entrance down below on Brookside Park Drive. When you come in, tell the woman who sells tickets you have an appointment with Mr. Huhtala."

I wrote down his name, and spelled it *Hootally*.

Leona said, "The woman in the booth will tell you how to get to the Administration Building. Walk through the front lobby. The offices are in the back."

After the call, I went down to kitchen and asked Dad, "Where's the zoo?"

He knew where it was and drew me a map. My stepmother overheard the conversation and added, "Wear good dress pants, and I will iron your nice white dress shirt. Wear your black church shoes. And don't chew gum, and say 'Sir' in every sentence. Sit up straight and speak in short sentences with quick answers, right to the point."

Normally, I would have had to listen to a second verse to this old tune– the one about getting a haircut– but the barber back in New Wilmington where I went to college had an aversion to students. In his idiomatic dictionary, "Don't take very much off" meant *buzz-cut*. The result was mortifying to a Beatles fan, but did spare me a second parental lecture.

While I usually did my own laundry, that evening my stepmother ironed my *church clothes* and hung them on the wrought iron railing at the bottom of the stairs leading up to my room. Things were looking up. I was probably going to live.

The next day I borrowed my sister's yellow 1967 Plymouth Valiant and drove to the zoo. I drove in at the upper entrance on Fulton Parkway. The parking attendant, a woman in her forties, let me in with no ticket. (If you ever want to get in anywhere free, just tell them you have a job interview and that your name is *Mary*. That's a common name in Cleveland, and the odds are that they are expecting a *Mary* pretty soon.) Anyway, the smiling woman pointed me toward the right building; I walked along a little curving sidewalk to reach it. On either side of the entrance to the building were two large limestone polar bears, sitting like circus bears on their knees. I opened the glass door and went into a large open space with great windows and a high vaulted ceiling. That room was very *echoey*, (sorry, but I had to make up words, like *echoey* or *sewery* as I wrote this book.) My hard-soled church shoes echoed as I made my way toward the back and through another door marked: *Offices*. I was now moving along a narrow corridor, and there was a gun case on the wall to the right. Inside, under lock, was a menacing rifle. It was the kind of rifle a big game hunter might carry. Further ahead on the right was a counter with little windows, like teller windows in a bank. Through it, I could see several women at work. One of them, an athletic-looking blonde woman about twenty-five years old, looked up and said, "Hi, I'm Leona. Are you Adam?"

After I answered, she came out to greet me and I followed as she led me along the corridor toward Gene Huhtala's office. "Go ahead in. Mr. Huhtala will interview you," she said.

In the room was a slight, older man sitting behind a desk covered in papers.

"Sit down, please. I'm Gene Huhtala."

"Thank you, Sir." (I said with no gum in my mouth and nice shoes.)

I took a seat and nervously began to answer questions which came rapidly. Mr. Huhtala was about fifty years old, with a hooked nose and gold-rimmed bifocals. His snow-white hair was combed straight back.

Of course, I called him "Mr. Huhtala."

We talked briefly about my college, my major, etc. Then he asked me point blank if I was *a good boy* and if I had ever been in trouble. This, I am sure, made me smile at the comical absurdity of such an idea. At that time in my life, I was a very good boy.

"Well," he said, "I need a tour train driver. You said you drive a stick shift?"

That, apparently was all the credentials I needed. I was in.

Mr. Huhtala continued in his businesslike manner. "All right. It pays three dollars an hour. But, before you do *anything*, you have to sign up with the union, the Teamsters." Very sternly and shaking his finger at me to make a point, he said, "I don't want you *touching* the train or doing *anything* unless you're signed up with the union, do you understand?"

"Yes, Sir."

"Because I've had trouble with them before and I don't want any more trouble with them."

Then he handed me a card with the name of some union guy, and it had the Teamsters' Local 507 address on it. It was down on East 19th Street. He told me to go there right away, that day, and start work the next day, which was a Saturday.

As I stood up to leave, Mr. Huhtala warmly shook my hand. With his Old World accent he said, "You know, Adam, we get all kinds of kids coming in here asking for this tour train driver job, but I wanted to hire a college fellow, and you are the first college boy who came in here with a nice, good haircut. All the rest have that shaggy long hair, and I don't want that. So good. Good. Welcome. Welcome."

That's how I became a zoo tour train driver in the spring of 1968. And I wouldn't get another haircut for four years.

CHAPTER TWO

Before I could start at the zoo, I had to join the Teamsters Local 507. In those days, Cleveland Zoo workers were all Teamsters. According to the true believers, there were no *filthy scabs* at our place of employment. During this time period, the Teamsters were extremely powerful in Cleveland. When I went downtown to sign up, Harold Friedman was the local President, and Jackie Presser was Secretary-Treasurer of Local 507. It hadn't been too many years since Jimmy Hoffa organized virtually all over-the-road truck drivers in North America into the Teamsters. At that time their power was legendary. I'll admit that I was proud and excited because I knew I'd be carrying a Teamsters' card in my wallet. I also knew that the union was behind the wheel if a nineteen-year-old kid like me could earn well over the minimum wage.

Once again, I borrowed my sister's Valiant and drove to the Union Building on the near East Side. The sign outside the headquarters said: "Bakers Local #19. Teamsters Local #507." Inside, everything was done through bars. It was a strange set-up in this older building which at first seemed to be an open expanse of wooden floor. The room was maybe forty feet by twenty-five, with nothing in it. Five feet inside the door was a barrier of metal bars with openings through the bars like a teller's cage in an old bank. It reminded me of an old western movie set. Beyond the cage wall, I could look across the width of the room and see that there was a wooden door in the center of the far wall. It didn't take a genius to realize that this whole place was fortified against intruders who would have more sinister things on their minds than I did. The place seemed deserted, but there was a little buzzer on the ledge of the teller's window. So I pushed the buzzer and waited. I imagined two dozen eyes were looking at me from peepholes, trying to figure out what sort of threat I might be. But I was only a skinny, fresh-faced nineteen-year-old in a white shirt, tie, and church shoes.

After a few minutes the wooden door opened, and the most beautiful woman I'd ever seen came out the door and closed it behind her. Her face was expressionless as she walked toward the teller window. It was a walk of about thirty-five feet. Wow, she was a good looking, slender brunette. She took a position behind the teller's window.

"Yes?" she said, very understated.

I told her I was there to sign up for the union. She said nothing. She simply turned around and walked away. She walked across the wooden floor and back into the other room. A few more minutes passed, and she came back out. Two huge men came out behind her. They looked like mobsters, or what I imagined mobsters to be. She walked back to the teller's window. They stood on either side of her, about five feet behind her with their arms crossed, looking very tough. They were barrel-chested and powerfully built although smartly dressed in suit coats, black shirts, white ties, and brogue-style leather dress shoes. They didn't say a word. The young woman had some forms, maybe two sheets of paper. She filled them out, as I answered questions: "Name?" "Address?" "Date of birth?"

The whole time this was taking place, the two men were glaring at me as if they suspected that I had to be more than I appeared. Little did they know that secretly I was a writer and this would be something to one day write about. I tried to take in everything, even the strong cologne which hovered around them like some chemical barrier. I could see the lumps under their suit coats near their left armpits. They were packing rods in case they had any trouble with me. I weighed a hundred and forty-nine pounds, but I was packing a black tube of ChapStick lip balm. Still, I was glad I was signing up with them, and I knew I would never be some filthy scab who might have to face them along some picket line. On the other hand, maybe they were fearful of my charm if I were left alone with this beautiful woman who was now ascertaining all my contact information. That would be my preference for justifying their staunch regard. Then again, I do tend to have an active imagination.

I needed no imagination with regard to the woman who worked efficiently as I tried to catch glimpses of her downcast eyes, which for some reason would look nowhere else than at what she was writing. I watched her pen moving across the papers. I can still see her eyelids, brushed in a purple-hued eyeshadow. The two men, wide as doors, just stood staring at me. I sensed that without looking at them. I could hear her pen scratching on the paper. It was like one of those uncomfortable dinners where, in the awkward silence, you can hear people chewing. She wrote as quickly as possible. I remained utterly humorless and unfriendly to her so that no one would beat the living snot out of me. The woman was like a prisoner, I thought. But, then again, I may have been wrong about that. She might have been very happy. When she had filled out the forms, she slid them under the bars, and said, "Sign here."

So I signed the forms. Then she took them without speaking. She and the two men walked out of the room. I missed her when she was gone. After what seemed like forever, the two men came out the door, but stayed across the room, standing on either side of the door. I probably had used the ChapStick when they were gone, and maybe they saw that through a peephole. So they came out, but stayed far away. They had their arms crossed and watched me closely, staring me down from a distance. The pretty woman emerged between them and walked solemnly across the wooden floor, head slightly down. In her right hand, she had a temporary, typed union card with my name on it. She didn't say a word as she slid the card out the teller window. Then she just turned and walked away.

"Thank you," I said very low-key, and then I left. I was a nervous wreck, but an official nervous wreck. I was signed up with the Teamsters Local 507. My career as a Cleveland Zoo tour train driver had begun.

The next day I reported to Mr. Huhtala who immediately asked, "Are you signed on with the union?" He seemed a bit apprehensive. "Let me see your card."

I showed him the temporary card and he said, "Good. Good," and was very pleased. Eventually, the union mailed me a plastic card, which I still have.

Mr. Huhtala said, "Okay. We want you to start driving today. The trains start running at ten." After that, he directed me to park my car (my sister's car, actually) down on a lower level. He also provided detailed instructions: "You must drive very slowly because there are visitors in the zoo, many with children. Just drive all the way down the hill and turn left the first chance you see, before the Children's Farm. There's a big red barn. Turn left before the barn, then keep driving, just follow the road, and you'll pass Monkey Island on the right. Keep going and just before the river is the garage. Right under the big bridge. Ask for Whitey. Whitey will give you a train to drive. He'll tell you everything. I phoned him and told him you are coming."

Then he handed me a single-spaced, five-page document. "Now here, here is your speech to tell while you give the tours. Take it home tonight and learn it for tomorrow. I don't expect you to learn it today."

"Okay. Thank you."

"Yes, yes, get going."

The happiest times of my life had just begun.

I drove down to the lower level of the zoo with only the vaguest recollection of the directions Mr. Huhtala had given me. I remembered *red barn, Monkey Island,* and *garage.* But it was really cool. I was driving a car inside the zoo. That was very dangerous since there were families and children in there. At that time, temporary zoo summer workers were allowed to drive inside the grounds to get to their stations to start the day. Now I was one of them, but had no idea where I was going. I drove around for about ten minutes, endangering babies and old nuns, and was completely lost. What threw me off was that I never saw a garage. But finally, I looked over to my right and saw about eighty scrawny monkey-like creatures sitting up on a big gray hill made of concrete. I figured that was Monkey Island. I was finally on the right road.

I drove past that, then past a bunch of big buffalo-like things and some weird large deer with long straight horns and some zebras, but I still didn't see a mechanic's garage. There was a meandering creek on the left. It was a shallow creek, sunk down below the lay of the land. The creek was orange with pollution, like a filthy soda. Not wanting to get more lost than I was, I parked the car on the side of the road and got out. The morning was bright and sunny. The air was cool and sweet.

Pretty soon I saw a zoo worker in his light brown shirt and dark brown pants. Why they decided that zoo workers, and especially animal keepers, should be issued brown clothing eventually became obvious. This employee looked a little like Curly Howard, one of *The Three Stooges* who says "nyuk nyuk." He had a canvas sack and a wooden stick with a pointy nail on it. He was poking papers and litter, even cigarette butts, and putting the trash into the sack with great speed and efficiency. The worker had a big gut and close-cropped hair, just like Curly. He even wore hard shoes like Curly.

"Excuse me," I said, "Mr. Huhtala just hired me as a tour train driver. Do you know where the garage is, where they keep the tour trains?"

The man became very animated and gestured wildly in every direction. He spoke loudly saying, "Oo ya ooo ya eeyoooo, a ee yooo." This was followed by "Da wheet wheet doo flibberruba."

The gibberish was delivered with great emphasis, and his face contorted when he talked.

I tried again. "Do you know a guy named 'Whitey'? Do you know where Whitey is?"

The zoo worker's face lit up with recognition as he said, "Buuu buh boh-whay." Then with great certainty, he added, "Ooo, weee, staj a abble sterb."

"Thank you. "Thanks," I said trying to leave the area as gracefully as I could. I started walking, but evidently in the wrong direction because I had gone no more than twenty feet before I heard a booming, "Ooo eaugh. Bueah. Yooo-Ooo. Eaugh."

So I made the *okay* sign, and he nodded vigorously.

Then I turned around and started walking back the other direction, quite aimlessly, heading along the fence near the big buffalo-like things that weren't buffalo.

The man yelled, "Myuuh myuhhh."

You have to understand how young I was. I was just a freshman in college, and this was an experience that went beyond anything I had known before. As it turned out, I had just met a man who some referred to as *The Dummy*. In fact, he was not dumb in terms of intelligence. He was a deaf-mute and a very faithful employee. I never did learn the guy's name, and eventually I would work around him for nine years and begin to understand some of his more unique forms of communication. On the first day, however, asking him for directions was a bit unnerving.

Suddenly, like a dragon roaring out of a woods, a tour train came clanking and speeding from behind a clump of trees under the bridge. It just appeared out of nowhere really fast. It zoomed right past me, and I felt the wind from it. Dust and little rocks flew out from behind the huge drive wheels of the cab. Rattling behind the cab were three passenger cars, each with two facing seats in the center and seats facing forward and back.

These cars bounced and shimmied every which way. It sounded as if twenty people were beating on garbage cans with rocks. The cab and the cars were painted a deep blue and trimmed in white. The   train   roared straight away toward Big Creek like the guy was going to drive right into the water. Then abruptly, he hung a big skidding doughnut to the left. The careening, sixty-foot-long train made a hard, counterclockwise turn off the road, ripping up black soil and turf. When the train came back toward me, I jumped backward about three feet as it zoomed back in the direction from which it had come. Unexpectedly, the cab skidded to a noisy, gravel-spewing stop right in front of me. The driver hadn't come out looking for me. He had just driven out into the open to turn the train around when he looked over and spotted a lost teenager standing next to *The Dummy*.

This enormous tour train had a cab with a huge flathead 8-cylinder engine. The sides of the big hood were open, and the tractor-style engine was in plain view. The driver was an older guy about fifty-five years old. He was wearing a dirty red ball cap, the bill of which was filthy with engine grease, smeared in the shape of fingers. His sweat-soaked cap had an emblem on the front that said something like, *Ajax Car Parts*. He pulled off his cap and wiped the sweat off his forehead with a red bandana, revealing a head that was bald except for a snow-white fringe around the edges.

He stuffed the bandana down into his shirt pocket and put his filthy cap back on his head.

"Hey," he said, "Are you the new kid who's gonna drive the trains?"

"Yes."

"I'm Whitey. I'm the head garage mechanic. Get on," he said, gesturing toward the train. I hopped up into the first car. Before I was properly seated, Whitey roared the huge engine, shifted the cab's big gears, and peeled out. I was bounced down onto the seat, heaved back against the padded blue vinyl covering. Immediately, Whitey took me on a very rough ride of only about eighty feet. I had a hard time staying on the slippery vinyl seat. We approached a battered, steel building directly under the Fulton Road Bridge. Big Creek was straight ahead of us down in a wide stone canal. Suddenly, Whitey slammed on the brakes and stopped the train from the speed of forty mph to zero in about six feet. As the train crunched to a stop, all the cars' hitches slammed together, and I held on for dear life.

"All right," said Whitey. "Get up here. Come on."

I climbed up from the front passenger car and sat on the hard metal plate that formed the deck of the cab. I was right next to Whitey. He was in the driver's seat, a black vinyl seat no bigger than a skinny man's butt.

Before setting the vehicle into motion, Whitey turned to me and said,

"You know how to drive a stick, right?"

"Yes," I said. "I learned how to do it in driver's ed…"

"Yeah, okay. Good. Well, this is just like that, except you gotta double clutch her, ya see? Watch this. I go to shift, and I push the clutch down once, and then again, and then I shift. Otherwise it's just the same as a car. You have four gears. Always start in first gear. You know where that is?"

"Yeah, upper left of the *H*".

"Right. Never start up in second gear. Don't be lazy. You have four gears, but you'll drive around in gear 3 when you have people on the train. Don't drive fast. Don't ever drive fast."

That struck me as humorous having just experienced what could only be described as a tour train driven by a wild man. What he meant was, "Don't drive really fast when there are people on the train."

Whitey said, "And never do any power shifting. Do you know what I mean? I don't want you getting in first gear and then power shift right into third gear. Never leave out second gear. When you power shift, you'll end up grinding the gears. That will ruin the transmission."

"Okay," I said. (In reality, in just a few hours, I'd learn that power shifting was easy and great.)

Then Whitey showed me the microphone, which was hung on the side of a homemade aluminum box that contained an amplifier. It was clearly outdated technology with vacuum tubes from a 1940's style radio and a microphone from a trucker's CB.

He said, "So you turn this dial on, and this is also the volume, and then you just hold in this button on the microphone to talk."

Whitey was assertive when he gave me instructions, but he wasn't a public speaker. When he held the microphone up to his mouth to talk, he was suddenly shy and awkward as if the whole idea of speaking into a microphone was alien to him.

"Hello, hello, hello. Testing One Two. Testing One Two." The fact was that, though he was speaking in low tones, the reverberating voice which came from the speakers behind us was loud. Each car had its own speaker, and I couldn't wait to start talking into that microphone myself. I would have a real audience for what could become a lounge act.

Whitey pulled the train over and parked it next to some other trains near the fence, which enclosed the yaks. We got down out of the cab and he said: "You just sit here and wait. We're going to be running all five trains today. Some of the older drivers will start arriving in a few minutes, and they'll tell you what to do next."

It was then that I noticed a line of five trains lined up, all pointing in the same direction and ready for a new day. At that time, Cleveland Zoo tour trains were painted blue. Calling them *trains* was really a misnomer since they didn't ride on a track. They were actually trams with inflated air tires, and the cab's back tires were bigger than those in the front. On the sides of the engine were vents on hinges which could be opened for air circulation on hot days.

I sat down on a dusty vinyl seat on one of the trains and waited. It was a pleasant spot under the trees, and a yak was grazing just a few yards away. I originally thought it was a buffalo, but I clearly saw a sign on the fence that said, *Yak*. The animal had a long shaggy coat. Other, smaller yaks were in the same pen. Each one had its head down in the tall grass of their paddock. A yak's life seemed pretty easy.

Sitting there next to the fence, I could see out onto John Nagy Boulevard, and every once in a while a car sped over the Fulton Road Bridge. The passage of the car overhead created impressive echoes in the valley where I waited. Eventually, two other drivers came. These were men, possibly in their midthirties, both high-school teachers from Brecksville, if I recall. One guy was a jovial and imposing man named Ron Marec. He had short black hair and a slightly receding hairline and stood about six-foot-two. The other guy's was Jack Hrbac. (A lot of people in Cleveland have surnames that seem a little short of vowels.) Jack had an obvious limp and couldn't bend his right leg. Though I never learned the extent of his injury, I knew that he had been wounded in the Korean War. Jack was stocky and powerfully built, like an football nose-guard. In time, I'd learn that he was also a football coach at Brecksville High.

Personality-wise, the two were quite different. Ron liked to laugh and was always talkative while Jack seldom spoke. His facial expressions, however, showed that he was quietly amused by things other people said. He didn't even mind when Ron sometimes spoke on his behalf. Ron would say something like, "Jack won't eat at the refreshment stands" even though Jack was sitting right there. When the two introduced themselves, Ron's outgoing personality immediately made me feel comfortable.

Holding the script Gene Huhtala had given me, I said, "I guess I have to learn this speech tonight."

Ron just rolled his head back and laughed.

"The famous speech. It's full of errors and otherwise superficial. The first time I saw it I took it home and after dinner I read it and laughed my ass off. It's a colorful collection of fact and fantasy. Just remember no one is really listening. But you could learn it. It's probably ninety percnt correct, wouldn't you say so, Jack?"

"Maybe ninety-two percent," said the laconic Jack.

Ron grabbed the speech from me and read the first few lines. He read something like, "The Cleveland Zoo began as a deer park located on the east side of Cleveland in the area known as Wade Park. After a few years, the zoo moved to its current location on Cleveland's west side, in

Brookside Park, between West 25th Street and Fulton Parkway."

The big man erupted in laughter and said, "Think about that. It's pretty goofy to be driving people around on a train in the zoo and tell them where the zoo is located. You'd think they'd have that figured out since they're already here. My wife and I laughed about that for ten minutes, but there's another sentence in there that says the zoo has tour trains. Wait till you read that one. A guy's going to be sitting on the train, and you're telling him the zoo has tour trains. That's great information."

Ron laughed at his own narration, and Jack was quietly smiling.

Ron was right. While the zoo speech had some peculiar or erroneous information, it was also poorly written. Nevertheless, I'd told Gene Huhtala I would learn the speech; and I intended to learn it that night.

"Well, we've got a little time to wait," said Ron cheerfully. "We don't head out until around 10:00. Did you pick out a train?"

"No."

Once more Ron laughed heartily and said, "Oh, you blew it. You were here first and you could have picked any train you wanted. Since you didn't choose, I've got dibs on Number 3. They're not all the same, you know. Number 3 is the fastest. Number 6, the lovely *Cinderella*, is the slowest."

Ron looked over at Jack sardonically. Jack smiled ever so slightly.

Ron said, "I'm just kidding. Jack likes *Cinderella*. Don't you, Jack? Of course, he's nuts, but don't worry, all the trains are fine."

I said, "But there are only five trains. Why is one of them called Number 6?"

Ron laughed, "Hey, Hrbac, this guy has too much brains to be a tour driver. Fact is, Number 5 is out for repairs. Whitey will get it fixed. It's in the garage in a million pieces. Whitey's had it apart since caveman days." Ron threw back his head and laughed again. "So *Cinderella*, Number 6, is the slowest and drives like a tank. It's hotter than hell in there in the summer. But naturally, that's the train Jack likes."

Jack said, "*Cinderella's* okay. I'll take *Cinderella* every time."

Ron exclaimed, "She's a torture chamber. Like being in a German U-boat."

All of Ron's jabbering was good-natured, and I was just a kid to these middle-aged school teachers. At that point, Ron took me under his wing. He showed me how to clean the train I would be using, and how to wipe the seats and sides with coarse yellow sponges. Afterward, he looked at his watch. "We still have some time," he said. "Come on, we'll get you a shirt."

Ron and I walked toward the Old Main Zoo Building, which at that time housed the cats and apes. It was far enough away from where we were that it would have been much faster to take one of our cars, but the rule was that driving through the zoo was prohibited once we had parked. So the entire journey gave Marec a chance to begin my orientation.

We walked past the yak, ostrich, Bactrian camel, American bison, Grant's zebra, eland, and guanaco paddocks. Of course, at that time, I had no idea what half these hoofed animals were. The walk took us past Monkey Island with its dismal and mangy inhabitants malingering near the water's edge. At the end of Monkey Island was a refreshment stand. Already, some cute teenage girls were hosing off the sidewalk in front of the stand, getting ready for a day of selling Dots candy, popcorn, hot dogs, and Cokes. It should be remembered that I was a young college guy and far more interested in the women than the mangy monkeys. They wore tight white dresses (the girls, not the monkeys), sometimes with a little button cardigan over the top. I can still see them laughing and joking as they began their workday.

I always enjoyed mornings at the Cleveland Zoo. The zoo's landscapers had ornate seas of flowers planted near the front of the Cat and Ape Building and in front of Monkey Island. The flowers were red and white and arrayed in vast beds. The green canopy of the mammoth trees near the Cat and Ape Building shaded the walkway beneath.

A shortcut behind the refreshment stand took Ron and me toward the western end of a building which was constructed of a dark, almost purple, brick which was moss-covered in places. The bricks' coloration came from decades of exposure to Cleveland's harsh climate. To the left was a little, shallow *fish pond* with several fat alligators lounging in their eternal coma.

Around the back of the building, we walked into sunlight and breezes with the scents of fish, wet pavement, fresh fruit, willow trees, truck exhaust, cigar smoke, cigarettes, hay, raw meat, and chlorine all mixed together and tingeing the air. We had walked into a vibrant marketplace which was just awakening for the day. Old flatbed trucks roared in and out. Cars arrived with men jumping out, slamming the doors loudly, and shouting.

In total, about twenty men scurried over a large area of concrete, shouting, laughing, and whooping inexplicably. Each man wore a light brown shirt and dark brown pants. They wore dirty old ball caps as they moved about to the endless sounds of leather soles on asphalt.

Every face seemed happy and alive as they shouted back and forth.

"Hoi. Hoi." "Look out." "Get outa me way, Jocko." "Box o' cabbage comin' in." "Hey. That's mine."

The shouting was good-natured, playful, often unnecessary. Some grins revealed teeth missing with the remaining teeth colored like caramel. The crews were giddy with the joy of work, and mornings at the zoo had the energy of a busy street market.

From the backs of flatbed trucks, men were throwing off wooden crates filled with cabbages or lettuce. Heavy cartons of frozen fish flew everywhere. The sound of those frozen blocks smacking down onto asphalt was constant. Near the old brick archway that led into the back center of the building, several men were ripping open wooden crates of produce or cutting open cardboard boxes with switchblades. It was the daily ritual of dividing the stores of bread, fish, and fresh produce into lots.

Near the center of the asphalt behind the building were several red plastic coolers into which other men dumped frozen blocks of fish with a distinctive *whump*. To thaw the fish, a man with a cigarette dangling from his lips jammed a hose down into a cooler and let the water run. Soon the cooler was overflowing with water pouring over the edge in an icy cascade. From time to time, the guy with the cigarette grabbed the end of the hose up out of one cooler and stuck it down into another. He was rotating the flow of water into the various coolers to keep all the fish thawing. Water was always running at the Cleveland Zoo.

That bustling outdoor place was the zoo's commissary in those days. It was the point of origin for the animals' breakfasts and dinners. All the supplies came into there, including stale bread loaves, crates of cabbage and lettuce, sacks of oranges and apples, eggplants wrapped in white paper, sacks of sweet potatoes, piles of carrots with the leafy green tops, huge bunches of bananas, and all those fragrant silver smelts and blue mackerels. From there all the stuff went to hoofed animals, bears, monkeys, pachys, sea lions, birds of prey, and every creature large or small.

The men shouted and joked, many with thick Slavic accents. Some yelled in a Cleveland slang, saying *youse* and *gim-me*. It was all new to me, a young college kid, as I watched them lug huge cane baskets overflowing with produce. Some of the scurrying, brown-clad men hoisted boxes and containers onto the back of an old flatbed.

Still joking loudly, a couple of men tilted the chilly coolers to dump off the water. The giant steel-blue mackerels and tiny silver smelt were thawed, or pretty close. And, as if that were a call to action, the heavy, fish-laden red coolers were hoisted onto the back of the flatbed truck along with everything else, and off it went.

When Ron and I reached the back of the Old Main Building, we walked through the open back door and descended a stairway into a moist, cave-like cellar. The place smelled old and musty, accented by the dank odors of urine, fur, moist feces, and body oil. I heard echoes of the faraway whooping of monkeys. We stepped down a few worn concrete stairs and turned right into a corridor of cinderblock walls. The ceilings were very low. Ron had to crouch down as he walked. The old, tomblike place had been built by men of smaller stature. Overall, the basement smelled like an old well full of algae.

In the middle of one section of cinderblock wall was a hole about one foot square. Ron called through the opening to an odd, nervous little guy who looked like an old jockey. His eyes bugged out like the eyes of a trout. The nervous fellow appeared to be getting the zoo's laundry sorted. He hurried around amid knee-high piles of starchy laundered shirts, pants, towels, red mechanics' work cloths, blankets, and neatly folded towels. Everything was stacked on the light gray concrete floor, and that room smelled like starch and bleach. The little man probably weighed one hundred twenty pounds and stood around five foot one. As he moved stacks of clean, folded laundry, a cigarette hung from his mouth. His hands were gnarled and bony. Heeding Ron's call, the little man grinned and popped out through the hole in the wall like he was the doorkeeper in Oz.

"Hello," bellowed Ron to the man. "This kid needs a shirt. New tour train driver."

That was the first time I ever saw the diminutive and energetic man they called *Little Johnny*.

"Yeah. Yeah. Three shirts he gets. We got plenty today. Three Train." said Little Johnny sucking a drag from his cigarette. "What size? What size?"

"Uh, medium," I said.

"Medium. Medium." he chortled. "Medium is *M*."

He found three laundered blue shirts and stuffed them out through the square opening. Ron took the shirts, then handed them to me.

To my eyes, wiry Little Johnny Ranallo looked about four hundred and fifty years old as he exclaimed, "That's it. That's got it." Then he went back to his duties in the dank cellar room.

"You're lucky," said Ron. "They gave you all three at once. I had to beg for mine for weeks."

"So," I said, "Do I turn them back in here to have them laundered?"

"You're supposed to. That's the theory." Ron laughed. "But sometimes it's tough to get them back in actual practice. I suggest you have your mom wash them."

Outside the building, the brown-shirted men and the trucks were gone. My shirt was a cheerful blue. I took off the shirt I had worn right there on the spot and put on the new one with a red-and-white *Cleveland Zoo* oval patch. Now, at least, I *looked* like a tour train driver.

CHAPTER THREE

That first day, I learned from Ron that it was in the driver's best interest to arrive early to get the pick of trains. Ron was always early and tough to beat if you wanted to get dibs on the Number 3 train, but since he only worked weekends, it wasn't too bad. I could get there and snatch up Number 2 and have a better shot for his favorite during the week. (There were even times on the weekend when I got there first and could have taken his choice, but I always respected his seniority, a fact he duly noted.)

Before long, Mr.Huhtala brought in other *college-aged* drivers to work with me during the week. The first one to come was Rich Kemper, an even-tempered guy with sandy red hair. Rich had driven the trams in the past and knew all about it. He was going for his PhD in Business Administration, I believe. So for a few days, Rich and I were the only ones who drove during the week, with Ron and Jack coming in on weekends.

All the trains (except *Cinderella*) looked as similar as pups in a litter of hounds. The average person might think them identical, but the drivers knew better. Each had been handmade so they weren't exactly the same. It was kind of like telling twins apart, but we could do it. The trim was just a little different on one train, or one rode a little higher, or one's paint was worn in a different place. For us, the difference was in the way they handled. Trains 2 and 3 were fast, but there were other things to consider, as I would learn in time. Number 4 was a tank, performance-wise, but its speaker system was perfect, loud and clear. Number 3 also had a good amp and speakers. As far as this litter went, Number 1 was not a puppy; it was an actual dog, slow and bumpy with a bad amp. It was a lousy day, if you were stuck on Number 1.

Then there was the dreaded Number 6 which Jack had dubbed *Cinderella*. This tram was both newer and totally different in appearance from the others. Number 6, with its enclosed cab, was slower than a turtle pedaling a tricycle in mud. It didn't have a floor shift; rather, it had some weird gizmo which the driver straddled. The driver shifted by clicking a big U-shaped lever up through the notches on the device. *Cinderella* had ten forward gears. The clutch was hard to depress, and on a hot day, the clutch pedal picked up heat that seared right through the bottom of the driver's left shoe. The steering wheel was hard to turn, and the metal seat was back-breakingly uncomfortable.

Inside the cab, there was no air movement and it was hotter than heck. *Cinderella* had tiny windows and a little battery-powered fan which moved about as much air as a gnat's wings. *Cinderella* didn't even have a gas pedal. Like some foreign cars, she had a metal throttle rod on the steering column so that the driver would have to lift his left foot high like a male dog taking a leak, then push it down on the hot clutch pedal while pulling down on the odd shifter with his left hand and moving the throttle back with his right elbow while still holding the microphone in his right hand and saying stuff like, "All right. Next stop, the Children's Farm. Keep your hands and feet inside the train, unless we go around a corner fast and you fall off completely." Number 6 was not the train you wanted. Even getting into the cab was like crawling through a set of monkey bars into a garbage can.

Lucky for the rest of us Jack, the Korean War vet, liked Number 6. He always drove her. He would pull himself in with his arms and drag his bad leg up through. Jack must have driven a tank in the military. Though he never said, he may have preferred Number 6 because of his bad leg; he needed a train with a hand throttle. "Yeah," said Ron, "Jack will drive *Cinderella*, so don't worry about that. He likes her."

As the crowds increased in the summer of 1968, the zoo needed to run more trams and have more drivers on staff. Gene Huhtala herded them in. One of these was Les Mertus. I remember the first time I met him. It was a chilly, early summer morning, around 9:15 a.m. Gene stopped my train as I was turning the corner to head toward the flamingoes.

"Hey, Adam. This is Les Mertus. He is a student at Kent State. You should have a lot in common since he is also a major in Literature. So take him around with you today, to show him the ropes. But don't let him drive or talk into the microphone. He needs to be signed up with the union first. Do you hear that?"

"Yes, thanks, Mr. Huhtala."

"Good. You are good boys. Both of you."

So the first day Les was hired, they had him go around with me all day. He sat next to me in the cab, sitting on top of the wooden ticket box.

"I met that older mechanic in the garage. That guy Whitey. He was so serious explaining everything to me about the trains, but the whole time he was talking to me, I was thinking, *Man, this guy looks like Walter Brennan playing Grandpa McCoy.*" (I thought the same thing when I met him.)

"Yeah, I know."

We drove around together all day on Number 3 without incident. The visitors to the zoo that day were few. At the end of the day, I recalled how Ron had helped me get my shirts. It was around 4:30 p.m. After putting the train away, Les and I walked through the zoo around to the back of the old Cat and Ape Building. I remembered the frantic pace of that part of the zoo and was surprised to find the area quiet. We were under the assumption that the laundry room, at least, would be open, but the old building was completely abandoned. Until then, I never knew that if punch-out time was 5:00 p.m., many of the workers stopped working around 3:30 p.m. just to make really certain that they wouldn't be late to the time clock. Some keepers liked *to put the critters in the barn* as early as possible to guarantee that they'd get out of work on time. From then on, I always told people to visit the zoo early in the day.

Still hoping to find someone on duty in the laundry, we went into the deserted Cat and Ape Building to get Les a shirt.

"Halloo?" I yelled to no response, except for the always eerie creaking of the structure itself.

We made our way down into the dank cellar. Les and I could look through the little square hole in the cinderblock and see the stacks of shirts, but the metal chain link door was padlocked. Les surprised me with his boldness, considering it was his first day. Without hesitating, he quickly squeezed through the one-foot square opening with no problem. He just put his arms through the hole and jumped through like diving into a swimming pool. If he could do it, I could, too, so I followed him in. We took three shirts for Les, and I took the shirt off my back and threw it in the dirty laundry and replaced it with a clean one. That was a great revelation. Instead of requesting clean, laundered shirts, we had figured out that after hours we could get new shirts anytime we wanted. Marec couldn't do that since his size restricted any attempt at larceny. On the other hand, it wasn't really larceny since we took only the allowed number of shirts and put back the dirty ones.

A few days after Les started, Mr. Huhtala approached my train again while I was parked in front of Cat and Ape. With him was another young driver he had just hired.

"This is Norm Tulodziecki," said Gene. "Norm is a pre-vet student at Ohio Wesleyan, so he knows a lot about the animals. He's going to be one of our drivers, so take him around with you today, okay?"

I had broken Les in so I felt fine about taking on another. I'd show Norm the ropes, too. I'd fill him in on little facts from the script, and get him started on studying the speech. That idea lasted about eight seconds. Norm already knew more about animals than I did, and he filled me in about them. I was soon humbled.

I drove the train twenty feet, and spoke into the microphone, "Up ahead on the right is Monkey Island, the home to over eighty rhesus monkeys."

I was just about to show off my knowledge by saying that rhesus monkeys live in India, but Norm matter-of-factly added, "Yeah, we use a lot of rhesus at Ohio Wesleyan University in the lab. I've dissected a lot of them. They're just so useful because of their morphological, anatomical, and physiological similarities to humans. I guess you know that Jonas Salk used the rhesus macaque in his research when he discovered the polio vaccine. But did you know that the Rh factor in human blood gets its name from the rhesus? By the way, you should really called them macaques, not monkeys."

I was breaking Norm in. So I said, "Uh huh… I better give some of the speech to the people back there." Into the microphone, I said, "Also joining the monkeys on Monkey Island are aoudad sheep from the Barbary Coast." I felt like an idiot the entire remainder of the tour.

Norm went on and on about a book he was reading called *Never Cry Wolf* by Farley Mowat.

He said, "You can borrow it when I'm done with it."

"Great."

"You'll learn a lot about wolves."

As I continued showing Norm the ropes, it was not too long before I was actually writing down all the stuff he was telling me. I was scribbling all over the back of the tour driver's script. I'd say, "Hey, repeat that, will ya, huh?" Or I'd say, "How do you spell that?"

And he'd reply, "d-i-m-o-r-p-h-i-c."

I wrote down the things he said, and studied them. From Norm I learned the words *dimorphic, feral, morphological, sedentary, arboreal, diurnal, crepuscular,* and many more. No one used the word *crepuscular* except Norm. Animal experts don't even use it. They use the words *nocturnal* and *diurnal* to denote animals that are active at night or in the day. But *crepuscular* refers to an animal that is active only during twilight. Many flying bugs, gnats, beetles, and moths are crepuscular, Norm said, to avoid hot periods of the day and to avoid predators.

I did the best I could showing Norm around. While he clearly knew more about the animals, I could introduce him to the ticket sellers at each train stop. For me, this was important since they were all pretty girls. The girl named Nancy at the Children's Farm pulled me aside and said, "I guess that guy is really smart. But I don't understand a word he's saying."

As I drove Norm around the zoo giving my tour, I said, "The white stork is the among the largest of all storks. Only the Marabou stork, in the next pen, is larger, some as tall as five feet."

Norm said, "Those white storks we just passed… Did you notice the one in the pen with the black legs? That one is a juvenile. Its legs will turn a reddish color, like the others, when it matures. Did you see the loose sack of skin on the neck of that Marabou? That's an air reservoir. It can keep extra air in that sack when submerged."

We continued driving. Into the microphone, I said, "On the right is the western crowned crane."

Then Norm said to me, "That species of African crowned crane is *balearica pavonina*. Whereas the Indian peafowl around here are *pavo crisatus*. So you can see that the *pav* in both their names refers to the *crown* on the top of the heads."

Of course, I was able to tell the people that there was a restroom in the Bird Building, if they needed it, but that's how Norm talked. Whether he was talking to a ticket selling girl, *The Dummy*, Chuck Voracek, or a bunch of old people from the home, Norm used big words all the time. For Norm a *big* word was something like *foraminotomy*. He threw words like that at us all the time, and we would just duck. He had no interest in refreshment stand girls, for whom a big word was *Marlboros*. Voracek was the only one whose vocabulary was on Norm's level. When the two of them got together, it sounded like Latin encyclopedias exploding.

Other young drivers who joined the crew in time included Bob Ulasewski, who went to John Carroll University. He was a tall, handsome kid. Everyone looks like somebody, and Bob looked like the actor Judge Reinhold. Ulasewksi shortened his name to Bob Ulas and eventually became a local disc jockey on *shock radio*. For a time he was the arena voice of the Cleveland Cavaliers when they played at Richfield Coliseum. He always took his tour speeches very seriously and used a deep *Radio Announcer* voice.

He'd say, "Good morning, Clevelanders, and welcome to the Cleveland Zoo tour train. I'm Bob Ulas, and I'll be your announcer. Today the temperature outside is 74° Fahrenheit. It's partly sunny and I hope you enjoy your tour."

Whereas I said stuff like, "Here we go."

Bob always said to me, "You never know when a radio station general manager is going to be on the train. They take their kids to the zoo, too, you know."

That was good thinking.

Another of our drivers was an "older" guy (probably twenty-five) named Al Marabito, who was a graduate student at the University of Chicago and staying in Cleveland with his aunt for the summer. Marabito was a pretty cool fellow. He had his hair slicked back like the Fonz (long before the Fonz), and was definitely was what we used to call a *Greaser* in high school. Now there were six weekly drivers: Les, Norm, Rich, Bob, Al, and me, with each guy getting two days off a week. Additionally, Ron and Jack drove on weekends for the summer of 1968 and beyond. Before anyone ever started driving, however, Gene Huhtala insisted that they sign on with the Teamsters. Marec told me a story that went behind this insistence:

"There was one period of time that Huhtala got a little lax about signing people up for the union before they would work. This was before I started driving. At one time Gene didn't think having people signed up with the union was so important. They might work a day or two before they were signed up. 'No big deal.' Or so he thought.

"Then one time, two of the really big guys from the union came to see Gene. I mean *big* physically. You know the type if you've been down to the local. Black shirt. Suit coat. Wingtips. White tie. Sunglasses. Each built like a brick house. Maybe with a toothpick in the corner of his mouth. Cigarette behind the ear. These two guys paid Gene *a little visit* up in the Administration Building one afternoon." Ron laughed as he told the story. "They like to do their business in the afternoon, since the mornings aren't good for them. These two guys came in late one afternoon when the only people in the building would have been Gene, some of the office girls like Leona or Marsha, and maybe Chuck Voracek."

Ron continued, "Anyway, the two union guys came in and asked for Gene. He said, 'May I help you?' And the union heavies said something like, 'I hear youse having people drive the trucks and haul the garbage and shovel out the stalls and what have youse whatever without foist being all squared up and copasetic with the Teamsters Local 507. Would that be correct, Mr. Hutaly?'

"And Gene said, 'Whu-whu-whu-whu.'"

Ron cracked up at his own storytelling. Then he went on, "So the heavy from the union said, 'In the future we presume that everyone will sign up with the union expeditiously before proceeding into doing any work. Right? Are we right. Mr. Hutaly?'

"Gene said, 'Right. So right. So totally right, obviously.'

"Then the union guy reached out and took Gene's wire eyeglasses off his nose and dropped them onto the hard tile floor. Then, he ground the glasses into the floor with the heel of his shoe, and said, 'Remember, this could be you.'"

When jocular Ron finished that story, he rolled his head back and laughed and laughed. "This could be you." he repeated. "I love that."

With that little bit of history, it was clear that everyone would be signed into the union *before* driving. Norm and Bob went by themselves and signed up right away, but Les and Al needed to sign up, too. Since I was now an old hand at that, I went with them. The three of us piled into my sister's car and drove to the near east side.

The same young woman was still working behind the bars. This time, she had on a blue-and-white striped dress and red high-heeled shoes. The dress had vertical stripes. She was a perfect *10* and as serious as she had been when I encountered her the first time. Les and Al stood in line, waiting in front of the bank teller cage. The heavies, however, weren't in sight. She had a stack of forms and interviewed Les and Al one at a time.

All business, she began with Les just as she had with me. "Name?" "Age?" "Address?"

Les answered every question quietly, politely, and seriously. He kept his eyes down in spite of the fact that a stunning woman was standing directly in front of him. I was sure that he was just as interested as I was to engage her in some casual conversation that would go beyond this name, rank, and serial number interview.

Then it was Al's turn. Cool, smooth Alan Marabito. Twenty-five years old. His thick black hair greased back, as always. He had on a print short-sleeve shirt, with a red pack of Marlboros rolled up in the left sleeve. As always, Al was chewing gum, and he had his customary toothpick in his mouth.

Very businesslike, the woman got out a clean form for Al.

With her eyes down and the pen ready to write, she said, "Name?"

Al leaned coolly on one arm, looked into that babe's face, and drawled in a gangster voice, "Big Al... from Chi-CA-go."

With no expression whatsoever, the woman said, "Just a moment."

She turned on her heels and walked straight away toward the large wooden door in the back of the room. It was a walk of about thirty-five feet, and she had our complete attention. She disappeared into the door, and not ten seconds later she returned, with the two very stocky and well-groomed men in nice suits with black shirts and white ties. They came and stood on either side of her like wide blocks of granite, expressionless and staring straight ahead.

Again she asked Al, "Name?"

"Um. Alan Marabito."

"Age?"

"Twenty-five."

The rest of that interview went without incident.

The bottom line: On that day, at that time, there were no scabs in the Cleveland Zoo. Everyone was Teamster, together as brothers.

CHAPTER FOUR

That summer, I settled into a daily routine. The tour drivers arrived between 8:30 and 8:45 a.m. Every morning we chose a train and washed it, anticipating the arrival of the crowds. The majority of the day was spent driving around in the sunshine. From my point of view as a nineteen-year-old, it was a great respite from college classes. My hair grew longer and blonder every day, and at each stop there was an attractive ticket seller who was near my age. In those days, transistor radios were still the rage and many of the girls had them in their booths sitting on the counter next to a big roll of pink tickets. From the radios came strains of Donovan or Neal Diamond singing. Most had extendable chrome antennas that were positioned for the best reception of WIXY 1260, the most popular AM music location on the dial. Interspersed between the hits was the station's own chorus of *Wixy Twelve Sixty– Super Ray-dee-oh.*

The illusion among the drivers was that each of these young girls lived and breathed in the hopes of dating (or even marrying) a tour train driver. They would smile mightily and perhaps wave each time a train drove past. Ultimately, it could have been that they were really bored sitting in the booth all day and were dying for anyone to come and talk to them, but again that depended on the individual. Many of the ticket sellers were, in fact, college co-eds from the westside suburbs. All of them were personable, and their fathers were doctors or business owners. A guy might find a great real girlfriend among these pretty and cerebral girls, if *they* were interested.

There was a cultural divide, however, between the ticket sellers and the refreshment stand staff. The young women at the food vendor booths were not from the 'burbs, and, though also very attractive (to my eyes), their style was more at home on West 25th Street. These girls seemed more open to the prospect of meeting one of the young drivers. They were dressed quite differently than the more refined ticket sellers. Maybe it was the way they shrunk in the wash, but all of them wore very tight dresses. These dresses usually had a wonderfully placed large bright yellow mustard or ketchup stain on the thighs or butt. On the thighs the stain was an accidental smear. On the butt, the stain would be clearly in the shape of a hand. For awhile the girls got into the habit of placing those smack marks artistically and on purpose. One of the girls would take the yellow plastic mustard bottle and carefully squeeze mustard over the entire surface of the palm and fingers of her right hand. She'd smooth the mustard carefully. Then, *smack.* She'd whack herself in the rear and have a sort of fashion accessory.

In contrast to the ticket sellers, these girls were junior high school-educated or thereabouts. Their fathers were car mechanics or bus drivers. In general, they were younger than the ticket sellers, maybe sixteen or seventeen, and, unlike them, the refreshment stand girls were never bored. First and primarily, they were always preoccupied with a cigarette. At first I wondered how these underage girls got cigarettes. I was told that they'd just remind their mothers to buy them some at *the A em P.* Other activities that entertained these girls were popping their gum and sitting cross-legged while bouncing one leg up-and-down.

The social contrast between these two groups can be best illustrated by describing how they interacted with tram drivers. A college-type ticket seller would sit demurely inside her metal ticket booth while reading something like Rachel Carson's *Silent Spring.* She would smile pleasantly when the tour driver looked her way. As the train left the stop, she included a little wave to let him know she liked him.

Refreshment stand girls, on the other hand, would run at the train and throw water balloons at the driver's head when he drove by. They ran in packs like jackals. This is how it could play out: The driver is delivering his spiel, "On the left are the Himalayan tahr. These mountain goat-like animals live up to thirty thousand feet above sea level and can withstand the coldest temperatures on earth. Unlike most species of mountain goats, tahr do not have beards…" Then, *splat*. He'd get a water balloon against the skull.

Sometimes, the girls would bring out the big guns. As the train ran past their refreshment stand, she and her partner would race out hauling a big black hose behind them. The lead girl, the one who liked the driver best, was at the nozzle end of the hose. She'd let the driver and the passengers in the front seat really have it. The next time the same driver drove past the refreshment stand, she would smile and give him a little wave.

Within the Cleveland Zoo of the late 1960s, there was a sort of hierarchy of employment. At the bottom were the kids who gathered trash with a pointed stick or painted metal posts green. Next up the evolutionary chain were the refreshment stand girls. They were in a surprisingly low position because they were stuck in one place and dwelt in a toxic environment. Next, were the kids who ran the Kiddie Land rides. After one of those operators turned on the Merry-Go-Round about fifty thousand times, he was bored, and sometimes even hostile toward the screaming children. Next up the Darwinian chain was the sea lion pool guy. This teenager had a cooler full of ice and he sold smelts to people, three for a quarter, all summer long. His primary personal friends were four sea lions and one harbor seal. He also smelled like fish. Continuing up the ladder, were the summer employees who worked in the Children's Farm. They took care of goats, pigs, chickens, and other barnyard animals. It was fun and healthful, but the one downside of that job was they had to help castrate goats. Then you had the tour train ticket seller who were the little "her royal majesties" of the summer scenario. They organized picnics and cookouts and thereby expanded their social status far beyond their intended job description. Just above those girls were the tour train drivers. They ranked higher because they moved all around the zoo. They also could conk themselves on the head with their microphone, or do something else equally absurd, to get a laugh and enliven the zoo's guests. This was the hierarchy I knew that first summer.

It might be said, "But that's not what the zoo's about. What about the animals' keepers and maintenance men?" The fact was that they did not exist in our world, not then. One glimpsed them rarely. After all, they were brown-clad and standing in the middle of piles of shit, quite invisible. Also inconsequential were the zoo's director, curators, managers, vets, etc. Who knew what they were for? The power of adolescent hormones and the proximity to the opposite sex trumped them all.

CHAPTER FIVE

Who would have guessed that a bad haircut would have landed me in a great position, both in terms of income, and in longevity? I was making three bucks an hour, and had the potential of driving a zoo tram during the summer for the next three years. I had fretted over the haircut inflicted on me by a small town barber, but it grew back. As my new outdoor life gave me a healthy appearance, so too my longer hair better fit my generational values. I remember once hearing a little girl's comment as I leapt from the train cab, "Look, Mommy, that man looks like a Beatle." Though my father might not have agreed, I took that as a compliment.

The actual routine was to drive around the zoo all day on a precise route while narrating highlights over the microphone. Each tour took about a half hour with four stops along the way: 1. Cat and Ape Building/ Monkey Island. 2. The Children's Farm/Kiddie Land. 3. The Bird Building/Waterfowl Lake. 4. Lions, Tigers and Bears.

The Cleveland Zoo was expansive, perhaps more than people knew. The *Talking Storybook* said, "The zoo's one hundred ten acres provide quite a workout." Other brochures and tour scripts gave different numbers, and they ranged from eighty-five to over three hundred acres. I think the larger number came when people counted the areas of Brookside Park west of the Fulton Road bridge. However large the zoo was, the trackless tour trains made getting around a lot easier for visitors, and there were many. The zoo was often brimming with thousands of northeast Ohioans, awash in sunlight and happy chatter. On Sundays there were as many as ten thousand people.

Jack would sometimes mutter at the end of a Sunday, "Gene Huhtala told me that there were eighty-three hundred people here today, and I think every one of them rode on my train."

This is how I conducted tour rides circa 1968, and it's a bit of a composite of actual events. Families arrive at the zoo, parking in Parking Lot Number 1, and enter through the main entrance, passing in front of the old sea lion pool. At this point the scope of the venue can become a bit overwhelming, and as guests are wondering over directions, a tour train swooshes past. The amplified voice of the guide repeats: "Next stop, Cat and Ape, sea lions, and Monkey Island. Please remain seated while the train is in motion."

This little introduction announces to guests that there's a more comfortable way to navigate the pathways and exhibits. The tram's stop at the Old Main Cat and Ape Building is not far, and it's easy to reach the spot where the long, rattling train has eased to a stop. On the opposite side of the road is a brown metal booth where a girl is seated. Over her head is a sign saying: *Buy Zoo Train Tickets Here.* It's an effective form of suggestive selling. The ticket seller peels off tickets from a roll of perforated stubs which, as the sign says, go for *10¢ per stop. 4-Stop Round tour 40¢.* Next to the pretty girl with the tickets is a small gray cash box.

In spite of the fact that the booth is both well-marked and only ten feet away from the cab of the train, the driver who is jumping down off the cab will be asked, "Where do we get tickets for the train?" Now, pointing is as good as speaking.

The next question often seals the deal for families with children: "What's the next stop?"

"Children's Farm and Kiddie Land."

Literacy often disappears in the face of family fun and the driver may be asked, "Do we buy the tickets from you?" Again, the sign is right across the way and in bold relief "BUY ZOO TOUR TRAIN TICKETS HERE," and patience is the driver's friend.

Cleveland's weather often gets a bad rap, but in the summer with proximity to Lake Erie's breezes and shade from enormous trees, it's difficult to beat.

The reality of this time in the tour is different for the people who quickly bought their tickets and boarded the trains and the driver who is supposed to wait at the stop until the schedule says "Go." Families who jumped into empty seats, feel that the delay which follows is entirely unnecessary. Young drivers, on the other hand, welcome slightly interrupted minutes of flirtation with the ticket selling girl who is so unbelievably cute, even as she peels off a string of paper tickets from the roll.

At this point some customers get antsy and ask, "When does the train leave?"

The fact is that the schedule is somewhat loose and stops can be shortened or lengthened slightly and in proportion to how pretty the girl in the booth is.

Management did not share this opinion, and if Gene Huhtala walked by, there would be an irritated directive: "Hey. Hey. Get the trains moving. These trains should never stop moving." On occasions when that happened, it was clear to the passengers that the tour driver had just been busted.

There are other delays, however, delays which also alter the *get moving* scenario. Families arriving late and asking questions must be accommodated even as the younger children already on board ask parents when the adventure will begin.

The newcomers ask the same questions as the early arrivals. A mother might ask, "How much is the train?"

For Les, this was the lead in to a standard punch line. "Well, it was around thirty thousand dollars when it was new, but right now you could probably get it for around five thousand." He had a number of good-spirited retorts to everyday questions. "How long is the train?" (meaning how long is the ride), "About sixty feet, ma'am." "Where do you get tickets?" "I don't need them. I'm the driver."

When an overheard joke made one of the ticket sellers smile, life was very good.

Eventually, it was time to walk the length of the train to collect all the tickets which verify a purchased place on the excursion. Invariably, this was interrupted by people still approaching the train. In that moment, an onlooker may think that the driver has attained some sort of rock star status as he is mobbed by zoo visitors; the fact is that they, like those who had gone on before, assume that he was into sales as well as show biz.

So they say, "Do we buy the tickets from you?" For the gorkabazillionth time, I would direct them to the booth, and add, if the ticket seller was listening, "from that pretty girl. That one right there."

"Oh. How much is the train?" "Well, it was about thirty thousand dollars when it was new, but you could probably get it for five thousand now." (But, this is a train and not a Merry-go-Round, so let's move on.)

"Please remain seated while the train is in motion. Keep your arms and legs inside the car at all times. Thank you," and the ride begins as the driver lets up on the clutch and the mighty train cab's tractor engine pulls the three cars loaded with humanity. Then double clutch with a Whitey prohibited power shift from first to third gear. The train moves away at five miles an hour, and since it's not actually riding on a track, it can go anywhere (within limits), and it's the driver's job to make the trip both fun and memorable.

"Immediately on the right you can see Monkey Island. The home of over eighty rhesus monkeys."

The train slows down to a near crawl, so that the riders can get a good look at the rhesus macaques. They are a dusty brown lot of dismal primates, arguably mangy. There are lots of them. The island itself is made out of concrete and looks like a parking lot that melted.

"Rhesus monkeys are from India. Due to their anatomical and morphological similarities to humans, the rhesus monkey is very valuable in human medical research. In fact, the Rh factor in human blood is named after the rhesus. Dr. Jonas Salk used the rhesus monkey when developing his famous polio vaccine. Now you will notice that there is no shade on Monkey Island. But, you will also notice that there is a telephone wire high above the island. See it? That thin wire, probably only one-quarter of an inch in width, provides the only shade, and indeed on a very hot day, you will see all eighty monkeys lined up shoulder to shoulder, side by side, to stand in the shade of that wire. But today is not a hot day, so the monkeys aren't doing that now. Our rhesus monkeys share their enclosure with a small herd of Barbary wild sheep. These are also known as aoudads (pronounced OW-dads), the only wild sheep found on the continent of Africa. As you can see, the freeloading rhesus monkeys often like to hitch a ride on the backs of the aoudads. (That line was from the official speech.) The aoudads can sometimes be heard complaining, 'I just can't get the monkey off my back.'"

Vroom. The train speeds up. Now it's really moving, zipping along at about fifteen miles per hour. There will be no more animals and no speech for a long time. The train moves past the enormous empty grass mall on the left, a souvenir stand on the right, then past a picnic ground on the right. The mall, a sprawling expanse of nothing but rough, weedy lawn, is six hundred feet by four hundred feet, large enough to devour four football fields. After going around five hundred feet past venerable Monkey Island, the snakelike train turns at the "Flamingoes Refreshment Stand." The train turns left onto a much smaller paved road that is barely wider than the train. As the train hits the uneven surface of the different pavement, the cars rock back and forth and passengers hold onto the arm rests.

Judy and Carol are working in the refreshment stand today. They are smoking filtered cigarettes behind the long counter of this, the widest, of all the food booths. There are no customers at the moment. Judy is a slim blonde with her hair *ratted up* into the size of a collie. Carol is a dark-haired girl who is somewhat endowed. Seeing them on duty, the excitement of the tour is really beginning.

Fatally, the tour driver takes the microphone off its hook and speaks, knowing the sound will be clearly heard by the two girls in the stand.

"On the left is the Flamingoes Refreshment Stand, and that's Judy and Carol. They hate it when I tell people their names. Please take the opportunity later in the day to buy a hot dog or a box of popcorn from Judy and Carol. That's Judy on the left... The other one is Carol..."

The train passed within fifty feet of the rhesus macaques. Those monkeys are pretty much harmless. But now, the big train moves dangerously close to the Flamingoes Refreshment Stand, which is oddly named since it's really quite a distance away from the flamingoes. Suddenly, the all-metal door on the right side of the building bursts open with a morbid screech. Rabid with enthusiasm, the pair race toward the train. The helpless driver is suddenly pelted with hard, frozen *ice balls*, covered in red, blue, yellow, or orange syrup. They are the decapitated tops of snow cones. *Ouch!* The icy missiles hit him in the head and ribs, and the people on the train cheer and laugh at the inclusion of these rebellious West High girls in the drama of the train ride.

Now the train is right next to the refreshment stand, in the center of the War Zone. All of this was premeditated. The snowballs were stacked just inside the door, ready. And a third *shooter* appears from behind the refreshment stand. This is young, gum-chewing Jane. She's dark-haired, slender. Jane approaches with the refreshment stand girls' classic *coup de grace*. As she moves forward, Jane is dragging a heavy black garden hose, with the nozzle attached. Her attack is a bit uncoordinated, but determined. With a turn of the nozzle, the driver gets a good blast of water in the back and does his best to respond like a wounded cowboy in a TV western. The kids on board like this part of the tour pretty well, as Jane reaches the full extension of the hose, and is pulled backward like an attack dog reaching the end of the chain. The people are getting their dime's worth of entertainment. Amid the chaos and wild laughter, the train speeds away, heading past the spot where Big Creek goes underground.

"As you can see, we have many primitive aboriginals running loose on the zoo's grounds."

The people in the front seats have been provided a bit of over-spray, and a cheerful, half-soaked seventy-five-year-old lady says, "Oh, they like you."

In the rearview mirror, Carol and Judy are firing up a couple of victory cigarettes, and Jane is dragging the hose back behind the brick rear wall of the building, coiling it up in the shade of a scruffy pine tree. Then she also lights up a fag. The girls are laughing. The day is sunny and bright.

After passing the Flamingoes Refreshment Stand Combat Zone, the train winds along the bumpy and very narrow asphalt road that lead toward the actual flamingoes, Humboldt penguins, storks, cranes, and pheasants. There are a lot of animals on display up ahead. The train is now moving due east, having begun the tour moving due west. Everyone on the train looks out toward the right as the driver slows the train down to a crawl to provide a good look at the area's outdoor bird exhibits. The train is now near the center of the zoo, not far from the original focal points of Brookside Park, riding right over Big Creek, which is running unseen beneath the grassy lawn. In 1906 there was a scenic bridge at the center of Brookside Park. The train passes by that very spot, but the bridge is long gone and forgotten.

The driver describes the large birds on display. Approaching on the right is a line of penned yards bordered with chain link fencing, nothing fancy. Each pen has a concrete water trough, with fresh water dripping into it from a pipe. Each pen has a stainless steel bowl, about twelve inches in diameter, set in a block of brown concrete. These pens go on in a long line for about a hundred yards, just down the ridge from the zoo's greenhouse.

"Immediately to the right of the train you can see the pink flamingoes. We have quite a few, as you can see. These flamingoes eat tiny microscopic life forms that they sift out of the water with their beaks, which act like strainers. You'll notice they are right now filtering food out of the huge mud puddle in their pen. Here at the zoo, the flamingoes' diet is supplemented by a food additive containing vitamin K. If it weren't, they would soon lose their pink coloration.

"Next on the right are the Humboldt penguins. These are warm-weather penguins that can survive the summers in Cleveland so we keep them outside. Our larger emperor penguins and the rock-hopping penguins are in the Bird Building in a refrigerated exhibit which you can visit when we visit there two stops from now. The cold-weather penguins are put outside here at the Cleveland Zoo in the winter. Getting the penguins from the refrigerated exhibit in the Bird Building to this outdoor exhibit is simple; the birds walk over. Somehow they even manage the stairs that you'll see coming up on the right.

"Next on the right, we have the first of a series of storks. In the first pen is the white stork. This is the species that folklore calls the stork that brings the baby, even though now modern science knows it's caused by something else. White storks build nests on the roofs of houses in Europe, and return to the same nest every year. The stork pair mates for life and over the course of many years, they keep making the nest bigger until it can weigh as much as nine tons. Having a stork building a nest on the roof is considered to bring good luck."

The train continues. The next enclosure houses the ornate western crowned crane, who is standing erect and surprisingly calm, considering that it appears to be sharing its space with a small lawn mower that is still running though there's no sign of an operator. (A little red rotary lawn mower is chugging away behind the fence, so the driver incorporates the scene into the tour.) "On the right is a four-cycle Briggs & Stratton lawn mower engine, one of the most deadly of all animals in the forest, complete with razor-sharp teeth and a fierce yell. As you can see, it ate whoever was working in the yard. In the same enclosure with the Briggs & Stratton is the western crowned crane. This and other subspecies of crowned cranes are the only cranes that can roost in trees. Of course, all these birds in this area have been pinioned, so that they are incapable of flight. That means they've had one of their wings clipped. The metacarpal bone and phalanges of one wing have been cut off so that the primary feathers of that wing will not grow back. When one of these large birds spreads its wings, you can see how it has been pinioned. This does not harm the bird in anyway. It simply means it can never fly again.

"In the next pen, the lesser adjutant stork, so named because of its military gait. Next we have the marabou stork. That sack on the marabou's neck is an air reservoir. It can keep extra air in that sack when submerged. Next is the kori bustard, the heaviest bird in the world capable of flight."

It's fairly clear that the official script has become a guideline for drivers who take advantage of the events on the ground to establish rapport with tour riders. Our boss, Gene Huhtala, always says, "stick to the script, " and if Mr. Huhtala showed up somewhere along the route, the driver's speech would default to the standard script or something very much like it. Mr. Huhtala had a limited travel range, however, so the drivers had options for artistic license.

"These large storks and flamingoes are kept here outside during the summer months. They spend the winter indoors, in the basement of the Bird Building.

"Also on the right from Asia is the black cormorant. This bird is a great fisher, diving deep into the water and out-swimming the fastest fish. Fishermen in China and many other Asian countries use the cormorants for fishing. They tie a cord around the bird's neck so that it can't actually swallow the fish it catches in its throat. Then they pull the cormorant back to the boat and remove the fish from the bird's mouth.

"And now on the right, these are some pheasants and things like that. You can read the signs; you're as close to them as I am." The train is now passing a very old stone stairway that is from the earliest years of Brookside Park.

The driver continues, "There's the Lady Amherst's pheasant. And there's the golden pheasant. The Japanese green pheasant. And the ring-necked pheasant. All of these birds are pretty good eating. None of these pheasants are indigenous to the United States, but they were bought here as game birds by English settlers, or later, by hunting clubs. In the same enclosure with the ring-necked pheasant, you can see that we're in luck. There's a Neanderthal man who just learned to stand erect this morning."

Everyone on the train laughs as they spy the tiny chain-smoking keeper, Little Johnny, working in one of the pens. He's scraping old feed out of a stainless steel bowl with his bare hand. The train stops completely, but Little Johnny doesn't notice the train at all. He lets water flow from a faucet into the stainless steel bowl to rinse it out, oblivious to the fact everyone is watching him. His work-focus blocks out everything else until the driver continues: "It is the opposing thumb that gives this species its ability to master simple tasks and tool-making, and the ability to smoke and operate a Zippo lighter. This particular individual smokes Winston cigarettes, as you can see."

Little Johnny, with a cigarette hanging from his lips, suddenly realizes that everyone on the train is looking at him and laughing. He waves and bursts into a wide grin.

The train resumes moving and passes the last of the outdoor bird exhibits. By now the children on board have glazed over with all the grown-up babble coming out of the speakers. The kids think, *Where's this Children's Farm and Kiddie Land that everyone was so pumped up about?* The tram approaches a turn as the driver announces, "Straight ahead of the train is the Pachyderm Building. From here you can see the eighteen foot tall giraffes. The male giraffe's name is Bert. Those are Masai giraffes. They have the same number of vertebrae in their neck as you or I. Seven neck bones. The female giraffe gives birth standing up, which means when the one hundred pound baby giraffe is born, it comes out of the mother's womb and falls six feet and lands on the ground. Inside the building are Nile hippos, pygmy hippos, a black rhino, Brazilian tapirs, and the two female African elephants, Simba and Tara.

"The sweat of a Nile hippopotamus is sometimes red in color, and that has given rise to the myth that hippos sweat blood." At this point, the train comes to a complete stop, right in the middle of the turn. I thought of something out of the blue, and decide I need time to say it. It is a narrative that will only be heard once in the entire history of the Cleveland Zoo.

On this day, the yard next to the Pachyderm Building is empty, and this vacancy allows for a sudden flight of imagination for a college student whose future career will include cartooning and advertizing. He lowers his voice as if to disclose a little known secret. "To the left of the giant log wall up ahead, you can see an empty enclosure where you would normally find our elephants. There is a reason why it stands empty. Ladies and Gentlemen, this was the scene of one of the most adventurous and ultimately disappointing scientific experiments in the history of the Cleveland Zoological Society. Last winter, our scientists succeeded in crossbreeding an African elephant with a canary. The baby looked exactly like an elephant, except it had little, teeny-tiny yellow wings on its back, but alas, one day... they let it outside for some air, and it... flew away."

When the train reaches the Children's Farm, families with young kids will likely stay and walk around for a time. By now, however, there is an apparent difference in the energy levels of those on board and those who have chosen to walk this far into the park. The pedestrians are looking for places to sit, and sometimes missing the sights along the way, and there are many animals yet to meet. Blue peafowl tend to congregate in the warmth at the foot of the concrete stairs leading to the Bird Building. Close to the train are peacocks with full feathers, and an albino peahen.

"On the left are the wallabies. Like their larger cousins, the kangaroos, wallabies are marsupials, but they are smaller with thicker fur. These hardy animals spend the entire year outdoors, even in the coldest winters of Northeast Ohio. Sharing the enclosure with the wallaby is the emu, the national bird of Australia. It is a flightless bird, and the female emus lay large blue eggs which are incubated by the males. In the same pen is another large bird, the cassowary. The building on the right is the Bird Building, which you will have an opportunity to visit after our stop at the Children's Farm and Kiddie Land.

"Also up ahead on the left, in the next pen, is the giant red kangaroo. That is the male and you can see that from his head to the tip of his tail, he is easily seven feet long. On hot days, a kangaroo will lick its fingers so that the evaporation of the saliva acts like an air conditioner and helps keep the animal cool. How the kangaroo got its name is interesting. Captain James Cook was the first European to discover Australia, and he saw a bunch of these animals. So Cook asked his native guide, an Aborigine, what the animal's name was. And the guide said, 'I don't know' in Aborigine. The Aborigine word for 'I don't know' is *kangaroo*, so Cook wrote that down as the animal's name." (Actually, the word means "I don't understand your question," but we drivers didn't know that at the time.)

The tour continues, heading up the grade toward Brookside Park Drive.

"On the left are more deer, including the spotted axis deer in the wooded area. In the large cages up ahead on the right are the birds of prey. From here, they are difficult to see. We have an American bald eagle, a golden eagle, a turkey vulture, falcons, red-tailed hawks, and a great horned owl. You can best see those large birds by walking from the Bird Building, which is just two stops ahead.

"On the left are the prairie dogs. Look over the concrete wall and you may be able to see them. These are black-tailed prairie dogs, from the American southwest. In the western states, they are considered a pest. Cow ranchers hate prairie dogs because a cow might step in a prairie dog hole and break its leg. That's the story everyone tells. But I know the real reason cattle herders hate them."

The driver slows the train to a crawl and looks back and forth to make sure no one overhears this insider information. "Here's what prairie dogs do that makes cattle ranchers angry. One prairie dog will walk up to a cow and engage it in a conversation. While he's talking to the cow and has her attention, another prairie dog sneaks up behind. This second prairie dog gets down on his hands and knees. When the second prairie dog is in position, the one talking to the cow pushes it and it trips over the prairie dog behind it and that's how the cow breaks her ankles.

"Next, on the right, the large deer are the rare Père David's deer from

China, which are now extinct in the wild. These are among the largest deer in the world. The Père David's deer is named after a Frenchman, Père Amand David. He visited China in the 1800s and brought some of the deer with him back to Europe. After the deer were hunted to extinction in China, there were as few as eighteen alive in the entire world. Today all surviving Père David's deer are descended from the specimens taken from China by Father David. Next on the right are the barasingha deer, also called the swamp deer. These are also extremely rare in the wild and in danger of extinction. As few as sixty-six were still alive in their native habitat just a few years ago. Now on the right, you can see that the Cleveland Zoo is proud to have two kinds of camels. The camel with one hump is an Arabian camel, and the camel there with two humps is our bactrian camel, and we have two of them, but the other one always stays in the barn. Camels don't store water in their humps. The humps are deposits of fat, and water is actually stored in a chamber attached to the stomach.

"Also on the right are the llamas. They are native to South America and are used for milk, meat, wool, and as a beast of burden. Remember… a lama with one *L* is a priest, and a llama with two is a beast. Also in this paddock is the nandu, the world's second largest bird, sometimes called the South American ostrich.

"The Children's Farm and Kiddie Land is our next stop. Here you can feed the lambs and pigs and chickens, and there are rides for small children. As we approach, notice on the left in the barnyard is the Sardinian donkey, which legend says is the kind of donkey Jesus rode into Jerusalem during his triumphal entry. You can see the markings of a cross on this donkey's back and shoulders and that may be how the legend began. Please remain seated until the train comes to a complete stop."

The children perk up at the prospect of getting off the tram and actually moving among the animals. Likewise, the driver is anticipating a brief stop with the chance to chat-up Helen, who is standing by the metal fence apparently waiting for the train to pull in.

When it comes to popularity, only the lions, tigers, and bears rivaled the Children's Farm and Kiddie Land as an attraction in the zoo on this day in the late 1960s. It was a magical place with a rustic split rail fence surrounding a large shady enclosure full of pigs, goats, donkeys, chickens, peafowl, ducks, bantam roosters, and geese. Generally, there was a lot of commotion from this domestic menagerie combined with the shrieking of happy children. The air was filled with bleating, oinking, braying, clucking, and quacking. Another very prominent noise is the ear-splitting crowing of the Children's Farm rooster who never cared a lick about the time of day.

The barnyard is on a sloping hill, with a fenced perimeter. Set back beneath the shade of giant tulip poplar trees and broad leafy maples, it was a lovely little spot, which stayed a cool retreat, even on the hottest day of summer. Donald Kuenzer was the Manager of the Children's Farm in 1968, having been promoted from keeper. Don was extremely energetic, and with his compatriots could be seen moving throughout the barnyard herding animals and dealing with any emergencies. An emergency might be when a baby goat drinks so much milk that it's laying there like a bloated rubber balloon. Were that to happen, Kuenzer would run out and scoop up the animal and put it into a bed of hay in the barn to sleep it off. All the kids who worked there in the summer thought him a great boss.

At the Children's Farm is a red wooden barn where kids can walk past neatly cleaned stalls filled with wood chips or hay. These stalls are inhabited by guinea pigs, baby lambs, piglets, rabbits, and baby goats. Children are often excited at the opportunity to offer a bottle of formula to one of the baby goats. These *four-legged* kids make out pretty well in all this and after awhile a baby animal waddles off belching into a soft corner of wood chips, and lays its full belly down to sleep.

Adjacent to the Children's Farm is a little amusement park called Kiddie Land which featured, among other things, a little mechanical helicopter ride. Most of the rides travel in circles, and here there were plenty to choose from helicopters, cars, and merry-go-round animals all join in this circle of a child's amusement. There was also a miniature train which, unlike the zoo tram, actually one rode on tracks. As exciting as that may sound to a railroad enthusiast, very little of the zoo can be seen from the cramped vantage point of the small train.

Tracks or no, the tractor/tram is the best to ride, and the driver has reached the limit of his time available for banter and flirtation with friends on staff. After collecting this round of tickets, another train pulls into the stop and it's time to resume the ride.

Just past the prairie dog exhibit, the tram turns left to circle around the 3½-acre Waterfowl Lake.

"Over to your right in the big cages are the American bald eagle, hawks, owls, turkey vulture, and the golden eagle. The best way to see these exhibits is to walk there from the Bird Building which is our next stop." The comment is a reminder from the earlier leg of the tour. It's given for the benefit of new passengers who have joined the tour from the Children's Farm and to those whose minds have become befuddled by the whirling motion of the rides in Kiddie Land. "In the early 1960s the bald eagle was nearly extinct due to the widespread use of DDT as pesticides. DDT in the diet caused the eagles' eggs to be thin, and they cracked before the embryo was developed. But now that DDT is banned, we are hopeful that the Bald Eagle will someday make a comeback." (Time would prove that very point. In the twenty-first century, Ohio's wilds are again home to the bald eagle.)

"Up ahead on the right is Waterfowl Lake. Home to over one hundred species of ducks, geese, swans, and other waterfowl. That is a wood duck on the right, and also Bewick's swans; they are the white swans with a bill that's yellow near the nostrils and black on the tip. Those larger white swans with the bills that are orange with a mask of black around the eyes are mute swans. The very large white ones with the all-black bills are trumpeter swans, and the black ones with the orange bills with the white tips are Australian black swans. As the name suggests, the black-necked swans are the ones with the black necks."

The view from the tram is especially good in springtime when the lake's bountiful variety of flowering trees are in full bloom. Out in the center of the water, a big fountain sends a misty spray of water up into the air. This may be the loveliest place in an absolutely beautiful zoo.

At the north end of the pond is the second stop at the Bird Building. The narration resumes. "Inside this air-conditioned building are hundreds of bird species, including parrots, macaws, bleeding heart pigeons, and several large naturalized bird displays. Also in this building in a special, refrigerated exhibit are Antarctic penguins, including emperors and rock-hopping penguins. At this stop is the zoo's greenhouse which is the work area where much of the landscaping magic takes place. You can't go inside the greenhouse, but you can see many of the exotic plants through the glass. Please remain seated until the train comes to a complete stop."

After a brief stop, the tour resumes and the driver knows that the next arena will be more popular than the last.

"The next stop is Lions, Tigers, and Bears."

At this point, the passengers join the act by chanting, "Oh, my," and then repeating the familiar words, "Lions and tigers and bears, oh, my. Lions and tigers and bears, oh, my."

The train moves directly toward the Bird Building, then curves down to the left, doing a one-eighty turn to head west past the zoo's greenhouse, then up a slight grade for hundreds of yards, moving past dramatically exposed prehistoric siltstone and shale cliffs.

As the train gets within a few hundred feet of the Fulton Road Bridge, the speech resumes. The tour driver tells everyone on the train to look high up to the left. There is a sheer wall of bare dirt cliffs rising about a hundred twenty feet upwards.

"On the left, up on those hills, if you look very close near the top, you can see mountain goats." People have to crane their necks to see the animals on the farthest height.

"In the first area are the Himalayan tahr."

People squint up into the bright sky and focus on the nearly camouflaged herd of tahr. There are probably thirty in all with short horns of similar length, but the larger males have manes, almost like a lion's.

"Himalayan tahr live at altitudes up to thirty thousand feet and are an important food supply to natives of the Himalayan mountain regions of India and Pakistan. They can survive in some of the most severe cold-weather conditions on earth, but they are endangered because of trophy hunters. Newborn tahr are able to walk up and down sheer cliffs within hours of the time they are born.

"In the next enclosure, also at the very highest part of the cliff, are Nubian ibex. The large male is leader of the herd. He's the one with the large curved horns."

The male ibex seems to pose against the sky, bearded with long deer-like ears and a striking white underbelly, and displaying a set of curved horns. The horns are scimitar-shaped, nearly a meter long, with pronounced knots on the forward edge.

"The Nubian ibex is actually a goat antelope, which lives in mountainous regions of Israel, Saudi Arabia, and Oman."

As the train approaches the next venue, the earlier observation of a woman on the train is expanded. After the last *attack* by refreshment stand girls, she said, "Oh, they like you." If that were the case, the refreshment girls at the tiger area *really* loved me.

The attack is swift and ferocious. With war whoops, Annie McGinty and her two sidekicks, Mary Ann and Ilene push forward. Ilene's aim is spot on, as should be for an athlete who has mastered fast-pitch underhand softball. After the ice balls, however, it is clear that this is play which keeps the staff engaged and the visitors entertained.

The train moves ahead as it slips into the cool shade under the Fulton Road Bridge. Directly ahead of the train are the lions, tigers, and bear exhibits.

"In this area of the zoo you'll find the African Lions, including the male lion, Rajah. We also have Siberian tigers here. You can see both of those exhibits directly ahead. You know that most cats don't like water, but the Siberian tiger enjoys swimming. That's why there's a pool in the tiger enclosure. Also, in the alcove next to the tigers is our gray wolf exhibit. Wolves have an undeserved reputation from stories like *Little Red Riding Hood*. The fact is, there is no record of a wolf attacking a human being in the history of North America. You'd be surprised to know that in the wild, the main food of wolves is mice. That is according to Farley Mowat's book *Never Cry Wolf*."

The train moves around the left side of the perimeter into this part of the zoo as the driver continues, "On the right you can see the zoo's giant grizzly bears, weighing in at up to twelve hundred pounds. Next on the right you might be able to catch a glimpse of the Kodiak bears, which can weigh as much as sixteen hundred pounds. These are the largest bears in the world, and they come from Northwest Canada and Alaska. A Kodiak bear, when standing on its hind legs, can be over ten feet tall. To see all these bears properly, you will want to get off the train at the next stop.

"Next are the European brown bears. These bears can be trained to dance, walk on their hind legs, and even ride bicycles, which is why this species is the kind most often used in circuses. Next, on the right is the American black bear.

"On the right is the Siberian reindeer and the capybara, the world's largest rodent. Capybaras can weigh up to three hundred pounds and are a favorite food of jaguars in the Amazon.

"Now we're approaching our stop. Straight ahead of the train is the zoo's polar bear exhibit. Please remain seated until the train comes to a complete stop."

Families alight to see these popular animals. This is the westernmost spot in the zoo. Everybody gets off the train to see the lions, tigers, and bears. That is a hot spot in the zoo on a busy day. But the train quickly fills up again with people returning to the starting point of the tour.

"Next stop. We'll be back to where it all began: The main entrance, Monkey Island, sea lions, and the Cat and Ape Building."

So the blue tour train pulls away from the bears' stop. The train is full and heavy with a load of over seventy people crammed in; so there is no power shifting when leaving. With such a huge load, the train is sluggish.

"On the right, that reddish antelope is the sitatunga antelope. Up ahead on the left we can again see the polar bears, and on the right is the Malaysian sun bear, which gets its name from the markings that look like the rising sun on its chest."

The train moves around the perimeter of the sitatunga veldt. As the train begins moving back toward the Fulton Road Bridge, it slows way down, and the driver whispers into the microphone, "Okay, everyone. We need to be careful now." The sudden note of caution draws all ears. "Please keep your hands and feet inside the train at all times. Hold onto your children. I'm pulling the train as far away as I can from the terrifying creatures coming up on the right in this enclosure. The animals you are about to see may leap out of their exhibit at any time. On the right... near that big tree... are the zoo's three elephant tortoises... The largest of these deadly tortoises weighs over five hundred pounds."

People begin to laugh at the thought of a charging tortoise, but the driver continues the charade. "Shh. Be very quiet now, so that we don't provoke an attack."

On the right is a large shady exhibit area surrounded by a cement moat around five feet deep and five feet wide. Within the exhibit, lounging in the dark green Kentucky bluegrass are three huge tortoises.

As the laughter dies, the driver says, "Those are the zoo's three elephant tortoises. The two with the high, round shells are the males. The one with the flatter shell is the female.

"One giant tortoise born in 1750 is still living in the Calcutta zoo in India."

After a long drive downhill where the driver has to ride the brakes to slow the descent, the tram and its three blue cars crosses over Big Creek.

After easing off the bridge and coming onto level road, the train passes the garage where Whitey works, and then turns right heading into the final stretch of the round tour.

"On the left are the yaks from Tibet, weighing up to sixteen hundred pounds. Tibetan natives depend entirely on the yak for their existence. They milk them, eat them, and use their hides for clothing. They use virtually every part of the yak for their survival.

"Notice that the yaks' fence is covered with huge dents, as if a truck drove into sections of the fence. The metal fence has clearly been battered and deformed. You might think that the yaks enjoy ramming the fence with their huge horns and shoulders. Actually, the dents were made by a previous tenant to that yard, a male American bison. The bison are in the next enclosure."

"American bison are sometimes incorrectly referred to as *buffalo*. One hundred years ago, in the 1860s, there were over sixty million bison living in North America. They were slaughtered by men like Buffalo Bill Cody for their hides until they were nearly extinct. Only a few hundred were left at one time. Now there are over fifteen thousand bison living in the United States.

"Next are the ostriches from Africa. These are the largest birds in the world, weighing up to three hundred pounds. The all-gray ones are the females. The black ones with white wings are the males. Contrary to popular myth, ostriches do not bury their heads in the sand. Also surprising is that the male ostrich incubates the eggs, tending to them for a period of about forty days."

"Next are the Grant's zebras, a member of the horse family. Unlike the horse, zebras have never been domesticated for riding. The zebra is a favorite food of lions.

"Next are the pronghorn antelopes, which are from the American southwest." They appear on the left as a herd of handsome and nimble brown antelopes with striped markings. "Native Americans hunted the pronghorn antelope, and if you've ever read *Little Big Man*, the novel, that book says Indians ate this antelope's heart raw on the site of the kill. Now I will tell you a little history of this part of the tour. We used to say here at the *Cleveland Zoo* that the pronghorn antelope can run at speeds up to fifty miles per hour. But one time, one of the women who works here as a ticket seller had a guide book from the *Detroit* Zoo. That guidebook says *their* pronghorn antelope can run at speeds up to *sixty miles per hour.* Ladies and gentlemen, there's no way an antelope from *Detroit* can run faster than an antelope from *Cleveland,* so I'm here today to tell you officially that the pronghorn antelopes at the our zoo are capable at running at speeds up to *seventy miles per hour.*

"Next are the guanacos." Here's a herd of skinny-legged fuzzy tan creatures that look a lot like llamas. The guanacos look like walking shredded wheat biscuits. They are the cousins of the llama and alpaca and are from South America. We have a lot of baby guanacos born here all the time.

"The lone antelope on the left with the long spiraling horns is the beisa oryx, from the Red Sea coastal areas of Africa." This antelope is very striking. It has two long, straight parallel horns that look like two foot daggers. The horns come out like corkscrews near the antelope's head and then become straight. The zoo only has one beisa oryx, and I bet that when it stands alone, it is wondering where the rest of the herd has gone.

"Next are the elands, the world's largest antelope. We have six elands here. The large male you can see weighs sixteen hundred pounds." On the left there are very large reddish-brown antelopes with fairly straight, long horns that arc back along their backs, ears flickering constantly to ward off insects.

The train heads toward the starting point, past Monkey Island, heading toward the front of the huge Old Main Building. There are no visible animals along this stretch, but the driver fills the time by saying, "The eland looks a lot like the bongo antelope, which is the rarest antelope in the world. The Cleveland Zoo is the only zoo in the world that has a mating pair of bongo antelopes. Our bongos are named Karen and Biff. They are located next to the kangaroo exhibits near the Pachyderm Building, which is near our destination.

"We are approaching the end of the line. Our next stop is the Old Main Building and Monkey Island. The Old Main Building was built around the turn of the century and houses leopards, panthers, chimps, baboons, gibbons, wolves, and the zoo's anteater. But the prize exhibit in the building is Timmy, the four hundred pound western lowland gorilla. He is very possibly the most spectacular animal in the zoo. Timmy was born in Africa in 1959, and arrived in Cleveland in 1966. And here we are. Please stay seated until the train comes to a complete stop."

That concludes a round trip on the Cleveland Zoo tour train, circa 1968. On a given day, there might have been a new eland calf being born and standing for the first time on its wobbly legs. The mother eland also struggled to her feet and licked her new baby clean. And, as alarming as it might sound, she would have seen standing spread-legged and eating the afterbirth. In the wilds, the scent of the afterbirth could attract predators.

It is also a source of nourishment that cannot be wasted by an animal that is adapted for life in the harshest regions of Africa. I always tried to provide entertainment for zoo guests, but understanding and appreciation of the natural world was our goal.

Drivers presented their *speeches* twelve times a day, five days a week. Adding jokes or antics was a way to try and keep the delivery fresh. There were times when every driver felt a bit humorless, and there were a very few who never quite got into it. Frank Sandusky was a case in point.

CHAPTER SIX

At one point during my tenure, the zoo hired a retired mail carrier named Frank Sandusky as a driver. Frank sometimes drove the train as a fill-in. He was never full-time, but he was a character. Frank would load his thick head of hair with Grecian Formula and drive the train around the park at about forty miles an hour. People wouldn't want to be on Frank's train if they had to go to the restroom. Frank said very little, but when he drove past the beaver exhibit, he'd croak in a very high voice into the microphone, "Up ahead on your right, get your cameras ready for your beaver shots." And then he put the microphone away and wouldn't say anything else on the whole tour. That was his whole spiel. I rode all the way around the zoo behind him once on my day off. He didn't recognize me among the group.

I told one of the girls in the Children's Zoo that "the old guy essentially only says one thing on his entire tour." I said, "The only thing he ever says is, 'Up ahead on your right, get your cameras ready for your beaver shots.'"

She laughed and didn't believe me.

So I came in on my day off to prove it to her. In order for her to have something to compare it to, we rode Ulas's train to the lake and got off. Then we sat on the cool stone wall and waited.

Other drivers, like Les and Norm, came by and said, "Hey, you guys want a ride?"

I said, "No, we're waiting for Frank's train. His speech is better."

Finally, from the distance down along the west side of Waterfowl Lake, Frank came roaring along in the Number 2 train. He squealed to a stop and jumped down with all the energy of a marmot on speed. Frank was full of energy.

There were only three people on the train in the back car. In a near frenzy, Frank ran back to them and demanded, "Tickets. Tickets."

We got on Frank's train and climbed into the front seat. We didn't need tickets, of course. Clutching the tickets from the three people, Frank hopped onto the driver's cab, tore the tickets in half, and shoved them into the slot at the top of the homemade wooden box.

When Frank said, "Next stop bears," I turned to the young woman and said, "That doesn't count. That's just his appetizer."

She said, "Sure. I'll give you that one."

We took the whole tour on Frank's train. The girl found it side-splittingly funny that he said absolutely nothing. He didn't give any commentary, and that only added to the absurdity of the one thing he would say.

We were grinning and giggling the whole time, anticipating the moment. As each leg of the tour began, Frank would say, "Next stop Main." Or, "Next stop Farm." Then he'd put the microphone back into the holder and drive away like a madman. People held on for dear life.

In the cab of the train, speechless Frank was cheerful and whistling to himself. He was over sixty-five and thin as a rail. Some days his hair was snow white, and some days it was jet black. If anyone fell off the train, like a kid or grandmother, he would probably not have noticed, much less slowed down. The girl and I rode with our feet up on the front rail of the car. Frank drove fast and cut corners hard. The train lurched left and right. It was like riding the Crack-the-Whip at the fair.

The girl turned to me and said, "Oh, you're just pulling my leg. He's not going to say anything. You just wanted me to ride with you."

While that may have been part of my motive, I said, "He will say one thing. Just wait."

Frank was actually a pretty cool guy. Well, okay, he wasn't. Frank was energetic, like a nervous ferret and weighed about the same. He looked a lot like Percy Kilbride, who played Pa Kettle in the movies. Frank would get on this kick when he'd dye his hair black for a week or two, and he looked ridiculous. Then he put it back to snow white. His hair was white the day we took the investigative tour.

Before retirement, Frank had been a postal worker. He told me once, "Back when I was twenty, I could have either worked as a mailman or as a mechanic out at Hopkins, but the Post Office paid a nickel more an hour, so that's how come I was a mailman for forty-five years."

She and I rode all the way around. Frank didn't mention the beavers on the way to the Farm. Starting up from the Children's Farm, Frank said into the microphone, "Next stop Lake."

The rattling train geared up. We were moving fast as we peeled around the corner past the barnyard since it was a downhill grade. I bumped my elbow into the girl's arm to make sure she was alert. Frank shifted into high gear, and the train really picked up speed. The cars were pretty full; the anticipation was tense.

We roared past the camels and deer on the left. Just before taking a hard, careening turn around the lake, Frank reached his tanned, bony hand toward the mike that was hanging on the engine wall of the train. His hand shook a little bit as he pressed the button on the microphone and announced in a fast and breathless manner, "Up ahead on yer right, get yer cameras ready for yer beaver shots."

He put the microphone back on its hook. Then he turned a hard left and the train shimmied back and forth like a flopping fish. The girl burst into laughter and tears rolled down her face.

That was pretty much the totality of Frank Sandusky's speech. Good drivers, however, took a lot of pride in giving the perfect tour.

For the younger drivers like myself, the quality of the speech and the humor varied, especially if it was an occasion when a ticket seller or concession worker was being ferried to her work station. The refreshment stand girls, in particular, became part of the entertainment. They were mostly local high school kids and it was easy to get them laughing in a way that would become infectious. I could start the sixteen-year-olds off into a giggling frenzy by saying over the speakers, "Welcome. We have a special attraction for you, Ladies and Gentlemen, on this portion of the tour. The girls from the Monkey Island refreshment stand are joining us. They're the ones in the white suits in the front car in case you haven't been able to spot them."

From the front car would come wild, high-pitched shrieks of laughter. The rest of the people on the train would laugh. Then they'd applaud the girls.

Some of the comedic material required to make these girls laugh was extremely unsophisticated. I suppose it would be called *slapstick*; especially effective was bonking myself in the head with the microphone. The more sophisticated ticket sellers, however, would only find it *mildly amusing* no matter how many times I hit my head. In fact, the more times I hit my head, the less funny it became to a ticket seller. So there was an inverse ratio to the level of humor and the number of times I did it. Whereas, for the younger girls, the hitting of the microphone on my head had a cumulative affect. And the more different ways I could hit your head, the higher the onslaught to their central nervous system. Two hits on the right side of the head followed by one more into the hard part of the forehead was overly funny to refreshment stand girls, who in their natural state, traveled in groups of three.

"Bonk. Bonk. Qwank."

Several of the monkeys observed this and tried it incorporate the basic idea of head bonking to attract females, but to no avail. It only worked on these humans.

It remains a topic for future study by social anthropologists, but Les, Norm, and I spent the major part of the summer pondering ticket sellers and largely ignoring refreshment stand girls. Although the refreshment stand girls were, no doubt, more fun.

CHAPTER SEVEN

One afternoon my tour train was parked in front of the old Cat and Ape Building. Suddenly a woman came up to my train. She was probably around fifty. She was carrying a large carpetbag.

"Excuse me," she said. "Have you ever seen the animals in that building?" She pointed toward Cat and Ape, which was right behind her.

I said, "Well, not really."

The woman's face burst into tears, and she said, "Well, it just breaks my heart." Then she hurried away sobbing.

This encounter pointed out the fact that, as drivers, we naturally saw animals everywhere all day long, but had very little real involvement with them. From our tour trains, we saw relatively happy animals. Those included kangaroos and wallabies hopping along big grassy areas. There were emus poking the ground for insects, seemingly as happy as the day is long. We saw yaks and elands grazing on tall grasses and having babies. We saw zebras humping. We drove past ducks and swans that were virtually free on the big lake, except that they could not fly. There were loudly barking sea lions relaxing in the swimming pool or sunning themselves. These were constantly entertained by people throwing fish at them all day.

Anyway, one pleasant afternoon after putting away the trains, Les and I started the long walk toward the back of Old Main Apes to punch out. We were a little bit early that day. It was around 4:45. There were even a few visitors still in the zoo. We had some time to waste since we really couldn't punch out until 5:00 p.m.

We walked past the zebras and fed them grass through the fence for a few minutes. I loved doing that. Then we continued east and hung out along the edges of Monkey Island. As usual, we were *bad boys* and threw the monkeys big clumps of dandelions and grass, including the roots covered with dirt which made their day, I guess. Gradually, we worked our way over toward the Old Main Cat and Ape Building. It was a pretty afternoon, and the building was still wide open. Before we even got anywhere near the door, we heard the ear-splitting howls of the gibbons.

Les said, "Hey, let's check out this building here. I've got to see what's making that noise."

"Norm says those are the gibbons," I answered.

"I know," said Les. "What I mean is, I've got to see them."

As tour drivers, we could hear the extremely vocal apes all the time.

In front of the Old Main Cat and Ape Building, the howls were almost omnipresent as if the gibbon inhabitants liked the acoustics of the old building. It was a giant amplifier that broadcast their powerful, haunting screams and yells throughout the lower zoo.

It was the siren cry of the gibbons that pulled Les and me toward the Cat and Ape Building. Until then, we were only familiar with the outdoor exhibits. We'd seen the pretty little fat-bellied lambs grazing, carefree waterfowl gliding on the zoo's scenic lake, but now, we would venture into the dark world of the Alcatraz of exhibits.

Looking back in history, the first and original "Animal House" built at Brookside Park was opened in 1908. Befitting the zoo architecture of that time, the edifice was an Edwardian prison, dungeon-like, essentially terrifying to behold, and not designed with the animal comforts and considerations the Cleveland Zoo and every fine zoo uses today. Originally the building had animals on display in its deep, musty cellars. By the 1960s, however, Old Main's lower levels had been flooded so many times, they were no longer used for exhibits. When I began at the zoo in 1968, the old Cat and Ape Building was functionally limited to one floor, but the ceilings on that floor were probably thirty feet high. (Note: In this book, I call the building the *Cat and Ape Building*, the *Old Animal House*, the *Ape Building*, *Main*, or the *Old Main Building*. That because people referred to it in all those various ways.)

Old Main had barred cages inside. The bars were perhaps an inch thick and made of square wrought iron. These were anchored in a concrete floor. With few exceptions, each cage was also connected to an outside cage, so that animals were either *in* or *out*. The animals didn't have a choice, however, they were either locked out or locked in.

Les and I began our tour of the building by walking around the outside. The structure itself was made of brown bricks, which by the late 1960s were furthered darkened by a patina of bacteria and covered with creeping molds in many places. There was a lot of black wrought-iron work, both rails and cage bars. The cages on the outside face of the building had floors of solid concrete so animals did a lot a pacing. The floors were about eye level so that we looked up at the animals in their cells. The discolored concrete was worn and weathered, but it was also worn down by decades of imprisoned animals. In over sixty years, stressed animals had literally beaten a path in the cement. In the first cage, we saw an American cougar, or puma, pacing back and forth. On its elbows and haunches were ulcerated patches of dark skin. The animal seemed mangy, with an old coat made of sparse, dry, orange fur and dandruff. It wasn't pretty to see that cougar.

The outdoor cages were about ten feet square. The cougar walked one way, turned around and walked back. He walked in haste, anxiously seeking to burn off excess energy. From time to time, the yellow cat let a hiss of air whoosh out of his mouth. The pads of his paws were black, dry, and cracked. His ribs protruded gauntly from his loose-hanging hide because no matter how much he ate, he paced himself toward starvation. The old, coarse concrete floor of the cage was still wet from a late afternoon hosing. The air behind us was fresh and green. The air before us pierced our nostrils with the biting scents of dry skin and cat musk. Dressed identically in our blue tour driver shirts and tight jeans, Les and I were somber.

"Well, this is really... sad," said Les. "Jeez."

In the next cage was a dusty-looking giant anteater, also pacing anxiously back and forth near the front of its outdoor cage. It was large, about fifty pounds, the size of a Irish setter. As the anteater worriedly paced, the loud *click-click-click-click* of his long black claws was a constant. There was a disturbing rhythm to the clicks, an intensity and urgency. The anteater drummed out an accelerating, repetitive percussion. *Click click click click click click click click click...* It was about nine clicks, getting louder and speeding up until the anteater stopped and turned one hundred and eighty degrees with a whoosh and headed back the way he had come. *Click click click click click click click click click...* We heard the same nine clicks speeding up in the opposite direction. This went on endlessly, back and forth. The anteater stared straight ahead as it paced. I don't think it had a thought in its head. It was just a zombie, dead of mind. The tips of its black claws were cracked, some broken.

That giant anteater was a big, bristly-looking creature. He was dark brown, with light-colored forelegs. There was a striking and magnificent area of dark fur sweeping back artistically from his chest. That dark fur ended in a point, like a spear, on his back. The anteater had a very long pointed head and nose, with a massive bushy tail nearly as big as his body.

Every time he turned, the tail swung around in a huge swath. But this anteater's fur was dry and coarse. He looked frizzy and ratty, and smelled like an old dog on linoleum.

Les and I knew an anteater like that had like an eighteen-inch-long black tongue, but he wasn't sticking it out since there were no anthills or termite mounds in his cage. His claws were gigantic, dark and saber-shaped, designed for digging into ant hills and termites mounds. It seemed that concrete had to be the worst possible pacing surface for such an animal. There was something wrong with the anteater's feet. Somehow the animal had to bring its weight down oddly with each step, to avoid putting pressure on the parts of its pads that were the most painful. It had sores on its feet. Yet, it could not stop pacing. What should the animal do? Pace and hurt its feet, or lay down and ulcerate its skin?

"Ah, man," said Les. "This is awful."

We moved along slowly, not saying much. In the next cage were two cowering, skittish hyenas. They jumped sideways when we came into view. Their ears turned toward us, listening. They looked terrified. Wide-eyed. But the hyenas were neither pacing nor lying down. They stood anxiously, as if waiting for something. They skittered a little bit sideways, every time we made a move. These animals responded to our presence with a recoiling, harrowing dread. I noticed their mangy, denuded tails.

The sign said *African Striped Hyenas*. They were doglike in appearance, with their front legs oddly much longer than their hind legs, but a hyena is really not a dog. Whatever they were, their eyes offered them stereo vision; they looked straight at us, staring right into our eyes. They seemed to be questioning us, posing the simple question, "Why?"

I said to Les, "Do people always ask you if the hyenas ever laugh?"

"Yeah," said Les. "I tell them they don't laugh."

"Sometimes people come up to me and complain that their children were disappointed because the hyenas didn't laugh. I tell them I don't know if those are *Laughing Hyenas* or what."

"Chuck Voracek told me that the spotted hyena is the one that laughs."

The next cage had two gaunt gray wolves. The two wolves didn't pace; they simply stood there, never laying down. The wolves were nervous and scared-looking.

As we approached them, they winced down fearfully. Those were the two wolves drivers sometimes referred to as *the mated pair*. Their paws were big. It looked as if there were wearing big shoes with toes, like a cartoon. They had huge heads, big feet, and diminished bodies.

I liked wolves. I was intrigued by the whole concept of them. I'd read *Never Cry Wolf* recently, so that wolves and their habits were top of mind for me. These two wolves had my sympathy. Their hide seemed coarse and dry, not luxuriant. A lot of their fur was a bright white, colorless like an old man's beard. The two gray wolves were lanky, angular and could be referred to as bony, I thought.

As Les and I watched them, the thought that bleached our minds was the unmovable realization that these wolves were in that hard and lifeless cage all the time. That was it, day and night. It never would end.

"This isn't any fun," Les said. "It's upsetting. When we walk away from the cage, I'm still going to see them."

The two wolves were the animals that immediately pierced my heart. After recoiling initially, the wolves leaned forward toward me, staring into my eyes. The tufts at the sides of their heads were squared toward me, like the head of the wolf on the old Cub Scout patches. I had the sense that they were confronting me with a plea, one aimed directly at me. Their eyes widened with a surprised and sudden look of hope. It was as if they said, *At last. You're here.* They expected something from me, it seemed. That may have been my imagination. Wolves are very doglike, and it's easy to attribute doglike characteristics to their actions. Whether there is mentality behind the actions or not is hard to say. One thing for sure, though, the two wolves gazed right at me, bending down and peering forward through the two sets of bars that separated us. I felt that they were reading me like a book.

"They're looking right at you," Les said. "Maybe they smell your dog or something. Your parents have a dog, don't they?"

"Yeah, I see it. I'm going to walk out of sight and come back," I said. I moved far off to the right. I walked away around thirty feet. Then I came back.

"Yeah, they watched you go and kept looking after you and waited for you to come back," said Les.

I felt hopeless about those wolves. I said, "Well, at least they've got each other, you know? That cougar and that anteater are like... just nothing."

Leaving the wolves, we moved on. In the back left of the next cage was a pile of lifeless black fur. It looked like a dead shag rug. That was a black panther, actually a black leopard. As it lay there, it seemed to be only four inches thick, like it was deflated. It was a pile of bones wrapped in an old fur coat. Les and I peered into the far corner a long time to see if we could detect any shallow breathing from the panther.

"It's breathing," I said.

Along the front were other cages with vertical wrought iron bars. One cage at a time, we looked inside. In successive cages, we saw a jaguar, a lynx, and a spotted leopard. They were all solitary animals, pacing. Like all the animals, they were closed out into their cages by a simple plywood door. They'd be let in before nightfall, but all of them were still outside. The keepers in that building were simply running late that day.

Those animals were out in the fresh air, but were anxious and miserable. All those animals had ulcerated sores on them. Some had sores on their sides and haunches. Some had spots where the fur was worn off or missing, like a mange. They all had black, worn ulcers on their *elbows*. That was from laying on concrete.

It was obvious their overwhelming dilemma was, "Should I lay down on the ulcerating, arthritis-causing concrete, or should I pace endlessly forever, to burn off this unquenchable energy and frustration?"

There was the overwhelming thought I often had when seeing zoo animals. I simply could not understand why any animal is deprived of dirt. How difficult can it be to give an animal dirt to lie on? It doesn't seem that on a planet made of dirt, that would be too much to ask. Maybe they were pacing in search of dirt.

We continued walking along the cool, shady front of the old building. It was a glorious spot, with moist green grass and towering leafy trees, all at our backs. At our fronts were metal, animal dander, and stone.

Next, past the leopard exhibit was an empty cage. That was the chimp's outdoor cage, but he was not outside. Then, we reached the end in a spot where the walkway was surrounded by lovely flowering bushes. On the rounded, front right of the building was one more very large corner cage. The largest of all Cats and Ape outdoor cages was always empty, never occupied, night or day.

The two of us walked back along the front the way we had come, passing all those animals again. Les was very upset. I started to feel uncomfortable because he was so unhappy. I'd never seen him that way. He was taking on an attitude of anger and frustration.

Les said, "Okay. We can walk away from this, but these animals will be here until they die. That's their only way out of here. I can't stand to look at it. If I could do something to help them, to make their lives better, I'd come back here every day. But since I can't do anything about it, I'm never looking at these animals again. This is the only time I'm ever taking a tour of this building."

We walked to the west end of the building amid a light breeze. Before we entered, we noticed there was an animal exhibit just before the entrance. It was about thirty feet west of the building. The small exhibit was walled in by chain link fencing. There was a canopy over the exhibit, a plastic canopy of red and white. Inside the fencing was a stone-edged pool that looked like a backyard lily pond. It was about a half-foot deep and maybe eight feet in diameter. On the concrete laying on top of one another, trying to lie on something soft, was a load of flabby-looking grayish-white American alligators. There were six or seven of those. These mold-colored animals simply did not move at all. I felt that they were simply basking in the warm day.

Les said, "They're laying there like they're dead. Man, this whole thing is bothering me a lot. I'm sorry we did this."

But the alligators didn't bother me.

"They probably just ate," I said. "I think alligators always lay around like that." I'd see those alligators lots of times after that. They could have replaced them with stuffed alligators and no one would have known the difference.

Turning right, we were at the bottom of the stairs, at the west entrance to the Cat and Ape Building. Beginning the long parade as early as 1904, the public had entered this building from that spot. From ladies in broad-brimmed feathered velvet hats and long Edwardian dresses and men in three-piece lounge suits and derbies, to 1960s women with see-through blouses and hippie men covered in biker tattoos, the Cleveland public had walked into the Main Building looking to see the world's greatest beasts.

Just as they had, we walked up a few deeply worn concrete steps to get in. There was a center-latching pair of old wooden doors, painted white, with glass panes. Those old, rattling doors were rickety. As they noisily creaked open, it caused eerie echoes. They shimmied and vibrated like the doors of an old china cabinet, with the glass loose in the panes. The putty of the old doors was hardened and falling away, and the doors' bright white paint was peeling off in dusty sheets. The door knobs were ornate, round like huge dark coat buttons.

Once inside, Les and I stepped onto a white marble floor. That was a tiny vestibule. Everything about the entrance way was small and demure, like the entrance to a historic house from the Civil War era. People were smaller in the old days.

There was hardly room in this foyer for both of us at the same time. We stepped over a warped wooden threshold. Going past another pair of white wooden doors, we entered a huge cathedral of zoo antiquity. We moved into a long arcade-shaped hall. Everything in the hall seemed dirty in color. There was a gray pallor over the walls, the floors, the informational signs, even the light bulbs. The atmosphere seeped with the moist stench of animal fear and urine. Every word we spoke and every footstep resulted in a series of hollow echoes.

Immediately we had to look up. The ceiling seemed miles above our heads, lined with skylights and old, wavy glass panes. Architecturally, that ceiling was vaguely reminiscent of the Old Arcade on Euclid Avenue. The Arcade was built in 1890, possibly modeled after Galleria Vittorio Emanuele in Milan, Italy. Well, the skylights of the old Animal House gave the building some of that same old-fashioned interior light.

In places, water was dripping from above. It was moist and moldy in the old building, with green algae and condensation formed on the glass panes far above our heads. Little wisps of vapor, almost like tiny clouds, floated near the high windows.

There were people in the old building as we entered. Moving toward us down the center of the long hall, a single woman pushed a dark, out-dated, spoke-wheeled baby carriage. It was like a scene in an absurdist French film. I remember her because Les said, "hi" to her and she made no reply. I looked down into the carriage, but there wasn't a baby in there, just a crumpled white blanket.

There was another group of people, maybe a dozen in all, farther down the center hall to the right. They were families with children. These happy families were noisy, sometimes shrieking. They were fascinated by the exhibits in the east end of the building.

As Les and I moved further into the hallway, every footstep and every word we spoke resulted in endless echoes. The floor was a hard, concrete aggregate, very uneven, worn down along the paths in front of the exhibits. Between the echoes, the moisture, the darkness, the faraway natural light source, the mold scents and algae, and the stone floor, it was like being in a cave. Les clapped his hands sharply, and a cascade of endless echoing claps bounced at us from every direction, up down, and sideways.

Surprisingly, there were hardly any animals in the building at all. Most were outside, and we had seen them. On the right as we entered were several barred cages in a row. Those were the indoor cages of the cougar, anteater, wolves, hyenas, etc.

But to the left as we entered, we soon found the very large gibbon exhibit behind a great glass panel on the north side of the hall. There were six or seven gibbons in an exhibit that formed the centerpiece of the structure.

By the standards of that old building the gibbon enclosure was huge. It also seems to me that the ceiling within the cage was high, going up to the skylights. The sounds the dark-haired gibbons made were incredible, echoing throughout the giant building with monstrous might.

"OOOOOO. OOOOO. Ah-whoop. Whoop. OOOOOO." It was like somebody cranking up a fire siren. "Oooo. Oooo. OOOOO. OOOOOO. Ahhh-WHOOOOOOOOOOOO. Eeeee."

There are many species of gibbons in the world, and I don't know what species the zoo had. They were dark in color is about all I know. They may have been agile gibbons. Those small apes were behind a glass wall, and didn't have bars at the front of their cage. It was a huge pane of glass about ten feet high. The gibbon group was very active, walking around on their hind legs in a slightly crouched and bent-over way. The gibbons were constantly milling around, back and forth, back and forth. Their way of walking made them look like a group of small, hairy men, little people about two and one-half feet tall.

I watched one gibbon who liked to mock the walking patterns of people. We approached the glass. Suddenly that one gibbon stood up straight, fully erect. He held his back as straight as a board, with his arms hanging at his side like a French puppet. Then walked around back and forth, like a human, mocking the way we walked. That was kind of funny. But that was about the only cheery thing in the Old Main Building in the late 1960s.

Les and I walked further, passing the many empty cages on the right. Each cage was nothing but a cement floor with steel bars on all four sides. Really, all those cages were like cells in a kennel. Some cages had a water trough with water trickling into it. A few of the cages had shelves, or platforms, for the animals to climb upon. These shelves were primitive, made from wide, long wooden boards, bleached gray from endless cleanings. Those worn planks were about four feet up off the floor. Some animals, such as the panther, cougar, lynx, or leopard could jump up onto a shelf and be up off the concrete.

Other than the wailing gibbons, there were only two animals inside the building that afternoon. Mertus and I walked further toward the end of the building to the east. Far down the hall on the right, there was a big chimp inside the second last cage. There was a tire hanging from a rope in the center of his small, barred enclosure. Up on a wooden shelf, the large chimp was curled up against the back bars of the cage, totally inactive. He looked like a pile of nothing.

Finally, at the other end of the building on the right, was one last exhibit. By the time we got there, all the other people in the building were there, also. There were ten or twelve people looking into the cage at this end of the old, damp, dark hallway.

Inside that last cage was Timmy. That was the first time I saw him, but it wasn't much of a look. The sign said western lowland gorilla with the Latin name *Gorilla gorilla gorilla*. But all we saw was a musty mound of dark fur in the back corner of the cage. He was curled up on the same spot of concrete where I'd seen the other gorilla eight years earlier. That chilly spot of concrete was where gorillas always curled up, doing nothing.

The people there were very disappointed.

Someone asked, "Is the gorilla sick?"

Then that family left.

A person from the other family concurred, saying, "The gorilla's sick."

It was dark in the corner. It was so shadowy that the black hairy form sometimes looked like an illusion, like a shadow itself. Timmy was curled up in a fetal position, with his curved back toward the people. But he wasn't asleep. From time to time he rolled over and peered back toward us, hoping that everyone would simply go away. I saw the wet glint of his eye. In this charcoal darkness, that was about all I could see.

"Yes, I think he's definitely sick," said someone else.

We all stood there quietly for five minutes, as if in a funeral home. Finally, a cheerful brown-shirted keeper appeared in the hallway behind us. He spoke with a European accent.

He said, "Hokay, folkses. Is time go. We close now. All right?"

Les and I had no special privileges. We had to leave, too. We walked back out into the sunny afternoon.

"Well, I'll never go back in there again," said Les, looking straight ahead with his jaw set.

And he never did. That I know.

CHAPTER EIGHT

Mertus didn't see Timmy again, but I became a frequent visitor to the front of the gorilla's cage. I found out something before too long. After the Old Main Building was locked and the keepers were gone, the back door to the building was still unlocked. The doorway that led down to the time clock wasn't locked for a long time in case anyone needed to punch out late. From time to time, I went in through the basement and up the stairs into the Animal Hall after hours, around 5:30 p.m.

Being nosey, I also went snooping around in the cellar of Old Main. I wanted to know where they had kept the snakes that drowned in the infamous 1959 flood. I made my way down into a bizarre labyrinth of small cinderblock chambers, all connected like the interior of a pharaoh's tomb. Every one of the little rooms was empty. All the floors, ceilings, and walls were painted with a thick white-green oil-based paint.

It was always broad daylight outside when I worked my way up into the now-quiet arcade hallway where the cages were. With the people and even the keepers gone, Timmy had his quiet time. The entire zoo was empty except for me and the night watchman, wherever he was.

Inside the big Edwardian Ape House, it was peaceful, serene. The cats, hyenas, wolves, and the anteater were indoors, but they never made a sound. The illumination indoors was a shade of deep olive green. *Murky* is how I would describe it.

After hours, Timmy was no longer hiding down in the back corner. He was always sitting up on his wooden ledge, with his legs pulled up under him. He tolerated me during those visits. As I approached his cage, he looked my way for a second, just barely turning his head. Other than that, he had no reaction to me. He simply continued in his quiet thoughts. At that time, Timmy was around nine years old. He was already majestic to view.

Timmy was born wild in Africa in 1959. The story was that Timmy was less than one year old when poachers culled him from a band of wild gorillas. The poachers probably shot and killed all the adults in the group, murdering them in front of tiny Timmy's wide eyes. He was plucked up by the poachers, undoubtedly torn away from his dead mother. The poachers were careful to not shoot him since he was a valuable commodity that could be sold for a good price to animal traders. The dead members of the band also had value; the most-magnificent members of the group were probably mounted, stuffed, and sold as curiosities. For the next several years, from 1960 to 1966, Timmy grew up in a tiny cage somewhere in Africa while the poachers waited for a buyer. The cage in which young Timmy spent a hundred percent of his time would have been a primitive one, perhaps just a few feet square. His cage may have been stacked among many others, teeming with leopards, hyenas, big cats, and monkeys. Perhaps they sometimes cleaned his cage by hosing it out while he was in it, soaking him with a spray of water infused with the foaming urine of other beasts. After six years in that cage, a market was found for the darkly colored lowland gorilla. The year was 1966. No doubt bewildered, Timmy ended up on an airplane, and finally arrived by a series of trucks and automobiles to the old Main Cat and Ape Building at the Cleveland Zoo. There the cage was somewhat larger, and Timmy no doubt had better food and cleaner living conditions than previously. When I first saw him in the summer of 1968, up to that point in his life, he'd been completely alone in a comfortless cage for eight years. That sounds like a long time to be sequestered in a tiny space surrounded by iron bars, but Timmy's prison sentence was just beginning.

Timmy was a male western lowland gorilla that would someday weigh in excess of five hundred pounds. In the zoo's Old Main Building, young Timmy had a *corner office*, on the east end of the building. His space was tiny, about ten feet square. But it was larger than most of the other cages. His cubicle, however, did not offer him access to an outdoor cage during the daytime. For some reason, Timmy was never let outside. If he had, it would have only been out onto a rock-hard concrete slab surrounded by dark iron bars.

At the back of Timmy's indoor cell was a worn wooden shelf made of gray-white lumber. It was bleached from cleaning solvents and urine. This shelf was perhaps eighteen inches wide. There was a tire swing hanging down from the bars in the ceiling. The tire was tied from a simple chain. In the daytime hours, when people were in the building, Timmy would sometimes swing on the tire. The tire would really get moving. At the height of its swing, Timmy would grab onto the bars, and hold himself and the tire high upon the side of the cage.

Back then, Timmy hadn't yet developed his glorious *silverback*. But he was an imposing brute, if you could get a good look at him. Most people went away disappointed because he didn't do anything. Timmy didn't like being looked at. Yet there was no place to hide from the gawking eyes of the visiting public. That's why more often than not, he would huddle down in shadows against the corner of the bars in the back of his cage. He kept his head down and out of view. Timmy hunkered into a ball, looking small, with his back turned and his legs and arms gathered into his chest. His appearance was generally that of a hairy round ball of non-movement. As I noted, the remark most often heard was, "Is the gorilla sick?"

Yeah, I guess he *was*.

In the daytime hours, only a few lucky zoo visitors went away feeling they had really seen the show. These were the ones who happened to be there when Timmy went into one of his periodic wild rampages. When one of these brutal fits started, every visitor in the building raced to see. Timmy would career berserkly around his prison home. He galloped around the iron-hard cage on all fours, running on his knuckles and feet. Then he crashed with his full force into the bars, making dramatic thundering sounds. *BAM. BOOM. WHAM. BAM. BAM. BAM.* It was a display of great speed and extreme violence. Anyone watching worried that he was harming his shoulders, chest, arms, and ribs. He'd just keep hammering and hammering and hammering his shoulders into the thick iron bars.

Timmy had the tire swing as a possession, but he also had a second tire that was loose in the cage. As people watched duly impressed and genuinely terrified, Timmy hurled that old 16-inch tire across the cage and screamed angrily. He took a lot of frustration out on that rubbery tire. Vocalizing constantly, the young gorilla moaned and hissed. He also gave the expected gorilla screams, *OOOOOO OOOOO OOOOO OOOOOOO.* As he screamed, his mouth opened wide like Kong, revealing deadly canine fangs, with his black lips curled back in a snarl.

Sometimes he'd charge the front of the cage and beat his chest. *BA-BOOM, BA-BOOM, BA-BOOM.* That's what people wanted to see. That's what people wished he'd do all the time. They could have sold tickets for that. The rampages were what people liked, but they were rare. During his tortured outbursts, Timmy would often slap his palms loudly against the concrete. *WHAM. WHAM. WHAM.* It had to hurt. Then he would charge the crowd again, his head bobbing up and down as he came forward in jerking stops and starts to the front limits of his cell. The display was morbid, disturbing, and dynamic. It seemed the manic gorilla was completely out of his mind with rage. When he charged toward them, people naturally jumped backward in fear. Timmy was separated from them by two layers of bars. But nonetheless people felt their hearts pounding.

When Timmy was in the middle of one of these frantic tirades, the floor and the walls were all the same to him. He could race right up the sides of the barred walls. He'd swing from the bars on the ceiling, then roar around the interior of the cage in a swirling whirlpool of speed. Then, suddenly, he would drop to the floor and sit down calmly. As quickly as it had started, the show was over. People watching would start to wander away. As one by one they looked away, then *WHAM....* Unexpectedly, with blinding speed and awesome force, Timmy would lower a shoulder and ram his great bulk into the unforgiving iron bars at the front of the cage. People jumped out of their skins. Their heads jerked, and they sucked in a hard breath. That was one of Timmy's favorite ploys. He liked to lull the people into thinking he was done. When they turned their backs, he'd scare them to pieces by a bone-jarring hit that shook the old building and echoed back in mighty waves. That old building was sensational for echoes.

During a tantrum, Timmy often watched the crowd out of the corner of his eye. He entertained himself by watching their reactions. The fear in their eyes interested him. They were puny, and the ease with which he could manipulate them, even from behind two barriers, reinforced his feeling of superiority.

But after the day was over, I saw a very different Timmy. At those times, he was sitting quietly on his shelf, with his knees up against his chest. He had his head turned to the right, staring out the tiny window at the east end of his cage.

What was Timmy's favorite thing in the world during the many years he was kept in a cage in the ancient Main Building? It was his *window*. It wasn't a window with a frame or glass, but merely a tiny opening, about one foot square, in the brick wall. It was very much an architectural oddity. Its reason for being seemed unexplained. It was simply a square hole in the wall, like a opening in the tower of a medieval castle. But it was open, with no glass and no bars.

Timmy couldn't sit as close to the hole as he would have liked. It was too high in the cage and too far from the narrow wooden platform. Looking up through the small square, all he could see were the upper branches of some nearby sycamore trees, mixed with the lower hanging boughs of black willows. At certain times of the year, he certainly saw patches of sky. He gazed sadly upward toward this small, high window in his dungeon. The alluring opening transfixed him and was his sole escape. It was good that he could spend two-thirds of each twenty-four hour period in solitude, free from the puny ones, comforted to a small degree by his little window. With his keen senses of smell and hearing, he could undoubtedly see far beyond the view itself.

Certainly he heard the evening orchestra of wild bird song. Perhaps he knew everything about the zoo's two-and-a-half acre lake. Did he also know about the glorious flower beds that surrounded his building? Did he detect the rich, moist scent of freshly dug soil as he distantly monitored the daily progress of the crews laying sewer pipe near the sea lion pool? Had he learned the seasons of the flowering willows along the railroad tracks behind Old Main? Did he surmise how delicious their leaves and branches would be? Did he enjoy the sunrise that slipped ever so briefly through that tiny window with a golden light that probably found its way inside for a mere ten minutes each day?

As I looked at Timmy in the late afternoon, it was very dark in the cage. By then, with the lights turned off, the window was pretty much the only source of light that reached him. So his face was dramatically lit by the warm afternoon radiance coming in through the window from one direction. Every line and feature of his black skin was accentuated. Timmy had a lot of tiny furrows around his eyes, making him look wizened. His eyes were searching, groping. When a breeze stirred, his head rose just a bit and his nostrils flared ever so slightly, like a dog sniffing a faraway world he could not know.

His head moved only the smallest amounts and rarely. But his eyes and nostrils were in nearly constant motion. The dark eyes were filled with hopeless longing, wistfully turned to the right, as he sullenly pondered his restricted view of a few yellow-green branches.

I thought at the time Timmy was very old. I had no idea that he was actually young. His face seemed so lined with worry and care. I'll never forget his expression as he sat there virtually motionless. I wish I could better describe the hopelessness, loneliness, sadness.

I remember saying to others in my age group, "You look at him, and watch his eyes, and it's just like some man sitting there."

All I could ever see in Timmy's face was humanity. He was a man, sad and wistful, with intelligence looming in his moist eyes. He wasn't crying, but his eyes were moist.

Walking respectfully away from him, I moved along through the center of the damp Ape House. I walked down the flights of concrete steps and came out behind the building, strolling out into the place where in the morning all the men would once more be a bustle of activity. Turning right, I walked beneath the canopy of the great sycamores and willows, moving past the very places toward which the great ape Timmy could only peek, sniff, and listen.

The next day, driving the tour train, I alleviated only my own unhappiness when I enthusiastically told the visitors to the zoo that plans were underway to build a new Cat and Ape Building in the upper levels of the park. I told everyone the new building would place the animals in larger outdoor, naturalized exhibits.

Indeed the management of the zoo was hard at work, trying to raise the three million dollars needed to make that possible. We expected it wouldn't be long before Timmy's day of deliverance was at hand. Soon, the zoo would build a new Cat and Ape Building and name it after the zoo's Director, Dr. Goss. (I don't want to tell story out of order, but ten years from that day Timmy was still waiting.)

As for me, I was young. Like all my friends, it was easy and natural for me to simply slip back into the world of summer friendships and frivolity. I wasn't any different from anyone else who worked in the zoo. At the end of the day, I just went home.

CHAPTER NINE

I remember sitting up on the cab of Number 3 one pretty afternoon. It was a slow day, and my train was parked at the Children's Farm stop. Some guy who was visiting the zoo was seated alone in the front seat of the first car. He was about thirty, small and nervous, but very talkative. He was chain-smoking cigarettes, and flicking the butts off toward Kiddie Land. He had dark, thinning hair, combed back.

"Yeah," he said wistfully, "You got it made. My job stinks, working inside all the time. I'm just stuck behind a damn desk. Look at all this here." He gestured with a broad sweep of his left arm up toward the huge, towering leafy trees that provided the cool canopy over the Children's Farm.

"You got all this nature, all this fresh air."

The guy left, and none too soon. On the other hand, he was right about one thing. The zoo was where I wanted to work in the summer. All the kids were nice. None of us drank. Well, Norm drank beer sometimes. None of us smoked or had even heard about drugs. We were good, clean, bright kids. Gene Huhtala had hired hard-working *good kids* in the late sixties when, from some people's point of view, the world was being populated by hippies and pot smokers. His wisdom had brought all of us together. He was a pretty shrewd judge of people.

Meanwhile, the older full-time employees were also everywhere, dressed in their brown, feces-soaked uniforms. Many looked like convicts. They *all* smoked. About half were European, with various accents. In 1968, all the keepers were men. Full-time female employees were relegated to being a matron or nothing. The matron's job was cleaning the public restrooms. All the animal keepers, groundskeepers, and mechanics were men. Most were older; many had teeth missing and gnarled hands. More than one limped. They often got up in the morning with *zookeeper's back*. This was stiff lower back that lasted two or three days, and had them hobbling around like hunchbacks. We thought they were dangerous, like winos hanging out near Municipal Stadium after an Indians game. Some of them had old floppy shoes that were taped back together with electrical tape. They were kind of like hobos in that regard. To a man, they spit an awful lot. I have to say that they didn't curse much, though sometimes a word slipped out.

I was only nineteen, and the *old guys* freaked us out. A description of a typical older keeper will give you an example.

One time my train was parked at the Children's Farm, and one of the *old* keepers started talking to me. Let's say his name was *Joe*. I was standing there by the split rail fence talking to a cute girl, and the next thing I knew

Joe was talking to me. He wanted to join the conversation with the girl. But she took one whiff of that old man and split, whereas I was too polite to leave.

I stood there listening to this guy. Again, the best way to describe it is that it reminded me of the times I was walking downtown and a panhandler started talking to me. This conversation with Joe is representative of how we viewed keepers at the time.

"Yeah, well, whatever the hell," he began. "Life sure is lousy. What day is it? What can a guy do about it? I feel better now than I did this morning. That's not saying much. I gotta go, but not yet. I don't know what day this is. I think the politicians are full of crap. The zoo is screwing me. It's like I told my old lady. What are you gonna do? Can't do nothing. I'm not happy. I've never been happy. Well, I gotta get back to work, but not yet. Where'd that girl go? This isn't my area. I need to get back to my area. I like it here better."

The whole time Joe was talking at me, he inhaled huge puffs off a crooked Lucky Strike cigarette. Dressed in loose-fitting, filthy brown garb, Joe leaned back against the fence, which gave him the illusion of being able to stand erect. If the fence had suddenly disappeared, he would have fallen off the planet. The man's yellow-green hair was slicked back as if soaked in SAE 30 motor oil. His fingers were stained with nicotine, and he reeked of cigarettes. At one point, when his cigarette was almost sucked down to the end, he put another cigarette in his mouth and lit it. For a few seconds he had two cigarettes going in his mouth. He held them flush together and sucked a double drag off the two of them. Then his leathery old face winced in pain as he took the last drag off the short cigarette. It was about a half inch long. With the new cigarette in his mouth, he, threw down the butt, and stepped on it. As he stepped on it, he was taking a drag off the other one.

I thought, *Now that's a chain smoker.*

Of course, these older keepers were covered with *dung, doodoo, dooky, tee-tee, pooh-pooh, stinkies, guano, ding-dongs, dingle berries, crap,* and *caca.* And they smelled like it. Pachyderm keepers had one aroma. Bird Building keepers had another. If a guy took care of the big cats, he smelled like cat feces and musk. If a guy was the sea lion keeper he smelled like chlorine, pee, and mackerel. A keeper from Old Main smelled like swimming pool chlorine and male gibbon. If a guy was a keeper in Bears, he smelled like moldy wet carpet that a dog peed on.

Every area of the zoo had a very different aroma. The waste of the birds and animals varied greatly. The smells of birds droppings were acidic and raced up into the tops of your sinuses, sour and biting. The bears' was a deep and heady waft that curiously smelled of rotten apples. The big cats' stools had a wicked hard pill of stench, and the hippos, elephants, and hoofed animals' wastes were extremely permeating potent manures. When you breathed this in long enough, it came out your pores. And this represented only a small sampling of the odors by which animals made their presence known. There were also various body odors and musks of animals, as in *wet-dog mixed with light skunk*. After a time, a person could walk blindfolded into a building and say, "Oh, there's a cougar in here," or "I smell gibbons." The fact is that the old keepers carried all these scents like albatrosses around their necks. We just kept our distance and observed.

The keepers in the late 1960s also had an amusing habit of *goosing* one another in a particular way. I mean that they would grab each other by the testicles as a joke, reaching through the cloth of another guy's pants. The main place where keepers did this was at the time clock where they punched in and out. Interestingly, the young women who worked at the zoo did not punch out at the same clock as the men. They had another time clock somewhere else. That way, the zoo managed to spare the young women from the obscene ritual of the keepers.

But tour drivers punched out in the same place where the keepers and maintenance workers punched out. So we saw the men grabbing each other by the nuts as a joke. While everyone was waiting for the clock to hit 5:00 p.m., there would be perhaps thirty men standing around, all dressed in brown. It was a relaxed and peaceful room with a lot of light conversation and men shouting and joking.

When a keeper entered the room, another one might yell, "Hey, there he is. You old son of a gun. Get in here."

As we silently listened to the conversations, we blue-clad drivers noticed that in the crowd, there would always be one sneaky keeper, who was on a mission. He had targeted another keeper whom he wanted to goose from behind. That is, when a zoo keeper was standing there talking, another old guy would run up behind him and pinch him in the testicles from behind. Really.

"*Yeowch*. Why you... *Ouch!*" the guy who got goosed would yell.

The attacker would giggle and scurry away.

"I'm gonna get you, Perkins," the man who had been goosed would shout.

And he would get even, too.

The next evening Bob Perkins would be standing at the time clock and he'd get his. They kept score in their minds, remembering who owed whom a grab on the nuts.

A likely scenario would go like this: Thirty guys are standing around, and the victim of the day is there, also. Casually, the attacker moves into a neutral position about twenty feet behind the victim. After hanging around innocently for a few minutes, the attacker begins approaching the victim from behind. Many people were seeing and understanding what is playing out as the attacker approached. The five of us stood together like ducks in a pen. Meanwhile, the attacker tiptoes up from behind intent on grabbing the victim by the testicles and squeezing. As he approaches, no one blinks an eye. Quite the contrary, they all become part of the plot, and one or two of them casually engages the victim in a distracting conversation.

The victim peers down into the face of the time clock to see what time it is.

Then someone says to him, "So what are you doing this weekend?"

"Well, my wife and I are going to see Perry Como in concert."

"Oh," says the keeper named Jackie, "you'll like that."

"Naw, I don't want to go see Perry Como. My wife's gonna make me get all dressed up. I hate that."

"Come on!" exclaims Steve Sandusky, "you'll have a great time. Is it downtown?"

The other keepers have now become part of the plot and the subterfuge as a conversation continues until the man strikes. He breaks into a run, tongue sticking out the side of his mouth as he reaches in from behind and, well, grabs the victim's gonads with a sharp, quick squeeze.

Then the whole room bursts into uproarious laughter as the attacker runs away.

In my zoo career I saw this happen fifty times easily. After learning how to shovel up a load of zebra shit while eating a Big Mac, nothing much bothers you. Drivers were bystanders in this game. We knew better than to warn the guy or anything. We were just spectators. The old guys were playing a game they thought funny. From our point of view, we'd never consider grabbing a co-worker by the testicles, yet this was apparently a popular game. A keeper named Vince Rimedio was a regular target. Evidently, he gained that honor by being easy to distract. All the other keepers had to do was get him talking about one of his pet peeves and a bull's-eye appeared below the belt. Let him go off on his ex and her husband and it was goose-city.

"Hey, he can have her. I oughta send the guy a Christmas card," would be a passionately delivered line just before an even more passionate yelp that always stretched into an exclamation: "Why you *sonofabitch!*"

At that time, the keepers were a rough lot, but there was at least one exception; his name was Perkins. Unlike many of his peers, Perkins was a gentle and polite man who actually carried on polite conversations at the ticket booths. The sellers liked him and would offer him popcorn and slices of apple. Perkins was the one guy, who was always called by his last name.

One of my friends relayed a conversation she'd had with him.

She said, "He walked passed my booth near the end of the day, and he was all dressed up. He didn't have his uniform on. He looked nice... well, you know... He looked pretty good for him. I said, 'Hey, Perkins, why are you all dressed up? Have you got a hot date?' He said, 'Oh, yes. I'm going to sneak out tonight on a date with my sweetheart.' So I said, 'Oh, your wife better not find out.' And he said, 'My wife is my sweetheart.' Isn't that cute? I almost cried."

For a bunch of naïve college boys, all this seemed like a crushing way to make a living. "I'm sure glad I go to college," said Les one time. "I mean, could you imagine ending up like one of those guys?" We had that conversation often, and most of us had alternative dreams of the future.

"That's why I'm going into radio broadcasting," announced Bob.

I was majoring in English Literature and just knew that a degree would open the doors to riches and opportunity. Norm was studying to be a veterinarian, and we were all quite sure we'd never face life as one of those giggling gnomes covered with dung. They scurried hither and yon amid the dark, wet shadows behind the barred cages, dispensing chow.

Big Al from Chicago might have been the exception. "But do you have any idea how much money those old guys make? That guy Joe in Apes made over thirty grand last year." (It was a princely sum in 1968.) "He gets time-and-a-half for overtime and paid holidays. It's because of the Teamsters."

In truth, the tour drivers never really got to know the full-time workers and, other than at the time clock, had little interaction with the keepers, truck drivers, maintenance crew, or groundskeepers. The only full-time person we really knew was Whitey.

Having said that, I did have an altercation with three of the zoo's truck drivers.

One morning, I drove my train to the Children's Farm. Being early and during the week, the zoo had few visitors and I had no passengers. This gave me a chance to visit with Mary Beth, who was in the barn caring for a piglet.

As I neared the building, I saw a big cardboard box full of lettuce, sweet potatoes, carrots, and apples. It was a slow morning, and I thought I'd be helpful so I hoisted the box onto one shoulder.

"YOU PUT THAT BLANKETY BLANK BOX DOWN– NOW!"

An old flatbed truck wheeled up just beyond the gate. An old, greasy looking guy with a cigarette butt hanging from his mouth pointed a crooked finger at me, while two other tough-looking guys glared at me from the cab. The guy yelling at me was Vern, the union steward.

"Put the box f—— DOWN. Right f—— back where you f—— found it."

"Oops, sorry," I said, setting down the box. "Sorry." Apparently, an apology wasn't enough and Vern moved toward me with a vengeance.

He yelled, "That's *NOT* your f—— job." Vern really laid into me, like an army drill sergeant. "Your f—— job is driving the f—— tour trains and that's f—— all. Every f—— job in this f—— zoo can only be done by one f—— person. Do you f—— understand?."

"Yes, sir."

"Hey, you don't be f—— acting like a damn f—— scab. You with the union? You better f—— be..."

"Yes, sir. Teamsters Local 507." But I was thinking, *Everyone's with the union. How could I not be with the union?*

Bulbous-nosed, slick-haired, foul-mouthed Vern came over the short fence and kept yelling at me. I was nineteen years old and weighed a hundred and forty-nine pounds. Vern and the other two men, in their forties, weren't afraid of me, not even a little.

Coming right up into my face, Vern yelled, "Listen. I'm f—— telling you right now, you f—— f——. Just do the job your f—— supposed to do, and you won't get into real trouble with the Teamsters. Got it?. You f—— do that again and I f—— personally will f—— kick your f—— ass right f—— here."

Vern shook his finger at me one more time. I looked over into the cab of the truck, which was about forty feet away. One of the other guys, whose name was Bobbie, had a small silver flask. He tilted back his head and took a snort. It was 9:30 in the morning. As it happened, this was just another lesson that union stuff was pretty serious.

CHAPTER TEN

Les Mertus was my best friend at the zoo in those tour train years. Like me, Les was an literature major. He aspired to be a writer and loved Henrik Ibsen's *The Wild Duck* (go figure). I was the only guy he knew who ever heard of Ibsen.

In the mornings after washing the trains, we usually sat around and talked until 9 a.m. which was *roll 'em out* time. The topics were (of course) girls, cars, and what good movie was soon to be released. In truth, we all had a great deal of ambition. Ulas was serious about becoming a local disc jockey. Norm was in the perfect summer job for his ultimate goal of being a vet. I was intent on being a cartoonist.

Les was attending Kent State as a drama major and wanted to be a theatrical writer. It totally preoccupied him. He would often say, "I know I can do this." By that, he meant that he could become a *writer*. Les kept a worn, green paperback copy of *Hamlet* stuffed in the back pocket of his jeans and read it over and over that summer of 1968. He was reading it to study its structure and to be close to the feel of the theatre. He felt that if he had Shakespeare's voices running around in his mind, it would affect his writing style for the project he was working on.

He was feeling an internal pressure that I sometimes felt as well. He felt that he had to create something remarkable before graduation so that he could step out into the competitive world of writing. Rightly or wrongly, he thought that he had two years to make it as a successful working writer. If he didn't have a hit on Broadway by the summer of 1971, he'd be a failure. I understood this because I believed that I had to have a syndicated cartoon strip by the time I graduated, and I had a drawer full of rejection slips at home to prove that my failure was not from a lack of trying. My failed attempts had not gone unnoticed at college where a friend of mine, Sherry Dodd, once told me about what happened in her American literature class. "Hey, Adam," she said. "Your name came up today in lit class. Dr. Cook was wondering what color of paper a rejection slip is printed on, and someone yelled out, 'Ask Adam Smith.' It got a pretty big laugh."

Another driver with plenty of gray matter was Norm. As his hobby, he kept pet snakes, tarantulas, and iguanas at his house on Cleveland's near west side where he also had a gecko in his bathroom. It made perfect sense when Norm explained it. "He likes the moisture. Sometimes I just let the shower run in there."

One time when I was hanging out at Norm's house, I went into the bathroom to use it. Just before I went in, Norm reminded me that the gecko was there.

"Close the door behind you quickly so he doesn't get out."

I went in, and saw that, indeed, a jeweled green gecko was loose inside. It leapt the width of the bathroom from wall to wall, right past my face. *WHOOOSSSH. Smack.* The bright lizard flashed past me like a Frisbee. Then it jumped again, smack into the mirror over the sink. Its little sticky toes grabbed right onto the bathroom mirror as its buggy eyes looked at me. I did my thing, and then went back out into the living room.

"That's pretty cool," I said.

"Yeah, I ought to feed him," said Norm, who opened the bathroom door just long enough to throw in a live white mouse.

Norm's expertise in animals made him an instant buddy with Chuck Voracek, the likeable Public Service Director at the zoo. Chuck would invite Norm to hang out with him and the vets when a chimp needed an injection or when Chuck was going to feed a guinea pig to an eagle. Chuck knew I existed, but just barely.

Because he was a snake collector, Norm's Volkswagen was often full of sacks of live white mice and rats. Norm knew a place in town where he could get nice good-eating ones really cheap. He was always bringing them to the zoo and handing them out like candy to keepers and Voracek. That was another way he endeared himself to Chuck and the vets. They all loved Norm.

Unlike the rest of us, Norm was also interested in going into the animal areas and becoming acquainted with animal keepers. He spent a lot of time in the buildings where they kept the bears and birds. He was already living in a different zone than the rest of the drivers. Norm would start a conversation with a keeper by saying something like, "Hey, your polar bear has *dermatophilosis.*"

The keeper would answer, "Yeah, I know. Dr. Wendt's going to give him an injection today at noon. Wanna come watch?"

So the next thing you knew, Norm was hanging out with the zoo vets and even giving animals injections himself on his off days. Soon he was friends with everyone from Dr. Goss down to the grubbiest baboon keeper.

It was through Norm that tour drivers were sometimes drawn into what seemed to us to be the bizarre world of the full-time employees. Through Norm, I met another full-time employee who quite candidly freaked me out. That was John Sich, the zoo's night watchman. I still remember the first time I saw this unusual and unforgettable man.

Norm, Les, Bob, Al, and I were near the yaks, sitting in the back passenger car of a parked tour train at the end of the day. The sun was in the west, beaming through the Fulton Road Bridge. The bridge cast massive shadows onto the rippling surface of the slow-moving Big Creek. The zoo was entirely empty of visitors.

Along came this late model Ford station wagon with faded paint. It was a zoo vehicle. That old rusty wagon was the color of yellow puke. Behind the wheel was an odd-looking man, grinning like the Cheshire Cat. Seen through the filthy front windshield, this ruddy-faced older man looked extremely happy, and the sun illuminated his face with a golden hue.

I could see that he wasn't very tall as he sat low in the seat as if disappearing into quicksand. He wore mirrored sunglasses and his rounded shoulders were squished up around his head so that he appeared to have no neck at all.

I'd never seen that man before. Of course, I knew he was an employee, but I didn't think he was one of the keepers since they would have been at the time clock by then. Who was this guy? That's when Marabito said, "Hey, there's that old night watchman, coming this way."

As the car approached at a slow speed, I thought *He looks like he just got loose from the loony bin.* Norm looked up and saw the man. He smiled broadly, "Hey. Here comes John. We're going to shoot rats up in the reindeer enclosure, up in bears."

It was a surprise to me that Norm knew this guy, and that he was driving over to see us.

The car stopped with a squeaking of tired brakes. The driver's side door creaked open with the sound of a steel girder being bent. Out stepped the short, stocky man, grinning broadly. He was in his early fifties, but to me he looked ancient. The man was wearing layers and layers of hooded sweatshirts, mostly dark green. He had a grimy red baseball cap pushed back on the top of his head, with short, dark hair peeking out, as thick as the fur of a cat.

As he walked slowly toward us, the old man jingled. Around the belt of his loose-fitting *old man's pants*, were several rings loaded with keys. His hard, brown shoes were scuffed. He shuffled his feet as he walked, kicking aside loose pieces of gritty sand on the asphalt surface.

The ruddy-looking man walked right over to the train where we were seated. Norm jumped up excitedly to greet him.

In a thick Slovakian accent, the grimy, stout watchman said, "Ah. There is he. It is Norm."

The man was warm and friendly as Norm greeted him. "Hey, John," he said, "you ready to shoot some rats?"

"I ready," said John, grinning from ear to ear.

Then Norm turned to us. "Hey, John. These are some of the other tour train drivers..."

Unimpressed, John shrugged and said, "Humph. Well... good. Good for them. Okay, Norm... we go."

"All right," said Norm. "Hey, Adam. You want to come up to bears and shoot rats with me and John? I'll take turns with you using my gun."

"Uh... naw," I said. "That's okay."

"Well, then will you punch me out when you get to the time clock?"

"Oh, sure," I said.

John rattled like a bag of bolts as the two of them got into the old, wagon. The doors of the car protested as they were slammed shut. I couldn't believe Norm had gotten in a car with that guy. As they drove off, heading up to bears over the Big Creek Bridge, the sputtering car's exhaust spewed a trail of dark, gritty particles. After they were long gone, the fumes hung in the air. "Whew," exclaimed Al, "Now that was a kooky old guy."

"You said it." remarked Les.

We couldn't understand what motivated Norm to spend his time shooting rats with that old man. We could understand why he'd want to shoot rats, but how could he hang out with such a grubby guy? But he did, several nights a week.

Every evening when Norm went to shoot rats with John, I punched him out at the time clock, finding the yellow card with the dot-printer type that said, "Tulodziecki, Norman."

Bob said, "Ah, you guys don't get it. Norm's comfortable with that guy because he's first or second generation born in this country himself. That guy's like his grandfather or something."

"I guess so," said Les. "I know one thing. It doesn't matter how hot it is in the zoo, that guy has on five shirts and two coats."

Norm and John Sich went two or three evenings a week to shoot rats. By that I mean wild rats in the zoo. The concept struck me as repulsive. Those were the sneaky, grubby, tan Norwegian rats, not pretty white pink-nosed rats found in a pet store next to the gerbils. Norm wouldn't go around shooting domestic rats, but he did feed them to his snakes. He shot the feral brown rats with a .38.

The next morning the bunch of us were again sitting on a train waiting for the day to start when Norm said, "I don't know why you guys don't come up to bears and shoot rats with me and John. It's a lot of fun. Last night, I shot two of 'em. John shot six. So it was a pretty good evening."

Norm was always saying, "John this and John that." He was very fond of the odd man. He was also able to see a larger picture and had a better understanding of the threats to zoo animals from the disease carrying pests that lived off the scraps left in the cages and food areas. Nowadays, there could be a public uproar over shooting rats; in the sixties, however, it seemed low-tech, efficient, and free of dangerous chemicals.

CHAPTER ELEVEN

During the time I was at the zoo driving the trains in the summers, there was a change that dramatically altered the appearance of the trains. When I began, all the trains were *country blue*, and the cabs were blue with some metal-colored trim. The seats were blue vinyl. In 1969 or 1970, however, all the tour trains were repainted. Most of the painting was done by a young guy who was brought on as Whitey's assistant for awhile.

Cleveland was an auto plant town in those days, with big Ford and Chevy plants out on Brookpark Road. So lots of teenage boys, like their dads, were capable of customizing cars, working on cars, rebuilding engines, and painting their own vehicles. Whitey's new helper was one of those. He was an expert at painting vehicles with a lot of different semi-transparent layers in the finish. His own car, for instance, was painted, with several different types of transparent greens. After that dried, he used a special nozzle that blew out elaborate layers of stringy fibers that flew out into the air like cobwebs.

He said, "I paint the base coat, let it dry, and then I shoot this stringy stuff out over the car, real fine, like spider webs. I float it out real thin. I let the wind grab it and move it in creative ways. After that's all dry, I give it a couple of layers of clear coat."

Whitey raved about that kid. So the management decided it would be nice if he painted the trains. He did a fantastic job. That had to be a lot of work, since each of the six trains had three cars. It took a lot of masking and a lot of painting. He also painted other equipment, like the zoo's big gas-powered vacuum cleaner.

After he was done, two of the zoo trains were painted black and white with zebra stripes. I think those were Trains 1 and 4. That was done by painting the cab and cars white, then putting stripes on with masking tape and newspaper strips and painting the black stripes. He even painted stripes on the roof. Trains 3 and 5 were painted a reddish-orange and black to look striped like a tiger. Using the same method of masking tape and newspapers, he painted the roofs, also.

Trains 2 and 6 (Cinderella) were the coolest of all. He laid down a base coat of khaki, and then in a very loose and artistic manner put freehand (no masking) airbrushed leopard spots on the trains. He added some of his special *spider web* frills on top with the hard clear coat over everything. So those two trains looked like leopards. That was the same style in which he painted the zoo's park vacuum. He even painted all the vinyl seats. He painted all the seats black, whereas they had been blue.

Thus by the summer of 1970, the trains looked quite different. After that it was, of course, really easy to tell the trains apart, and visitors liked that. It wasn't unusual to hear a kid yell, "I want to ride the zebra train," or some other animal reference to a particular tram.

During that time, I remember meeting Dr. Goss, who was the director of the zoo. The occasion was a *Friends of the Zoo* evening party. We were sometimes opened for special events, in this case for patrons who had supported the zoo with major donations. Though it was after hours, all the exhibits were open and the trains were running to ferry the *Friends of the Zoo* to the various places in the park. The patrons were dressed in evening gowns and tuxedos; the drivers worked very hard to make sure every train was utterly spotless. Les, Bob, Norm, Rich, and I wore white shirts and ties that night.

I was standing next to my empty train right in front of Refreshment Stand Number 1 when Dr. Goss walked past me. I knew it was him and risked speaking first.

"Good evening, Dr. Goss."

He didn't look at me, but as he passed he said gruffly, "There are a lot of important people here tonight so let's not get involved in any extracurriculars." Apparently, the drivers' reputations (or mine?) had preceded us. The second time I saw him was the next summer at the next *Friends of the Zoo* gathering. That time, I kept my mouth shut.

From my point of view, the antics of the drivers were not the real extracurricular activities. As coworkers and friends, our work life spilled over into our personal lives. Linda Stojkov was the unofficial social coordinator of the young employees in the zoo at that time. She planned picnics and brought the food and everything. The entire Stojkov family was wonderful, including Linda's sister Maria, who also worked selling tickets. I also remember their younger siblings, Joey, Carol, and Teresa. They came to the picnics even though they were just kids.

Sometimes several of us went to concerts at Blossom Music Center. The best concert we saw was when Linda got six of us great tickets to see Bette Midler. We were in the fifth row. The problem was the people in the audience were a little too sauced. They kept talking and walking around. I kept wishing they'd be quiet.

I whispered to Linda, "If they were just a little drunker, they might pass out."

At one point Bette Midler stepped up to the microphone at the very front of the stage. She started to sing *The Rose*. But the obnoxious crowd was making a lot of noise. Bette sang a few lines. Then she stopped and smiled. The whole orchestra came to a halt and she held up one finger and said, "Just a second."

With a Mae West sashay in her glittery tight gown, Bette walked back to the orchestra and said something to the piano player. Then she glided over to a violin player and said something to him. She smiled and nodded. She walked over to the drummer and looked at the music on his stand and made marks on it with his pencil. She nodded as if she had fixed the problem. Then she walked back to the microphone, smiling all the way like a model on the runway.

She put the microphone to her mouth and said, "SHUT THE F--- UP!"

The audience roared in laughter and cheered as the offenders were squashed. *The Rose* was sung to a remarkably quiet crowd.

Sometimes, Les and I would double-date with women we had met on the job. We went to see the plays at the Great Lakes Shakespeare Festival. Or we would go to Huntington Park on the west side in Bay Village. At sundown we observed that you can even see the gleaming downtown of Cleveland from Huntington Park. At the movie theaters we saw *M*A*S*H*, *Butch Cassidy and the Sundance Kid*, and a rerun of *Romeo and Juliet*. On our dates we would end up in good discussions about Christianity, iambic pentameter, Keats, and Simon and Garfunkel. We'd even discuss the difference between Newtonian physics and physics as redefined by Einstein. All of us were interested in the life of the mind.

On the other hand, double-dating with Norm, who liked shooting rats and knew the Latin names of fungi, was a little different than with Les. I recall one double-date in particular, which was a disaster. Early one morning, before the day started, Norm and I were near the sea lion pool when a guy who worked as a keeper in the Bird Building scurried by.

"Hey, Norm," he said.

"Hey, Joe." The man's name was Joe Vallo, but he went by *Snakey.*

Snakey Joe was around thirty-two years old. (I was nineteen, and he looked ancient to me.) He was a short, thin, wiry, dandruffy guy, balding but with long hair. I noticed pretty soon that his one eye didn't have a pupil. He reminded me of the actor who played Fagan in the musical film version of *Oliver.*

"Hey, Normy. I got that big rattler you wanted. It's in my car. You wanna go get it now?" asked Joe.

Norm seemed delighted. "Sure," he said.

So we walked out to where Joe had parked his car in the Number 1 Parking Lot. This was near the big old round swimming pool that no longer held water. As we headed toward Joe's car, the two were engaged in constant chatter.

Snakey recounted the capture. "I was walking down Madison Avenue, and I seen this big old piece of refrigerator cardboard lying there in the sun, ya know? Refrigerator cardboard laying in the sun, right on the side of a building next to some bushes, and I thought, *Man, I'll just bet you there's a big old snake heatin' himself up under that cardboard,* and so I whipped the box off, and sure enough, I grabbed up this big rattler. If I took it home, my wife'd leave me for sure, but then I think, *I'll just bet old Normy would like to have this'n..*"

We got to the car, and Joe wiped his long thinning hair out of his eyes, and opened the driver's door of his old beat-up green 1960 Pontiac Bonneville hardtop. He'd left all the windows open for the sake of the snake.

He reached in and pulled out a big heavy burlap sack tied with a drawstring. Then he whacked the side of the bag with a couple of hard hits, and a furious rattling sound emerged.

"Heh. Heh. Hear that?" Joe chortled.

Then he opened the top of the bag, and he and Norm looked in. Joe faked a hand thrust into the bag a couple of times. Then he bounced the bag up and down a few times and shook the bag like a martini to try and get the snake turned over. Then he faked a couple more hand thrusts into the bag. Finally, he darted his hand in and pulled out a fat six-foot rattlesnake by the tail. He held it out away from himself and worked his other hand until he'd grabbed the hissing reptile tightly by the neck, close up behind the jaw.

"Oh, yeah. That's a beauty," said Norm. "Oh, hell yeah. That's a nice hog nose. *Heterodon platirhinos.*"

"If you say so," countered Joe. (They were evidently more into herpetology than I would ever be.)

"Let me have 'em." said Norm.

Norm reached around behind the snake and took him by the neck and held him up, as the snake hissed, bared its deadly fangs, and spit all over the place.

"Well, thanks," said Norm.

"No problem, man," said Joe. "No problem at all."

Norm lowered the snake back down into the sack and spun the sack to seal off the top and retied it.

"This is just perfect," said Norm. "I have a couple of other rattlers in my Volkswagen now, and this one can keep 'im company."

Meanwhile, Snakey Joe had hauled another bag out of the back of his car and opened it.

"I got me these blacks snakes this morning, too. I can keep these babies."

"I've got a bunch of frozen rats at home in the freezer," said Norm, wanting to reciprocate the gift. "I mean, I've got lots of 'em. I got 'em for nothing from my college Science Department. I'll bring you some tomorrow."

These guys were really bonding. Norm rolled down all the windows in his dark-green VW Super Beetle, and tossed the burlap bag with the rattler on the floor. It landed next to another bag and there was plenty of dry rattling going on for a few seconds.

"Well, I gotta get going to the Bird Building," said Joe. (His real day job was taking care of birds.)

Needless to say, I hadn't enjoyed witnessing this exchange; rattlesnakes are just plain freaky to me. Just when I thought it was all over with Snakey, Norm called to him as he headed off.

"Hey, Adam and I are going out on a double date this Saturday. How about we bring our dates by your place so they can see your spiders?"

"Sure, what time?"

"Oh, about 8:00 or 9:00."

"We'll be there," said Joe.

Yeah, that was great, Norm. Good one. Way to go, I thought. My date was this girl I really liked, and I wanted her to like me. I thought maybe we'd go to dinner and a movie, and then a romantic walk at sundown at Huntington Park along the lake. Meanwhile, Norm's date was with some girl he's been out with lots of times so he was probably trying to figure out a way to make her not like him. I really think he had hit on a good plan.

So after dinner on Saturday night instead of going to see *Take the Money and Run* in a nice dark theater with my arm around my date, she and I got into the back of Norm's car to drive to Snakey Joe's rented house.

As we sat down in the car, Norm said, "Now don't open the burlap bags back there. They're full of rattlesnakes."

"Are these the same snakes you had last week?" I asked.

"Naw. These are some new ones I got today when I was out with my cousin. Don't open 'em, but you can pick the bags up and shake 'em to hear 'em rattle."

"That's okay," I said, turning down his offer. Now, I was both terrified *and* looking like a *wuss* in front of my date.

We drove over to the house where Joe lived. It was a big, old Victorian down on West 101st Street not far from Madison Avenue. He had no furniture, not one stick in the enormous parlor and living room. It was just a bare wooden floor. The only thing in the room was a record player on the floor, and a stack of early Bob Dylan records. One of them was playing. I think I remember noticing the phrase *corduroy dwarves*.

By way of introduction, Joe asks, "Hey. You wanta see my tarantulas? And I got a new alligator in the basement."

Norm seemed completely up for the idea as if the man had just said, "Can I offer you a cola or something else to drink?"

Norm's date had on high heels. Somehow in the context of the adventure that seemed funny. I'd bought a whole new outfit for the evening. I had on very stylish bell-bottom pants, and my date looked great. She, too, had dressed up, and now she was probably thinking, *I passed up a date with that guy who operated the Merry-Go-Round for this?* It was our first and only date.

To get to Joe's basement we had to go through the kitchen so Joe warned us. "Now listen. When you go into the kitchen you'll see a circle made out of yellow tape on the floor. *DON'T* step inside the circle. *WHATEVER* you do on God's earth, don't step inside the circle."

"Why not?" I asked, and my date looked at her watch. I'm nearly sure she was thinking, I can still make it to TelStar in Lakewood with my fake ID and hook up with whatshisname.

"You'll find out." chortled Joe excitedly.

We walked single file into the kitchen. The room had two wooden chairs, a bare wooden table, and a gas stove. On top of the stove, right on the burners, was a nine-inch black-and-white television. Joe's wife was sitting on one kitchen chair intently watching the TV. She was barefoot, and had on a simple blue floral blouse tied at the waist.

Sure enough, a circle made of yellow tape was right there on the dirty linoleum floor. The second chair was in the center of the circle, and tied to it was a gigantic great horned owl. It just stood there on the chair and glared at everybody with its flashy round yellow eyes.

Joe pushed me forward saying, "Act like you're going to step into the circle, and then step back. See what happens."

I wanted my date to be impressed; so I stepped into the circle with one foot and stepped right back out and stood just beyond its edge.

Enraged, the owl flew off its perch directly at me. *VA-VOOOSH...* Those two giant wings took about one big, clamoring stroke through the air and made a wild, loud swoosh. But then that owl hit the end of its rope, and was jerked back. The chair made a screeching noise as it was pulled a few inches across the floor. The bird landed hard and muttered a few little owl vulgarities. It beat its wings awkwardly a few more times, then made its way back up onto the chair. The wings churned up a lot of air and scattered some loose Cheerios that had evidently fallen to the floor. Feathers realigned, the great bird settled back down into its hateful, silent glare.

"Ain't that great?." said Snakey. (I was thankful that I was still alive.)

Joe's wife never looked up from the TV, but made an offer. "You guys hungry? I've got some Eggos."

The musty cellar was next. It was a zoo in itself. Joe had a whole wall covered with chicken wire cages, a few smaller cages, and some big tubs full of crabs and lizards. He had a collection of twenty or thirty snakes in various aquariums, buckets, rubber tubs, and stainless Revereware pots. Among them were three alligators. Two of them were babies which had needle-like teeth, and kept hissing like they were pissed off. The third gator was much larger and looked like a bowling bag stuffed with extra shoes. He also had some scorpions, and an aquarium which was covered by a piece of cardboard weighed down by a rock. Inside this were a coule of geckos. Another aquarium had piranhas in it, and he tossed in a couple of goldfish to make the tour complete. (I felt sorry for the goldfish.)

As part of the show, he let several of his tarantulas free to crawl on his face. Ever the gracious host, he asked us if we wanted to try it, but we passed as politely as possible. (I think my date's actual words were, "Oh gawd, hell no! Are you nuts? Are you friggin' nuts?")

In all, we hung out down there for about an hour, listening to the Latin names of everything except *exeunt* (which is the stage direction for leaving). As soon as we got outside, my date begged out of the evening with a headache.

"That was bad," I said, "but we can do something more fun now."

She said, "Well, maybe..."

Norm said, "Hell, yeah. We can go over to my house and watch Big Chuck and Hoolihan and drink some beer."

Norm's date said to my date, "That will be fun."

"Well, okay," said my date.

We all piled into Norm's Volkswagen and drove to the near west side where he lived with his father. Norm's cousin was also hanging out there that night.

The livingroom was very dark. The only light was from the television. We all sat and watched Channel 8. It could have been romantic except that Norm's grown cousin and his father were watching with us.

Back in those days, I didn't drink beer, but the other three did. In fact, my date seemed to be trying to get hammered as quickly as possible. Looking on the positive side, at least we were no longer in a basement full of snakes and alligators. On the other hand, Norm's enormous green iguana was also up watching TV with us. From head to tail it had to be six feet long. It was gigantic with a huge leathery stomach stuffed with God knows what. This dinosaur had free roam of the living room. It was moving all over the place as my date made pained faces and squirmed.

Norm's cousin, who was in his twenties, said things like, "How you guys doin'? Your dates are hot. *Ha ha ha.*"

The television was a small black-and-white TV with a terrible picture. We watched a skit featuring *Soul Man*. That was when mild-mannered Chuck Schodowski went into a phone booth and turned into a black superhero. "*Sooooooooouuuul Man.*"

After five minutes, the massive iguana began to climb up the old green drapes behind the sofa upon which Norm's father was leaning back snoring.

The iguana had long toenails and kept licking the air like it was gagging.

Then it climbed up the dark green drapes like a dragon climbing up jungle vines. The iguana weighed about twenty-five pounds, I'd guess. I thought the drapes would fall off the wall at any second. The curtain rod was springing up and down like a swing set with kids on it.

Finally, the enormous lizard reached the top of the drapes and climbed out onto the white metal curtain rod, right in the center.

The iguana settled in, hanging over the curtain rod, with its gigantic gut sagging down like a bag of potting soil. On the couch under the lizard, Norm's father was snoring and snoring. Norm's Dad was completely bald. He was an older man, near retirement age. After awhile, the iguana began to imitate a bombardier, and white droppings fell in ample quantities on a regular and repeating basis.

I would like to say that this was as bad as it got, but remember where Norm's dad was sleeping.

His date seemed amused by the nightly entertainment, but my date said, "I really have to go," and that was it for her. Earlier, I had parked my car at Norm's house, and the ride home was long, icy, and silent. I never saw her again.

It wasn't long after that when I learned that Joe Snakey's wife had walked out, too. Norm didn't seem to know why, but Joe said that there was no longer any reason that he couldn't keep rattlers.

CHAPTER TWELVE

The Cleveland Zoo has a long and dramatic history of floods. The original Brookside Park was laid out on the bottomland of a gorge. When heavy rainstorms hit Cleveland, volumes of chocolate brown water roared violently into the valley. The normally lazy trickle called Big Creek would suddenly come to life as a cascade of frothing water. After really bad storms, Big Creek overflowed her artificial walls and raced through the lower zoo, carrying leaves, sticks, garbage, grass, tires, trash, and dark wood chips. When this happened, it unleashed a frenzy of activity.

At stake were the exotic animals. The main area of flooding flowed through the vast center mall and threatened the storks, flamingoes, and penguins. It also swamped the paddock near Parking Lot Number 2 with its yaks, zebras, antelopes, elands, bison, and guanacos.

During the worst floods, water was waist-deep in the basement of the Pachyderm Building, which became a flowing aqueduct for escaping water seeking a direct path toward the storm drains.

Other areas were no less affected. The moat around Monkey Island quickly filled up and spilled over. The concrete island looked like a gray iceberg in a filthy sea. Near the main entrance, the sea lion pool looked like it had been hit by a Gulf Coast hurricane. On one occasion, water overwhelmed the prairie dog exhibit and animals drowned in their tunnels. Beavers and otters could ride out the troubles, but their exhibits were also inundated and became nothing more than a dirty brown lake, heavily clogged with floating sticks. The flooding was so dramatic that even these aquatic mammals sought the higher ground behind Children's Farm. They were gone when the storms hit their peaks.

The ungulates like camels, deer, and llamas joined the large birds like cranes near Brookside Park Drive when their enclosures became a pond. The animals sought the highest ground at the back of their areas.

Among the first areas to flood was the low ground around the old Cat and Ape Building. The alligators were soon underwater, which was sort of natural for them. They were okay since they could surface for air. When water cascaded down the back stairs of the old Cat and Ape Building, as it had done a number of times since 1904, the only things that could be saved in the useable rooms of the basement had to be set up on high shelves.

As odd as it sounds, one place that didn't flood or overflow was the zoo's lake which was simply a basin propped up on higher ground.

One morning I was parked near the Children's Farm and got into a conversation with Don Kuenzer, the Children's Farm manager. He was probably in his late twenties then, and this was the only conversation that I had with him when I was driving trains. (For those who think my commentary thus far is critical of the full-time employees, I need to confess that my life at the zoo changed over time as I became a night watchman and an animal keeper.) A group of summer employees gathered around to listen to Don. We were debriefing a recent flood. Everybody was shell-shocked because of the devastation we had seen the day before. The air smelled like wet dirt and soggy wood. Down in front of the camel exhibits, crews were still clearing away tons of brown silt. Broken tree branches littered the barnyard in the Children's Farm area. We all started talking about Big Creek, whose surging waters created the deluge.

"It's strange how people who visit the zoo aren't even aware of Big Creek. It's been diverted and just disappears into tunnels near the bison exhibit. Was it always like that after they built the zoo?" I asked.

"Oh, no," exclaimed Don. "Before the zoo was here, this area was simply Brookside Park. It was one of the biggest and most popular spots in Cleveland. I guess that was back around 1910. At that time, Big Creek was the centerpiece of the park. It ran through the area where the mall is now, in front of where the flamingoes, wading birds, and sea lions are. The creek continued on down to join the Cuyahoga. Within the park were bridges over the creek and walkways along the shores. In the 1930s when the zoo was built, Big Creek was simply channeled underground. It now runs underneath Parking Lot Number 1."

That was such a wild idea to contemplate, that there was a meandering river underneath the huge parking lot that we all knew well. It seemed strange that they would literally bury what had been an important feature of the park.

I asked the obvious question: "Why?"

"I guess to help control the flooding," he said.

Over time, we heard more flood stories, the most notable of which was *The Flood of 1959*. It happened at the end of January, and there was flooding statewide as the result of heavy rainfall on ground that was still solidly frozen.

Because all the storm sewers and drainage paths were filled with ice, the water had no way to drain. Even in the city, the water was two feet deep on the main streets, and the water that flooded the streets eventually sluiced and found the downward paths into Cleveland's gorges. The zoo is about a hundred feet below the level of West 25th Street. When the city flooded, the zoo was doomed.

In the 1959 flood, Old Main had water rising in the animals' cages.

People say that the big cats, which included lions and tigers, had to tread water or leap up on their shelves to escape. The caged snakes, lizards, turtles, and alligators, which were housed in the basement, drowned. I suppose it remains the greatest animal disaster in the history of the Zoo.

It's really exciting and dangerous to be down in one of the gorges in Cleveland when a monster thunderstorm hits. Down in *The Valley*, picnic tables, trees, logs, bushes, and pieces of lumber float by at breakneck speed. Once, being young and feeling immortal, I climbed onto an upside-down picnic table and rode the thrilling torrent of Rocky River for miles, whooping the whole way. I'm lucky I didn't drown. Doing that was really stupid.

What was exciting (and not stupid) was how the zoo's managers and maintenance departments went to battle with the water every time flooding threatened the zoo. The first time I saw them in action was when I was driving trains. The day seemed completely normal until about 3:00 p.m. when a summer storm blew in. It wasn't raining, but the sky was very dark, and Gene Huhtala sent word to the summer workers that we all needed to clear out. They closed down all the refreshment stands, Kiddie Land, and the Children's Farm. We were supposed to take off early and go home, but I delayed longer than I should have. I drove for a time under the threatening skies, which seemed more invigorating than scary. The animals were antsy, pacing in their pens, or galloping in their paddocks. I was in Train Number 3, which was noted for its speediness, and drove around the lake a couple of times as the wind started rolling nice waves across the surface, and the waterfowl disappeared into the cover of bushes along the shore.

I drove up to the abandoned Children's Farm where every animal was in the barn and the red building was boarded up. I began to think that I might have waited too long before heading for the garage. Near the kangaroos, the wind began to whip severely and huge black cumulus clouds hurtled in off Lake Erie. I was caught out in the open. Lightning and thunderclaps boomed out of the dark northern Ohio sky. The hairs stood up on the back of my neck. I was pretty sure that I had felt electricity coming up through the tram's carriage.

I stepped on the gas and roared past the sea lion pool. At that moment the rain came like an icy cold wall of water exploding with force. I was only wearing a thin short-sleeved shirt, but found that the coldness was nothing compared to the blindness visited upon me by the sheeting rain. Within a few seconds I felt the flow of water starting to drag against the sixteen inch tires of the train. I lowered my head to try to avoid the punch of the rain, but it found me and the cab soon had two inches of water in it. Hissing, whirling wisps of water vapor flew up off the hot tiger-striped hood. In one instant, I was panicked, soaked, and humiliated, but that was quickly followed by another emotion. I felt that it didn't matter, and suddenly I was into a great adventure.

It was like when you jump into a cold lake, and you get used to it. As the storm smashed into me, I was really alive. I raised my arms high in celebration and shouted at the sky.

I once saw a documentary about John Muir, the nineteenth century Scotsman who came to America and helped establish the national park system. Once, before a thunderstorm, he lashed himself to the top of a tall pine so that he could experience the storm's fury. This was kind of like that.

Huge thunderclaps exploded in the distance. I double clutched and shifted the fastest train in the Cleveland Zoo into fourth gear. The cars of Number 3 rattled and shook in terrified obedience to the pulling engine. I hydroplaned through two or three inches of rising water, with the trailing cars whipping around like a fish's tail. Racing toward the garage, I left a wake behind me as I plowed past Monkey Island, no rhesus monkeys in sight.

At some point, I stood up in the cab, and held my arms out sideways holding the steering wheel between my thighs and my right foot straining forward to stay on the gas. The train droned as if in flight with the cars fishtailing as I went past the elands, zebra, and bison. I saw the soaked yaks standing amid the gloomy downpour. I thought that they, too, were not troubled by the storm.

On my left, Big Creek was rising fast, churning with brown water which swirled in little spinning eddies of foam built up like the suds in a washing machine. At the violent center of the creek, a vast flotsam of branches, boards, bottles, and leaves sped past. Big Creek was contained in a manmade channel, but rising more quickly than the engineers had bargained for. When the roaring water spilled over its containment, the entire lower zoo would flood. That seemed to be coming pretty fast.

I downshifted into second gear to turn toward the garage, just past the yaks. As I neared the turn, I was having so much fun that I just kept going.

Accelerating the train, I zoomed across the concrete bridge directly over the churning Big Creek and headed up the severe incline up toward the lions, tigers, and bears. At the top of the hill, I turned left amid a cascading waterfall falling off the Fulton Road Bridge. Fast-moving sheets of water fell a hundred feet and slapped onto asphalt with a whacking sound. The rain was now blowing sideways.

I wondered what was happening at Waterfowl Lake, but realized that only a moron would go there amid all this lightning. On the other hand, I was currently demonstrating a high capacity for moronic behavior, so I went to check it out.

On the right, as I headed toward the greenhouse, new brown waterfalls were cascading down the hill from the upper levels of the zoo. As I passed the structure, I caught a glimpse of several zoo workers huddled there, out of the storm. I gave them a wave and started to hang a hard right up toward the lake, but the train had other ideas. It hydroplaned nearly straight sideways. Fearing I might tip over to the left, I *went with the skid* and kept going straight down past the Bird Building on my right.

Once past the Bird Building I turned left and headed toward the main entrance. By now, that area of the zoo was awash with rivers of brown water everywhere. I saw streams flowing over the lawns of the mall, and they were over a foot deep. The grassy areas of the lower zoo had been transformed into a huge delta. The sounds of a raging river were all I heard as the water rushed to find a way out.

As I passed the sea lion pool, I saw Joe Matyas from the Maintenance Department. That was the first time I ever saw Joe in my life, and it was a pitiful sight. He was probably twenty-one and out in the storm, wearing hip boots and a tan raincoat. He looked like a lobsterman during a storm at sea. I braked the train and made a sloshing stop in front of the Main Refreshment Stand.

Joe was fighting his way through the storm. I could hardly see him, it was raining so hard. In a grim mood, he staggered along near the edge of the road, which was lost under ten inches of brown water. He kicked around until he found where the sewer grate was. Then he bent over and began pulling leaves and debris off the grate. It was an endless job. He hauled off big armloads of leaves and sticks, as water rushed around him, down into the sewers. Immediately a new flotilla of debris was sucked down onto the grate, clogging it once more. But Joe kept struggling against the sticks and leaves, maintaining some flow into the storm drainage system beneath the zoo.

As I looked around, I saw other maintenance people out in the severe storm. Many of them, like Joe, were fighting the buildup of debris over the sewer grates. It seemed a fruitless task. They'd strip away an armful of rubbish, and new junk immediately flooded over the grate. Though the task seemed endless and futile, it was utterly necessary especially since Big Creek had not even burst over her walls yet. Within the hour, Joe and those others would be up to their thighs in dirty cold water, desperately trying to keep the grates open against tons of chilly, muddy torrents. I would hear later that they did this into the night.

Rain continued to fall in cold, hard sheets all around me. I toggled my train's gear shift into first gear, and eased up the clutch to head away.

Other crews of men were gathering by the east end of Monkey Island. They were nearly shrouded by dreary weather when I heard them shouting to one another, planning their battles against the inevitable wall of water that would soon roar down into the Monkey Island moat and into the basement of Old Main Ape. It was a real emergency.

I built up speed, and drove on through water that was perhaps six inches deep. To the left, the vast grassy mall had become a collection of snaking rivers. The grass which was still visible had been matted down by the runoff. The uneven lawn became an archipelago of tiny green islands covered in bent sea grass.

All around, the storm continued to rage. Overhead were more cracks of lightning, and the rain came sideways in sheets. The large trees were whipping back and forth like dogs' tails.

I had been playing, but the veterans knew that we were caught in a massive park-wide emergency. The animals sensed it, too. The flamingoes and storks showed their agitation with great wing flaps and a whooping call. The warm weather Humboldt penguins were swimming around, but not in their pools. They were swimming in their yard.

Men in the area of the greenhouse came out with nets and poles to capture the terrified penguins. I had never appreciated the older men, but here, in the driving rain, they moved with athletic agility to capture the slippery birds.

Not all the birds seemed as distressed as the little fellows in tuxedos. The pink flamingoes faced the wind and stood tall as they vigorously flapped their pinioned-wings as if they were flying at altitudes of hundreds of feet.

The flooding was deepest down at the zoo's lowest areas, so I headed back there, to make another run past the hoofed mammals. When I saw how high the creek was near where Big Creek went underground, I stopped the train to watch. I was near the guanacos pen.

Big Creek had risen quite high, yet was still contained within its manmade walls. It had another three feet to go before it spilled over. How deep it was I couldn't tell, but it was easily ten feet higher than the last time I looked. The creek was normally half a foot deep. Now it was a torrential river, churning brown and sounding like Niagara falls roaring by.

After a few more minutes, the zoo's Assistant Superintendent, Ron Seeley, arrived in the zoo van with two guys. They jumped out and staggered through the monsoon to the high side of the creek, standing up on a tall concrete wall. They were right next to the open tunnel Big Creek disappeared into.

The men had an extendable white metal pole with numbers on it to measure the depth. They walked around to the high bank of the creek with the depth gauge. The bank where they were standing was a slick slide down to the water. I thought that I was about to witness the death of all of them. The men had no rain gear on at all, just the usual brown shirts and pants. The one guy gripped a tiny shrub with one hand as an anchor and held onto the belt of the other guy who was lower down the line. The second guy held the pole and lowered it into the spate. The intense current just caught the pole and nearly ripped the two off the hillside, but they managed to keep hold of the shaft and pull it from the water. The two moved around to a different spot, often slipping down the muddy hillside. One completely lost his footing, but the other guy caught him by the back of the shirt. After a lot of testing, they found a little eddy where the current wasn't so strong and slipped the pole down next to the concrete wall. The depth of the water was twelve feet at that point, but what they really wanted to know was how fast the water was rising. As the two held the gauge in place, Seeley, watching from above, pulled a stopwatch from his pocket. It didn't take him long to determine that the flood was winning the battle. If nothing changed, the zoo was screwed. Ron signaled dramatically to get the men back to safety.

They knew that they literally had to turn the tide, and orders went out to every available hand. There would be no visit to the time clock to end that day, and every tactic was employed to mitigate damage. Gasoline-powered pumps, sandbags, and bulldozers were mobilized. I was just a kid on a joyride, who was suddenly awakened to the realities of the adult world.

Seeley was racing back to his van when he saw me. He stood right next to me, but had to cup his hands around his mouth so that I could hear his voice over the storm. "Well? What the hell are *YOU* doing? Get going."

His words scared me, and I frantically toggled the train into gear. Suddenly, his expression changed as he burst into a huge grin and winked.

He cupped his hands over his mouth and yelled again through the storm, "Hey. I'm just kidding. This is funner than hell." Then he threw his big head back and laughed. He ran back toward the van and jumped into the passenger side. The van roared away.

Near the old bridge, I hung a big U in my train and went back driving down the main drag toward the main entrance. I took Seeley's big grin and wink as if he was giving me the *okay* to continue. I drove up back around the Children's Farm and Kiddie Land, honking my horn in case any summer workers were still in the barn. As I turned for the garage, I sped along past the submerged otter and beaver exhibits which had become a huge grotto, filled with silty brown water which extended all the way to the Pachyderm Building, a distance of hundreds of feet. The otters and beavers were long gone, lost somewhere in the zoo. This wasn't a big problem. The animals would return themselves to their respective exhibits when the water went down. They all knew their correct places when it came to feeding time and wouldn't miss a meal.

The water was getting deep in places, and I drove along, past a partially submerged refreshment stand where long rows of rental strollers were half underwater.

I passed Joe for the second time, and he was still pulling debris off the same sewer grate. In this direction of travel, the rain was driving right into my eyes so I kept my head down as much as possible. Fortunately, however, I looked up in time to see another tour train in the center of the road heading right at me. I was directly in front of Monkey Island when I jerked the steering wheel hard right, and the other train zoomed past on the left. Through my dripping wet glasses, I looked to see who was driving the other train. It was the Number 2, and her driver also had turned the wheel hard at the last instant to avoid hitting me. Shaking a triumphant fist at the torrential skies, Les turned back to look my way for the briefest instant. Like me, he was soaked to the bone, and was grinning widely as he let go with a big war-whoop.

I answered back echoing his call , *Wahoo!"*

That was a great moment.

CHAPTER THIRTEEN

Whitey, the zoo's auto mechanic, was a wonderful man, but we didn't always make him very happy. Whitey's real name was Garth Goede, Sr, but I never heard anyone refer to him by Garth. The only way we knew this was from the name printed on his card at the time clock.

Just about every day, impetuous drivers did something wrong and made Whitey's job more difficult. We'd drive the tour trains way too fast, grind too many gears, wear out the clutches, or accidentally pull the microphone cords too hard, and rip open the soldered connections. While unintentional, all this was pretty stupid.

Chief among our sins was engaging the train's emergency brake while chatting with a cute girl for ten minutes. In that amount of time and distraction, it was so easy to wave a cheerful goodbye and drive off without disengaging the brake. It was amazing how far we could drive before noticing, and the first clue was the smell of burning brake pads (usually accompanied by a little smoke coming up from the wheels).

We were also prone to damaging starters by trying to crank an engine which was already running. Clutches, brakes, batteries, tires, gears, fly wheels, engines, and starters were like *throwaway* commodities for us. To Whitey they were like scarce supplies on the battleground of a volcanic island in the Pacific in WWII.

We had no doubt Whitey liked us, but we drove him nuts. We liked to drive fast when no zoo visitors were on the trains. When the trains bounced and rattled over rough roads, things like distributor caps, batteries, and even radiators often became loose from their corroded moorings. Exhaust systems, spark plug wires, and microphone boxes could fall off. Even though he warned and specifically prohibited power-shifting, we all did it, going from first gear straight into third. This was, in fact, our standard practice.

It was tough for Whitey to keep the tour trains running. In the first place, they weren't off some assembly line, so he couldn't simply call the manufacturer to order a part. The trams had been custom-made, and were over thirty years old when I started at the zoo. There was some discussion among the drivers about the origins of the zoo's first trains. Jack insisted that Cleveland purchased the trains for the 1936 World's Fair in Cleveland.

"Where did they run them at the World's Fair?" I once asked.

"All over," said Jack. "They went up and down Euclid Avenue, taking people back and forth from the hotels and the train stations to the fair. When the World's Fair was over, they drove them here to the zoo."

But Norm and I secretly mumbled that there had never been a World's Fair in Cleveland.

"I would have heard about that," Norm once said. "If there had been one, my old man would have been one of the exhibits."

A modern search of the Internet clarified part of the story. There's no record of a World's Fair, but there was a centennial celebration of the incorporation of the city. Old photos of this Great Lakes Exposition, however, showed the trains in action, and they were not the ones we drove at the zoo.

Still, the trams were already plenty old and getting a little run down when I drove them. (My guess is that they were from the early 1950s.) Whitey worked hard keeping them running every day. Sometimes he'd cannibalize one train to keep another one going. If Number 2 needed a starter and Number 3 needed a clutch, he would, of course, order a clutch and a starter. Then he'd take the starter out of Number 3 and get Number 2 back in service. That made more work for him, ultimately, since when the clutch came for Number 3, he'd put in the clutch and put in a starter. He was always juggling parts to keep the trams in service.

Whitey also didn't appreciate our fondness for train Number 3. When Train 3 was down, we'd say, "Hey, Whitey. Could you fix Number 3 first?"

He'd say, "Drive Number 4," which, in translation meant, *I've been working on Number 4 all day*. We were a bit insensitive.

Whitey was always down in *the pit*. The pit was a large concrete hole in the floor of the mechanic's garage. He climbed down into the pit to be able to work underneath a vehicle. As an older man, climbing down into the pit was tough, especially in cold weather or when the dampness of the pit made his rheumatism act up.

In spite of our insensitivity, the drivers loved Whitey. At heart, he was a kind man. He was a rarity in that he didn't smoke. His work ethic could not be doubted. He was one hundred percent dedicated to work even though he was his own supervisor. He never goofed off. I never saw him reading the paper or engaged in horseplay. He was always working.

Flat tires on the passenger wagons were also a regular occurrence. For this repair, Whitey always had an assistant. These were not tubeless tires that had to seal against wheel rims. They worked off the old inner tube system and could be patched with solvent and rubber patches.

Whitey's assistants came and went. I remember one whose name was Walter. He was a lanky kid who was working to change a tire one Saturday, Whitey's day off. He was using a screwdriver to pry at the tire as he inflated the innertube which then exploded in his face. The screwdriver flew back knocking him unconscious for about twenty minutes. The incident left him with a worm-shaped scar about an inch under his left eye. Everyone thought it lucky that he did not lose his eye, but Walter used up all his luck that day. A year later, however, someone told us that Walter drowned while swimming, or as Les corrected, "No. He drowned while *not* swimming."

Whitey and his assistants were constantly charging and switching out batteries in the trains. We got used to arriving in the morning and finding dead batteries. Whitey just seemed to take it in stride and go scrounge up another used one from somewhere. Actually, the mechanic kept a supply of old batteries charging side by side on a table in the garage. Since the batteries were often being rotated in and out of service, the mechanics never bolted them down securely under the hood. Sometimes they were not bolted at all, but just sitting on the metal platform. That's why when we hit a bump the battery could fly out.

While I'd like to be able to write up all the blame as a mechanical error, the fact was that we often drove the empty trains too fast. I remember once when I came flying over the old Big Creek bridge heading for the garage. The train was jolting and rattling since I had built up a lot of speed. I hit a big bump at the edge of the road just outside the yaks, and the battery got launched up out of the engine compartment. As this happened it took with it the black ground cable which had been bolted to the engine block. Whitey was standing close by and saw it all as the big battery hit the pavement. He just shook his head and gave me *the look*.

"Oops. Sorry," I said and jumped down off the train. I scampered to pick up the battery. "I'll put it back."

"No, no," said Whitey. "I'll take care of it." I tried to press my case, but it was too late. "I'll do it," Whitey repeated. "Just get out of my sight." (Whitey said that a lot.)

Like the guy in Greek mythology who was doomed forever to push a rock up a hill, Whitey's twin torments were tram repair and young drivers who knew nothing. I remember one particular day when I kept wondering what the strange smell was in the zoo. I completed several tour runs before I found out that the smell was from my train. My second clue (I had missed the smell clue) was the radiator boiling over and sending big billows of water vapor steaming up into the sky. That was followed by a green puddle under the cab. Apparently, I had been driving while low on coolant. After the breakdown, my passengers were shifted to Ron, who was not far behind.

When something like that happened, someone had to go get Whitey. This was before cell phones so we'd first try to make it to a zoo phone and just call the garage. If the zoo's animal refuse truck drove by, we'd ask them to relay the message, "Tell Whitey I'm broke down." In time, Whitey would show up in a flatbed truck with a big black rubber five gallon container of coolant. He'd fill the radiator, and maybe tighten a clamp.

I remember him once asking me, "Didn't you notice the steam coming out from under the hood?"

"I thought it was just the clutch." This probably wasn't the best answer.

"So if you thought the *clutch* was burning, you'd still keep driving?"

It was hard to get Whitey to laugh and smile, but with what we made him endure, that was completely understandable. He always had a half-inch open-end wrench in his right hand. This wrench was the size of a battery cable connector, and he always had it with him.

There was a day when five of us, Al, Norm, Les, Bob, and I were sitting in the back car of another train joking and talking at the end of the day. Someone had parked Number 2 next to the garage, and suddenly, in the middle of our conversation, we noticed that it was on fire.

We all jumped up and ran to her cab. Somebody, Al, I think, flipped open the big side vents, and sure enough there was a small flame around the base of the carburetor. So what happens when you have five college kids standing around a burning engine? Naturally they embark on an intellectual conversation of the preferred methods for extinguishing various types of fires. You have electrical fires, wood fires, paper fires, and gasoline fires. Whitey wasn't there to see that. He was down in *the pit*, where he lived most of the time. Meanwhile, what had been a tiny fire was expanding into something more impressive.

"I'll go get the hose," was my first response. After all, the hose we used to wash trains was only about twenty feet away.

"Now, wait. Wait," said Al. "I'm not sure that's a good idea. This is an electrical fire."

"It's not," said Bob. "It's grease. It's a grease fire. But you are right, and Adam's wrong. You do *NOT* want to use a hose. This is a grease fire, and you need a CO_2 extinguisher."

"I think you'd need a Soda extinguisher," said Les. "It's really a gas fire."

"I think it may have been started electrically," said Al. "But I think what's burning there is grease and gasoline now."

"And," said Bob, "Not one of those three kinds of fires should be put out with water. I mean, really, this is a moot point. If it's electrical, or gasoline, or grease, we need an extinguisher."

I'm embarrassed to say that we went around like this for quite awhile. Each arguing the merits of specific techniques to put out various types of fires. The fact was we were on the verge of an electrical, grease, vinyl conflagration. What could have been easily smothered or doused easily became a mass of melting wires, burning grease, and a cloud of black smoke.

I wanted just to let loose with the hose, but I was outvoted and Norm ran off and found a red CO_2 fire extinguisher. By that point, it was too little too late, and even the paint on the radiator was ablaze. The white cloud of CO_2 literally fizzled without taking the fire with it.

Al blamed the extinguisher, and I opened up the water nozzle on the hose. It wasn't pretty, but the fire didn't spread, we didn't blow up, and what was left was steam, not smoke.

"We oughta go tell Whitey," said Norm.

"Who's going to do the telling?" asked Al.

"We'll all go," said Norm.

So the five of us walked into the garage where Whitey was down in *the pit* looking at something under the illumination of a bare, hundred watt trouble light hooked up on an undercarriage. The cab he was working on had him trapped down there, and that may have actually saved our lives.

We were clouded in contrition as we approached the area where the mechanic was working. Al did the talking.

"Uh, Whitey?"

"Yeah?" said Whitey, too busy to be bothered.

"There's been a misfortune and an accident."

Whitey squinted up to see us through the correct part of his bifocals.

"Huh?" asked Whitey. His face was smeared with sweat and engine grease.

"I think something went wrong with the fuel line on the Number 2," said Al.

"What's wrong with her? Won't she start?" (Whitey always called trains *her*.)

Al was taking the long way around. "Anyway," he said, "I suspect that there was a leak in the fuel line."

"Oh, Jeez. Is that all? Just leave her there. Jeez, leave me alone."

"Well, no, that's not all. It caught fire."

Whitey wasn't sure what he had just heard, but Al suddenly had his attention.

"What are you talking about?"

"The train. Number 2.... The fuel line... The carburetor... It was unfortunate."

"What the hell are you saying?" yelled Whitey.

He came over to the edge of the pit, his sweaty, reddened face poking out from under the aluminum sheet on the side of the cab.

"The Number 2 burned up," confessed Al.

"You mean the engine? The cylinders? Did it lock up? What do you mean about fire?" exclaimed Whitey.

Al yelled back, "Number 2's engine caught on fire and it burned up. Fire, you know, like flames."

"Like actual flames?"

"It was pretty big, all-engulfing, in fact."

There was silence from below and we were all hoping that Whitey was counting to a hundred before giving an answer.

Trapped below as he was, he needed his assistant to move the train so he could get out.

"Go get Walter," said Whitey. "I need him to pull this train off me."

"We can drive it off you," said Norm.

"No!" said Whitey. "No. You don't want to be here when I come up out of this pit. You all need to go away, and I'll go home and I'll drink a six-pack of beer. Tomorrow I will come back, and I will deal with it. Go get Walter. Tell him to smoke one cigarette, and that will let you have time to all get out of here. Then tell him to get this train off me when his cigarette is done."

"Okay."

"And I don't want to see any one of you until tomorrow. Understand?"

We understood completely.

We were still sticking together when we found Walter and told him to take a cigarette break.

"When the cigarette is completely done," said Al, "go into the garage and drive the tour train off Whitey. He's in the pit."

"Why?" asked Walter.

"That's what he said to do," said Al. "He wants you to smoke a cigarette, and when it's completely gone, go drive the train off the pit.

He's your supervisor, so I think that's what you need to do."

At that point, we were gone. Whitey spent many long weeks getting Number 2 running again.

We caused a lot of trouble for Whitey, but, as I said before, it was unintentional. I was glad that on one occasion, at least, I could do something good for him.

Terry Semple, a friend of mine from John Knox Church, gave me two box seat tickets to an Indians' game at Municipal Stadium. It was for a Friday night game, and I was pretty excited about it. There was only one thing that could stop me from going, and that one thing happened. A pretty ticket seller named Linda and some of her friends announced that they were planning a big picnic after hours, and I was invited.

Terry had made my taking the tickets conditional. "Now if for any reason you can't go to that game, make sure you give those tickets to someone. Those are really good seats." He was insistent about that, and I had agreed to the terms. (Apparently, they were his boss's season tickets and the seats were *not* to remain empty.)

The decision to go to the picnic would have violated my pledge to Terry, but the easy solution presented itself at the time clock. Whitey was there, all cleaned up, and standing right next me.

"Hey, Whitey. A friend of mine game me a couple of tickets to tonight's Indians game, and I can't use them. Gaylord's pitching. You want them?"

Whitey's face lit up. "You bet, and I know a guy who'll want to go with me." He used a nearby phone and ended a short conversation with, "I'll pick you up in a half hour."

That night Gaylord Perry pitched a six-hitter and struck out eleven. That was the year he won twenty-four games. The next Monday, Whitey came up to me with a huge grin. He looked invigorated like he was thirty again.

"Do you know where those seats were?" he began. "They were in the first row behind the Indians' dugout. We were right there." Whitey was grinning like crazy. "Gaylord was great."

That didn't make up for all of us letting Number 2's engine catch fire, and the million other horrible things we did by accident, but it was something, and I was glad that Whitey got the full benefit.

CHAPTER FOURTEEN

Reportedly, the fossil record of the Big Creek area goes back at least three hundred and seventy-five million years. The Cleveland Zoo was built along the flat bottom of a gorge that had been carved by the melting of Ohio's last glaciers, which occurred during the Tertiary Period which was between twenty-two and sixty-six million years ago. This great expanse of time was sub-divided into epochs, the first of which was the Paleocene. Ohio, or what would one day become Ohio, was at that time covered by a long series of glaciers which deposited silt and rocks in a geological formation know as a moraine. Big Creek cut its way through one of these moraines, and, in doing so, cut a cross-section in the glacial sediment. Water and erosion provided natural excavation and exposed layers of stratification which are clearly visible on the craggy cliff sides of the modern gorge.

The streams and rivers, which cut the rock over the ages, formed the Great Lakes Watershed, which divides the state between water that flows toward the Atlantic and water that escapes through the Ohio and Mississippi to the Gulf of Mexico. As the valleys widened, they also created many basins which eventually became the Cleveland Metroparks system. The network of parks and reservations are an important part of life in northeast Ohio, and add to the livability of the region. For all the jokes about Cleveland and winter snows, there is a lot to commend the city and area.

Because the zoo was built in a deep, natural watercourse, human intervention has been a key player in shaping the land. I have already noted the frantic responses of zoo personnel when the Big Creek defies the engineers who diverted its flow, but designers were also at work overhead. Two great bridges dissect the sky that touches the valley floor. Looming overhead on the East side was the 25th Street Bridge, but that bridge was more remote than the Fulton Road Bridge, which ran over Big Creek and spanned the gorge at the western end of the zoo. This structure towered over the middle of the zoo's activities. [Editor's note: The original Fulton Road Bridge has been demolished and replaced. In 2010 a new bridge was opened.] The tour trains passed under it, and the tigers' refreshment stand was beneath it as well. The roar of lions echoed down from the bridge's underside, which also sheltered Whitey's garage. For fun, some of us would throw rocks against the bridge abutments to create a loud retort which may have freaked out more than one motorist.

Of more concern to us were rocks coming from the other direction. There were a few brainless Cleveland juvenile delinquents who apparently liked to drop rocks off the bridge for the purpose of hitting moving tour trains. If a large rock, dropped from one hundred plus feet, ever hit a tour train driver or a passenger, it would kill them. Every tour train car carried young children, young mothers, loving dads, and miscellaneous other citizens who rode in pleasant ignorance of the possible danger. But just over their heads, the roof of every tour train car was peppered with dents from rocks dropped from atop the Fulton Road Bridge.

Several engine hoods also had dents, just a few feet in front of the unprotected driver. *Cinderella*, which was the only covered cab, had a few rock impacts on her cab roof. The corrugated metal roof of the garage itself was strewn with rocks, bricks, bottles, cans, and pieces of metal. Some rocks there were larger than a foot in diameter. Since there were no loose rocks lying around on top of the Fulton Road Bridge, the brainiacs obviously moved with premeditation.

Rocks had been dropped onto the passenger-car roofs of my train several times when I drove under the bridge. The people were startled, but had no idea what had happened. Once a rock actually hit my cab while the train was in motion, just as the train passed the Nubian ibex enclosure. A rock about four inches in diameter crashed into the hood from the heavenly heights. *BLAM.* It hit three feet in front of me on the hood. I looked up and saw two or three young heads ducking away against the bright mid-day sky. They disappeared like winks, in an instant.

CHAPTER FIFTEEN

In the morning, the zoo is a lovely park sitting down in the bottom of a misty bowl. The chilly air of my early morning arrival would gradually give way to sunlight creeping into the valley like an intruder. The appearance of the sun during the first tours in the morning were all the announcement a driver needed to tell whether the days would be sunny and warm, or not.

Similarly, because of the sheer valley walls, direct sunlight disappeared in the late afternoon. At the lower levels of the grounds, shadows started to slide in on the soil, flowers, and lawns around 4:00 p.m. It was sort of sundown within parts of the park, and the hardwood trees in that area grew tall with wide-spreading leafy canopies. These gigantic trees had few low branches though no zoo employee had pruned the old trees that high.

When the morning mist settled in the valley, the lower zoo was always wet. The lawns were soaked as if from heavy rain even when there had been none. The result was a lush green which brought on smells which I imagined to be native to rain forests. I smelled damp hay, rotting wood, and wood mulch all bathed in heavy dew and carrying the thick forest scenaromas of algae, water, and oceans of flowers.

The local fauna brought a native beauty with busy clusters of small flying insects and speeding blue-black dragonflies that seemed the size of sparrows. The road around the lake was littered with white flower petals in the spring and strewn with gold and brown seeds in the fall. Wild Canada geese and mallard ducks took refuge in the park, along with dozens of other bird species, like coots and kingfishers. Waterfowl Lake was a haven to a blend of zoo animals as well as native and migrating species of ducks, geese, coots, kingfishers, and swans.

In terms of ambiance, the screams of the peafowl were heard quite regularly throughout the park. *Wuh-RAW- RAW- RAW.* The sounds carried for what seemed like miles, and keepers would stand around and say things like, "Peacocks are the best watchdogs ever." There were many dozens of peafowl in the zoo, wandering everywhere. When alarmed, they let out a cacophony of screams like in a jungle movie.

The peafowl ran wild, but they are *sedentary birds.* Peafowl will never wander more than a mile or two from the place where they were hatched. And plenty of peafowl were hatched in the zoo. Early in the summers, docile brown peahens walked their halting walk among the grass looking for bugs. Zipping in and out behind each mother was a long string of six to ten speckled brown chicks.

Of course, when the peafowl mating season was on, the peacocks grew their long blue-green tail feathers. When the male peacock saw a prospective mate, he'd fan that giant six-foot round tail out and shake and shimmy. You'd hear the feathered shafts clicking away, like hollow reeds in a gusting wind. The hens seemed to not care much as they continued to keep looking for sow beetles and crickets. On the other hand, the show must have had the desired effect because there were always plenty of peachicks running around about a month later.

After mating season, the feathers of the male's long train fell out, but not all at once. A big fellow would lose them over a period of a week or two. Toward the end, when he just had three or four beat-up feathers, he looked a little pathetic. Still, a male with only one lousy big feather would try to display. He'd approach a female and raise his tail (with the one feather), and seem to say, *"How do you like these apples, baby?"*

Of course, the long pretty feathers with the distinctive *eye* shape on them were prized souvenirs to a zoo visitor who saw one laying on the ground. They were snatched up quickly. The zoo also had female summer employees out looking for them every morning during mating season. They wanted to corner the market on peacock feathers and sell them in the gift shops. Friends and relatives often asked me if I could bring home a feather, but I never found any, so brief was the shelf-life (or is it *path-life?*) of a discarded plume.

Peafowl are actually good flyers. Many times we'd be standing around talking when a peacock in a nearby tree suddenly zoomed out over our heads, soaring past. When the large males in full plumage passed over, they cast a large shadow, and why not? After all, it had a wingspan of about eight feet.

Once, Les and I were standing by the old stone steps near the Bird Building at the end of the day. Actually, we were talking to a ticket seller when she asked, "I wonder why can't they fly?"

"Peacocks can fly all right," Les answered.

"No way," said the girl. "If that's true, why wouldn't they just fly away? I don't believe you."

"They're sedentary," said Les. "They never travel more than a few miles from where they were hatched. They could get away, but they don't want to."

"I've seen 'em fly lots of times," I added.

The girl laughed, "That's crazy. You guys are just kidding me, right?"

Well, the gauntlet had been thrown down, and, as it happened, a great big peacock was walking along on a nearby patch of lawn.

"Watch," I said as I started to move toward the animal. I was quite confident that Les and I could outrun a dumb, lazy bird with two scrawny legs and many pounds of feathers dragging on his caboose. We moved quickly toward the big bird, thinking that as soon as we got too close, he'd take off.

That's when we learned peacocks are fast on their feet. We chased it in circles all over. This bird didn't want to leave the general area, and just kept running, turning, doubling back, and staying five feet ahead of us. It wouldn't fly, and we looked ridiculous.

Suddenly the zoo's old yellow Ford station wagon screeched to a stop and Assistant Superintendent Dick Merrill jumped out of the cab. A heavyset man, he nonetheless charged toward us, leaving the car door open. He was pretty pissed.

"What the hell are you doing? You guys are fired. You're both fired."

That scared me plenty. "Sorry," I said. "We were just doing an experiment."

"We wanted to prove that peacocks can fly," said Les.

"Well, you're fired..." Merrill yelled again, as he got back in the car and slammed the door shut. Then he sped off.

Worried, the girl asked, "Are you guys fired?"

I had no idea, but Les thought about it for a few seconds before he spoke. "I don't think so. He doesn't know our names."

CHAPTER SIXTEEN

From time to time, Gene Huhtala told us to reverse the order of the tour, so we might run clockwise one day, and counterclockwise the next. The *reverse* went from Main, to Lions, to the Lake, to the Children's Farm and back to Main. One such morning I was driving the Number 2 train around the park. It was a weekday, and pretty slow in terms of patrons; in fact, there wasn't a customer in sight. As I passed the large birds of prey near the Waterfowl Lake, a young woman, an employee from the Children's Farm, ran up to my train.

"There's something wrong with the beaver," she said quickly as she pointed with her left arm toward the beaver exhibit.

"C'mon, get on," I said, toggling Number 2's gears.

There was an asphalt path that led down to the beaver area. It was a pedestrian path, but I knew that the train would fit down there, and I carefully maneuvered the rumbling sixty foot train down along the walkway to where it leveled out by the exhibit.

Once there, the girl leapt off the train even before I came to a stop. I soon followed to where she was now pointing straight down into the pool.

"Over there," she exclaimed.

The pool itself was a shallow oval about ten feet down in a big concrete pit. In the water, a nearly lifeless beaver was struggling to keep his head above the surface. Barely moving, he would suddenly give out a little weak spastic kick to get its little snout up for a gasp of air. We could hear each raspy intake of breath.

"He'll drown," said the girl, imploring. "We need to go down there."

This was the first time I ever had actually entered an animal exhibit. I hopped over the three-foot metal rail, then, from the concrete coping around the enclosure, I hang dropped into the exhibit. I was followed by my companion, and held her by the waist as she dropped into the damp concrete pit.

Wading into the thigh-deep water, I took hold of the beaver by his little front left foreleg, and gently pulled it along toward me, very slowly bringing his head up out of the water.

"I think he's dead," I said, as I floated it in toward the shore.

The girl knelt down by the side of the pool and cupped her left hand under the beaver's chin, lifting his face up out of the water. The beaver gasped and convulsed. It was still alive.

At this point, we were not sure what might have happened to the poor animal. "Maybe, he hit his head," she surmised, "and so was starting to drown."

The animal's breathing shifted from the terrible gasps to a heavy, but regular pattern. his droopy eyes moved slowly between me and the girl. The eyes were so dark, I couldn't see the pupils. We stayed like that for awhile, trying to comfort the hapless creature.

"I'll go find a keeper," she said. "You stay here."

It was my turn to cup the beaver's chin. "I'll be right back," she promised.

She went to the base of the wall and jumped up to grab the top of the concrete wall. She missed and fell back. Before I could help her, she leapt again more desperately, and caught the fingertips of both hands on the top of the sheer wall. After readjusting her grip, she hauled herself up, with a single swift *oomph*. Then she hurried away.

I kept my vigil as I waited, my feet in the water as I supported the head of the animal who was still bobbing up and down amid little waves that lightly traveled back and forth across the pool. I tried not to think about things like rabies. Now and then, a hind leg would twitch a bit, but for the most part, the only part of the animal moving were his eyes. Except for the eyes, the creature was just a dish rag of nothing.

When the beaver began shivering in the water, I reached underneath the limp animal, down toward its belly, and floated it out of my shadow and into the warmest rays of the sun. It was warmer where I sat on the edge of the concrete, so I hoisted the limp body up out of the water, laying it across the soft blue jean fabric of my lap. The animal continued to shake, and I wondered if it was shock, not cold, that drove its convulsions.

I knew what might be done for a small child, and instincts stepped in. Softly, I began to stroke the top of the beaver's head and began to speak to it. "It's okay, okay. That's it. It's okay, I'm sorry, poor old fellow."

Only the distinctive, pebbled flat tail of the beaver was still touching the water. That's when I noticed. The beaver had a large gash across its hind quarters, a wide gash, about six inches long. The flesh was open and dark. I hadn't noticed it at first, because wet matted hairs lay over the wound.

It had been more than a knock on the head. Looking closer, the gaping gash was full of white, wormy maggots, so I splashed handfuls of water up across the wound, and plucked the maggots away with the back of my right hand.

Somehow I hoped that this first aid would be a turning point. The shivering had stopped, but, like a new parent watching a newborn, I was now afraid it would get too hot. I tried to help it regulate its body temperature by moving my body to create a shadow when it started getting hot, and by splashing water when its fur started to show signs of drying. Oddly enough, I started telling it a story:

"You belong in a wild place where a stream is flowing, quick and clear. You are in a wide, wonderful river, and that is where you have spent your life and not in this place. Your fur is thick and soft, from all of the wonderful places you swim to freely. This is not how it is. This is not the world. This is not your final destination. Beyond here are rivers and places you are made to live in. You dive deep underwater into your family's secret burrow in the river's bank. It is cool and safe. That is you. This is not you. No matter what has happened to you, you are who you are and not what you have been made to become."

I described rivers and otters and muskrats. I described the building of dams and roaming far for the best bark. I told the beaver of a place when it would walk for miles at night to find good trees to cut down. They were white trees, with soft bark.

As a boy I had read *Chip, the Dam Builder* by my favorite childhood author Jim Kjelgaard. Diving deeply into the remembrances of that book, I described the way a wild beaver builds a burrow under the bank of a river. I told of a time in North America even before there were people. I believed my heart was producing emanations that an animal would recognize. I bent down closer to the beaver. I was still a child myself in America. And my ways were still the ways of innocent foolishness.

I was so focused on the little fellow that I had not noticed that three or four people had arrived at the top of the wall, and were listening in on my reverie. Suddenly self-conscious, I stopped talking. Just then, two people, a man and the girl, dropped down into the exhibit.

The man was a stocky animal keeper with dark hair.

"We'll take care of him now," he said.

He picked the beaver up in his arms, much more aggressively than I had. And he carried it away, handing it up to another man leaning down from the top of the wall. This they did in a corner of the enclosure. The other man was tall and slender, also, with dark hair.

The stocky keeper climbed up out of the exhibit easily, by climbing out in the corner. Then he was gone. But I didn't feel that he was mad at me for being in his exhibit. He was kind and sympathetic. But I had no business being there.

The girl and I climbed up out of the corner of the exhibit with ease. I walked back out to the pathway. Number 2 was still there, running. Idling. There was a wooden-bed truck pulling away. The girl said, "Thanks."

I said, "Can I take you somewhere?"

And she said, "No."

So I climbed slowly up into the cab of Number 2 and went back to my route.

About an hour later I was driving from Kiddie Land and the Children's Farm, heading toward Old Main and Monkey Island. The same girl suddenly materialzed out of the wooded area near the farm. Serious as always, she gestured with a tiny wave, and I eased to a stop.

She looked me in the eye for just a heartbeat.

Then she said, "I just wanted you to know the beaver died."

I nodded. She walked away, and I never saw her again.

CHAPTER SEVENTEEN

Gene Huhtala regularly hiked through the zoo, especially on Sundays when it was crowded. He went to all the ticket booths, and always had a camera case slung over his shoulder. Some ticket sellers speculated that Mr. Huhtala carried a pistol in his camera case, since the purpose of these *visits* was to collect money from ticket sales so that the cash boxes wouldn't attract felons. Every time I ever saw him, I felt a certain gratitude for the fact that he had given me a chance to work at the zoo. He, however, had only one thought on his mind.

"Hey. Get the train going. No waiting. Just load and go," he would scold us, and we'd jump to get the trams moving.

After he caught us dillydallying five or six times, Mr. Huhtala issued a written edict to all drivers: "No waiting at a stop. Let the passengers off. Load new passengers and go."

Everyone knew that when his edicts were set in writing, he was ticked. We immediately got the message and gave full compliance, at least for several days.

One summer a little Brooklyn Street *rat* became my buddy, and rode my train every day. The first time I saw him he jumped up into the first seat and said, "Hey. Can I ride the train for free? I don't have any money."

"Sure."

As I would learn, this tow-headed little kid hadn't paid to get in the zoo either. That didn't stop him from sitting right behind me in the first seat. After awhile, he convinced me to let him collect the tickets from the people.

"So how do you get into the zoo for free?" I asked.

"There's a big hole in the fence behind the Bears Refreshmentstand. All the kids sneak in through there. I come into the zoo every day, all summer."

At that point, he collected the tickets. That was the first time I heard about the *hole in the fence* up behind bears.

I can't say why I did it. Maybe it was the memory of being in a family which couldn't afford the additional cost of a fare, or maybe it was a belief that the zoo was a better place than the street for these kids. I guess if you added up all the money I gave away with free tour train rides it would be enough to buy a yak.

I was a soft touch for a sad story. An example of this was one day when a large woman with two very subdued children climbed onto the center car on the train. They were the only people on the train, and I'll just say that they didn't look as if they came from money. When it was time for the train to leave, I walked back to her car. "Tickets, please."

She acted as if an arrow had just hit her in the back and her head snapped back convulsing. "Tickets. My Lord Jesus, why do I have to pay for everything?"

Then she clutched her children into her side with her huge meaty paws, ready to stomp off the car.

"Okay, lady. It's okay. You can ride for free, today."

Free rides were not entirely alien at the zoo. In fact, every Tuesday was *Free Tuesday* when I started driving.

One bigoted employee (who shall remain nameless) called it *Black Tuesday*. His attitude made us hippie era drivers very uncomfortable. After all, it was the dawning of the *Age of Aquarius*. In any event, since admission was free, all the innercity kids came to the zoo on Tuesdays. They arrived in a fleet of school buses that covered a large area of Parking Lot Number 1. There were, perhaps, ten buses in all. This made Tuesdays at the zoo a madhouse, with hundreds of joyful innercity children running around everywhere having a blast.

When a train came into a stop, the kids swarmed over it setting a new record for occupancy. About a hundred and eighty children squeezed on. The first time that happened, I naively walked to the back of the train and shouted over the boisterous screams of the prospective passengers.

"Tickets. Tickets." Well, those kids didn't have any money. The first time it happened, I made everyone get off. As I pulled away with the empty train, all hundred and eighty kids just ran after me and jumped on again. It didn't take long for me to figure out that on Tuesday, all school kids rode for free.

"Why do you think they call it *Free Tuesday*?" Les noted later.

For about four hours every Tuesday, all five tour trains just drove around overflowing with innercity kids. They were all excited and their energy exceeded any thoughts of caution. I was afraid they'd kill themselves jumping on the train when it still was moving. So I'd always start tours with my version of a *keep-your-seat-belts-fastened* speech.

I'd walk back to speak with them directly rather than use the microphone.

"If you jump off and on while the train is moving, you could get hurt, so here's my deal: you can all ride for free— but to get a free ride, you have to hold on real tight. Okay?" For the most part, they all did their best to hold on, but sometimes a little kid would fall. When that happened, they'd jump up, run after the train, and climb right back on. I'm sure this level of safety would not be tolerated today, but in the sixties, grownups accepted a higher level of childhood risks.

Speaking of grownups, I sometimes confronted patrons who were not so happy with *Free Tuesdays*. The *free ride* system worked fine as long as there were only kids on the train. By 3:30, however, most of the school buses were gone and the more suburban types reemerged wanting to ride the train. These would buy tickets and get on, and that was *business as usual*, except for one detail. There'd often be a group of fifteen or twenty innercity kids in a group with a later departure time. I'd collect the tickets from the suburbanites, as usual, but the kids in the middle car didn't have tickets.

A woman in the front car might ask, "How come they don't have to pay?"

"They're with a school group."

"But it's summer. There's no school."

"Well, but there is. You can see the school buses in the parking lot."

"You're just letting them ride free because they're black. They don't have to pay for anything. I want my money back. We paid a lot of money for these tickets, and if those black kids don't have to pay, we're not going to pay."

"I'm telling you, they're with a school group. They're with Mrs. Anderson's Class. Honest," I said, lying through my teeth.

I stepped back toward the black kids and asked, "What's your teacher's name?"

They all answered in chorus, "Mrs. Anderson." (The kids were quick in the mind.)

The woman said, "Well, we're getting off. I don't want to ride this train anyway."

She gathered up her kids, and the others in her group, and the strollers and everything and walked over to the tour train booth.

"I want my money back. He's already ripped up the tickets, but I want my money back. $2.80."

The girl in the ticket booth gave her money back.

"That tour train driver is the worst liar I've ever seen. I'm writing a letter to the zoo about him. What's his name?"

"Sam," she said. (And I thought, *Thank you Linda Stojkov.*)

As the woman walked off in a huff, I realized an important lesson, and came up with a new subterfuge. My first plan was to modify my ticket collection technique. I'd go down the side of the train yelling, "Tickets. Tickets." When I'd reach the free riding kids, I'd say, "And you're with the school group."

That usually worked, but sometimes it didn't. Sometimes someone would ask, "Where's their teacher? That doesn't look like any school group to me. Why aren't they all the same age? They aren't in a class. How come the black kids don't have to pay?"

I was really just a kid myself, but could not tolerate the venom I felt from a few people. There was no way I was going to throw these kids off the tram, but, at the same time, I was being watched like a hawk. The worst scenario was when the train was full, and people were standing there with a fistful of tickets and insisting that the black kids get off the train.

This predicament led to the creation of the *Imaginary Ticket*.

Imaginary Tickets cost *ten imaginary cents* each, and you had to have one or you couldn't ride the train. The kids would absolutely have to get off if they could not procure an *Imaginary Ticket*. I was pretty strict about that, while the paying customers were watching from a distance.

My usual *modus operandi* was to brief the kids before it was time to collect tickets. I'd stroll over to the train car and strike up a casual conversation.

"Are you children enjoying your day at the zoo?" "Did you see the elephants?"

When the coast was clear, I quickly whispered, "Listen. You're supposed to have a ticket for this ride, but it's okay. You don't need one. I'll let you ride for free. But, when some people get on the train, they will give me a ticket. They'll get mad if you don't have to pay. So when I come back to this car to get your tickets, *pretend* to give me a ticket. Okay?"

This was usually understood instantly, but, in some cases, an older child would explain it to a younger one. When it was time, I walked very efficiently back toward the cars and said, "Tickets. Tickets, please."

The children were solemn and businesslike as I collected an *Imaginary Ticket* from each of them. It was a magician's trick to collect each one so that onlookers would be absolutely certain of something they hadn't seen. It was a great inside joke that evoked smiles and lit faces.

Sometimes a child would tug back on the ticket as if wanting to hold on to it.

"No, you have to pay."

"Oh... All right."

The more inventive children had a surprising amount of trouble locating their *Imaginary Tickets*. They would all reach into their purses or pockets to come up with it. One little kid stood up and went through every pocket over and over, trying to find his misplaced ticket. He found it in his back pocket.

"Whew," he grinned. "Here it is," he said with great relief.

One kid said, "Oh. It's all dirty. Sorry." And he wiped the ticket off over and over, rubbing it across the front of his flannel shirt before handing it to me. He held it daintily by its imaginary edges, since it was such a mess.

Taking the dirty ticket by the edges, I feigned disgust and said, "*Ughhh*. What did you do? Put mustard on it? *Ooo. Ooo.*"

The kids knew exactly what was going on, but they never laughed.

They were completely poker-faced. Not one child out of hundreds ever giggled or gave it away.

I recall one girl who was about twelve years old. She took forever to find her *Imaginary Ticket*, and put on quite a show. She had younger brothers with her and took on the role of a fussy old woman.

"Oh, I know I have it here somewhere," she said impatiently. "Me, oh my, my, my. What next? What next for me?" (That girl should have gotten an Academy Award as she rousted her little brothers up from the seat.) "Get up. Get up. I have to find it."

One of her brothers rolled his eyes and stood up reluctantly. Then she made all the kids in the whole car get up, on both sides. Her searching for the ticket took forever, and I tried to think of a decomposing dog so that I wouldn't laugh. (When I was four years old in Youngstown, I was crawling through some underbrush in a vacant lot near our house when I discovered a big, dead, rotting dog. I got out of there as fast as I could. Whenever I found myself in a laughable situation where I was not allowed to laugh, I'd call up the image of that horrible dog's head, and that would sober me up. So, I guess I learned method-acting as a child, too.)

Finally, the muttering girl turned around and dumped the entire contents of her beaded handbag out onto the vinyl seat.

"It's here. I know it is."

Anxiously she poked and rummaged through a sprawling pile of yarn, notes, keys, jacks, gum, coins, hair pins, brushes, and collectibles, but no ticket. Finally, she turned to her hapless younger brother and said, "Michael. Do you have it? Is it in your pocket?"

He only shrugged. "Look in your pockets."

Dutifully, little Michael searched all his pockets and came up empty. At that point, Michael had not grasped the concept of the *Imaginary Ticket*. The girl shoveled all the stuff back into her purse, pushing it off the front edge of the seat as she held the homemade purse open just below the edge of the seat.

"Just let me think a bit," she said finally. "Oh, yeah. I put it in my hat."

"It's a good thing you found it," I said, "Or I'd have had to throw you off the train."

At the next stop, her little brother reached out to hand me his own ticket as I collected them, but big sister had a second act. Stopping him, she said, "Michael. I already paid for you."

Poor little Michael looked very confused. The girl said to me, somewhat insistently, "I gave you two tickets, one for him and one for me. Now don't tell me I didn't give you two tickets."

"I know," I said. "I got 'em right here. No problem."

I could tell, however, that little Michael was practically in tears from being left out of the game. There he was, still holding an *Imaginary Ticket* between his little thumb and forefinger. I could see he was pinching it tightly.

"Michael, I think you still owe me a ticket from the last time. Otherwise, why do you still have all these tickets? You have lots of tickets there, and you better give me one."

Michael ceremoniously handed me an *Imaginary Ticket*, but the Oscar nominee had the last word, "Put the other tickets in your shirt pocket, Michael, so you don't lose them."

The truth was that I thought I invented collecting *Imaginary Tickets*.

But when I told Les about it, he said, "Yeah, I collect make-believe tickets from kids all the time. If you don't do that, the paying customers say, 'Hey. How come they don't have to pay?' You'd think that they'd realize that those kids don't have any money? I think some of them just don't want black kids on the train at all."

Marec chimed in as well. "Besides, how are little kids going to acquire our vast knowledge without riding the trains?" The mischief in his voice was not lost on any of us.

"I'd rather have a train full of school kids than regular people," said Jack. "That way I don't have to get out of the cab with my bum leg and collect tickets at each stop. People come up to the cab sometimes and say, 'When are they getting off? How come they're not paying?' I just say, 'Look, lady, can't you see it's a school group? The train's booked.'"

CHAPTER EIGHTEEN

Something happened in the summer of 1969 that should stun all Clevelanders. It was the fateful Sunday when the tour train drivers of the Cleveland Zoo risked life and limb. That makes us sound pretty brave, but it wasn't our lives and our limbs that we were risking. It was the lives of the zoo visitors. That was the day we became a danger to the general public. If you were there that day and survived, count yourself lucky.

The day before, we were waiting around to clock out. We were sitting aboard a train near the yak enclosure. It was *Big Al from Chicago's* day off, so Jack, Ron, Norm, Les, and I were there.

It began with a comment by Les. "I was driving Number 3 today, and she was really tuned up nice. Man, she could go today. I bet without the cars, she'd hit sixty."

"Number 3 is the fastest," I offered, "but in a race I'd rather have Number 2. It's nearly as fast, and the battery stays in place when you're hauling over the rough road by the storks."

Les was in an argumentative mood. "2 and 3 are both fast, but 3 is the fastest, especially today. I think Whitey put in new plugs or something, and she was roaring." (We all knew when Whitey had been working on a particular tram. The proof was in the performance upgrade.)

"It doesn't matter how fast the cab is," said Norm. "The point is, at what speed do the cars of the train bounce so that they become unhitched from each other? There's a limit to how fast you can go. I think that in some places on 2 or 3, your cars are going to become unhitched if you go too fast. Now Number 1 is slow, but those hitches stay together."

"That's true," said Les, "I have to hold Number 3 back down the main drag in front of the hoofed animals because when the cars start whipping back and forth it's pretty scary."

At that point, Ron joined the philosophical debate. "For going uphill, though, Number 4's strong. Its gears have a lower ratio. So on hills or with a heavy load of people, Number 4 is best. 3's okay when there are no people on the train, but how often does that happen? You guys are always just tooling around in it after hours like maniacs when there's nobody on board. So what? That's not reality. For hauling a load, I want Number 4."

"And what good is speed," asked Norm, "if the cars all come unhooked?"

Ron said, "Of course, Jack'll always take *Cinderella*. No matter what."

"Hey, there's nothing wrong with *old Cindy*," said Jack in defense of his usual ride. "She could whip any train's butt."

The rest of us knew that was a ludicrous statement.

"Let's get this straight," said Norm. "Les, you're saying that you'd beat us all in a race if you had Number 3?"

"You bet. There'd be no contest."

The discussion had become a challenge and Jack, the handicapped Korean War Veteran, was first to sign on. "I'd still take *Cindy*."

"You can't race in *Cinderella*," I said. "That wouldn't be fair to you."

"It's not just the train. It's the man. You guys couldn't stay away from talking to the girls long enough to win a race around the zoo."

Them was fighting words as far as the rest of us were concerned. *Cinderella's* acceleration was plodding at best. It took that train twenty seconds to go from zero to four.

"I think this needs to be settled fairly," said Norm. "It'll be a race, but Jack, you don't really have to race."

"No, I'm in, too."

"Okay," said Ron, "how do you propose this race take place?"

"Right in the regular work day," said Jack. "Do you guys have no guts? I just heard a lot of big talk. Do it right in front of everyone when the zoo's open. It's not just about who has the fastest train. Hauling a load, taking the tickets, and dealing with people has to be part of it."

"How 'bout tomorrow?" exclaimed Les, "All five of us will be here, and Al will be back."

"Al can't race," said Ron. "Whitey's only got five trains running now."

"Well then," said Jack, "Al can't race because he's not part of this, and we won't need him as a relief driver tomorrow because there'll be no break for lunch. No breaks. No stopping. No wimping out. But I'm racing, and I'm driving *Cinderella*."

"I don't think we should race on a Sunday," said Ron, the school teacher.

"They'll be ten thousand people in the zoo," added Les. "That's too dangerous."

"Oh, it's going to be dangerous," said Jack. "That's my edge. You guys don't have the guts to drive right at people. None of you college boys will drive a family with a stroller off the walkways. That's how you'll be slowed down."

"Aw, c'mon, let's race Monday," said Norm.

"The zoo will be empty Monday morning. What kind of contest is that? What are you guys? Chicken? I want Sunday," said Jack. "The crowds will be to my advantage."

"No, no," said Ron. "We can't race on Sunday. Not with ten thousand people and babies in strollers and old people. It has to be Monday."

"*Whitey* will be here on Monday," said Les. These were sobering words. Whitey would see what was happening and put a stop to it before it could resolve any dispute. "Sunday is his day off, so tomorrow has to be it."

Jack was normally a quiet man, but for some reason this had set him in motion and he already was writing the rule book in his head. "All right, here are the rules: We start at the beginning of the day, 10:00 a.m. All five trains lined up side by side. Main Booth is the starting line. All drivers in the cabs to start. We end at 7:00, when the zoo closes. Whoever goes around the zoo on the regular tour hitting all four stops the most times during the day wins. The winner is the train with the most trips around the zoo." (I had pictured a flat-out drag race for about five hundred feet, but Jack was describing a nine-hour grind. If pride hadn't kicked in, I think most of us would have backed out.)

"Well, who's going to keep score? So nobody cheats?" asked Norm.

Ron said, "No one's going to cheat or lie about it. Gentlemen's agreement. That girl in the Main Ticket Booth, Linda. She'll be the scorekeeper. We have to talk to her today." (No one would argue against this choice. Linda Stojkov was brainy and reliable. Linda would be lap counter and official referee.)

"That settles it," said Jack. "We line up at 10 a.m., and Linda says,

'Go'."

"Wait. Wait," said Les. "What about the people in the zoo? What if you're taking tickets at 10:00 a.m. and she says, 'Go'."

"That's part of the deal," said Jack. "You have to pick up people at each stop if there are people there. Just like normal. You can't just race around the zoo and not pick up people. You have to give the tour. You have to give the spiel. You have to be polite. If a zoo visitor asks you a question, you have to answer it. If there's a lady taking forever to get her stroller on the train, you have to let her do it. But if you come to a stop and there's no customers, you can just drive right through, and no blocking the other trains. When you pull into a stop, you have to allow room for another train to pass through if it has no passengers. Those are the rules."

We couldn't argue against that. All the visitors would still be expecting the tour and the speech. The other thing that seemed obvious was that Jack had given this more than a few minutes' thought. Maybe he'd been laying awake at night planning this for a year.

I drove a tour train around the zoo and found Linda near the main entrance. I told her about the race. She bought into it and said she'd come in a little early with a bag lunch.

On my way to the time clock in the cellar of Cat and Ape, a ticket seller called out to me.

"Hey, Adam. I hope you win the big race tomorrow. Everyone's excited about it." Clearly, the word was out, and that's how *The Great Tour Train Race* came about.

The next day, everyone came in a little early, and took to our favorite engines. Les grabbed the flat-out fastest train, Number 3. I drove Number 2. Norm took Number 1, the slowest of the floor shift cabs but with a stable trio of hitches. From my point of view, the race was between Les and me. We had the fastest engines, and didn't suffer from middle age like Ron and Jack. Besides, Ron was not the least bit competitive. Norm's brain was simply too large and heavy. Les and I could both jump from the pavement into the cab in a single bound. While Jack limped and was basically driving a bulldozer, he seemed awfully cocky, and that was worrisome.

Big Al from Chicago came in as relief driver, and we told him he would not be needed. Of course, he would be there all day and get paid. The rules were that each of us would drive without a break for the whole nine hours. Al would merely be a spectator. He was good with it.

At ten minutes to 10 a.m., the five idling trains were lined up side-by-side, right in front of the old Cat and Ape Building and facing west. That was an unprecedented event in the history of Cleveland. Five enormous trains were waiting abreast, like ocean liners about to launch. Since the zoo's gates had opened at 9:30, people had already had tickets and were boarding the trains. I suspect that, in the annals of the Cleveland Zoological Society, the paying customers never had so much service.

My train was soon loaded to the max which meant I couldn't go too fast. It had never occurred to me that with a full train we were talking about many tons of humanity. Les's train was dang near full, too.

Naturally, with five trains side-by-side people asked, "Which train goes where? Are they all they same?" In other words, the set-up confused the baloney out of the people. Everyone was milling around like chickens in a coop. Over and over, I said, "They're all going the same place. Pick any one you want. They're all the same."

"Do you have any anacondas here?" "How much does the hippo weigh?" "Where's the nearest restroom?" "Where is that?" "Does this train go there?" "Where does this train go?" Do they all go the same place?"

Yes, they would all go to four stops in this order: (1) Kiddie Land and the Children's Farm, (2) Bird Building and Waterfowl Lake, (3) Lions, tigers and bears, and (4) back to the start, to Monkey Island and the old Cat and Ape Building.

While all the commotion was happening, we were all getting antsy knowing that we had to wait until 10:00 before starting. There I was sitting in the cab with my hand on the gear shift, like a race driver awaiting the flag, as the clock ticked towards ten.

Just then, another person bothered the baloney out of me by asking walking up to my cab and asked the most-popular question yet again, "Do you have snakes in this zoo?" I had to answer him cordially according to Jack's blinking rules.

"No," I said.

"Why not? I would think you'd have snakes."

"Because there was a flood here in 1959, and they all drowned."

"Really? How did that happen?"

"They were down in the basement, and the building flooded. They were in cages and they drowned."

"Do you think you'll be getting snakes again?"

"Maybe."

"When will that be?"

"I don't know. We haven't had any for twelve years, so it may not be anytime soon."

"Don't you have any snakes at all?"

"No. Well, in August there's a Reptile Fair in the Pachyderm Building. You can see some snakes then..."

"Do you have any snakes at all right now?"

"No."

On the outside, I was talking and trying to answer all the questions, but on the inside I was freaking out. After all, this was a race. Oh, no. A house-sized lady in the last car just got off the train. She was seated and we were ready to go, but now she's getting off. What's she doing? She's walking over to the trash barrel and putting a soiled Kleenex in it. Now she's walking back. Oh, no. Now she's taking a picture of her grinning friends on the train. Her big, floral muumuu dress is blowing in the wind like a king-size sheet on a clothesline. Now she's getting back on the train, and in slow motion, one leg at a time. Oh, no. She's getting off again. The whole train tilted. Now's she's walking toward me to ask a question. She's so slow. I'm aging. The sun is moving in the sky like a flare. Here comes the question.

The large woman said, "Excuse me, but my little niece went over to the refreshment stand by Monkey Island to get some cotton candy. You will wait for her, won't you?"

"I... I guess so."

But Jack was sitting in the cab of boxy *Cinderella*, and he was reading a book. He was inside a tank with tiny little windows, and he had his head in a book. When people started to get on *Cinderella*, Jack saw them in the rearview mirror. He picked up the microphone and said, "This train is leaving last. The other trains are leaving before this one. This train is leaving last."

"Oh," said a nine hundred pound man. "I'll get on another train."

Then a family boarded Jack's train and sat down. Jack painfully got out of the cab with his bad leg, and walked back to the family. He pointed to Ron's train and told the family, "*That* train's going to the lions, tigers, and bears before this one."

So they quickly got up and got on Ron's train. What Jack told them was true, but not the entire truth. *All* the trains were going to the lions, tigers, and bears, eventually.

Ron realized what was happening and made a defensive announcement into his microphone, "All trains are going the same place. All trains will end up at bears." But, the people who had moved to Ron's train were already very comfortably settled by this time.

A couple walked over toward *Cinderella*. "This train is leaving last," Jack said into the microphone. "If you want to get started on the tour, take one of the other trains."

Over and over again, he announced, "This train is leaving last." Though *Cinderella* was clearly the *dog* of tour trains, it had one superior feature. It had the newest, biggest speakers. "All the other trains go to the Lions, tigers, and bears. And *all* the other trains leave before this one."

What a genius! His strategy was to get the slowest start. Soon our trains were full, and Jack's train was empty. At three seconds to 10:00, another man asked me, "Does this zoo have snakes?" and I heard Linda Stojkov yell, *"Go!"*

"No snakes," and I jammed my train into gear and let up the clutch. At that very moment in time, all hell broke loose in the Cleveland Zoo.

Jack was the only driver who seemed to maintain his calm. He did not make an empty train run to the head of the pack. Instead, he held back, as promised, and let everyone else go ahead. We took off and also took the bait.

Trains 2, 3 and 4 took off loaded with customers. Three trams running side by side was bizarre. Ron was sandwiched in the middle, and his speech would become pointless when he said *look to the left* or *to the right.* The only thing the visitors would see was another train running parallel.

"Next stop is the Children's Farm and Kiddie Land. Please remain seated while the train is in motion." The three trains were ready to lurch ahead, but a lady on Number 1 suddenly yelled, "Hold it," and Norm was dead in the water.

She got off the train and pulled her baby carriage off. It was a big, dark blue pram, with a roll top. She wasn't happy with the way the carriage was sitting and needed to reposition it. I saw this from my rearview mirror as Les, Ron, and I headed away past Monkey Island.

When Norm finally got away, it was also with a full train. I was driving along as fast as my train would go with seventy-two hundred pounds of beef on board. My train started out on the far right. The three lead trains were neck and neck, trying to be the first to make it to the turn at the Flamingoes Refreshment stand. Norm was about a hundred feet behind us. The three lead trains ran along side by side about three feet apart.

We all stuck to the rules and gave our speeches at the same time, and speakers in twelve cars blasted out three different speeches. Like a distant echo, Norm's speech followed just thirty yards behind us.

Now, my rear view mirror, showed me something else, Jack's empty train slowly leaving the main stop. He was not a man in a hurry.

For me, the crucial move was to be first to make the left turn at the Flamingoes Refreshment Stand. That would be the point of separation since only one train at a time could turn that corner.

Les had the inside track all the way, and was hugging the rail. When he powered into the turn, Ron and I actually had to slow to practically nothing. *Dang.* Then Ron followed closely after Les, and I had to get in behind Ron since I was on the outside.

That's the order we made the turn: first Les, then Ron, then me, and the bottleneck at the turn gave Norm plenty of time to close the gap. Norm caught up and was soon immediately behind me. I barely beat him into the turn. Three refreshment stand girls in white dresses came out of the Flamingoes Refreshment Stand and yelled encouragement as we turned right past their stand.

Now in single file, we passed the flamingoes, warm weather penguins, several varieties of storks, sand hill cranes, western crown cranes, kori bustards, secretary birds, and pheasants. All the while, four speeches blared into the morning air. Jack was still hundreds of yards behind.

After the excitement of the terrifying race to the first turn, I gathered my thoughts. Since my train would be faster than Ron's on this stretch of flat road, I decided to pass right there in front of the flamingoes and storks.

I gunned Number 2 and went off the road to the left. While giving the speech, I was soon running alongside Ron. My train was bouncing and shimmying over the uneven turf of the lawn, but Ron was on the pavement.

Into the microphone, I said, "On the right, on the other side of the train next to us, is the white stork from Europe."

The people on my train laughed, but I was noticing that Les, in the first train, was opening up an even bigger lead, and there was a good gap in front of Ron's train for me to pull back onto the path, but straight ahead of me was a stand of pine trees just to the right of the brick wall that surrounded the sea lion pool. I had to get ahead of Ron before I ran my train straight into those trees. If I didn't get ahead of him, I'd have to stop, and Norm would pass me on the right.

I begged the train for speed. The ride across the lawn was bumpy. My kidneys were bouncing. I recall looking into my big side rearview mirrors. The mirrors were shaking, shimmying with multiple images of vibrating people holding on for dear life in the cars of my train.

Gradually, I pulled ahead.

"Up ahead on the left, the sea lion pool. Those are California sea lions and one harbor seal. Fish are three for a quarter."

A mere twenty feet short of the trunk of a pine tree, I pulled over to the right in front of the other train. I was back onto the pavement, and the entire left side of my train missed the lowest pine boughs by three feet.

Into the microphone I said, "Please keep your hands and feet inside the train while the train is in motion." The people onboard were still laughing, and I was now in second place with only a little less than nine hours to go. Les, however, had been extending his lead and was about a hundred and fifty feet ahead.

My train, loaded with people, and this section of road that went past the kangaroos had an uphill grade. The incline gave the edge back to Ron who was driving the lower-geared Number 4, and he had a notion to try and pass me on that long uphill straightaway. I countered with a strategic move. As I saw Ron gaining, I decided that my best bet would be to hold the inside lane for the turn, which was fast approaching.

With the gas pedal already down hard on the floor, I wasn't going to get any help from the engine. Even so, pedestrians scattered as the trams approached. It was not long before Ron came up beside me on the right, his cab half a train length ahead of mine. Large, jocular Ron looked back at me and chortled as he passed, but the grade lessened slightly in front of the prairie dogs and beavers, and, on the level, I took back much of his gain. All I had to do now was remain even with him until the next turn.

We quickly exchanged glances, and it was my turn to laugh. Playfully, he shook his big fist back at me and grinned. Meanwhile, our speeches battled in mid-air, and I'm sure the paying customers were hearing a strange blend of descriptive phrases.

"On the right the birds of prey– kangaroos lick their fingers– including the bald eagle our national– wallabies, smaller with fur. On the left is the American prairie dog– where over sixty species of waterfowl– which is considered a pest– the great horned owl. Next, the deer– and that's how otters stay dry..."

Our trains were just two feet apart with the speeches running neck and neck. People on both trains were actually enjoying this. They had mounted the tram for a sedate tour and found themselves at an amusement park with a lounge act. In my rearview mirror, I saw the distant bouncing image of Norm's train. I saw Norm giving his speech in his open cab, but he was slowly, slowly slipping further behind. I had suspected all along that his love of explanation and scientific accuracy would ultimately be his downfall. That was now proving the case.

Up ahead, Les was out of sight, already at the Children's Farm and Kiddie Land.

I held onto my position heading toward the next turn. As the grade steepened near the Bactrian camels, Ron's train started to pull ahead on my right, but he was out of room. He couldn't get far enough ahead of me to pass me cleanly, and I turned into the Children's Farm ahead of him. Norm arrived within a minute or so. So, at the first stop, we had four parked trains, and patrons were milling around everywhere.

Obeying the rules, we left a path for other trains to pass. All four trains were in single file in the order they had arrived, curled around the cul-de-sac. In the immediate area of the cul-de-sac, there was a massive, chaotic logjam of people getting off and on the trains. An absolute nightmare. Utter confusion. It took forever to get people on and off these four trains. They never got settled so that a driver could go. People were taking strollers on and off the trains. Kids were running from train car to train car like it was some sort of amusement park attraction. Anxiously, we collected pink tickets from anyone who sat down. Each driver hovered like a buzzard, waiting for people to finally sit somewhere and give up their tickets, and, as always, people asked questions about everything.

After about three minutes of this mayhem, *Cinderella* showed up. Jack, with no passengers, simply kept on moving through, and away he went, taking the lead with him.

It took another five minutes before any other train could depart that stop, and that train was driven by Les. He took off, to try and catch the long gone Jack.

As Les sped away, I could see the trailing cars of speedy Number 3 buggy-whipping behind him and people holding on for dear life. Les was going for it. He was aggressively speeding away on the downhill incline. I didn't know if I could be that daring.

That left Ron, Norm, and me at the stop. Norm was running around among the cars of his train, encouraging people to get on his train.

He said, "Here's a seat. Here's a seat. This train leaves first. Right this way, ma'am. I'll take your tickets."

Norm's strategy was to get fully loaded quickly while Ron and I were hoping for fewer passengers to lighten the pull. People were still boarding my train, when I heard Norm say, "Next stop, Waterfowl Lake. There you'll see the Cleveland Zoo's fabulous collection of fine, feathered friends…"

If I was going to have any chance at all, I needed a strategy. I had thought that speed would be the main element, but I was wrong. Other factors were at play, and I had not thought clearly about any of them. This was underscored as I finally pulled away from the stop. I had watched everyone else go on ahead, including Ron who left twenty seconds earlier.

"Ladies and gentlemen, our next stop will be Waterfowl Lake and the Bird Building. Please remain seated while the train is in motion. To prevent injury, please keep your hands and feet in the car at all times." Judging by the way that the day was progressing, it was only fair to underscore the warnings.

I drove as fast as I dared. It was a downhill stretch. I was actually holding the train back, with my foot on the brake. It was all downhill, and I could feel that Number 2 was eager, even straining, to really get moving, and the weight of the people added to the potential velocity. My main concern was to not let the train roll out of control.

"On the right, the Sardinian donkey, blah, blah, blah…"

I turned and looked back at the sixty people on board. It was clear that they were enjoying the ride and modifying their impression of tour trains. They looked a lot like what became the *Dawg Pound* at a Browns' game. They might not have known exactly what was happening, but they wanted to get into the action. I decided to let them.

"All right, everybody. You probably have noticed that the tour trains are in a race. And we're getting our butt whipped. We were in second place for awhile; now we've dropped back to fifth. I don't like to say this, but we're last."

People laughed.

I said, "Coming up on the left is the Bactrian camel. Its hump is not really full of water. But that's not important now. We've got a fast train, one of the fastest. But, I have been holding back for fear of your safety. Should we just have the tour, or should we try to win this race...?"

From behind me came the force of a great roar of affirmation... Everyone yelled, "RACE. RACE. RACE." A giant cheer erupted from the Clevelanders on my train. It *was* the *Dawg Pound.*

"HOLD ON."

So I floored it and we really started moving. That was a steep downhill grade out of there, I kid you not. We roared down the incline next to the Children's Farm, shimmying left and right like an old roller coaster.

I was fighting with the steering wheel and made a wild, hard turn to the right and the train lurched to the left. The bounce of the train's unforgiving suspension could be heard even as I gave the required speech, but the jostling played havoc with my vocal chords.

"O-o-o-o-on the right, the prairie dogs. Cattlemen ha-a-a-a-a-te them. Listen, every-b-b-b-b-ody... When we come to th-uh-uh next stop, ev-ev-everybody stay *on* the train. Th-uh-uh next stop is the Bird Building, and birds are for o-o-o-old people... If no one gets off at the B-B-Bird Building, I won't ha-uh-ve to stop there. On the left, the Père David's deer ag-g-g-ain. So will you all stay on, all the way to th-uh-uh Lions? The tigers. The bears... How about it?"

I can't say that the voting system met all the international standards, but the *Ayes* had it, and I pumped my left arm in the air. The people behind me cheered.

We passed the prairie dogs, beavers, and otters, skidded sideways in front of the birds of prey, and took the turn around the lake. Very refreshing, all in all, and we were able to employ the *full train rule* and just went right through the next stop.

From behind me, I heard singing. A few people began, and others joined in until it was rousing. We had become a team.

"Don't stop singing," I said, "but I have to say that above us on the cliffs to the left are the Himalayan tahr and the Nubian ibex. Mountain goats that live at very high altitudes."

Beyond the Fulton Road Bridge, we caught up to the plodding *Cinderella,* and Jack now had passengers. The road was narrow in this stretch, and I wrapped my arms around the steering wheel to get a good grip on it. Those circa-1937 trains did not have power steering. It took everything I had to turn the wheel.

"Hold on, everybody. We're going off road now."

The people onboard cheered and screamed continuously, shouting encouragement and even taunting the people on Jack's train, yelling *"YOU. YOU. YOU. YOU. YOU."*

"On the right. The capybara, the world's largest rodent. Let's hear it for the big rat."

The people whooped and yelled like the *Dawg Pound* they had become. We were actually kicking up dirt and gravel when we passed *Cinderella*, and I could hear Jack mumbling his speech.

"The reindeer is a staple of Eskimos. It provides food, leather, and everything needed for survival."

Rules were rules, so I continued my speech, too.

"In this area, you'll find the biggest carnivores in the zoo. At our next stop are the lions, tigers and bears, oh my." After a few minutes, I said, "You'll want to get off here. I promise you'll love it. When the train comes to a complete and final stop, please exit the train *QUICKLY*, but in a safe and orderly manner. When the train behind us stops there, stand in front of it for awhile. Ask the driver questions. He loves answering questions. Have a nice day. I thank you...."

The people got off and flooded the area with pedestrians so that Jack had to pull in cautiously. On the other hand, my train was empty and back on track.

Number 2 could really fly without a load. So that's what I did. I made excellent time heading around past the sitatunga antelope. I almost lost it on the downhill that bottomed out where the bridge crossed Big Creek. More cautious, I resumed accelerating right down onto the center of the old, crumbling bridge. I turned and looked back up the hill. From beneath the massive pillars of the Fulton Road Bridge, I saw Ron's train emerging, heading toward the tigers.

The path ran along flat ground now, and with an empty train, I had a great advantage. Ahead in the distance, I could see Les, already departing the Main Stop. (That was the last glimpse I had of Les's train in that race.)

In my fantasy race, there would have been no people waiting for a train as I approached the stop. This, however, was reality, and I had no such luck. There was a older woman standing in front of the ticket booth, waving a fistful of the pink train tickets. With her were a younger woman, two children, and a baby in a damn stroller. It took them forever to get on the train, and I rued the fact that I could have already gotten away if it weren't for them. I had that one little window of opportunity, and it passed. As they boarded, other customers arrived, and I was back at the start, in front of Linda's booth where the usual questions would roll.

"How much are the tickets?" "Where does the train go next?" "Where are the snakes?" "Will you wait for my cousin? He's in the restroom."

Before long, I had a rather diverse collection of riders getting on the train. They got up and took pictures of the train. Some of them were buying Monkey Chow. Eating Monkey Chow. I had to wait while more people bought tickets and boarded in the usual manner. Approaching in the distance was a snail called *Cinderella*, and even further behind, Ron's train. An old guy pushing a cart with a bottle of compressed oxygen and a respirator was getting on my train.

"Come on, Grandpa. Come on," a kid yelled to him. And he came along, walking like the last living member of the 1903 Boston Red Sox.

I ran around among them, collecting tickets, trying to get everything ready.

"Tickets? Tickets?" I said.

One guy said, "Tickets? I didn't know we needed tickets. Where do we get them?"

"Over there at the ticket booth."

He cheerfully said, "All righty." Then he started to get up.

I exclaimed, "I'll get 'em. I'll get 'em. Get forty cents ready."

I ran to the booth and got four tickets from Linda. Then I ran to the train and got forty cents from the guy. Then, of course, I had to run back to the booth and place the money on the brown metal counter in front of Linda. Finally, we were ready to go. I got away from the stop about twenty seconds before Jack came in. He was loaded with people.

With all these old folks and babies on the train, I was obligated to drive slowly and normally, which I did. But the trains in the race had spread out a lot now. I had to think... How could I convince the old people to get off at Kiddie Land? It didn't seem possible.

I gave the normal tour and headed up to the farm and the kiddie rides.

Of course the old lady and the guy with the oxygen tank didn't get off at the Children's Farm, but they were a good bet to dig birds. So I began touting the great things to be seen at the Waterfowl Lake-Bird Building stop. "At our next stop you will have immediate and easy access, including handicapped access, to possibly the most-spectacular exhibits in the entire zoological gardens. The Bird Building, the incredible award-winning Bird Building, *WINNER* of the Audubon's Society's Award for eighteen consecutive years, with literally thousands of exotic birds available for your viewing pleasure in climate-controlled comfort. Indeed, the Bird Building also features the finest and cleanest restroom facilities in the entire zoo. You won't want to miss the Antarctic penguin exhibit, where both emperor penguins and rock-hopping penguins are kept in a special award-winning refrigerated exhibit. Perhaps no other area of the zoo is more worth seeing than the Bird Building, and the zoo's Award-winning Greenhouse."

I laid it on thickly; they bought it, and got off. Eighteen other people, however, got on at the Bird Building, and I gained nothing from that salesmanship.

So that's how the race began. There was a lot of jockeying back and forth for about the next hour. I would get somewhere, and Ron would pass me at a stop. I would pass Jack while going around the lake. Then I'd pull in to a stop and Norm would be helping some lady with her baby stroller, and I'd pass him.

But I didn't see Les anymore. He was uncatchable.

Once near the ibex cliffs a strawberry blonde refreshment stand girl came out to meet me and ran alongside my train in her tight white dress. She was from the stand under the Fulton Road Bridge.

She yelled, "Go faster. Go faster. No one's at the bears right now. You can go right through."

"How do you know?" I shouted, not slowing down.

"They called me on the phone from the Bears' Refreshment Stand. I'm rooting for *you.*"

"Have you seen Les?" I yelled.

"He's way ahead. Hurry."

(I should have married that girl.) Anyway, between all stops, I drove as fast as possible. All the drivers did. We were really ripping around the park. Those pretty refreshment stand girls were like runners, like the Pony Express. They'd run fast and jog alongside, with their white uniforms smeared with mustard.

From one girl I heard a rumor that Norm had dropped out of the race. It was scary stuff because when you drove one of those trains too fast, the hitches buckled and snapped, and the cars whiplashed behind the cab. The people who rode on the trains were brave, but some of them were looking a little green.

Finally, after about an hour, I was driving with a full load past the main entrance. There was a ton people there (probably more than a ton). As I slowed down to make it through the crowd, I heard someone yelling at me. "Adam. Adam."

I turned and saw Linda's sister, Maria, running at the train, waving her arms.

"Stop. Adam. Stop!" she yelled. "Stop..."

"I'm racing."

"The race is over."

I brought the train to a complete stop, and Maria ran up alongside the cab, out of breath and panting heavily. "Mr. Huhtala's in the park.

Everybody's stopping. The race is off."

The Great Cleveland Zoo Tour Train Race of 1969 was over.

Later, at the end of the day, we were all sitting on the train, waiting to clock out. We were relaxing in the same spot where the race was conceived.

"Well, Huhtala would have blown his top if he caught us," said Ron. "We're just really lucky that the girls told us to put the *ix-nay* on the *ace-ray*." (Marec was educated and spoke several languages, including pig Latin.)

I was willing to concede that Les had won. After all, he had gotten ahead of us all and never relinquished the lead. But Jack wouldn't concede, and declared *no official winner*.

"Well," said Les. "I'm glad it was called off. At one point I had this old lady on my train going around the curve by the greenhouse. She was the only one on the train. I was moving fast when I looked back in the mirror and saw her all white-knuckled and holding on tightly to the back of the seat. It was getting pretty scary."

CHAPTER NINETEEN

Monkey Island was a pivot point at the zoo. As a driver I passed it and described it dozens of times a day. "On the right is Monkey Island, home to over eighty rhesus macaques…" When the tour began, Monkey Island was the first point of interest. At the end of the tour, there it was again.

It had been a fixture at the Cleveland Zoo for a long time. The blueprints from 1935 show the design for the sandstone display which was constructed in 1936. When it was new, it was topped with an elaborate array of trapezes, walking ladders, swings, and a spinning wheel for the monkeys to play on. That monkey entertainment center persisted until the early 1960s, but by 1968 all those playground elements were gone. Only two heavy vertical poles remained with a barren, flexible metal ladder strung between them.

Monkey Island was also home to a small herd of Barbary sheep, or aoudads. These were fairly large. One of them, in particular, was very big with huge curved horns.

Sharing the island was a good arrangement for both the sheep and the monkeys. The Barbary sheep were comfortable on the island's rocky concrete hills and steep pathways, and people threw them peanuts, which were easily stolen by monkeys at play. From the sheep's perspective, the favorite sport was *stampede*, the point of which seemed to be to make the noise of thunder by running together and slapping hooves on the concrete. The circular design of the island defined the racetrack, and the wild sheep could run for miles around and around.

One image that stays in my memory is see a herd of galloping aoudads circling the enclosure with several large monkeys riding on their backs. There they were racing around an upper level of the island, shaggy hair and manes flying in the wind, with the macaques holding on to their backs. The monkeys on the island liked jumping on the backs of the mountain goats, and apparently the sheep were fine with that. One large ram consistently seemed to have a rider. It wasn't that the rider seemed to be actually in control of its steed; rather, it was more like a parrot on the shoulder of a pirate. Sometimes, however, the monkeys would balance themselves like surfers on all fours waiting to catch a swell. Even better for the monkeys, once a day the keepers threw a pile of Timothy hay with a mix of grain added on the west end of the island. Though intended for the aoudads, the monkeys enjoyed picking through the hay and finding treats.

Sometimes, I'd spend a twenty minute lunch break watching the shenanigans on Monkey Island. If I had an apple or an orange, I shared it by tossing pieces of fruit onto the island. The place was a free-for-all of greed and selfishness. The bigger, greedier monkeys bullied the other ones. So I'd aim my piece of orange towards the biggest part of the group of monkeys. The greedy, aggressive ones would swarm around it, screaming and fighting among themselves. Meanwhile, a timid little monkey would stay back from that awful free-for-all of the larger animals. He'd have no chance of getting the fruit. As in a game of street football, the little monkey was now wide open and in the clear, and I'd throw another piece of orange right at him. The little monkey would snatch it up and clutch it to her body and run for it. That was a game I played, trying to get a piece of fruit or a peanut to a small monkey who was very low in the pecking order.

It was kind of funny that visitors purchased Monkey Chow at six chows for a quarter and then be disappointed that the monkeys on the east end of the island would ignore the offering. What the tourists couldn't know was that the monkey cave on the west end of the island contained around ninety-five thousand tons of Monkey Chow, their standard grub.

Most of the macaques on display just sort of blended into the monkey crowd, but there was one monkey who had a name. He was pointed out to me by a keeper as I was having lunch one day. I was sitting on a stone pillar at the east end when a keeper came hurrying by. He slowed down to talk when he saw me studying the monkeys. It was through him that I learned some of the secrets of monkey society.

High up on the island, atop one of the metal poles, sat the largest macaque who seemed to be pitching a fit. The keeper pointed toward the animal and said, "You see that big rhesus up there? His name is Brutus; he's the king."

Brutus was a monster, in size and in savage behavior. The keeper explained to me that Brutus's job was simple. He had to have sex with all the female monkeys, and he had to kill all the other male monkeys who became a threat to his monarchy. This meant watching all the other monkeys all the time, and especially during mating season.

"Old Brutus is the daddy of all these little monkeys that you see. Now, you see that other monkey right there?" The keeper pointed to an angular macaque sneaking down by the moat's drainage area. He moved in short cautious steps, keeping a watchful eye on Brutus looming above. "That's a male, too. A juvenile male. See there? There's a female over there." At this, he pointed to a monkey near the water, right across from us. "That one's in heat. The young guy has his eye on her, or more likely his nose. Now look up there, at the top of the island. See how Brutus is going nuts? He's watching them. That's why he's up there, so that he can see it all."

The keeper lit a cigarette and sat down next to me on the stone pillar. The man loved to teach, and I was willing to listen. The keeper gestured broadly over the hoard of about eighty animals. "They're mostly females, 'bout ten to one, right now. In the wild, it would be four to one. Can you spot the juvenile males?" (I really couldn't.) "Eventually, the males would be bigger than the females. The rhesus macaque is dimorphic. Do you know what that means?"

This was one of Norm's words, and I knew the answer. "The males and females aren't the same size."

"Right. Just like most people. Just like gorillas. These males are small because they're young. They live under a death sentence. Brutus won't let them get big enough to threaten his kingdom. He's the king. He'll kill 'em all. All the males. But there aren't that many males here. The females outnumber them. You can count the males of breeding age on both your hands right now. That's because females naturally outnumber the males in the birth ratio, and Brutus will try to kill any male that gets big enough, or drive 'im off.

"In the wild, the young males would leave the group and roam away to establish a new territory. But here, where are they going to go? It's unnatural, but that's the way it is. So, Brutus is the king, for now. He tries to kill them when they're still smaller than he is. But Brutus lives an awful life. I bet he hardly sleeps, not now when they're mating." The keeper laughed, "He's got to be always watching. Look at him."

He was right. Brutus had his hands full monitoring his kingdom. At the top of the island, Brutus frantically scurried hand over hand across a chain ladder, sometimes dropping to the top of the concrete portion of the island. There he'd run back and forth along the top, letting loose a shrill chorus of screams.

"In some ways," he went on, "the odds are in his favor. He won't let 'em mate, and that's not easy for them, even to try it. You see, sex is a process. A mating male has to mount the female repeatedly before he'll ejaculate. Because it takes time, Brutus can stop it, and the young guy really has no chance of breeding. Brutus would kill any male before that happens, or the younger fellow would have to kill him. Now watch, watch."

The thin and smaller young male monkey had been inching closer to the female, and she actually presented herself to the young hapless suitor. She did this by standing up on all fours and showing off her backside. She was ready if he wanted to mate with her.

Meanwhile, Brutus saw it all. He screamed his displeasure and increased the volume and intensity of his rants. Loosely translated from monkey, he was saying, "I see you. Hold it right there. Don't make me come down there. I'll kill ya, man. I'll kill ya."

On the other hand, Brutus was hesitant to abandon his vantage point to intervene directly. Doing so could unleash a huge rash of monkey business when the other macaques saw his empty perch. As it turned out, however, his reputation made his threats real and imminent. The juvenile male hesitated and dropped back away from the female.

The keeper said, "You see, Brutus is in a dilemma right now. During the mating season, I mean. He has to stay up there to see ALL the monkeys on the whole island. Look, over there. There's another female presenting to that juvenile male right there. See? Same thing's happening all over the island. Brutus has to keep watching with all those male hormones raging down below. During the mating season he can't get any rest. He knows, and they know just how close they can get to a female before Brutus attacks. Now, watch. Watch."

The diminutive juvenile male tried to make a quick move to the female. As soon as he was within five feet of her, Brutus screamed and came roaring down from the top of the island. He swooped down like a lion, and let loose repeating shrill barking sound like a giant squirrel that was freaking out.

Brutus scurried after the younger male, who also screamed. Lots of other monkeys screamed, too, and there was a general commotion. The juvenile ran, of course, yet Brutus didn't give chase once the other monkey had run away. Instead, Brutus immediately scurried back to the top, to his vantage point. Then he screamed in warning again, yelling down at another male.

Immediately, Brutus charged down from the top again. Quickly and forcefully, he mounted the female hussy from behind. He copulated with her, for just a few seconds. Then he broke off and hustled back to the top of the island, but another male was getting too close to a female in estrus on the other side of the island. Brutus ran half way down toward him and drove him off.

Brutus raced backed around to our side and mounted the first female. He thrust into her a few times, then ran back up to the top of the island. He leaped to the top of a metal pole, screamed, and went crazy once more, resuming his endless patrol of his harem. There was no peace for the big monkey, or any other monkey at a time like that.

"You see, it's like people," said the keeper. "Those other male monkeys got to try and sneak and cheat. Get it? That's how it is. As long as he's the dominant ranking male."

Those were the words he used, "dominant ranking male."

He went on. "Next, there's going to be all these babies. Those will be Brutus's babies. Then, they'll be a new generation of males coming up. When they get to be around five, he'll kill them or they'll have to get off the island."

"But how can they get off the island?" I asked, "They're trapped there."

"Oh, hell," he scoffed, amused by my naïveté. "They can all get off anytime they want to. You think that little wall and that little moat keeps them on the island?" He laughed. "No, they're monkeys. If they chose to, they could get off just like that." He smacked his hands across each other with a loud crack.

"They could climb over the Empire State Building if they wanted to. They just don't want to get off the island."

"Why not?"

"Where are they going to go? Back to India? They got nowhere."

So huge and mighty Brutus ruled the island in the late 1960s. It was, apparently, a murderous world syncopated by the prancing footsteps of a herd of aoudads.

That's was the only serious conversation I had with a keeper the whole time I was a driver, and it created a crack in my opinion of the keepers. A few days later I made the connection this was *Vince* who was always getting goosed at the time clock.

My conversation with Vince changed my tour speech.

"Up ahead is Monkey Island. It may surprise you to know that the monkeys could get off the island anytime they want. They're excellent swimmers and could easily climb over the wall at the edge of their moat, but they simply choose to stay on the island. If you look at the top of the island right now, the very large macaque is the island's dominant ranking male. He's king of all our rhesus monkeys. His name is Brutus."

CHAPTER TWENTY

Life in the adult world was slowly creeping up on me after graduating from college in 1971. I figured this would be my last summer job before I had to begin a *real* career, whatever that was. After working at the zoo, a new job was bound to be both boring and lower in pay (at least in the beginning from the bottom rung). On the other hand, I hardly felt prepared for life on my own. I recalled the words that Paul Simon sang, "When I look back on all the crap I learned in high school, it's a wonder I can think at all." John Lennon also captured the doubts when he wrote, "When they've tortured and scared you for twenty odd years, then they expect you to pick a career..."

As my time of innocence ended, I had not the first clue where to turn or how to live. I could read Camus easily in French. I could tell you all the books of the Bible, and trace the genealogy from Adam and Eve to Joseph, the husband of Mary. I knew the Periodic Chart. I was quite the expert on the poetry of Keats, Blake, and Shelley. I knew all the basic Newtonian laws of physics, and the formulas whereby I could compute the velocity of an object sliding down a ramp, if told the mass of the object, the angle of the incline, and the friction coefficient of the material comprising the ramp. But I was utterly screwed and unhireable.

In previous periods of civilization, childhood was an apprenticeship for adult life. Children's farm chores, for example, prepared them by literally placing them in the field to work alongside older people until they had the strength, stamina, and knowledge to master the craft. Apprenticeships are still a part of the trades, but for me at least, a college degree meant that I would be on my own to convince some prospective employer that I could do a job that I had never done before.

I suppose it worked both ways. After convincing an interviewer that I should be given a chance, I had to ask myself if it was the sort of thing I *wanted* to be doing. There was a generational split over this in the seventies. My father, who had known The Great Depression, was of the opinion that you took whatever work you could find and stick with it. My generation saw the end result of that, and people, who seemed to be trapped in little boxes, devoid of the spark of life.

I had been an English major. My ideal job would have been as a syndicated cartoonist with my own characters and strip. My father could not envision this sort of dream. He was a high school graduate who had gone to work for the telephone company before World War II. He volunteered for the signal corps and watched two of his brothers shipped out to the European Theater. He felt somewhat guilty that he had never been deployed, but, in hindsight, I think that the army realized that he had both an aptitude for electronics and for instruction. He was an instructor for years at Fort Monmouth, and after the war came back to Ohio Bell. They too, saw his ability and eventually he became a telephone engineer with master's degree engineers working under him in his department. His experience was that you just needed a foot in the door, and a company would reward hard work with promotions and loyalty. That culture was, however, in a state of major flux. An applicant now needed credentials, and companies were beginning to believe that turning out higher paid workers in favor of lesser paid new recruits was a smart way to do business. I didn't have time to be too picky.

The tour trains would stop running after the first few weeks of September, and I would be jobless. My father got me an interview at Ohio Bell. I'd work on the company's monthly newsletter, and have to write an article on some guy who was retiring or a woman who gave birth to something. It would have been easy enough to do, but it would be just routine, and that terrified me. They showed me the little cubicle where I would be kept beneath a constant hum of blinding florescent lights. It wasn't as appealing as the places they kept castrated goats penned at the zoo; I couldn't do it.

I had other interviews, one with a company that made industrial components. They made actuators of some kind. After the plant tour, the friendly manager showed me his work area which was equipped with a bottle of pills he kept on his desk for blood pressure.

I went to an employment agency and showed a guy my cartoon strips and some books I had written and illustrated, like *Willoughby Flask*. The guy said, "Wow. You've done well. I've never seen anyone your age so advanced in writing. But I don't have the first clue about where you might find a job. Usually writers don't establish themselves until they are much older. They begin to have success in their careers around forty."

It sounded like I had to keep working and tread water until I was middle-aged. In the meantime, I had saved around $600 (a considerable sum at the time). So I moved to Edinboro, Pennsylvania where a college friend and his wife now lived. I rented a room in an old house that was broken up into apartments. My housemates were mostly college kids from the nearby campus. It was clear I did not fit with this particular crowd.

Beer and marijuana were the most shared commodities there at that time. Though I had gone to college in western Pennsylvania, New Wilmington and Westminster College was approximately seven light years away from this scene. My rented room was the size of a Ford Econoline van. There was no furniture, just a bare mattress on the floor. My diet consisted of Hostess pies, bologna sandwiches with ketchup, orange soda, chips, and an occasional can of Dinty Moore stew, which I ate cold. My possessions were a blue record player, my original manuscripts kept carefully in my Mom's old 1940s suitcase, a portable typewriter, and a heavy crate of vinyl LPs. Those consisted of the Beatles, Donovan, Ramsey Lewis, Booker T and the MGs, Dionne Warwick, Simon and Garfunkel, Arlo Guthrie, and lots of Beethoven (including music for mandolin and harpsichord), Mozart (including Symphony No. 40 in D minor), Hayden, and my classical favorite, The Nocturnes of John Field on Nonesuch Records. I would lay on the floor and play the records over and over and over. I missed the zoo with all my heart.

Within a few days of my arrival, a delegation of my neighbors burst into my room. They were concerned that I did not participate in any of the house's recreational activities. It takes a great deal of effort on my part to write of this encounter so politely. I think the exact words of the spokesman were, "A lot of guys think you're a narc. Are you a damn narc? 'Cause if you are, you're dead. We'll kill any narc that comes in here, you f——."

At the time, I had no idea what a *narc* was. I was trying quickly on the spot to figure out what it was through word context. I thought, Well, *maybe a narc is a narcotics addict.* But why would they think a guy is a *narc* if he doesn't use drugs?

I said, "I swear to God I'm not a *narc.* I'm just a cartoonist and a poet. I really don't even know what you're talking about."

"Well, we don't need no eff'n narc in here. And if you don't smoke pot, you must be a narc."

A few of the guys didn't look quite as intent on killing me as the others; I could feel the mood softening. "Look, I really don't have the first idea what you're talking about. I'm just listening to some Hayden. I'll turn it off if it's bothering you. I just graduated from college last year, and I'm just trying to figure out what to do with my life. That's it, honest. I'm just a guy."

They seemed satisfied and disbanded. I went back to my non-existence. I got a part time job for a regional branch of the Pennsylvania Department of Education. My job was to inspect filmstrips and sound 16mm educational films to make sure they weren't torn. If they were torn or broken, I would splice the films back together with a splicing machine and plenty of nasty-smelling acetate. That job was awful since I went in and did it at night, all by myself. I think I made $1.10 a hour.

I drifted further and further into isolation. I focused on writing yet another novel that would be roundly rejected by publishers everywhere. That was *Three More People Will Be Eaten by Thursday.* How could the publishers pass on a Vonnegut-inspired masterpiece like that?

I had no car so I walked or hitchhiked to get places, and had some weird rides. In the end, I bit at a sign on a strange looking car parked near a local motel. It read: *For sale. Inquire room 28.*

The car was a 1964 Peugeot, and I had never seen anything like it. The man was upfront. First, he was in the process of selling a home in Erie and was relocating to Edinboro. He also pointed out why he needed to get rid of the odd little French car. It had bad brakes and would no longer pass inspection in Pennsylvania. As I explained, that wouldn't be a big problem for me since I would be living in Ohio where there was no regular vehicle inspection.

We took a long test drive together, and it was clear that the likeable, Mr. James T. Linn, loved this little car. Fact was that I did, too. When we got back, I gave him $100 cash. He had the title notarized, and the next day when I came back to pick up the car he said, "I called my family last night, like I do every night, and I told my daughter I sold the Peugeot. She was so excited, because we all thought it would go to the junk yard, and we've really loved this car for a long time. She said, 'Who bought it?' And I said, 'Oh, some nut.'"

That car changed my life. Now I had my only friend in this big world. It was an old gray car with leather seats that smelled like a giant baseball glove inside and had big rust holes in the fenders. Within a few weeks I was able to drive to a series of job interviews in Boston and New York. That was where I felt I needed to be. There were hundreds of book publishers in those cities. I always parked way out of the cities and took a train into town. I carried around all my novels and cartoon strips. I wore a navy blue sport coat and gray slacks. I walked up and down in New York and Boston until my feet were killing me.

In New York, during one interview, some old guy told me, "I'm telling ya, Michelangelo could be walking up and down the streets of New York and not get a job." I became a case in point, and was utterly rejected everywhere I went.

I took the train back to the Peugeot every night and drove off down the Turnpike or parkway until I saw a rest stop, and I slept in the car. Mr. Linn was right about the fact that the 404's seats folded back into a dandy flat bed. I washed in the restrooms of the rest stops, and shaved there, and ate fruit pies and Hostess cupcakes.

After about two weeks of walking the streets of New York and then Boston, I drove back to northwest Pennsylvania where my friends, the Van Wagenens now lived. They had moved from Edinboro to Cambridge Springs. It was just a little crossroads spot, so when my Peugeot needed repairs, no parts were available locally. My car definitely needed repairing. The brake lines were leaking, and the gas pedal cable, that went to the carburetor, broke.

I worked on the car on a little gravel parking lot right next to a railroad track. The trains roared by within twenty feet of where I had the

404 jacked up. There was a sign right next to the tracks. It said, "Halfway point between New York City and Chicago." Those trains weren't stopping. I was literally in the middle of nowhere.

Not being able to get parts didn't stop me from fixing the car. I replaced the throttle cable with a metal guitar string. Then I walked miles and miles to an appliance store and bought coils of copper gas lines which I would use to replace all the leaking steel brake lines on the car.

To begin the brake line repairs, I had all four wheels off and had the Peugeot up on precarious stacks of teetering red bricks. I was next to the railroad tracks flaring the ends of the copper tubing. A funny little guy at the gas station on the other side of the tracks lent me his station's flaring tool.

So I was down on my knees, flaring the copper lines when a big wind came up. It was really gusting. Minus its wheels, the Peugeot leaned this way and then that way and finally just fell off all the bricks so that it was laying flat in the dust with no wheels.

When I had finished flaring the copper tubing, I took the tool back to the little old man at the gas station on the other side of the tracks.

"You gonna get that car running?" he asked

"Well I'm almost there. Do you have a shovel I can borrow?"

"Why do you need a shovel to fix your car?" His confusion evaporated into laughter when he looked across the tracks and saw the Peugeot laying on its belly like a sunk washtub. He rousted everyone in the filling station including some of the customers, the mailman, and even people from the nearby convenient store.

"Hey. This feller needs to borrow a shovel to fix that foreign car he's got. Look at it over there."

So they all walked around the Peugeot, and my circumstance was the laugh riot of the day in Cambridge Springs, which was generally weak on laugh riots. On the other hand, he lent me a shovel, finally. I had to excavate under the car to dig out the jacks and bricks until I got the car back up in the air. I'm just lucky the car didn't fall on me when I was working on it.

I was still in Cambridge Springs and rented a room for that winter (or was it an arctic blast?). By comparison to my previous room, this one was large, but musty and stagnant. It had a big old dresser, with a mirror, a bathroom, and a king-size bed. There was also a hot plate, but there were no outlets.

To say that the room was cold is an understatement. It may have been warmer than the minus sixteen degrees that it hit that winter, but not much. Fact was that ice sometime formed on my sheets. One night as I was lying awake listening to the old man next door alternating between coughing and snoring, a dog barking to some deaf master who would not let him indoors, and wearing all my clothes to keep warm, I realized that I had no plans and no future, but I did have an idea.

I jumped out of bed, dressed myself as if for an interview, and sat down at my typewriter: *Click tap tap click click.*

Feb. 12, 1972
Eugene M. Huhtala
Comptroller, Cleveland Zoo

Dear Mr. Huhtala:

Hi. Remember me? Even though I graduated in 1971 with a Bachelor's Degree in English Literature from Westminster College, I've decided to continue my education. So I will still be available to drive the tour train in the coming summer. Would it be possible that I could return and drive the train this coming summer, in the summer of 1972?

Sincerely,
Adam Smith

I knew the address for the zoo was incomplete, but it's what I had stored in my memory, and I was quite confident that it would be delivered. As a writer who sent out many query letters, I had stamps and return envelopes on hand. It was around 4:00 a.m. on a Monday when I finished. I was so intent on getting this in the mail that I braved the horrid cold to get to the mailbox in *downtown* Cambridge Springs.

On Wednesday, the landlord said to me, "Hey, you got some mail today."

It was a letter from Eugene Huhtala on small, off-white zoo stationery. The typist's initials on the letter told me Leona had typed it.

Dear Adam,

So nice to hear from you. How wonderful that you are continuing your studies.

We will keep your job open for the summer. Call me when you return to Cleveland, any time after the middle of May.

Sincerely,
Eugene M. Huhtala
Comptroller

CHAPTER TWENTY-ONE

The letter from Gene Huhtala gave me a new purpose in life. I left Cambridge Springs the next day. I drove south and finished off the winter of '72 as a dishwasher at Porter's Diner on Route 208 just outside New Wilmington. Around April 16th, I moved back to Cleveland and called Mr. Huhtala, just to let him know I was back in the area. He assured me that it was too early in the season to start running a train, but would call as the need arose.

To my delight, summer temperatures arrived early that year, and so did the call from Mr. Huhtala. Three days after my call, he phoned and said, "You know, we had about five thousand people in the park today. So I think we could be generating some revenue if we started one tour train running early this year."

I began driving around the twentieth of April. The pay rate had even gone up a nickel so that I was making $3.05/hour. There were no ticket girls on duty that early so I sold the tickets myself from the cab. They gave me a big roll of pink tickets and a metal cash box, and I stayed close to the tram so that the box was never unguarded.

I drove for about ten days straight during that spell of nice weather. I was making around $170 a week, working seven days. That was a lot of money in those days. One day Gene Huhtala walked up next to my cab and said, "You know, Adam, we really want to run the train every day, BUT if you were to need a day off..." (I suspect that he was beginning to fear that I would complain to the union about no time off, but I was quick to interrupt.)

"No. No, I don't need a day off--ever. I'm very happy to drive every day." So it was that I kept driving and hoping that the weather would stay warm. Being Ohio, it didn't last and during that period I saw days of cold rain, and even snow. I was never told not come in, and Mr. Huhtala let me keep working day after day, even when not a single soul came to the zoo. I'd sit at each stop for ten minutes with an empty train, then I went on to the next stop and sat there. The only reason I got the hours was because of the kind heart of the zoo's comptroller.

One day a school group of innercity kids came in, and I finally had someone to drive. It was one of those rainy days, and I told the teacher, "Hey, there's no one else here, so I'll be your class's personal tour guide. This train is chartered just for them."

I drove those kids everywhere in the zoo, and I mean everywhere. I drove to out-of-the-way places that weren't even on the tour, anywhere the train would go. I drove along the narrow walkways in front of the bears, getting really close to them. When the school kids went into a building, I was waiting there when they came out. I drove completely around the Pachyderm Building. The train meandered along the narrow walkway next to the beavers and otters. I drove within a few feet of the bongo barn, where we were within a few yards of the emus, nandus, and the cassowary. From there, I took the train the back way over a utility road to Kiddie Land.

Kiddie Land and the Children's Farm were closed, of course. Looking into the mirror, I noticed the children looking forlornly at the silent rides, so took the microphone and announced, "Boys and girls, Kiddie Land's rides are closed, *BUT* this train is better than those dumb old rides anyway. Those rides can't really go anywhere. They're all on tracks. In *THIS TRAIN*, we can go on a wild ride anywhere we want. *HOLD ON.*"

I gunned the speedy Number 3 tiger train down the long straightaway past the Père David's deer. I made the train go in a crazy fishtailing ride as the kids shrieked with joy. The rattling, flexible train snapped back and forth like a snake, jolting the cars sideways against the hitches. I repeated *Hold on* many times. We drove all around the zoo in that crazy, carnival style, and I made the drive as rough and *scary* as possible. Glancing into my big rearview mirror, I saw the teacher right behind me. She was grinning the whole time, having a blast and laughing; I knew it was okay.

Splashing through puddles along rutted gravel roads with the cars lurching back and forth, I drove behind the Old Cat and Ape and into Parking Lot Number 2. We saw the zebras and yaks from the other side of the paddocks by driving extremely close to their barns. We came back out going past the reverse side of Monkey Island. I drove as fast as possible as we roared down the main drag. We left the exhibit areas entirely, and I took those kids way off the beaten path to see the tour train garage. I powered the surging train right up onto the dirt area by Big Creek under the bridge. We hung a big U-turn right there in the garage area where I brought the train to a complete stop. All the other tour trains were visible in the open garage, directly under the Fulton Road Bridge. The children were interested.

I said, "This is the garage where the tour trains are kept. You are the *ONLY* visitors in history to see this part of the zoo."

Hearing my voice coming out the speakers, Whitey, our chief mechanic suddenly appeared walking out of his work area. He was wiping his hands off on a red rag and was very surprised to see a trainload of innercity children within twenty feet of where he was standing. Whitey grinned sheepishly, realizing that over fifty children were staring at him.

Into the microphone I said, "That is the man who fixes all the tour trains. His name is… Garth."

At the day's end, I drove the class out into Parking Lot Number 1 and back to their buses. I was very proud of that particular rainy-day tour.

CHAPTER TWENTY-TWO

I was the lone train driver for over a month. When June arrived, I knew Les Mertus would be returning to Cleveland from his graduate studies in the Drama Department of Kent State. Les had written me during the winter, telling me that he expected to continue driving the trains during his summers in graduate school. With this in mind, I gave him a call. I was ready to go hang out with him at Westgate Mall or go on double dates to the movies.

Les originally lived in Rocky River near Center Ridge Road, but his family had since moved further west, out in the North Ridgeville area where TV actor Martin Mull grew up. (Martin Mull had been a member of my sister's class at North Olmsted High School.) Anyway, Les sent me a postcard from Kent State, telling me his new address and phone number. I called him from my parents' home, and his mom answered.

"Hello?"

We already knew each other, so I just went right to the point. "Hey. Mrs. Mertus. It's Adam. Is Les there?."

There was a little rustling sound on the other end of the line, and then a hang up. Ten minutes later, the phone rang. I answered it. It was Mrs. Mertus. She spoke in a halting voice, taking deep breaths from time to time, fighting to stay composed.

She began with an apology. "Adam. I'm sorry I hung up the phone." Then she burst into sobbing, and clutched down a hard breath and kept going. "I'm sorry, but when you called, and what you said... Oh..." She kept fighting to gather herself. "It's just that... Les passed away in March... I have to hang up. I'm sorry." And she hung up.

About twenty minutes after that, Les's sister called. She told me what had happened. Les had a heart defect from birth. I had not known about that, but apparently he became bedridden during the winter for a period of time. He was having a rough time, but he recovered and they gave him a clean bill of health. Then in the early spring, and for the first time in many weeks, he went outside. He got together with some friends at Kent State. They played kickball, and Les was having a great time. He kicked a home run, and ran the bases. When he crossed home plate, his heart failed and he fell over, gone. He was just four months shy of his twenty-third birthday.

After learning this, I went and visited with his family. They were the nicest people. I think about Les often. I feel as if he's up there, pulling for me, because we shared a kinship as writers. I hope his newest musical is a big hit among the heavenly choir.

CHAPTER TWENTY-THREE

My job continued into the warm summer months. By mid-June, all the trains were running full-time. Of course, Les, Norm, Ron, Jack, Al, and Bob were all gone. A new group of characters had taken their places riding atop the big trains. Many things had changed. For one, I was different, and for another, colleges and college students had changed. Opinions over the Viet Nam War had fragmented the nation and many college kids busied themselves between free love and marijuana. The result was that for this season I would be an alien in a strange new world.

I didn't fit with the new breed of driver (perhaps that is why I can't remember their names), and even the ticket sellers, always the cutest co-eds in the park, were reading from a different book. Actually, I'm not even sure they were reading any books.

Oddly enough, my best friends that summer were the much maligned refreshment stand girls. My big pals were Annie, Ilene, and Mary Jane, the woman, not the drug. That this was a real change of heart on my part is attested by the fact that Annie was the girl I had once blasted with a garden hose. The truth was that these women had not changed so much as I had. They were still just *themselves*, and unapologetically so.

They did spend much of the summer trying to convert me to their way of thinking. For example, eighteen year old Annie McGinty set out to teach me the art of smoking. Though not the normal classroom fare, she even had lesson plans which included units that could have been titled: *Introduction to Smoking, Flicking Ashes, Blowing Smoke Away From Others*, and *Butting a Lit Fag*. I was shown how to hold cigarettes, tap the pack, how to light them. They elaborated extensively regarding the difference between how men should flick off ashes and how women should do it, how to inhale and look cool, how to exhale and look cool. Annie postulated that smoke should always be exhaled by blowing it upward by sticking out the lower lip. This was polite to others. Blow smoke toward the ceiling and not into people's faces. She also taught that a woman can hold a cigarette between her thumb and middle finger and flick off the ashes by tapping down on the cigarette with her index finger. This was very feminine and pretty. The woman made a little, ladylike tap downward onto the cigarette, held horizontally away from the body.

"The woman can say, *Dah-ling*, as she does this," she insisted.

For men, there was a different technique, and there was also instruction on the finer points of that aspect. Fortunately for me, I sat through the classes, but I was a such poor student that I never mastered or appreciated the habit.

The three girls also tried to teach me how to throw litter out of a moving car, but I wouldn't do that. They encouraged me to run red lights by yelling "Pale pink. Pale pink," every time we drove toward a light that was just turning red. That was a cheer that was supposed to make me run the light, but I couldn't do that, either.

One thing that I really enjoyed, however, was when they taught me to ice skate. Two girls held me up when I skated. I had one pretty one on each arm, holding me up. We did that for a couple of hours, and that was pretty nice.

Then Annie said, "Are you getting it now? Do you want us to let go?"

I said, "I think I got the skating now. But I don't want you to let go. That was my idea of skating. Don't ever let go."

I also learned more about their food service habits than I wanted to know. They were not at the zoo to learn about animals. Could they tell the difference between a giraffe and a pelican? Probably. Could they tell the difference between an aardvark and an antelope? Now we are getting into a gray area. Could one of these girls tell the difference between an African lion and a cougar? No way in a million years. Not even if they were being chased by one.

On the other hand, they were very adept at free food and snacks. My stories here are legion, but it suffices to tell just a few. For instance, the vendor kept an accurate count of the number of hotdogs sold, but not the buns. Bread and condiments could make a lunch tastier if it's all free. When the boss came by, he might notice that there were plenty of hotdogs, but why such a shortage of buns?

"Some of them were going moldy and had to be thrown out."

For dessert (and this was in the days before tamper-resistant packaging), a missing box of Mason's Dots would show up on an inventory report. A Dot or a Junior Mint missing from each of a dozen boxes, however, would not. After awhile, some of the boxes were much lighter and lower in calories. They didn't pick on the Mason's Black Crows at all; so that remained the consumer's best value.

The girls never reached their hands into the till. Money was safe enough in their hands, even if the Junior Mints were not. There is one final statistical bit of information which I share here: The amount of time it took a girl to change from the refreshment stand uniform into some other clothes after the stand was closed was .0004 seconds.

The summer I spent as best friends with three girls came in gloriously amid flowers and bird song. In time, it eroded into the empty fall days of dwindling attendance in the park.

As all the other summer help went back to school, I made several mentions to Gene Huhtala that it would be okay by me to keep driving the train indefinitely. He agreed to let me drive as long as the crowds warranted it.

So, in 1972, I drove into September, and the weather stayed warm into the early days of October. As in the preseason, here in the postseason I sold the tickets myself out of the train cab. As the temperatures dropped, I was driving in a winter coat and gloves until that day when Mr. Huhtala, on one of his vigorous walks through the park, said, "Adam... We need to stop the train running now for the season. We'll see you next summer. Drive to the end of the day, but we will be done now until the spring."

What could I say? It was snowing.

CHAPTER TWENTY-FOUR

I had, once again, managed to use the *pursuit of happiness* to postpone the inevitable *pursuit of a career*.

In the beginning, I took any employment I could find. I worked at an Arby's, and then in the men's department at Sears. I applied for a job with the Cleveland Indians to be a member of the grounds crew, but, at that time, those jobs were a sort of family business. My interview went well, but I was told that, though I would fit in with the crew, most of the employees were members of the *Bossard* family. (I include this now, only because the joke was on them. Later in life, I would come to learn that my great-great-ever-so-great grandfather was Philip Johannes Bossert, the progenitor of the Bossard family in North America.)

Still, I needed a job, preferably one in my field. Eventually, I got a break, I guess. I became a proofreader at a Sunday School Publishing Company out on Brookpark Road. Working there was awful. It was less than boring. It was penal. I toiled there all day in a work environment where no one was permitted to speak. They actually had little yellow lines painted on the floors. You had to stay inside the yellow lines at all times, so that the bosses could see you on closed circuit TV. On the positive side, in the six months that I suffered there miserably, I was compelled to learn the intricacies of proper grammar and punctuation.

At the time, my Uncle Ollie asked me what I was doing for a living. I told him that I worked as a proofreader for a book company.

"Well, that's good," he said. "You can't get hurt in a job like that."

There was that. He, on the other hand, spent his whole career working at the Brier Hill Steel Mill in Youngstown. And his brother Bill fell to his death at the Campbell Works of Youngstown Sheet and Tube.

I left there and landed a job as a workbook editor at Modern Curriculum Press on Prospect Road in Strongsville. I also got a new apartment. My beloved Peugeot was now beyond resuscitation so I bought an old ex-Ohio Bell Plymouth Valiant for $350. I painted it brown with spray cans.

Over the next few years, at Modern Curriculum Press, I helped develop math readiness teaching materials for grade schools, phonics workbooks, preprimary readers, remedial reading materials, and so forth.

I guess I was never cut out for life beneath the glare of florescent lights or the bar scene, either. The party people in shipping could leave their drudgery behind, but I was trapped in words and beginning to believe that ecstasy was finding a typo in a two hundred and fifty page manuscript.

Meanwhile a lot of people were getting rich, but not me. The sales skyrocketed into the many millions of dollars within a three-year period. They went from $900,000 gross sales to $24 million in the few years I was there. I started to get bitter about my low wages and long hours. My salary at the Sunday School Book company had been $6,000 a year, and that was lousy even by the standard of living then. Now my salary was a less than stellar $8,000 a year. By comparison, my boss made $50,000 a year. The two things my boss said that I remember were, *These little things aren't big*, and, *Make sure the artist did what he did.*

I vented my frustration by writing a bizarre parody of a kindergarten workbook which I called *Diamondback Palomino*. You'd have to read that to know what I'm talking about. During the time I worked there, I was always writing something else, like poems and books. I remember writing the lyric to one country song that included the following:

I spend my whole time dreaming
Of a life out on the farm.
Where a man in his working day,
Gets a chance to move his arms.

I realize that this portion of the book is not about the my life in the Cleveland Zoo. It is meant to give you perspective on what comes next. I was at the zoo for a few summers; this *new life* was turning out to be no life at all, and it went on for nearly six years.

I snapped out of my life of sleep-walking after a series of troubling wakeup calls. One morning the Office Business Manager had a stroke and fell over dead. His name was Sweeny. Some months later one editor had a massive heart attack and died at his desk. A man named Hughes had his truck rammed by a freight train at a crossing, but he survived. The owner's son-in-law was killed one morning in a motorcycle accident, and then another guy in editorial blew his brains out with a shotgun right there in the office late one night.

The real epiphany came one Friday night. As usual, I was working at the office by myself until around 7:00 p.m. I got in my car and headed home to my apartment on Joan Avenue. As I made my way over to Pearl Road I realized that it was a fine summer evening. I saw a car pass me going the other direction, and for a moment, I could see the people in the other car. They were lit up in the golden sunlight like angels. It was a young man and his family, and they were happy. Someone in that car must have said something funny, because they all burst out laughing. The driver also threw his head back and laughed. It was then that I recognized him; it was Don Kuenzer from the zoo. I knew who he was, but he wouldn't have known me.

The words just came out, "I don't want to do this anymore. Oh, God, I miss the zoo, I want to be back there."

My place on Joan Avenue was a dive. After I was there for several months, the landlord told me that the old lady who lived there before me died in my bathtub. There was another old woman across the hall from me. She always wore the same green-floral housecoat and fuzzy blue slippers with matching veins on her ankles. Eventually, I saw that the editions of the Cleveland Press that the paperboy left outside her door were starting to pile up. After about five days, I told the landlord. He went in there and found her dead and covered in flies. The smell was pretty bad. It seeped all the way into my bedroom. It never went away, but I got used to it. If I had a date, I had to say, "Let's light an incense stick."

Everyone was literally dying all around me, but it got worse, at least from my perspective. I played softball on a lot of teams in the Cleveland area during those years. I played in Strongsville and North Olmsted. After one game in Strongsville playing for the MCP team, I woke up the next day with a pain in my left ankle. After playing more baseball and walking around on it a few days, the ankle began to swell. Before long it was double its normal size and throbbing in pain. I went to two doctors who x-rayed it and found nothing broken. They couldn't see any physical cause for the extreme swelling, joint heat, and faint blue-red discoloration. They said I could keep walking on it. So I did. When it didn't improve, one doctor gave me tests for rheumatoid arthritis. His name was Molina. I had to write him a check. The tests came back negative.

"But," he said, "Even though the tests are negative, I am going to treat you on the assumption that you have rheumatoid arthritis nonetheless. It can be that, in some cases, the tests results are negative, but the condition is present." (Basically, I had a broken ankle or a torn ligament and he treated me for rheumatoid arthritis.)

That doctor spent the next year loading me up with just about every kind of anti-inflammatory medication he could prescribe, increasing the dosage as he went since they didn't seem to help. There was one drug I can't recall that began with the letter A. Then another one, Azolid (phenylbutazone), then prednisone. He also told me to take up to eight aspirins a day on top of those drugs. Like a dummy, I took the drugs and kept going back.

He was always poker faced. He was one of those doctors who went into the next room to look things up in a book or a Reader's Digest or something. Then he'd change the drug or increase the dosage, but he told me to walk on the ankle normally since an injury was not the cause. Though my ankle stayed in its massive swollen state, my stomach and gastro-intestinal system paid an even higher price. The pain in my gut soon exceeded the throbbing knife in my ankle. I had sick feelings and often lay awake in hot sweats. I sweat so much the bed was utterly soaked. This awful time continued for a couple of months. But I went to work every day.

Then one day at the office, a middle-aged lady named Marie stopped me in the hall. "That doctor of yours isn't doing you any good. You need to get off that ankle. It's probably broken."

The next day she brought me some wooden crutches from home. I got on them. Within twenty-four hours, the pain in my ankle had dramatically subsided. Within three days on the crutches, the pain was gone. I threw away all the drugs. I took up swimming at the YMCA in Berea every night. I would walk on my crutches, and then hop on one leg to the side of the pool and jump in. Everyone else in the pool was a senior citizen, and I was trying to figure out what I was doing there.

Despite throwing away all the medicine, the gruesome condition of my ulcerous digestive tract continued for years. My youth was done. I was completely screwed up. I stayed on the crutches for six months. After that, I finally had the nerve to test the ankle with a few tender steps. The pain did not come back.

In an effort to put my life in order, I moved to a duplex on West 117th Street. Quite physically devastated, I left Modern Curriculum Press for a job as Media Relations Director at Channel 25, the PBS station in Cleveland. I tried to be normal. It wasn't easy. The most notable thing I did there was become the first person ever to draw the WVIZebra, the station mascot. The Station Manager Betty Cope said that everyone who volunteered for the station was a WVIZebra. So I drew cartoons of the mascot. I still have some of the first renderings, and that zebra remains the station mascot to this day.

I was still having a lot of pain in my stomach, but couldn't face the idea of dealing with another physician. So, I resorted to various tricks to lessen the pain. I took hot baths which seemed to anesthetize my body. A turning point came one day when I was doing just that, soaking away the hurt in my gut. My little thirteen inch black-and-white television was on in the next room. I had clicked the channel selector to a show called *The Way It Was* with Curt Gowdy. They were recounting the 1960 World Series between the Yankees and the Pittsburgh Pirates. The Pirates' victory in that series had been one of the joys of my childhood. I really would have liked to watch the show, but there I was, sitting in the bathtub after taking six *stomach-friendly* analgesics. There came a moment, however, when nostalgia trumped pain. The Yankees had tied the game in the top of the ninth, and I knew what would come next. I crawled out of the tub, wrapped myself in a towel, and made my way toward the grainy image of Bill Mazeroski's Game 7 home run, and the exuberant commentary of announcer Bob Prince as he tried to describe the ball flying out of the park at Forbes Field. Yogi Berra could only watch as Maz crossed the plate and was greeted by the team, among them, my childhood hero, Roberto Clemente.

Then suddenly the juxtaposition of one of the most-deliriously happy moment in my life against my current miserable caricature of existence hit me. Tears poured out of my face in a massive flow. I hobbled shivering back to the bathtub.

At Channel 25, I kept a bottle of Maalox in my desk at all times. For those people there who knew me then, like Bob Olive and Kent Guist, I am sure I was an oddity. I looked like hell, and felt like it, too. My body was falling apart, and I was convinced I had the onset of crippling arthritis in every joint of my body. I believed I'd be in a wheelchair in five years. I was twenty-eight years old.

Was God punishing me for something? Often, big clumps of my hair fell out. I recalled Dr. Molina telling me "hair loss could be a side effect" of the drugs I had long ago discarded. I didn't laugh for a year. I kept track of it and wasn't capable of laughing for an entire year. Nothing gave me the semblance of any pleasure.

I'm sure that my malaise did not improve the quality of my work at WVIZ, and everybody was affected by the harshness of the winter of 1976-1977. One day, the first melt of spring appeared in Cleveland, and it was suddenly spring. The roads cleared, and people become more active. Relief and optimism spread like breezes through the city. Clean invigorating water, icy cold, began flowing like sheets of purity out from under the drifts of collapsing wet snow.

The sun was warming Cleveland for the first time in many, many months. I stood next to the window and let it all wash over me, but I was hardly feeling anything anymore. Shouldn't I have been feeling something? I should, at least, have been contracting spring fever or baseball fever. The arrival of spring meant the whole planet was tilting, so I decided I would finally let it move me.

Around 11:30 that morning, a thought came to me, and the thought turned into the energy of motion. I had been raising potted plants in my apartment all winter. I drove home and selected the best specimen that I had, a bloom of *purple passion* which I had grown from a cutting, but now filled and overfilled a hanging basket. I carefully moved it to the back seat of my Dodge Dart, and turned the wheels toward my safe haven near the Fulton Parkway.

Gene Huhtala was in the lobby as I entered. It was as if he was waiting for me. The slight, white-haired, older man was busy with something, moving a stack of papers, or adjusting a table. I'd say he had a little bit of spring fever. He peered at me over his wire-rimmed reading glasses.

"Adam," he exclaimed. "How are you? What a surprise." I must have shocked him with my appearance, but he showed no reaction. I looked like hell.

"I brought you a present," I said, before I could say anything, he already knew what it was.

"It's *purple passion*," he said, "My mother's favorite." He took the plant and turned back toward the offices. "Come with me. Good. Good."

I followed him all the way to his large office where he set the plant on a file cabinet, but it trailed down to the floor, so he chose, instead a hook high up on the ceiling near the large window that looked out over nothing, but the ancient woods of Brookside Park.

He stood on a chair to reach the new location, then stepped down and admired its beauty before turning to me. "How are you?" he said again.

"Well, I've been working over at Channel 25."

"Oh, that's good."

"Well, not too good…" I confessed.

"Oh?"

"I've been a little… ill lately. I think it would be really a good thing for me to get outdoors. I was wondering if I might come back and drive the tour train this summer."

Mr. Huhtala was very surprised. It was the last thing he expected for me to say. "Well, you know it only pays three dollars and five cents an hour…"

The hourly pay seemed inconsequential to me. What I was hoping to earn was my life and health.

"We'll work something out," he said.

I took the next few weeks to try and regain my strength by riding the bike trail in *The Valley*, as we called the Rocky River Reservation. In early May, I went back to the zoo, to drive the train yet again. The very first day, I realized that there were changes at the zoo. Now summer employees weren't allowed to drive their cars into the zoo as we had once done. Full time employees could still drive to their stations, however, and I remember someone telling me that I could catch a ride to the garage with Ray. I turned around, and there was this zoo emloyee in a brown Metroparks shirt. That was another big change. This was no longer the *Cleveland Zoo*; no, it was the *Cleveland Metroparks Zoo*. It was not a part of the county park system, and not solely controlled by the city. It turned out that Ray was the current mechanic, and Garth "Whitey" Goede had retired. When I first saw him in the parking lot, he was driving the cab of the leopard train, Number 2. There were no cars attached to it, and he was just using the cab of one of the zoo's fastest trains as a vehicle to zip around the park. I thought, *this guy's a wild man. He cherry-picked this speedy cab and took off the cars, just like Les and I used to do.*

"Hey, they say you need a ride to the garage," he said. I hopped on, but with a Grandma Moses vitality rather than the vigor of my earlier days. I would work on that, however.

My first impressions of Ray as a mad man were instantly confirmed as he rammed it into reverse, slammed on the brakes, popped her into a forward gear, and literally peeled out, burning rubber. Then he power-shifted from first to third gear. From there he rammed the floor shifter back into the lower right 4-gear of the H, and we were soon blistering through the parking lot at about fifty miles an hour. Unbelievable. Whitey would have had a cow. Whitey would have had a herd of cows.

Ray was acting lively and giddy with happiness, simply enjoying life. I couldn't believe how different people's lives can be. In the world I had escaped from, a misplaced semicolon mattered greatly. In Ray's world, the world of the blue collar worker, all that mattered were muscles, moxie, and rock and roll. I saw vividly, at that moment in life, I had been corralled into an existence no young person should choose. I looked at Ray and thought, *He's alive, and I'm dead. He's in the normal world, and I have to somehow return to it.*

As Ray pushed the responsive leopard cab to its eager limits, he didn't know how difficult the moment was for me. I was not right. He had no idea how much I envied his vitality.

Over the roar of the engine, Ray turned back to me and yelled, "Hey. I gotta run up to the commissary, so we gotta make a little stop first." I was holding on for dear life all the way to the new commissary area. I waited in the cab as Ray went to the maintenance department to get some part or tool that he needed. If I had been shocked by the uphill speed that Ray had achieved, I was not ready for the downhill trek into the lower zoo. I now guess that we hit sixty-five miles an hour in that train cab, and I held onto both poles, nearly sick at my stomach, but things were looking up.

The contrast could not have been greater as the muscular young man jumped down off the cab and I climbed down gingerly, aching from stiff joints. He was about to tell me all about what it involved to be a Cleveland Zoo tour train driver.

I quickly said, "Hey, I got it. I was a driver for five years when I was in college."

"Good," Ray exclaimed. "That makes it easy."

I was embarrassed by my appearance and atrophied health.

Trying to explain, I said, "Yeah, but I kind of got into white collar jobs. I've been a bit ill for awhile. Everything kind of sucked."

"Well, hey, man," Ray blurted with a huge grin. "That's all behind you now."

In my head, I was singing along with Gene Autry that morning with the words *back in the saddle again* playing in an endless loop in my brain. At every corner there was another change. None of my friends from the past were there, and the blue button-up shirts of our old uniforms were replaced with brown Metroparks tee's.

Among the drivers, I was an alien from another planet. Most of them smoked and seemed unhappy to be in the zoo. When washing the trains in the morning, they didn't talk to me. I was totally gung-ho, and apparently that made me a freak. I understood their willingness to waste time by chatting up the ticket sellers, but something was different. The conversations they had among themselves and the girls were not open and friendly. In fact, they stopped any conversation when I approached. They seemed so serious, even worried. When one of these young drivers was ready to pull out on his train, he'd throw a cigarette down onto the pavement and climb up into the cab. He was smoking in front of the people and littering. Then he'd say, "Next stop, Farm." I watched him return the microphone to its little hook. I realized they didn't even give a speech. What kind of weird parallel universe was this? Somehow the space-time continuum had been altered. I, who had been in the Great Tour Train Race of 1969, was the voice of company-minded responsibility. I was finally adhering to Gene Huhtala's continuing mantra. "Come into a stop. Get the tickets. And go." I never stopped, and enjoyed being productive. As a result, I was always pushing the trains in front of me. That kind of pissed off the other drivers. But I didn't scold them or say anything about it. I would just pull in behind them, but could read their lips as they said to the ticket seller girls, "Aw, f— he's here already."

I tried to take it in stride by yelling, "Hey, don't worry about it. I'll take the people off your train and just go. No problem."

Over the speakers, I'd announce, "Attention: This train will be leaving first so if you wish to continue the tour immediately, climb on board."

When out of earshot, I'd say, "Congratulations, good people of

Cleveland and the Western Reserve, on your decision to choose the 'leopard train.' I suppose it's obvious that the leopard train could kill and eat the zebra train. You'll find that this tour contains four hundred and eighty-three percent more fun facts about animals. Now, on the right are the rhesus macaques of Monkey Island. These were the type of monkeys used by Dr. Jonas Salk to develop his polio vaccine. Notice also that telephone wire at the top of the island..." The people laughed seemed glad to have a traveling narrative.

I can understand why I was isolated from my fellow workers by age and, perhaps by work ethic, but it was more than that. It didn't take long before I saw a hip flask passed between a driver and a ticket seller and was hearing rumors of inappropriate sexual encounters during work hours.

For my part, I kept my mouth shut and did my job. Apparently, that was not the solution that the other drivers considered best. One day, a very attractive ticket seller asked why I didn't ever stop and chat with her. She understood that I made more tours during the day than any other driver and thought she'd like to talk.

I tried to take her up on the offer, but could never find anybody home behind the come-hither smile and the name of Karyn with a *y*. The fact was that she had a boyfriend, no interest in the zoo, as far as I could tell, and seemed oblivious to music, art, and the life of the mind in general. I, on the other hand, had a train to catch.

Soon after I clearly gave up on that potential relationship, I got an invitation from another knockout to spend some quality time along the tour's route. Regina, like Karyn, was uncomfortable and not really there when I tried to pick up a friendly conversation at her stop. Perhaps I was a little paranoid, but I think there was a pattern beginning. It was a game being played in order to slow down an old codger who seemed to be getting stronger as the season progressed. I might have been nearly a decade older, but not stupid. I was, however, ignorant in the sense that there was more going on than I would have guessed. After all, how did my tours interfere with their social agenda?

I resolved to stay focused on following Gene Huhtala's vision of the ideal Cleveland Metroparks zoo tour train driver. It was clear that this younger crowd of summer zoo workers and I simply did not mix. We were like cats from two different litters.

Through it all, more and more, I kept to myself and found a new fondness for the innocence and sanity of the zoo's visiting families. Grandpas still made comical remarks about their aching knees when trying to board the train. Children still liked cotton candy. Moms still pointed at the swans. People still chanted "lions and tigers and bears, oh my" as the train headed up the long incline toward the Fulton Road Bridge end of the park. The vast universe of sunshine, gentle breezes, people, and families had not altered, except that now I found them all more refreshing than ever.

When the plan to slow me down didn't work, they tried to recruit me in their underground business. It was then that I understood this cluster of what social scientists were calling the *me generation*. Apparently, some enterprising ticket sellers were now in the business of reselling tickets. Their driver partners were no longer tearing the used tickets, but returning them to the women in the booths. These could then be resold with no hint of suspicion to customers. The invitations to *chat* were really given to try to figure out if I could be recruited for their scheme. I was a problem for them. Somewhere in their fiscal calculations they realized that I was ripping up one-half of their potential profits. On the other hand, they also realized that since all my torn tickets meant money for the zoo, their skimming would be harder to detect.

Of course, the young people's entire financial enterprise was based on the fallible assumption that Gene Huhtala was an idiot. He would know the attendance at the zoo on a given day, the exact turnstile count. He would walk around the park, and could no doubt see if the trains were active or not. He could see people throwing biscuits to the bears and rhesus monkeys. (They had also taken to selling animal treats at three for a quarter instead of six for a quarter and pocketing the money from every second sale.)

I learned all this on a Friday. I had been raised on the strict warning against tattling, but this was so far over the top that I didn't think it could be ignored. The fact was that Mr. Huhtala was off on Friday and Saturday, so I resolved to pay him a visit on Sunday.

So two days later, I came in to start the day. Sunday was the biggest day of all in the zoo. Sometimes as many as thirty thousand people visited. Amid the warming light of a fresh new morning, I took the long walk from the Main Parking lot to the garage area next to the good old yaks. When I came into the garage area, Ray the mechanic was there already, and he had a metal cash box.

"Hey," he said in his usual cheerfulness. "You're it today. You have to sell the tickets off your train." He plopped the cash box onto the seat in the cab of the leopard train, knowing that since I had my choice of all the trains, I'd pick that one.

"You have to sell the tickets yourself," he repeated.

"I've done that before," I said, "but why?"

Ray jumped up onto the cab of another train to drive it into the garage. He grinned and yelled above the engine as he raced it. "Huhtala fired all the other tour drivers and all the ticket sellers. All of 'em. Everyone in Kiddie Land and the Children's Farm got fired, too. All gone. They were all stealing from the zoo. And the girls were giving the guys in

Kiddie Land bj's up on top of that hill up there."

Ray thought that was hilarious. "He fired every freakin' summer employee in the whole zoo except you, my man."

That was a great day. I never stopped hustling all day, and the train was one hundred percent crammed with customers for the next ten hours. The trains ran until 6:30 on Sundays. And I didn't even think for a second to take lunch. How could I? So I was really running ragged that day.

Sometime during the course of the day, Gene Huhtala walked up to my train. He said, "We'll get some new drivers in here right away, Adam."

I said, "Hey, it's okay. I think everyone who wants the train tour is getting on eventually."

The next day, Mr. Huhtala had new drivers starting already. He had Rich Kemper coming back. He was even older than I, and he was still working toward his elusive PhD. On Tuesday, a big football player type named Vic Kaminski came in, all six foot five inches of him. He was a great guy. I broke him in, and we got along fine. Mr. Huhtala had new kids coming in left and right over the next several days. He restocked the staff at the Farm, Kiddie Land, and all the ticket selling booths. This crew was a great collection of good kids. All were hard-working, moral, and honest. The whole summer became like old times again. The only ones I remember by name (besides Vic and Rich) were a girl named Donna in the Main Booth, and another driver named Dean, a young black college student.

That summer was a time in which I recuperated fully. Within a few weeks I could run fast and laugh once again. That summer lots of us from the zoo went on cookouts and played lots of softball and football together. Vic even joined my church softball team, the John Knox Pews. I had designed the artwork for the team uniform. It showed two guys in church sitting on a pew. The one guy was smiling and listening to the sermon with his hands folded neatly in his lap. But he had B.O. Little wavy smell lines were coming out of him. The other guy next to him was holding his nose and saying, "pew."

I was still living in the duplex on West 117th as the summer passed in sunshine and health. When August came, I had no idea what would be next for me. The driver job would be ending soon. I was about to face another fall with no job.

According to union rules, full-time job openings had to be posted on the bulletin board by the time clock in the commissary building up on Fulton Parkway. Above the time clock was a cork bulletin board with a sign-up sheet so that employees could sign the list if they wanted to be considered for a job. The selection, however, was based on union seniority among full-time employees.

Job qualifications, at that time, meant nothing compared to seniority, and to tell the truth it was a good system. It meant that if a common man grew up on a farm taking care of cows and pigs all his life, he wouldn't be shoved aside for someone who had gone to college for a few years, but knew nothing about the real world of animal care. So, oddly enough, the system worked though I doubt that any zoo does that today.

Early one August evening around 5:30 p.m., I punched out from another day of driving, and noticed a job posted on the bulletin board. It was an opening for zoo night watchman. The position, at that time, paid $5.65 a hour. Plus, a person also would also get double time on twelve paid holidays a year, double time on his birthday, and a free frozen turkey at Christmas. That was $12,339.60 a year before taxes plus a free frozen turkey. That was more money than I had ever made in any job.

I suspected that I didn't qualify to sign up for the job. I was only a driver, and part-time summer employees weren't supposed to sign sheets like that. But as I stood there, Mary came into the room. She was the zoo's restroom-cleaning matron. Heavyset Mary had long black hair, flecked with gray, and looked like the stereotypical Italian *Mama*. I could easily imagine her in a big kitchen, tending to bubbling pots of spaghetti sauce, meatballs browning in an iron skillet, and baking bread, with her big family filling the house with laughter and stories about *l'Italia bella*. She was, instead, a widow who never had children.

"Well, there it is… the answer to your prayers," she said.

I probably appeared startled by her unexpected insight. I wouldn't have thought that she even knew I existed, but she had me figured out.

"I don't know… Isn't this for full-time employees?"

"Who cares? It can't hurt to put your name on there. Go ahead," she said reaching into her pocket and pulling out a ballpoint pen. She even clicked it to make the writing point pop out. Smiling in encouragement, she handed me the pen.

"Sign it. This is your chance."

I don't think Mary usually went around with a pen in her pocket. She knew I was in there and had come in to motivate me to take a chance. So I signed the sheet as she watched approvingly.

The next morning I came in expecting another day of driving, but as I was punching in, I noticed the list was gone.

An older man walked around the corner. I recognized him as Joe Chery (pronounced *cherry*). He was the zoo superintendent. I'd always seen him at a distance, but he seemed to be walking straight up to me. He was a kindly looking gentleman, with a short sandy crop of hair, flecked with gray. He had thick, calloused hands, like the working man he had been all his life. Though he was the manager of the entire zoo, he always wore the simple light brown workman's zoo shirt and dark work pants, just like the one worn by keepers and maintenance. He also wore steel-toed black shoes, even though he was nearing retirement, and his was a desk job.

With his office just around the corner from the time clock, he gestured me to step in and talk. Neither one of us sat down.

"You know, Adam, summer employees are not eligible to sign the list for full-time jobs here in the zoo," he said apologetically. "Even though you are a member of the union, that's not provided for under the Teamster's contract. Only full-time employees can qualify to sign for a job that is posted."

That's pretty much what I had said to Mary. He let his words cook for a minute or two before a smile betrayed him. "But no one else wanted the job, and Gene Huhtala recommended you. So you can have it if you want it."

I was pretty much speechless except for *yes*. That was a really wonderful day for me.

"Go home," he said. "You won't be driving the trains today. Get some sleep and be back here at 4:00 this afternoon. You'll need to go on a couple of shifts with John Sich. He'll show you the ropes as night watchman. Do you know John?"

"Oh, yeah. I sure do."

John was the older fellow who used to shoot rats after hours with Norm. I could remember the look of satisfaction he had when he drove to the bear area with his .38 loaded and ready to blast vermin.

"All right then, be here at the time clock at four, and don't be late. For the next two nights, John will take you around with him on his shift to break you in."

I had been awake about an hour, and I was already headed back home to hang out until 3:30. I was now the late shift night watchman at the Cleveland Zoo. How cool was that?

BOOK II: THE NIGHT WATCHMAN YEARS

For John Sich,
the most-punctual person in human history;
a rock of unfailing dedication.

CHAPTER ONE

I was twenty-eight when I became one of three night watchmen who served on three different shifts, 4:00 to midnight, midnight to 8:00 a.m., and a relief watchman who gave the others two nights off. I was hired for the midnight to 8:00 shift.

Instead of the t-shirt of the late 1970s which I wore as a tour driver, I was issued light brown button-up shirts and matching trousers made of one hundred percent polyester. The shirts had button-flap pockets with sewn-on badges all over them. *Cleveland Metroparks Zoo* was emblazoned on the left sleeve and also in a smaller patch above the right pocket. And above the left pocket, in gold embroidery was *Adam*. I surmised that detail was provided so my interaction with intruders could be friendly. It was kind of like having a *Hello. My name is...* sticker on my shirt to greet murderers, arsonists, and thieves when they illegally entered the park at night.

I figured that the late shift would be the most dangerous and resolved that any tough guys who dared set foot on *my turf* during *my shift* would soon find out that I could run like hell and that I was pretty handy with a telephone. By way of orientation, I was to accompany the legendary John Sich, Senior Night Watchman, on his 4:00 rounds.

I met him by the time clock at 3:30 in the afternoon. I was a half hour early, but he was already there. This punctuality enabled me to engage in conversation for an extra half hour prior to that first shift on the job. I would correct that by arriving at 3:59:59 on the second day of my training.

When Joe Chery introduced us, he explained that John had been pulling a double shift during the vacancy that I was now filling.

"Long time. Two shifts long time. I make lots money but ready for rest," Sich explained.

John, like many other zoo employees of that era, had been born in the Old Country. John was sixty-one years old. He was short and stocky, powerfully built with a thick neck and a barrel chest. He looked like a muscular Nikita Khrushchev, but with thick brown hair cropped in a crew cut. John smiled easily with a wide gap-toothed grin. Other than a change of ball cap, not one particle of the stocky man's appearance had changed in the ten years that had passed since I first saw him. He always seemed to be buried under layers and layers of flannel shirts, t-shirts, hooded sweatshirts, his zoo shirt, rubber raincoats, and a thick winter coat. He was a memorable person, charismatic, and picturesque. I want to make this perfectly clear. He was a wonderful man, quirky, but wonderful.

John's hobby was spitting. To get good at it, he practiced a lot. Since we had a half hour before punching in, we stood just outside the door to the commissary talking. During this time John leaned sideways every minute or so and let loose a voluminous stream of fluid. He'd squirt off a three-foot long thin line of spit sideways onto the sidewalk. After awhile, there was a large puddle forming on the cement about two feet to his right. I took great pains to avoid this when we finally went into the building.

Several times during the half hour, I said, "Well, should we punch in?"

"No. Four o'clock. On time we punch in. Four to midnight shift. You punch in right on time to minute and out on time to minute. Very important."

"Well, okay. You know some places it's okay to punch in earlier, not later, but earlier."

"No, four o'clock we punch it. We wait. We watch clock." John smiled and said, "You will like to be watchman. It is good job to do. No one here except us to guard whole zoo." John was being humorous when he said that.

I asked, "How long have you been a night watchman?"

"Twenty-eight years. I begin as Pinkerton. We was all Pinkerton. Zoo did not have watchman, so they use Pinkerton."

Then John pulled up the left sleeves of about six coats and sweatshirts to see exactly what time it was. One minute had passed so far. It was 3:31 p.m.

We continued talking; well, John talked and I listened. He was wearing mirrored sunglasses like a character out of *Cool Hand Luke*. He never ran out of spit, and he had a charming manner of adding an extra syllable to nouns ending in *S*. He would say, "Wipe your bootses on the stepses. These are the best clockses they make, and the car-ses they make in Detroit are good, you know?"

During the interminable first wait, he showed me the Detex Time Clock and the weighty ring of keys that I was to carry. We virtually carried every key to the zoo on that ring, several dozen of them, most differing in size, shape, and color, but some nearly identical. It was now 3:32.

"These are the keyses, but you don't need all these keyses. Only five of them needed. I just got 'em all. Who knows what they all are for? There are fifty keyses here." Then, one by one, he singled out and introduced me to each of the five significant ones: "All you need is Bird Building key, and you need *this* key to Commissary, *this* Administration Building, *this* Greenhouse, and all other lockses open with *this* one key right here. Is zoo master, huh?"

He showed them to me on the ring, but he wouldn't let me touch.

"Zoo master opens every lock in zoo, except Commissary, Bird Building, Administration, Greenhouse. It too opens locks of outside gates everywhere." It was 3:33 p.m.

John then showed me the night watchman's clock. The big, heavy Detex clock probably dated back to around 1915. It was made of brushed aluminum, and about the size of a stack of fifteen pancakes. It had a black leather carrying case with long leather straps. Inside the clock was a replaceable paper disk about the size of a CD. Chery put the paper disk in. Only Joe Chery, Ron Seeley, Al Sironen, or Don Kuenzer could open the clock to wind it.

Throughout the zoo there were stations where a type of key was chained to a metal box bolted to the wall. As the night watchman made his rounds, he would insert the suspended key into the Detex. As the key was twisted, it created an imprint of the numeral of that key on the internal paper disk. In this way, it provided a permanent, accurate, and infallible chronological record that was essential to the zoo security team, that is, it prevented the night watchman from sleeping all night in the car.

Finally, at 4:00 we punched in and John added one more installment to the ring of spit collecting on the sidewalk.. We got into a beat up, green 1970 Chevrolet Chevelle station wagon that was the official coach of the security force. It was equipped with an exhaust system specially designed to feed fumes into the passenger area.

The car had alternative uses, which left its mark in the smell department. It had been used to carry animals in small cages, to haul buckets of meat, engine parts, tubs of fish guts, dead things, grain sacks, muddy tires, and an occasional bale of hay. The result was a less than refreshing blend of cat and gasoline.

As we began the shift, John turned and asked, "Where's your pencil? You gotta have a pencil to write down all the things I'm going to tell you."

At first I thought he was kidding, but he wasn't. After finding a pencil and a scrap of paper in the glove compartment, I dutifully began writing everything I was told, and even managed to work in some questions of my own. For example, I wanted to know what I should do if someone came into the zoo with a weapon.

"Knock him unconscious." His answer was that simple, but without the obvious detail of "How?" That explanation, as it turned out, would come later.

I wrote down *knock unconscious*.

"First stop Yak Barn," Sich announced as we drove down behind the Old Cat and Ape Building and through Parking Lot Number 2. Near John Nagy Boulevard, John turned the car around and parked outside the little wooden Yak Barn. It was around 4:03 p.m. and still broad daylight.

When the car came to a stop, John turned toward me, stared and smiled. "Well? Write it down: First stop Yak Barn, we hit it at 4:15."

I quickly scribbled: *Stop 1. Yak Barn. 4:15 p.m.* Next to that, I wrote, *12:15.*

John had his eyes on me the whole time. "Good. You are smart," he said. "I hit Yak Barn at 4:15. You hit Yak Barn at 12:15, because you midnight shift. Now, we wait."

It was 4:04, and I was officially bored.

"Do you ever get out of the car and walk around?" I asked. "Maybe take a little stroll?"

"No. Why would I do that? What if criminal nearby with gun on railroad tracks? We would be sitting duckses. We wait. Wait for 4:15."

John talked for nine minutes, before saying, "Okay. Is time. Now we hit 'er."

He unlocked the brass padlock on the wooden back door to the rustic Yak Barn. The heavy dark wood door creaked open, and we were nearing the time to *hit the clock.* In John's world, hitting a Detex station was about as complex as performing brain surgery. First, he showed me how to insert the station key into the clock, and then he waited until exactly 4:15. Holding the heavy clock in both hands, John stared down into the face of the clock and counted out the last forty seconds.

"Now is time. Now I hit 'er." He turned the key in the clock with a little bit of force, recording our visit to the Yak Barn.

He was trying to instill his punctuality; I, however, was enthralled with the yaks. I'd never seen one up close, and thought them impressive.

But John hurried me along. "We go. We go. Too dangerous to stay in barn."

We went out into Parking Lot Number 2 and got back in the wagon, and John drove the car about fifty feet to the Zebra Barn. It was technically still 4:15, and he turned to me and said, "Now, we wait."

At this point I was praying that someone would start shooting at us from the B&O railroad tracks nearby just to break the monotony, but John talked some more about values and politics for eight minutes before saying, "This is Zebra Barn. We hit 'er at 4:30. You will hit 'er at 12:30. Write that down."

Once again, we watched the clock, and once again, I was enamored with the animals. It was magical to see zebras up close. I loved them.

"Pay attention," said John. "Soon we hit 'er." He stared down into the clock face for fifty seconds, with his thick fingers wrapped around the black leather of the case. His chest went up and down as he breathed beneath his huge collection of sweatshirts and coats.

At exactly 4:30, he said, "Now." And he turned the station key in the clock.

Jeazels-measles, I was dying.

Next we drove to the back of the Old Main Cat and Ape Building. That killed about twenty-six seconds out of the eight-hour night. We parked right behind the dark brick, hulking form of Old Main. John spit out the driver's side window, and we waited for fourteen more minutes to pass. John pointed to a large black willow tree about ten feet from the car.

"You see that tree there at fence?" John asked. "You know keeper in Apes, that guy Dick?"

He was a big heavyset guy. I knew who he was.

"Well, Dick was here in this spot one night when was night watchman. Only he wasn't night watchman. He was Pinkerton. This long time ago. I was Pinkerton, too, then. We was all Pinkerton.

"Well, Dick was here and he was with this guy Bill. Bill was with him. But he wasn't Pinkerton. He worked for the zoo. Riding around with him, you know? Well, Dick was going into Main Cat to hit (the clock), and he saw this man standing up on fence there like he was sneaking into zoo, holding real still so Dick not see him in branches. It was real dark. But Dick gets out of car, and he sees him. He says, 'I'm going into this building and when I get back, you better be gone. The zoo is closed.'" John turned toward me and said, "He tells him the zoo is closed, you see?"

"So Dick he goes to hit 'er, but when he comes back out, the man is still there." John turned his head toward me and broke into a huge grin. "And the man is dead. He had hung himself and was dead hanging on that tree right there by the fence."

John laughed and laughed. "So let's go hit 'er." he said.

I didn't write that down, but made a mental note: *sometimes there might be dead bodies hanging from trees.* Great. Anyway, then we got out of the car and went down into the ancient cellar of Old Main. John and I went in single file in through the smallish back door. The check station was in an old furnace room, and once again, we waited until the second was right before *he hit 'er.*

John talked all night. For eight hours. He spit into the night every thirty seconds. I wrote down the important stuff he said. I thought eventually he'd become dehydrated and stop talking, but he never did. I also figured out why the car smelled like B.O.

John hit all the Detex stations during the first four hours. He let me hit them for the second four hours. It was kind of boring. But I wasn't discouraged. The plan was that I'd go around with John for two middle shifts, and after that I'd be on my own doing what seemed to be the world's easiest job. We went to buildings and barns and *hit the clock* in each place throughout the zoo's huge grounds. We never played the radio in the car or walked around. John was always cheerful and grinning. I think he was glad to have some company.

For John, being night watchman at the zoo ranked somewhat higher than being President of the United States. The responsibilities were similar, except that the president had people to help him. There was a precise way of doing everything. Buildings had to be visited according to a strict schedule.

"You got to check all doors," said John. "Check every one. If you see something that a keeper has done wrong, left door unlocked or water running, put him on report. If teenagers drive into parking lot, try to see license plate and put them on report. If you are to notice animal doing anything funny, sick, or loose, put him on report."

At 8:00 p.m., midway through the rounds, we pulled in next to the Bird Building to go hit the clock in there. We stopped by the entrance near the Waterfowl Lake, right under the tower with the sculptures. "Now another lesson," John began. "Very important. We watch for pee on doorknobs of Bird Building. Bad kids they come into the zoo at night for trouble. They torment the night watchman. So right here, be careful."

By that time it was pretty dark. John had a flashlight, and he carefully examined the brass doorknob leading into the main level of the Bird Building. Then, he stooped over and smelled the doorknob carefully before touching it.

"All right. Is good. Okay," he said. "No pee tonight." As he unlocked the door, he said, "These kids come in to trick John. They think is funny to piss on doorknobs so I touch to get a hands full of pee. One time they trick me. And on the locks, too, sometimes. Look for pee and smell to be sure."

He looked at me and waited. So I wrote that down. *Check for kids' piss on doorknobs.*

"Sometimes they move picnic tables, huh? I drive and suddenly is picnic table middle of road by the Monkey Island. It not there before, so I know something is funny up. Then one time, I pull into Birdses here, and hit 'er. Then I come out and there is a garbage can behind car, to block me in. So I got to move it."

Maybe if he wouldn't be so predictable, I thought. After all, he went around the park with his headlights on, and hit the clocks in the same order at exactly the same times every night for twenty-eight years. The kids knew where he was at every minute. That gave me something to think about. I was going to have to deal with these punk kids.

During my years as night watchman, I had plenty of time to do the math. By my calculations, twenty-eight years, John waited for the clock to get right to the minute 232,960 times before hitting it. He also followed a similarly precise schedule when he punched in and punched out for his shift. He punched in at 4:00 p.m. exactly, and out at midnight on the dot. He'd stand by the clock and wait for it to *click* over to midnight, and then he'd punch out. So that was an additional 14,560 times he waited for the minute to be exact. Without counting extra shifts, that comes to 247,520 times of his hovering over a clock waiting for the exact minute to arrive. He would also continue for three more years after that, adding another 26,520 times, but who's counting? With overtime he probably hit a clock over 300,000 times in his career.

John and I went into the Bird Building right in the middle of his shift. We walked up to the kitchen on the top floor. That was where he took his lunch break. His wife had prepared sandwiches, a slice of homemade pie, and carrot sticks.

I hadn't brought a lunch.

"Now that I know, I'll bring one tomorrow," I said, "But you go ahead and eat. Don't worry about me." He wasn't.

We were sitting at a table in the Bird Building kitchen. Sich ate his lunch there every night, but it would not have been my choice. As I have noted before, animal smells are specific to each type. While many people thought the Pachyderm Building was the worst, for me, the smell of bird droppings topped the list. This kitchen was a large room used for preparing diet for the many birds. The room had windows that comprised a whole wall of glass. In the daytime I'm sure it was very bright and cheery. There was a dining table for keepers, a large stainless steel table for food preparation, two huge stainless steel sinks, and many folding chairs. There were wire baskets on a counter near the sink which were used for washing lettuce. The floor was brown stone tile. Everything in the room was immaculately washed, fresh, and clean. Still, the building smelled like a thousand birds. This was not a place where I would eat a meal, but all this was just my opinion.

As he ate, John recounted various experiences with wet doorknobs, and reminded me to write it all down after our break. He said a lot of other things that night which I remember very well.

"The clock she is heavy," he said, "it's protection as weapon. You hit the man with the clock. Knock him unconscious. That is why clock heavy. To swing and hit. Tough luck for them."

"Are you married? You have children?" he asked with an abrupt change of subject. I wasn't married at the time, and he gave me his opinion of that: "That is not good. No good. You can do what you wish, like young people today. They do what they want, have fun. But to be an old man some day and not have someone calling you *Poppa*, is not good." From there, it was back to official business. "If you see a lion loose in the zoo, don't mess with it. Call on the phone. Call Kuenzer. You call Kuenzer. Or call keeper who's in charge in this area. Leave the lion alone. If man in zoo, that is different. Hit him with your clock. Knock him unconscious. If he blocks you so you can't hit his head, hit him in the knee. Then hit him in the head with the clock."

Then he was back to the benefits of the union, and getting a frozen turkey every Christmas. (Evidently that was an important extra bestowed on members who stood in line at the union hall every December. Who knew?)

"Never leave the zoo during your shift when you are supposed to be here. Never. Not to store. Not home. Nowhere. You stay here. This is your job. What if you leave and something happens? What then? Huh?

"If you see a sick animal, put it on report. Dead animal, put it on report. If boilers not work, put on report. Tell Joe Chery in the morning. In winter, is very important that boilers work. For heat. For animals. So that the pipes not freeze and break from cold. In the winter at night if not heat in the building, call maintenance. Joe Matayas. His number is on the sheet. If boilers not work, call maintenance. Joe Matayas. Even three in morning, you call. Wake him up. Get him out of bed. Is his job. Get him out of bed. Man in the zoo. Knock him unconscious. Then call rangers.

"Bear loose in the zoo. Call keeper. Don't mess with her. Stay in car. Don't mess with a big bear.

"You can't have a gun. Not allowed. So if you have gun, is not allowed. So no one must know that. I don't know it. You don't know it." Grinning, John said, "What gun? I don't have gun. What gun? Do you see a gun? No, not allowed.

"Fire in the zoo, call the fire department. Very important, be at gate, let fire trucks in. How crazy would it be to call firemen and not let them in gate? Write it down: *Call fire department. Let fire department in zoo.*

"Never do this, also. Never steal gasoline. You fill the watchman's car with gas, okay, that is what you're supposed to do. But never *your* car. These rangers even, lots of people. They steal. I see them stealing gas from pump, for their own car. From all over the park system I see them come into the gas pump, into the zoo, stealing. They have no business in zoo. Why they in zoo? For gas, they come. John knows. How can man steal from company that gives him bread, the living for his family? Never steal. Never touch anything not yours at work or in the whole life of a person. If I see a dollar, I ask whose dollar is this that I found? It goes to lost and found. Not me. Something in refrigerator in Bird Building is not mine, I don't take it. Someone may left his lunch. What does he do with no lunch? If I see people steal, I put them on report, even a ranger. So they better not let me see them anymore. They know. They know now. One or two of them learn hard about John Sich.

"When you shoot at rat or skunk, watch where you shoot. Where bullet goes. Huh? A zoo animal may be there, a deer or zebra, so you be careful, not stupid. Watch behind this rat. Watch where you shoot. If you miss, huh?" John grinned again. "Uh, but that could not happen. Who has gun? What gun?

"This is better than when I was Pinkerton. Very good. The zoo is good and Teamsters are good. Thank God for Teamsters. I was here many years, with only hourly pay, nothing else. No benefits. Who cared about John? Now, I have retirement, pay for my birthdayses, holidays, sick dayses, all because of Jimmy Hoffa and Jackie Presser. Some say being Teamsters is bad. They should be without it, like we was then. Ask Dick about them days. He will tell you. Ask anyone. Teamsters very good to me and my family. For long time."

For the second half of that shift, John let me hit the Detex stations. The second half was a repeat of the first four hours, with one exception. At around 8:30 p.m., we parked the Chevrolet wagon behind the Old Main Ape Building.

"All right," said John. "Now is time. The end of daylight is come. Time to take down flag. Every morning 6 a.m., on your shift, you will raise American flag. Now, on my shift, I take down flag for nighttime."

There was a tall steel flagpole about fifty feet in front the old building. A small concrete walking path went from the center of the front of the building to the main roadway. The flagpole was at the halfway point between the building and the road, and the pole had a circular walkway around it.

"The flag of America," said John, "Must never be left out overnight or in rain. But must also be on display, for pride. Never just to take it down like job with no thoughts. Up and down she goes with ceremony, each day, each night. If on your shift and it begins rain, you must take down flag. After rain stops, you put flag back up. It may be cold and dark in dead night, and you are alone, still it is necessary. Now, you watch me."

John climbed up onto the concrete base of the flagpole. He was a short-legged man, putting his knees onto the cement as if in prayer. He loosened the flag's woven ropes from their hooks and, hand over hand, lowered the big billowing flag downward.

"Now you watch," he said, demanding my attention. "Flag must never touch ground. Never. You know? And there is proper way to fold this flag that must be done."

Without letting it touch anything, John adroitly flipped the flag into a neat half fold, then in half again, and again. When he had it down to a square about one foot wide, he folded it into a neat, tight, star-spangled triangle.

"Now, you do it," exclaimed John, and he flapped the flag open while being careful to keep it off the ground at all times. He handed it to me. Without too much trouble, I endured his scrutiny and managed the task.

"All right," he said. "Now we put it away in Main Apes." There was a place for the flag in Old Main, and though it shared a shelf with paint cans and brushes, mouse traps and d-CON®, it was reverently set in place by short, stocky John Sich.

His manner said more than his words, and every morning at 6 a.m., I went to that shelf and got the flag. I walked to the flagpole and raised it over the zoo. When rained threatened, and that happened a lot, I went and took the flag down.

Since this 4:00 shift was actually my orientation, not my first night solo, I was sent home at midnight. It was then that I realized that Sich was going to stay and pull a double. The next day, I phoned Joe Chery. "John doesn't need to pull a double shift again tonight to break me in, unless he wants the extra hours. I feel bad for him. I can do it. I'm really familiar with the zoo from driving the train. I can handle it by myself if that's good for everybody, but it's up to John. Whatever he wants is fine with me."

Both John and Joe thought that a great idea. So on the second night, I went out alone on the midnight to 8 a.m. shift. Of course, I did manage to forget the two pages of hand-scribbled notes, which I had made the day before. They were safely at home in my other pants. Since I knew the zoo, however, it wasn't a big deal.

CHAPTER TWO

During the midnight shift, the zoo was more desolate than at 4:00. When John went on duty, there were still keepers, administrators, and even some of the public lingering in the zoo. Additionally, there was a contingency of Metroparks rangers who often stayed right up until midnight. These were adult, law enforcement officers complete with squad cars and guns. They were assisted by a junior ranger. The term *Junior* might connote childishness and even a juvenile, amateurish status. In comic book vernacular, you might picture Huey, Dewey, and Louie from one of Carl Barks' Uncle Scrooge comic books. You may also picture a plastic toy badge, and a baby-faced neophyte in the sense of a novice or beginner. These are misleading images when you consider that Huey, Dewey, and Louie, in Donald Duck terms, were bright, brave, plucky, honest, resourceful, and dependable; therefore, the comparison is invalid.

If John Sich ran into trouble on the early shift, he was in walkie-talkie range of a real ranger, who could shoot people, and, of course, he also had access to a junior ranger, who could bore anyone to death in four hours with adolescent drivel.

When I arrived at the zoo to start the midnight shift, the real *adult* ranger left the Park. He turned off the TV in his office and left. John had told me that the junior ranger would stay on duty for four more hours after I got there. Though never introduced, and never actually seeing any variety of rangers at orientation, John assured me that somewhere in the park there was a junior ranger who would be my backup for my first four hours.

I began alone at midnight. I punched in, then drove the old green station wagon on my rounds. I followed John Sich's schedule with an almost religious devotion. Midnight, punch in at the Commissary Building. From there the rounds commenced. Detex clock and building keys on my person, I hit the stations on a schedule that any observant intruder could document. Wait at each station in the car. Turn on the dome light to see the clock and also provide a clear target for snipers. Visit the yaks, visit the zebras, unlock and walk through the dark shadows of Old Main. (At this point, the former tour train driver learns that zoos are very different in the dark than in daylight.) Turn on the radio for some company, then realize that intruders will hear you coming. Turn the radio up to fight boredom and realize that its sound will cover a scuffle and cries for help. Keep the walkie-talkie close, a junior ranger is just a battery-powered hail away.

Walking through the buildings, the animals stir to the left and right. The cages have not been hosed for twelve hours and urine is draining along concrete gutters in a cavern dimly lit by two bare hundred watt light bulbs dangling in green metal fixtures.

Baboons move to the front of the cage. They are extremely close and reach through the chain link like lunatics in an asylum. Anyone walking there has to keep hands in close to the body or behind the back so that an animal cannot grab hold of a finger along this gauntlet of countless small hands and flailing hairy arms. Behind each arm is a face showing a needy hunger and desperation. After passing, the baboons run ahead to renew their assault further down the line. For a watchman, the goal is the Detex station, and after *hitting* the clock, it's back along the same route.

Then it's 1:00 a.m. and back in the car heading toward the tigers' area. Parking in front of the Wolf Alcove, it's now a matter of waiting fifteen minutes before getting out of the car. The wolves aren't afraid, and on the other side of the bars they look almost dog-like. They do not, however, act like dogs. No tail wagging or friendly reactions as a greeting. In contrast to the primates, the wolf's cage is spotlessly clean. This is because the animals eat each other's dung. It may be a survival tactic that is useful in the wild where the scent of scat would give away the predator's location. It could also be the result of boredom, an emotion that would be understandable here where they now watch your every movement.

The Detex is what always dictates the path. Opening the padlock to the Tiger Building at night is an experience. Walking here is a role play game of hunter and hunted. In this case, the watchman is the prey. Siberian tigers watch closely from a few feet away, and bars seem a feeble defense from even the vibrations from their enormous lungs. They race back and forth along the bars, panting in excited snarls and huffs. They pace. They pounce. They turn every way with energy and a restless, incessant eagerness to be upon me, shredding my flesh into nothing. Readers may think this an exaggeration, but the reality is that they are salivating. The clear drools hit into dark gray circles on the smooth floor of their enclosure. The Detex station is straight ahead.

The lions are next, and they are so like their feline cousins from Siberia in the sense that they are focused on the intruder whose only ambition is to punch a digit on a paper disk inside a heavy clock.

Pay no attention to the bears. Get past the Kodiaks and grizzlies and feel the wave of relief when the outside door mercifully clicks shut. It's 1:15 a.m., and the wolves seem more dog-like than ever.

Breathing can slow to normal now on the drive around the perimeter of the capybara and Siberian reindeer enclosure. According to The Gospel of John Sich, Chapter 1, Verse 1, there are exactly fifteen minutes between hits. The night is cool and pleasant, and the sound of the crickets is calming and peaceful. If there are punks in the zoo somewhere pissing on doorknobs, suddenly it isn't so infuriating. I get out of the car, unlock the padlock, and go into the Reindeer Barn. The smells inside are fresh and sweet. Hay and wood. Rich earth and molasses. It is not the stench of baboons, or the pungent hard stools of cats and bears. 1:30 a.m. *hit 'er.*

Next it's the Sitatung Barn. Like the Reindeer Barn, it's a newer building, constructed of dark wood that smells of cedar chips. The air there tastes like sweet alfalfa hay and barn wood. After this brief respite, it's back to the beginning at the Main Entrance. Soon it will be time for a second tour around the zoo. There's been no sign of the mythical junior ranger. And the new, squeaky clean Commissary Building is a good place to sit down and wait here for the next hit. The Detex station is in the autopsy room, and at 2:00 that visit is registered.

Then it's back in the Chevelle driving along the upper level parking lot until coming to the Education and Administration Building. Inside it's dark, and the only light in the outer lobby is stealing in through great windows from the streetlamps outside. One of the keys gives entrance, and this clock station is deep in the building, just outside Gene Huhtala's office and toward the rear. Moving in that direction means passing the ominous locked glass case that contains a loaded .30-30 rifle for emergencies. Over against another wall is Gene's safe, a small black safe with painted gold filigree. Part of the job is protecting that safe. After a turn of the key in the time clock, it's time to retrace the path back to the entrance.

This time, there's no waiting in the car. The drive down to the lower level will absorb the minutes between twists of the key in the Detex. The road runs parallel to Fulton Parkway and then left along Brookside Park Drive. It goes past the Arabian and Bactrian camels, the axis deer, and the Père David's deer. These animals are on the left, but hidden in the darkness of their enclosures. Over the years I took pleasure in driving around Waterfowl Lake with the headlights off, especially when the moon was high so that visibility was not an issue. This was a magical world of darkness filled with the fresh natural scents of water and woods. At times like that, it was easy to forget that I was moving along the very cusp of urban neighborhoods. On the left is a thick forest, rising up the side of a step ridge. On the right is the peaceful lake, with starlight and moonlight revealing its shiny dark surfaces. The only intrusive sound is my car's engine which continues to sputter after the ignition is switched off and the noise and fumes come to a dieseling halt under the canopy of the sycamores. This is the location of Wade Memorial Hall, the oldest structure in the park.

I confess that there were times when I found the place too captivating to adhere to Sich's letter of the law. I'd stay here a little longer than the allotted time and make up the loss later in my rounds.

Inside this one hundred year old building, a clock station lies hidden in a utility room. The drive there is short, and it's easy to correct the time loss of the extra minutes spent near the lake. It's then a quick loop to the left and the zoo's Greenhouse. Walking into that building is a trip to the tropics, and a perfect sanctuary in winter.

I had actually been to this greenhouse before. In 1959 I was a fifth grader with an assignment to collect leaf specimens in a scrapbook. After gathering every variety I could find in North Olmsted, I still wanted more. My Dad asked me if I remembered seeing the trees at the zoo. That was enough to spark my interest. That Saturday I took the bus from Lorain Avenue, transferred at Denison Road, and walked the rest of the way to the zoo. It was quite an adventure for a little kid, but kids did stuff like that in those days. It was like taking the bus to the Indians' game, but getting off at a different stop. I took a roll of wax paper with me, and my large blue cloth notebook. While wandering around inside the zoo on that Saturday, I ended up outside the Greenhouse, where they had a lot of trees in huge pots outside as well as inside. The dark haired man who managed the building saw me carefully examining the trees and came out to talk with me.

He asked if I was interested in botany and I explained my school project.

"You've come to the right place," he began. "That tree you're looking at now is a ginko, or maidenhair tree. The Latin name is *ginko biloba*. It's unusual among trees, very ancient and primitive. It has been on earth unchanged since the time of the dinosaurs."

I left the zoo that day with a great many new finds, and the greenhouse manager was my early mentor.

Now, eighteen years later, as night watchman, I was in that greenhouse again. Alone at night. That place also held other memories. Once when I was a tour train driver, the same greenhouse manager flagged me down and said, "Hey come inside the Greenhouse for a second." I stopped the train and he said, "Here. There is a lovely orchid flower at the height of its bloom." He cut it and put it in a tiny glass water vase. He said, "It won't be good tomorrow. Why don't you give it to your girl?" I gave it to Annie McGinty, a food service worker whom I had once sprayed with a garden hose during a water fight around the refreshment stand.

Two-thirty a.m. and the key is twisted at the Detex station in the greenhouse.. The next bit of a drive is only about thirty feet to the Bird Building. At this stop, however, I always made it my practice to enter by a different door than John. This was my way of avoiding any possible wet doorknobs. John always used the public door so I'd climb the concrete stairs up onto the loading dock and enter on the north side of the lower building. Two forty-five a.m. and now the Bird Building has become a documented stop.

Next was the Children's Farm. The Detex station was outside, on the back of the barn. These places were all so familiar. At night, however, they were quiet except for an occasional roar of an engine or a drunken hoot from late night revelers moving fast along Brookside Park Drive. The life of that place was loud only in the memory of high school and college employees laughing in a dance we called a *summer job*.

Actually, this was an old crime scene. As the night watchman, I'd be obligated to report it, but when it happened ten years earlier, I was one of the perps. It started when I noticed a tree growing through the chain link fence. I knew that as the tree enlarged its girth, it would be strangled by the wire mesh. One Friday night at two o'clock in the morning, Annie, Ilene, Mary Ann, and I drove to that very spot. We had become a gang of four, three refreshment stand girls and a tour train driver. We brought wire cutters with us and went to work on the fence to create a hole large enough to give the sapling a fighting chance. The escape vehicle was my beloved Peugeot, and we became the noisy revelers of Cleveland's west side. Ilene actually stood up in the car and whooped out of the sunroof. I did, too. The tree is still there, the reminder of a summer long ago.

This leg of the patrol is not lonely or boring. Instead it's the familiar haunting grounds of pleasant memories. A right turn past the kangaroos and around the outside giraffe and elephant yards leads to the rear employee entrance of the zoo's large and ominous Pachyderm Building. After unlocking the brass padlock, I step inside and get hit in the face by the most powerful manure smell anywhere in the park. The intense aroma obliterates all other senses and duty requires a long walk past bales of hay, grain sacks, wheelbarrows, and large coiled fire hoses. The hall is long and narrow, and well-lit by hundred-fifty watt bulbs in green metal fixtures hanging down from above. At the end of the building is a small keeper's room with a few soft chairs, a tiny table, a coffee maker, and a small toaster oven.

By now, my clothes have already picked up a barn smell which will stay with me for the next few hours. The main volume of the pungent odor is drafting in from the public area of the Pachyderm House and swirling down the canyon of the tiny hallway where I entered the building.

Within the cavern of the public area are noises of slow, heavy rattling of chains. Something's moving in there, something massive and rumbling. Deep, deep growls, throaty and menacing, loom unknown within the chamber in front. The sounds come from all directions, and it sounds like the building itself is speaking some primeval language that's deeper than the roar of a lion, and strong enough to vibrate the floor beneath the feet. Step into that room. Fortunately, the Detex station is by the door. Hit it and leave.

At 3:30 a.m., it's back through the hall, and down a long metal stairway into the building's steamy basement. The room is full of water pumps and roaring oil-fueled boilers. There are two of these big boilers with tanks which are four feet in diameter and ten feet long. The room is a maze of massive pipes and oversized valves. At the end of each boiler the pilot flame is checked to make sure it's still lit. If one of the boilers is not working, there's a red reset button to make it roar back to life. There is a Detex station bolted nearby, and after making the hit, it's back up the stairway. The odorous belly of the Pachyderm Building is *not* a favorite place to be.

Waiting the rest of the fifteen minutes in the car, near what was then called the Ostrich Barn, is a great relief to the nasal passages. When the time is right, it's a pleasant walk up a garden path, open the padlocked door to the dark brown wooden building, and step into the total darkness while feeling around for the Detex station.

As I describe this, the dark room sounds more benign than the actual experience. The fact is that there are sounds in that place. There is a growling roar that sounds like a lion just inches from where I am standing, on the other side of a thin burlap barrier. I know intellectually that it is *not* a lion, but some kind of enormous bird. Whatever it is, it's separated only by a thin veneer of a wall. It knows I'm there, and slams against the wall while bellowing loudly. This is the final stop in the freakiest area of the zoo. Ahead is the home stretch and back to the commissary and a modern building that includes everything (showers, kitchen, and vending machine area). The 4:00 a.m. station is in the lobby of the Commissary Building. Now, it's time to rewind and start again. The next round will find me back in this place at 7:30 and the actual end of the shift. At that time, the Detex-Newman clock goes back to Chery, who opens it to remove the paper disk and winds the clock for the next shift. Now, I will wait by a different clock to punch out for the day. As with the Detex, this *other clock* is hit with the exactitude required by John Sich's timetable. Once there, I am instantly transformed into a fly on the wall. The full-time keepers, managers, and maintenance people are coming in, one at a time, to start their day. They roar up in old cars and leave them running. Most punch in and drive away toward their areas, but some of them hang around, shooting the breeze. It's fun just to watch and cash in on the jokes and laughter.

Once again, I found myself in a world of flip-flopping self-images. A few days earlier I was an *old* train driver compared to the others in the trade. Now, at twenty-nine, I am suddenly young, slender, and fresh-faced.

The old guys, however, are just beginning a new day and a sudden wave of fatigue hits from the long night that has just passed. It was lonely, but it took this sudden early morning comparison to bring that into perspective. The world of laughter and people belonged to the day.

CHAPTER THREE

It didn't take me long to get the hang of the night watchman job, and I started to realize that the time clock in the Commissary Building was the zoo employee's equivalent to a water hole where all animals gather. Over time, I met people that I did not expect. One of them was a childhood friend, Alan Sironen. When we were in elementary school, I'd bug him to play baseball so that we could reach my brother's quota of at least three on a side. He was pretty studious, even then. He had his life's goals mapped out by then. He wanted to start as an animal keeper at the zoo, and work his way up into management, maybe even curator.

He greeted me with a smile one morning at the watering hole. He was now the Assistant Curator, and I recognized him immediately. For me, his story was the best example I've ever known that a person can visualize his destiny and have it come true.

There were also other memorable meetings that took place there. Sometimes they were related to Don Kuenzer, the Curator who was often there greeting the employees as they came on duty. He had worked his way up the hard way, first as a keeper, then as manager of the Children's Zoo. He was a charismatic, hands-on leader who was good with animals.

In those days, zoos were changing with the times and moving away from the idea of warehousing animals and recreating natural habitats. Don was in a sort of collaboration with a relatively new director of the Columbus Zoo. Jack Hanna had come to Columbus from a small zoo in Florida and was trying to increase the popularity of the zoo in Ohio's capital city. Don helped out by loaning Columbus *new* animals such as a lesser panda or Kermit the caiman as a way to increase interest. This was all done on the up-and-up and in the name of cooperation between zoos. It was not a surprise when Jack would appear around 7:30 a.m. and seek out Don near the time clock. The two would put some caged animal in the back of Jack's truck, and he would drive off with a thank you.

Anyway, I was hanging out by the clock talking to Don on maybe the fourth day after I started. I told him about the orientation that John had provided and his strict adherence to the clock. This brought a knowing smile to Kuenzer's face.

"I was thinking that if a crook wanted to, he could observe me, like from the Fulton Road Bridge, and figure out my schedule after a few days."

"Yes," said Don. "I've always thought that."

"Like the Administration Building," I continued. "I go in there just after midnight and don't come back until 4 a.m. So anyone could figure that out. Does it matter if I hit the stations at random, as long as I hit them all, one every fifteen minutes?"

"Absolutely. I think that would be good. Just hit them all twice a night in any order."

I wasn't trying to pull a fast one or anything, but a little flexibility with the route would make the time move along, or so I surmised, and maybe even add to the zoo's security. Within a week of the time I started, I did not follow Sich's schedule, and even started patrolling on foot. I figured that driving around behind two headlights was more of an announcement than a thief deserved.

After two weeks as night watchman, I still hadn't seen one of the fabled *junior rangers*. The real Metroparks rangers were on patrol outside the zoo grounds in an area known as the *Emerald Necklace*, a reserve that surrounds the city. While they were too far away to help me in an emergency, I could hear them all talking on the police-band walkie-talkie I carried.

I'd hear things like, "Leaving Rocky River Reservation." Or "Leaving Huntington." It was interesting to hear their chatter, but if there had been a real emergency, I could not reach them with my little radio. I entirely relied on the junior rangers on duty to appear if I were to need any quick help.

My other back-up was an aluminum baseball bat. Sich had told me if I had any trouble, I should simply *hit 'em with the clock*. The fact was that I was better wielding a bat. After all, I could hit a baseball thrown at ninety mph and was certain I could hit a man in any part of his body that I chose. I even had a batting strategy all worked out: at full-speed I would feint a swing at the man's head. He would then raise his arms in defense, and I would retract the bat in one blurring motion, whip the bat handle past my face, and come in low and hard with a left-handed, back-handed swing to the kneecaps or shins, after which, I would bring the bat back instantly, again in a continuous motion, and quickly deliver the second hit. In my mind, it always worked with my Harmon Killebrew-style swing from the heels. I had total confidence in this tactic. In fact, I practiced it from time to time on small dead trees. I defeated them all quite easily; I was sure it would work.

On the other hand, I had serious doubts about the swinging Detex theory. Sure, it could be swung around on its leather strap like a mace, but achieving any accuracy with the single hit would be impossible, and probably only piss off an opponent who would be armed. Besides, the heavy clock was like a brick at the end of a thin leather strap. What if the strap broke away from the wimpy clips that connected it to the mechanism? Just swinging the clock might cause this before any impact was possible. I could see that happening with a loud *whirring*, and there goes the clock flying away like the head coming loose on an old wooden golf club.

Using the clock as a heavy battering fist, on the other hand, would mean getting close to a guy who probably had a knife. No, using the clock as a bludgeon had its drawbacks. If I tried using the clock as a heavy blackjack, a guy who was bigger and stronger than me would get it away from me and beat me to death with it in no time.

John clearly said, *Hit 'em with the clock. Knock him unconscious*, but this was the guy who officially didn't have a gun (apparently, the .38 he was packing under his layers of sweatshirts didn't count). The aluminum bat was my weapon of choice, but I also had a Plan B.

I was in the sporting goods section of Uncle Bill's, a local discount store on Center Ridge, when I saw a .22 caliber starter pistol. Of course, it only fired blanks, but the cardboard box it came in said that it also fired teargas pellets. This was a completely new technological advantage that had fallen in my lap. The cartoon image on the box showed a criminal totally engulfed in massive billowing clouds of debilitating teargas. Perfect.

I bought the pistol, the .22 blanks, and a little wax-cardboard container of teargas cartridges. Of course, I'd need a holster, and I didn't see any in sporting goods, but I found a plastic toy gun with a rubber shoulder holster in the toy department. I took everything home and assembled my new arsenal. I freed the holster from the shrink-wrap and threw away the toy gun. Then I slipped the .22 blank gun in the shoulder holster for a perfect fit. From that time forward, the little .22 was with me on my rounds. I seldom wore it, but I took it along, just in case. I loaded the chambers with six of the teargas cartridges, but never actually tested it. The little graphics on the box told me all I needed to know. This baby would blast big clouds of incapacitating teargas, plenty to stop man or beast.

CHAPTER FOUR

A few more nights went by, still no junior ranger in sight. It didn't matter to me. I was packing a rod by that time. I made my rounds in a more random pattern and on foot, and by late August I was completely settled into the new job.

When I arrived for my shift after my two nights off, John had some news. "They finally hired junior ranger. So you have help tonight. It took forever, but he is on job. This is his third night. He started on your days off. You will meet him tonight. He is nice guy. He stays here until 4 o'clock. That's all. Then he go."

Evidently, I had been looking for a person who had not existed, but now I would actually have some human backup in an emergency. To date, however, nothing eventful had happened, and I expected that was a watchman's way of life. All that was to change at around 3:00 a.m. that night.

At that time I was taking a break from my foot patrol and sitting along the wall near Monkey Island. The Detex clock was slung over my shoulder on its leather strap. The walkie-talkie was set upright on the stone pillar next to me. Then I heard a voice on the dark gray radio.

"Two-fifty-two to zoo night watchman. Two-fifty-two to zoo night watchman." It took a few seconds to realize that someone was actually calling me.

"Zoo night watchman to Two-fifty-two. Go ahead."

"This is the junior ranger Two-fifty-two. Where are you?"

"I'm at the wall around Monkey Island."

"Stay there. I'll be right over." *Two-fifty-two* actually referred to the vehicle he was driving that night. The full-time park rangers drove squad cars on outside patrols, but within the zoo, they sometimes drove a tan-colored, three-wheeled police-style Cushman. These were also driven by junior rangers.

People are most familiar with Cushman *motor scooters*, but this model was known as a *truckster*. It was a three wheeler that was powered by a noisy propane engine that produced an ear-splitting *bam-bam-bam* when it was started. It had a tiny enclosed cab with a small truck bed in the back for hauling. The zoo had two of these units which went by the unglamorous names of *Two-fifty-one* and *Two-fifty-two*.

As I sat there, I could see the approach of the Cushman, its headlamp winking in and out between the glow of street lamps. They are relatively slow, and I watched for quite a while as it zigzagged a path through the zoo to where I was waiting. Finally, the single, bobbing headlight was coming straight at me and the hammering engine was announcing its arrival. The noise was soon eclipsed by the screams of nearby peafowl calling out in protest.

A dark-haired man of nineteen mercifully quieted the night by killing the engine.

"I was just over inside the Pachyderm Building," he began. "I went in there with my flashlight to check it. There's about a million snakes crawling all over the floor in there. I didn't know the zoo even had snakes."

Normally, the zoo didn't have snakes, but this was August and the annual Reptile Fair was in progress over in the Pachyderm Building. I could guess what must have happened, and my first thought was *holy crap*.

The reptile event was the brainchild of Public Service Director Chuck Voracek who, in the 1960s, '70s, and '80s, invited local snake owners in Cleveland to place their collections on exhibit. Norm Tulodziecki brought in his snakes, and so did the guy with the blanked-out eyeball. The zoo's education staff and a couple of maintenance guys lined up dozens of folding tables along the wall, and the local herpetologists loaded the tables with cages full of snakes, lizards, geckos, iguanas, toads, frogs, and box turtles. There might have even been a baby croc or two.

"Yeah, there's lots of cages in there," continued the man, "but they're all open. There are snakes everywhere. Some of them are big. Do you think any of them are poisonous? This is my first night on the job. I don't need to get bit by a rattlesnake."

I reassured him that none of them were poisonous. That was one of Voracek's stipulations. The guy was relieved, especially when I suggested that we go take a look.

"By the way, my name is Tim." After exchanging greetings, we both hopped aboard the Cushman and lurched our way to the back keeper entrance of the Pachyderm Building.

"I locked the building behind me," said Tim. "Since the snakes are loose in there."

"Smart thinking," I assured him as I unlocked the brass padlock and opened the door.

We stepped into the well-lit back hall, and I wasn't the least bit concerned about anything. The snakes were harmless after all. We'd just check it out. This was, however, my first time as a night watchman to enter the big public room of the Pachy. By entering through the keeper's entrance I had avoided that mysterious dark space of animal rumbles and growls. Now we had an excellent reason to turn on the building's overhead lights. John Sich had shown me the breaker box on the wall in the grimy little keeper's room, and after looking at all the panels and confusing breakers, I said, "Let's just turn on everything."

The breakers snapped on one at a time, *Schtoink. Schtoink. Schtoink.* There were probably sixteen in all, and throughout the building 150-watt bulbs in large arrays started coming on. This set off a great stirring and rattling of elephants' chains, and noises of lapping water in the large center pool that was the lair of the big Nile hippos. A choir of grunts vibrated and echoed against the walls.

We placed all our stuff, the walkie-talkies, flashlights, and my clock and keys on the table in the keeper's room before stepping into the public area. The great room was subdivided into various zones to isolate and protect zoo visitors, keepers, and the animals themselves. A three foot high stainless steel fence separated the visitors from the keeper's work area. (The low barrier might seem feeble for such massive animals, but the fact is that three feet is a veritable high bar to these great beasts.)

The keeper's area ran parallel to the pedestrian walkway and was about six feet wide. It was both a work area for the employees and a buffer zone for the public. In this area were fire hoses which could be used to wash down the stalls, and the runoff would drain into stone gutters.

We were now making our way past all the exhibits including a deep central pool area for Nile hippos. The humidity inside the building was always high and ripe with the smells of wet hay, manure, and urine.

The outer walls of this area were brick and entirely unremarkable. The building was made to focus all eyes on the center of the room where the animals were housed. Who would turn their backs to elephants and rhinos to count bricks? There was no reason to look out from the center *except* for two weeks in August when the zoo invited locals of the reptilian sort to be displayed on folding tables set against the brick walls in temporary display.

When Tim and I walked down the concrete ramp at around 3:10 a.m. and opened the stainless-steel swinging gate to enter the public area, the floor was slithering, shimmering, and glimmering with thirty to forty crawling snakes and lizards. These included a few iguanas, more than one boa, and a four-foot python or two. Every single cage had been opened, and every snake and reptile had escaped.

The only saving grace was that this room was designed to be a giant sink for the purposes of easy cleaning, and the loose reptiles were actually contained in a huge cauldron which was sealed by tightly fitting doors.

The majority of the cages were homemade from wood and wire mesh. The doors of each cage had a latch held by a little pin or nail. I had few doubts about how this could have happened. The same sort of vandals that peed on doorknobs had probably loosed all the closures just before closing time. Sich hadn't noticed the escaped snakes on his shift because he never went into the exhibit area of the pachyderms.

Tim and I had disrupted all the buildings' residents when we turned on the light and entered the room. The gargantuan animals had been thrown into a giant conniption. I didn't know the first thing about any of them, but they were all up, about, and agitated. The little pygmy hippos paced around on the concrete floor in their stalls. The Nile hippos snorted repeatedly at their displeasure. Though I could not see them, I heard the thundering stomps of eighteen foot tall Masai giraffes.

To my right, in the elephant cage, the two big African cows, Simba and Tara, rocked back and forth angrily. Their metal chains rattled heavily as they rocked. The presence of the colossal Africans made me uneasy. We were stepping into another world, their world. Simba and Tara growled and snorted.

All the while, the enormous Nile hippos continued snorting and blowing like whales, *OomPAH, OomPAH, Whoop. WHA-OOF-OOF-OOF.*

Just to my left, one of the pygmy hippos came to a frozen position, her head held low in a threatening posture. She was glaring at me with hatred. True, it was a *pygmy*, but to add some perspective, it weighed over five hundred pounds and had saber-sharp tusks. Thank God it was in her stall.

Meanwhile, the snakes appeared to be having a blast. They were writhing and side-winding everywhere all over the hard concrete floor, dozens of them. Many were twisted together into piles like Medusa's hair. As for which snake belonged in which cage, we couldn't tell. The signs on the cages had words like *Opheliais hasstreptococcus* or *Leobloomorophis jerrysherkisbighereallyis* or *Daddywags sirtalis* or *Studebakerfloorshiftmodelis* or *Eatuslotsa whitemouseswholeis* and stuff like that. We would have put the correct snakes in the correct cages if the signs had been more helpful, but there was no use in even trying.

"Let's just put them somewhere and someone who knows what they are can sort it out in the morning," said Tim.

I agreed. "Just don't put two things that look like they would eat each other into the same cage."

Tim picked up a pair of entwined, slithering critters. "These two love each other," he said. "I'll put them together. Since I can't get them apart."

So what we did was pick up a snake or lizard and lock it in a cage—any cage. Big snakes we put in big cages. Little snakes in little cages. We put turtles into a cage that had a nice bowl of water. Itsy bitsy snakes we put into cages with a very fine mesh screen.

Totally relaxed, Tim picked up a big old constrictor and it wrestled with him.

"Look at this thing," he exclaimed.

"That'll probably go in the biggest cage," I suggested, but we looked around and the biggest were already occupied.

"I'll just cram it into this one. It'll fit," he said as he crammed it into one that was a size too small. We relaxed after we had everything caught and placed somewhere. By then, the larger residents of the room had quieted down.

Eventually, we took a stroll along the front of the hippo pools and pens, but we forgot where we were. Instead of staying in the public area, we walked along on the wrong side of the safety rail, right along the front of the exhibits. We watched a feisty little pygmy hippo for a minute, the one who had been in the threatening posture. She was still pretty pissed. Then we continued down along the exhibits.

"Holy cow, look at that!" exclaimed Tim, as we stepped in front of an exhibit where a giant black Nile hippopotamus was stretched out on the concrete like a beached whale. This thing was huge, dry docked, and trying to get back to sleep.

We stepped in front of the large center pool next.

"Hey," Tim said, "There's another big hippo in here. The relief watchman showed it to me last night. Watch this. Here's a trick he did."

I couldn't see anything in the big pool, since the water was a filthy brown, swirling slowly with bits of yellow foam bobbing on the surface. Tim leaned out over the water and loudly smacked the interior concrete wall of the pool, to try and make the unseen creature surface. His hand came down inches away from the water.

"Hey. Hey," he yelled and the whole room began to echo.

The thing, whatever it was, never surfaced, but large ripples of water raced along the surface. Something large was vigorously swirling around within the depths.

"Hey. Hey," yelled Tim again, smacking the walls some more. *WHACK. WHACK. WHACK.* "Oh, well," he said, giving up.

We naturally hung out to shoot the breeze for awhile. Pretty soon, every animal in the building had quieted down. We stood in front of the big hippo center pool and talked. Tim had his back toward the way we had come in, and I was facing toward the keeper room, which was about a hundred feet away.

"This is my third night," said Tim. "It's pretty easy, but I'm not crazy about working at night since I have a girlfriend. But I'm starting back at Cleveland State in January. So this is okay till then. I figure I'll do this for about five months and then be back in school."

Tim did not know at that moment he would have that job for about one more hour.

Next, Tim described some work he was doing to his car, and I made an appropriate remark. As he was saying something about using over-sized replacement piston rings, his eyes suddenly lit up with terror. He looked right past me, over my left shoulder, toward something behind me. His face contorted and went pale.

At that moment, I heard a tremendous sound, half splash and half wallop. Tim's eyes grew wider and he evoked the name of our Lord in a loud voice.

"Jesus Christ," he exclaimed. That was all either of us said. His face seemed glued in the air for a moment, but already his body was turning and starting to run.

I whirled around to look, and I was running, too. What I had seen in a flash is recorded in my brain as one still frame of action. It is a picture of an off-balance pygmy hippo, having just vaulted his heavy body over a concrete wall. He had hit hard on our side of the wall, enduring a four foot drop. A wave of water washed over him. It was actually pool water that was drawn along with him as he launched himself out of the pond.

His tubby, slippery stomach smacked heavily against the rock hard floor, and he was shaking on his legs. What wasn't shaking was the dark eyes that I had seen earlier. Eyes that had been, and were now, trained on me. He was running.

That was all I needed to see. I turned my back to him and took off. I turned on the jets. Tim had already been running for a few seconds, but I was soon speeding up his back and he was in my way. We were in a five-foot-wide corridor between two walls, each about three feet high.

Over the wall to our right were pools and stalls filled with more hippos. To the left was the public area. It was like being the pins in a bowling alley, and the hippo was the ball.

We were racing for the keeper room which was about seventy-five feet ahead of us. The upper tusks of a pygmy hippo sharpen themselves against the broad inside surface of the lower tusks each time it closes its mouth. They are also not known for their even temperament.

Tim wasn't looking back. To do so would be to lose speed and risk tripping. He was running hard and maybe thinking that, well, hippos are not gazelles, and we'd outrun this pygmy.

I, however, remembered the tour speech that I delivered sixteen times a day when I drove the trains. In particular, one of my *fun facts* came to mind: *You may be surprised to know that a hippopotamus can easily outrun a man.*

That dripping wet, slimy pygmy hippo was coming up on us like a shot, nearly upon me, anticipating the moment of attack. We hadn't gone ten feet and he had gone twenty. All this drama was within fractions of a second. One quick look was enough for me, and I reached out with my left hand, grabbed the stainless-steel rail, and vaulted over.

I yelled with all I could at Tim. "GO OVER THE WALL." To my relief, he grabbed the rail and flew over. Our feet weren't even safely on the ground when the hippo barreled past on our right. It had seen our escape and tried to change his own direction when his feet slid out from under him on the slippery floor. We were still running on the other side and wondering if our pursuer could scale this wall, too. Would he even try? I don't pretend to know hippo psychology, but it seemed like he abandoned us for bigger ideas. He started running again, this time past all the hippo exhibits and out into the areas where the other animals were housed.

Everything was chaos. The elephants trumpeted and pulled against their chains. The Niles called out, *OMP. OMP. OMP.* The giraffes stampeded in awkward circles in their pen, and the other pygmies ran back and forth in their stalls.

Tim and I had stopped running since the pygmy was now running away from us. The elephants told us where he was by raging as he raced toward their cages. I wondered if the angry animal could manage to get to them by sliding between the bars.

He was on the move again, back toward us, but apparently unable to negotiate the barrier that separated us. His sudden change in direction made me realize a new danger. What if the gate at the end of the keeper's work area was standing open? If it was, the animal would be in the public area.

The gate *was* open. We had, in fact, opened it ourselves when we came into the lobby to pick up the snakes. The hippo barreled through the opening so fast that his momentum threw him against the brick wall. We expected him to come back at us, but instead he went the opposite direction, heading toward the already terrified giraffes. When he was around a corner and out of sight we heard the crash of breaking glass. He had broken through an outside door. He now had an exit to the zoo grounds, but apparently, he had second thoughts and remembered the unfinished business regarding two idiots who had been herding snakes.

He was coming back, head down and accelerating, but this time, he was on our side of the barrier with nothing but locked doors to our backs.

There was nothing else to do but vault over the rail again, back into the corridor between the hippo pools and the public area.

If he kept running in his current direction, we might have time to reach the safety of the keeper room. He had seen our move, however, and reversed until he was running alongside us in a race back to the open gate. It was a race he'd easily win. In fact, he careened through the open gate and was facing us on the same level once again.

We vaulted the wall, and, like *déjá vu*, we were back with the hippo on one side, and Tim and I on the other. It seemed like it was going to be a game of leap-the-wall until the animal tired. What we had not anticipated was that the pygmy might think up another game to play. As   if   with forethought, he made a turn, ran out of sight, and was gone.

Now what? Would he suddenly reappear, running back at us? As it was, the speeding slate-gray rubbery missile had rocketed into the keeper room where I left my night watchman's keys. With those keys, I could open the glass doors behind us, and we could get out of the building and find help.

We inched toward the keeper room. Tim was suddenly moving forward with quickening strides, turning his head sideways to listen carefully. When we were around ten feet from the door, Tim peeked around the corner.

"I don't see him," he whispered. "If we can get into that little room, we can close the door and trap him in the back hall."

No hippo was in sight, but we weren't in any hurry to move forward. In the distance, there was a sudden crash of metal, like a wheelbarrow toppling over or a Coke machine falling down.

"He's way back in the hall. Come on."

Tim ran into the keeper room and I followed. We both reached for the wooden door on the other side and slammed it shut. If the plan had one major drawback, it was that the door had no latch and no door knob, no mechanics at all.

"We need to barricade this," said Tim. "Use everything we can find."

Most of the stuff in the room was pretty feeble compared to what we had seen on the other side of the wall, but there wasn't a single moveable thing in the room that we didn't cram onto the pile, which was around chest high and went halfway across the tiny room.

"That should be good," said Tim. "I put two rubber wedges beneath the door under all this stuff anyway."

Everyone knows a five hundred pound hippo can't bull his way through a rubber wedge, I thought.

We could hear more commotion on the other side of our barricade. The animal was in a room full of rakes, shovels, hay bales, wheelbarrows, and bags of grain. From the sound of it, he was having a field day, but I knew that we had another big problem. The door in the back of that hall opened outward and it was not padlocked. He was hitting everything, and it would not be long before one of those objects would be a door that swings open to the grounds beyond.

I decided that the only chance of corralling the hippo was to run outside the perimeter of the building and set the padlock before Mr. Pygmy tried for the exit.

I took an enormous breath, grabbed my watchman's key ring and the Detex clock and ran back out into exhibit area of the building past the trumpeting elephants. I was racing as fast as I could, but my mind was going even faster. If the animal got past the metal exterior door, he could get down into Big Creek. From there he'd have two exits out of the park. He would have the run of the city.

On top of that, I had every key in the zoo, and this was a door that I had never unlocked. Fifty keys on a ring. Where do you start? The master didn't work. I tried a few other keys that were cousins to the master, and they didn't fit either.

Eight keys later, I found one cut from a blank that at least fit the tumbler. Though it didn't turn, I now looked for its sisters and found a couple. The next one worked.

I left the key in the lock with the key ring and the heavy clock hanging from the door and raced outside past the giant mastodon relief sculpture. It was done by artist Viktor Schreckengost in 1956, but this isn't a time to conduct a tour.

As I ran, I had a wary eye ahead, and expected to see the hippo charging at me. If I got to the door before the hippo came outside, it could save lives, mine among them.

I focused on the green metal door, visible under a hundred watt porch light. I could see that the door was still closed. Of course, if the animal were already outside, the door could have swung closed again, but I was betting that it was still inside. Of course, the closer I got the more I realized that the hippo could blast through the door just as I reached it. I ran faster, but I took care not to actually slam into it myself. After all, I didn't want the animal to hear me. I reached the door and listened. Nothing. (The hippo was probably in the keeper room, eating Tim.)

I grabbed the open brass padlock that hung on the metal latch and locked the metal door shut. Oh, God. My hands were shaking. I retraced my steps and ran back to the front of the building reentering through the glass doors. Tim had been busy fortifying the barricade, and I turned off all the breaker switches to the lights in hopes that the elephants would settle down.

Soon the building quieted, but we heard nothing in the back hall. Perhaps the hippo had gotten out the back door. Maybe he was gone before I padlocked it. Maybe he was up on West 25th Street by now. But then we heard noises—in the back hall. Garbage cans, rakes, and shovels were being knocked over. It was a big commotion.

"I have to call the keeper who works in this building," I said. "That's my instructions. I think it's a guy named Brent." Of course the phone numbers were posted on the wall in the Commissary (no such thing as a cell phone in that era).

"It's not like this every night," I said from the back of the three-wheel Cushman as Tim was driving up the winding road up toward the Commissary. Once there, I called Brent Sanchez from the old black Bakelite phone, which was on the table. It was half past three when his sleepy wife answered.

"This is the zoo," I began, "Is Brent there?"

She handed off the phone, but kept talking in the background, "Holy *bleeping bleep*. It's three o'clock in the morning."

I didn't know Brent but he knew the pygmy in question. "WOLEE?" he shouted into the phone as I explained how the hippo had launched himself with a swimming leap over the barrier. "Wolee," (he used the name again and pronounced it like *wooly*.) "Jesus Christ!" he said without even a hint of piety. Recovering his calm, he very deliberately said, "Don't mess with him." (We knew that *now*.)

"We've got him in the back hall. He ran through the keeper room, and we barricaded the door with desks. He's back by the grain bins."

"Good. Good. Just don't mess with him. I'll be right there."

"We'll meet you by the back door to the Pachy," I said.

"Ten minutes," he said. "Do you have a gun?"

"Well…" That kind of came out of nowhere, so I had to think about it. I said, "There is a loaded .30-30 rifle in the Administration Building for this sort of thing."

"Get it."

Tim and I walked out into the otherwise pleasant night. "I'll take my station wagon and get the rifle," I said. "I'll meet you down there. Be careful. Wait for the keeper. We'll all meet by the back door."

I started up the station wagon, all my night watchman stuff piled next to me, the Detex, my baseball bat, teargas starter pistol, and a sandwich. Pretty much everything I needed except a .30-30.

Outside Mr. Huhtula's office, I used the tiny key on my key ring to unlock the gun cabinet. I took down the heavy rifle very carefully. John had told me it was kept loaded, and firearms terrified me. Riding the uneven roads down to the Pachyderm Building with a rifle across my lap was not my idea of fun. I thought for sure that I'd hit a bump and it would go off. It might have been more terrifying than being chased by the hippo.

It wasn't long before a bedraggled keeper drove up in his piece-of-junk work car. Brent was a small, handsome, dark-haired guy, probably thirty-something, mustached and wearing black pointed shoes. As he got out of his car, he had a bunch of stuff in his hands. He kicked the car door shut with the bottom of his right foot. *BAM*. One hand held a huge box of Nabisco Saltines, the other, a plastic-ringed six pack of Budweiser beer.

"Wolee loves beer," said Brent in a businesslike manner. "He goes ape shit for the stuff. And saltine crackers, too." (Years ago I wrote about this in *Cleveland Magazine*, but said that Brent used ginger ale, but it was beer. I cleaned up the story to keep Brent out of trouble.) It was Budweiser in the red, blue, and white cans. A person would expect that Brent would bring either Budweiser or Miller High Life since they are the two major food groups in Cleveland.

Brent said, "So the Booger's loose, huh?"

I said, "Yeah. Is he dangerous?"

"He's very dangerous," replied Brent. "It all depends on what kind of mood he's in. You got the gun?"

"Yes, and I've got this teargas gun, too." I held up the little snub-nosed .22 starter gun.

"I'll take that," said Brent. "Do you know how to handle that rifle?"

"No," I said.

"I do," said Tim, seeming a bit too eager to blow something away.

Thank God I didn't have to have anything to do with it. Tim took the rifle as Brent used his own key to unlock the padlock on the back door.

"All right," he said, popping the top off a beer. "I'm going to pour these beers down Wolee's throat and feed him those crackers. He just loves beer and saltines. So I'm going to walk ahead of him, pouring in the beers, and I'll lead him to his stall."

Brent was very insistent with Tim. "Listen, you keep that rifle pointed at his head, and if he starts mauling me, let him have it."

"Right," said Tim.

Brent creaked open the door slowly and looked inside. "C'mon," he said.

The three of us went in cautiously. There was a bank of light switches just inside the door, and they weren't all turned on, so I flicked them all on.

Brent immediately began calling, "Here Wolee, Wolee. Here, boy. Hey, Wolee Booger. It's your Daddy. Here, Wolee, Wolee."

We saw Wolee in the back hall, his head buried in a wheelbarrow of giraffe feed.

"That's good," whispered Brent. "Eating puts him in a good mood."

Wolee saw us and moved our way. He didn't charge like before, and he noticed Brent straight off. The shiny metallic-hued animal now looked duck-footed and clumsy. He opened his huge mouth like a baby bird opening up for food. He actually sort of waddled toward us slowly. Brent was talking to him a great deal. Tim had the gun in position, aimed at

Wolee's head, and was peering down the barrel.

Brent gushed, "I've got a beer for you, Wolee. Daddy's got beer. Wo-LEE. Wo-LEE Booger."

Brent called him Wolee Booger because he looked like one, a big wooly booger.

"Wolee. That's a good Wolee. Come to Poppa," said Brent in a syrupy voice. Later I would learn that Brent considered himself to be Wolee's actual father.

Wolee was by this time foaming over with a white mucus that appears around the neck and ears of pygmy hippos when they've been out of the water for awhile. Hippos sweat mucus. The bigger Niles sweat mucus, too, but Nile *sweat* is often red or tan-colored as well as white—whereas pygmy hippo mucus is almost always white and foamy. If the red *sweat* seen on Nile hippos gave rise to the myth that they sweat blood, I could start the rumor that pygmies sweat Barbasol shaving cream.

Wolee recognized Brent instantly by the exaggerated mindless sort of babbling Brent was doing. Later in my zoo career I learned that pygmy hippos have generally one of four reactions when they are in the same enclosure with a human: (1) timidity, (2) a total indifference, (3) an instant and quite noticeable desire to tear the human being to bloody shreds, or (4) they beg for food in a manner reminiscent of many dogs.

Fortunately for us, Wolee Booger realized he was being approached by the man who fed him twice every day. And the man had beer and saltines. Wolee was like a pit bull. Now that his master was in the room, he was under control.

Wolee walked forward comically, slowly, clumsily. He threw his head back and opened his mouth wide, chomping at the air. He made a little guttural noise, like, "*Arrga arrga arrga.*" As he worked his jaw, thick saliva frothed around the long, yellow menacing tusks.

Brent was quite an act. He wedged the crackers under his left arm, the beer under his right. In his left hand he held the teargas gun pointed at Wolee's head which was just a foot away. That left his right hand free to pour beer down Wolee's throat. He started him off with two quick ones, and Wolee chugged 'em down.

Stooped like a mad scientist conducting an experiment, Brent walked backwards, shuffling his feet. He held each open beer out in front of Wolee like a carrot, sloshing it into the eager maw. He was trying to lure the pygmy back to the rear entry to his stall. At this point, I was only a spectator. Tim was intently peering down the barrel of the gun, and walking in procession. Thus we made an erratic progress along the back hall. Tim kept jockeying for position, with the rifle pointed alternately at Wolee's head or Brent's back, and Brent just kept shoving stacks of crackers into Wolee's gullet and popping open beers. The bad news was

Brent was running out of beer. The good news was the hippo was getting sloshed and starting to feel pretty good.

The pygmy's regular spot was still a fair distance, so Brent improvised and threw the remaining crackers into the *Bull Room*, an area designed for keeping bull African elephants. He poured out the remaining beer as Wolee single-mindedly licked up the suds with his huge pink tongue. Brent pushed the huge metal door shut and put a pin in the latch.

"He'll keep in there," said Brent. "Tomorrow I'll get him back in his pen when the other keepers are here to help me."

As Brent hosed Wolee down through the bars. The hippo seemed pretty pleased with the way the adventure had ended. He had a full belly, a cool shower, and a warm buzz.

Tim, who had been fiddling with the rifle, came up behind me and whispered, "You know what? This gun ain't loaded for shit."

"Don't tell Brent," I said.

Later that night, I went out into the big field which was the mall area, right in front of the stork exhibits, and just down the ridge from the Greenhouse. I went far away from all the exhibits to actually test fire my Saturday night teargas special.

I knew enough to get upwind before firing one of my *exploding* cartridges. I squeezed the trigger. It made only the tiniest pop, far less noise than a child's cap gun, no hint of any teargas at all. So much for truth in advertising. The little green cartoon on the package indicated the cartridges were supposed to go *BOOM*. And release huge billowing clouds of teargas, totally incapacitating everyone in the country except the guy who fired the gun. There was neither *boom* nor cloud, just a little *pftt* like a bug sneezing. I never bothered carrying it after that, and I never saw the junior ranger Tim again, either. He'd had enough zoo adventures, and never returned. Personally, I thought he was a pretty cool guy.

CHAPTER FIVE

A lot of people go their whole lives without being chased by a pygmy hippopotamus. During that first evening with John, my fear was that the job would bore me out of my skull. Now my opinion had just double-clutched into high gear. I couldn't guess what was yet to come.

Of course, I was tempting fate the moment I asked permission to vary the watchman routine. Sich's inviolate routine would probably never surprise an intruder. On the other hand, is that really something a lone employee would want to achieve? Now, I was on foot and exploring every nook and cranny of the zoo. The only place I had avoided was the exhibit floor of the Pachyderm Building. I'd never gone in there before the incident with Wolee, and after what happened, I was sure that I didn't want to go there again. Let the big animals sleep soundly in their big dark room. I never wanted to footrace with a hippo again, and I'm sure the other big fellows had been watching me as well, and had my measure down pretty well.

The truth is that a watchman spends most of the time in solitude and out of touch from the daily interactions of zoo life. What didn't happen on my watch might have been talked about all day, but I would only find out by accident. A distressing example of this was the last time I saw Tara, one of the great African elephants that had been in the building the night of the great snake grab and hippo chase.

I was on foot, walking on my rounds. It was a warm September night, around 3:30 a.m. The moon was high and stunningly bright. I walked around the big perimeter of the giraffe and elephant yards, heading toward the back door of the Pachyderm Building to make the Detex hit.

Suddenly I walked right up on a sight that froze me in my tracks and made my mind go utterly blank. I was confused for a minute and didn't understand what I was seeing. I didn't know much at all about the daytime operations of the zoo and was not prepared to see a wide pile of heavy slabs of slaughtered meat along the fence. The neat and organized pile was around three feet tall and five feet wide and as much as thirty feet long. The sight of it shocked me, baffled me. I stood still.

What was strange and other-worldly about the whole scene was that the moon was high and right over my shoulder. The angle of the moon in the sky was perfect to illuminate the lifeless heaps of flesh. It was as if there was a blue-white spotlight aimed right at the pile. So there was an odd juxtaposition of images with a fairylike hue to everything that was utterly morbid.

What I was witnessing was an elephant, Tara, in fact. She had died rather suddenly leaving her companion, Simba, in a state of mourning. Zoo personnel could not, however, get bogged down by the emotions they surely felt. The problem was the disposal of the body in a timely way. Such practical realities in a public facility don't allow room for sentiment. In the end, the keepers had helped to butcher the corpse with chain saws so that the meat could be hauled away for burial. I had not heard the news and stumbled on a sight that I would always carry with me. The next evening, when I returned, the area was spotless and a casual visitor would have no idea about the life that had been lost or the sorrow that the loss carried for both the humans and her animal companions.

The fact was that, as a night watchman, I spent about ninety percent of my time without human interaction. I did, however, become aware of the personalities and quirks of a great menagerie of captive wild animals. These generated an intelligence and a consciousness that permeated their immediate areas. They are *there*, and they knew who belonged and who didn't. It's not so different with people. We can sometimes intuit what others are thinking, or get a sense of another's emotion. That's kind of what I felt about the animals. I think they enjoyed a certain peace at night. They appreciated the general absence of people. I was the only intruder into their peace.

Sometimes I could hear them chewing as I approached, then they'd stop to listen for me. This was especially true of the sitatunga antelope. I'd enter their barn, and they'd stop. I would sometimes sit quietly in that darkness for five minutes before I'd hear the chewing resume.

I found it interesting to go into any area and just sit until the animals resumed what I guessed was their normal night behavior. Of course, I don't know if the animal was simply thinking, *Hell, I'm not going back to sleep while this guy is here, so I might as well eat something.*

Over time, some animals seemed to tolerate, maybe even welcome, my visits. This was especially true of the gray wolves. At that time, they were housed in what we called *the Wolf Alcove*. It was a sprayed-concrete enclosure, with metal bars on the front and open to the sky. It was just a few feet away from the door to the keeper areas of the Lions, Tigers, and Bear Building. When the two wolves had a litter, there were a total of six wolves in the pen. The pups matured quickly, and it wasn't long before there was a pack of six with nearly identical markings. They were so in tune with each other that they did everything in unison.

What bothered me was that the wolves' exhibit was so empty and utterly sterile. It didn't seem so different than I had seen years before in the Cat and Ape Building. Why were they still on concrete? The wolves somehow got into my brain as if conveying their frustration with what had become the reality of their world. Their every look toward me was a plea for understanding. They seemed to trigger all my sensitivities.

Every time I passed them I'd stop to look and interact. I wondered if I could get them to play with me. Would they chase a ball? I was afraid to try that. What if they swallowed it and choked? I wondered if they would tug on the end of a rope like a dog. I wanted to do something, but mostly they just stared back.

Whenever I approached the wolves' cage, they greeted me, though not with wagging. They would all come to the front of the exhibit and face me, waiting. I talked to them at length, but they didn't react like dogs. I had the feeling, however, that there was something they wanted from me. They were trying to tell me something.

Eventually, I made suggestions to management on their behalf.

"You know that ridge in the bear area, on the hillside, opposite the reindeer exhibit? Three-fourths of that area is already fenced in. How easy would it be to fence in the front of it and put the wolves in there? They'd love that. The crews could just sink a concrete wall a few feet down all around the fence line so they couldn't dig out. That would be a great exhibit."

The objection at the time had something to do with non-indigenous diseases or catching rabies from feral cats. But in my mind, it was easy to imagine the six wolves roaming in the enormous sloped *pen* opposite the reindeer veldt. That piece of land was so narrow that the public would be able to see the wolves, too.

I'd tell the wolves I had made a suggestion, and that I'd even written it up in my report. Not an arm's length away, they would just stare intently, totally focused, six sets of unblinking eyes.

I found an old corn straw broom, held onto the handle, and stuck the straw end into their cage. "Take it. Take it." I said. "C'mon. C'mon. Play."

One wolf ventured slowly toward the broom and clomped down on it with his mouth. Forever, he just stood there holding it, with no idea about how to have a tug of war. When I pulled on the handle, the wolf just let go. I slid the broom back through the bars, and the same wolf bit again. As before, when I pulled against him, he simply gave it up. It took several visits and attempts before one of them began to feel possessive of the broom. When I tugged, one particular male chomped down on it and held on. We began tugging the broom back and forth between us. Eventually, the other five joined in the game. Still, they were extremely sullen and oddly subdued as they played. They seemed to like it, but they didn't get into it the way I'd hoped they would.

I had read Farley Mowat's, *Never Cry Wolf*, a fictionalized account of his study of wolves in the Arctic. In that book he also described the relationship of native peoples with the wolves. The howls of the packs convey information about humans and animals passing through their territory, and Inuit are able to understand these communications. Citing this is the best way I can describe the interaction that I was working to establish.

Sometimes I'd just sit cross-legged in front of their pen. All six of them would stand in front of me at arm's length. After a time, it dawned on me that these creatures had lost all contact with the earth itself. They were stranded on an island of concrete, hearing the choruses of crickets and katydids through the trees and echoing from the nearby cliffs. With the wolves in front of me, I imagined them roaming the ridges and sniffing along the ground. Then came an epiphany. I could bring the ground *to them*.

Behind the Bears Refreshment Stand I could access a natural area beyond the park walls. I went there and scooped handfuls of the black topsoil and carried it back to the enclosure. I pitched it into the alcove expecting that they'd sniff it or roll in it. I figured in the morning people would see the black soil in there and figure out that the watchman wasn't minding his own business.

I was surprised by what actually happened. In a ravenous manner, they greedily ate all the dirt, licking up every particle and sniffing around for more. So I gathered more soil from a wooded area near the pillars of the bridge and threw that in. That was the first time they made me their errand boy.

A few nights later, I offered a clump of wild grass, and they pounced on the meager offering and scarfed it down. Then all six scurried around the pen, sniffing for any little tiny piece that was left. They were craving it. All they wanted was dirt and grass.

After this, they greeted me in the low-key and serious way that wolves behave. I became bolder and bolder, throwing them sticks, branches with green leaves, a big dandelion with the root clump and dirt ball, some smelly old moss, an armful of leaves from the forest floor, or a piece of a rotting stump. After a few days, their cravings subsided and they didn't eat the stuff. I figured that I wouldn't get busted for this because things like leaves could have blown in naturally.

Since this book is turning out to be true confessions, I also have to come clean about the mandrills which were caged just inside the door of the Baboon Building. A mandrill is a member of the Old World monkey family. When I was at the zoo everybody seemed to think it was a type of baboon, but nowadays, the zoologists put it in its own class. It is simply the world's largest and most spectacular monkey. They're the ones in which the male of the species has an incredibly ornate bright red nose and blue cheeks, and a long beard almost like an old shaman. When a big male mandrill yawns, he shows incredibly long and terrifying fangs. They are really nasty. Mandrills live in groups in the wild, with about fifty in a group. It was a dismal thing to see that magnificently colored male all alone in the big cage in the Baboon Building. It really wasn't anybody's fault because for a long time the zoo's vets and curators were concerned about that one poor male.

For some reason, the big monkey fell into the habit of gnawing off its fingers. This went on for years. It ate its own fingers, chewing them down. I saw it many times, and that was distressing. Maybe it needed calcium. I'd be in there at night, and it was chewing its fingers. So I figured, maybe it just needs something to chew on. I went up the side of the fence behind that building and broke down some green leafy willow branches. I put them it its cage. The mandrill took them readily and ate the leaves and chewed and swallowed the little branches. By morning, all that was left was the thickest portion of the stump of the branch. He was chewing the sticks. I would come in and he'd be chewing his fingers so I gave him branches instead. Well, that didn't seem fair to the other baboons and monkeys there so I would slip them some sticks, also. These, they were all eager to take.

That's all I did. Oh, no, wait, that's not right. There was also the thing with the grapes. I don't know how this started, but I developed the habit of taking a large paper sack of red grapes with me into the Baboon Building every night on my first hit of the Detex station there. I never took grapes on the second hit, however. I wanted the animals to know it was the first visit only. I gave the mandrill a nice clutch of grapes, with the little reedy sticks from the bunch. It broke my heart how the big monkey struggled to grasp a grape, with so many of his digits missing.

There was a baby hamadryas baboon in a cage, about eye level in the center of the building. He was quiet and slow-moving with a little rubbery face. I'd give him a single grape, which he would spend a lot of time eating. The mesh of his cage was very fine, and I could barely get my fingers in a few inches, but I would pet his little back or the top of his wide-eyed face. On the other hand, the little guy was so small that he could reach his whole arm through to me. He would clutch my old army coat with his little humanlike fingers and not want to let go. He was fascinated by a freckle that he wanted to pick off my arm. After a few minutes I had to pry his little clutching hand off the cuff of my coat or my jacket lapel (wherever the baby had latched on). I'd leave a few grapes on his shelf when I left. On the other hand, I never gave any to the adult hamadryas baboons. It would have been the opening salvo of World War III, and pity the unfortunate animal who got the first grape when all his mates came at him to steal it away.

Grapes went to many other cages, and were enjoyed by raccoons and monkeys alike. Granted, this was something that I ought not to have done in the first place. Anyone of those animals could have been on a special diet prepared by the vet. It was also expensive, but once I'd started, I could never disappoint them. I was a regular visitor in the fruit and vegetable section of the A&P.

I do need to take special notice of the difference between most monkeys and baboons and especially the colobus monkey, my favorite. Its face was so humanlike, it was amazing. They all look as if they were wearing a black knit cap and a ski mask, with a big nose that's almost comical, like Jimmy Durante or something. Their dark little eyes always noticed everything so that they appeared as wise old priests.

Though there were six of them in one cage, unlike the other species, they seemed to respect their individual spot in the pecking (or is it *feeding*) order. I could reach into the cage with a single grape and they would all sit quietly until the largest came down to take it with its fingertips. I'd offer a second grape, and the next in line would come down, take my offering, and return to its place. This would continue until each had taken a grape, at which point, an equally civilized second round would begin if I had enough grapes. I wondered what they'd do if I offered an entire cluster. I suspect that somehow they'd be doled out fairly. I once read this description of the colobus: "A shy and retiring aloofness sets this species apart from other monkeys and may be the reason they are considered holy in West Africa."

I made friends with a part-time ranger, who was there only a short time. One night I was walking around the park, and he pulled up to me in a Cushman.

"Adam," he said. "I was just in the Baboon Building, and I need you to help me with something." (Clearly, he was spending time going into the cage areas and hanging out with animals. As far as I know, he was the only ranger who ever did.)

"You know that mandrill in there?" he said. "Well, he likes to be up on that plank, and it fell down. That thing's about twelve feet long and I don't think I can lift it up back into place myself. I don't have a key for the cage, either. Do you think you do?"

Of course, I had the key to everything so we drove over there in his truckster.

There he was, the big, nearly fingerless mandrill sitting on wet concrete on the floor. At the back of the cage, the large wooden plank had fallen to the floor. (Now, this shows how dumb and naïve we were since this largest of monkeys has giant fangs that could kill a leopard on a lucky day.) I opened the cage, and we went in. The mandrill, not in a panic, kind of sashayed into the far front corner away from us. So together, the ranger and I lifted the twelve foot heavy plank back into place.

"We were kind of dumb going in there," I said, as I closed the padlock after we got out. "How would we know he wouldn't attack us? Have you seen his fangs?"

"I know," said my companion. At that moment, the mandrill climbed up onto the plank, but didn't go to his normal spot. Instead, he moved over toward where we had entered the cage. All of a sudden it became clear that the ranger and the mandrill were friends. That's why he hadn't been too afraid to go in with him. It was suddenly like I wasn't there. The two looked at each other face-to-face, and then he spoke.

"Here, buddy," he said softly. "I wanna show you something. You see this?"

The mandrill rolled his oddly orange eyes downward and tilted his head a bit to look. The ranger held his hand up to show the creature that several fingers were missing from the man's left hand.

"You see that? That's just like you, buddy. Now stop chewing those fingers, huh? You need those, pal."

The mandrill looked wistfully at the ranger's mutilated hand; I'm sure he noticed the missing digits. The animal stood perfectly still, except that his constantly searching eyes moved thoughtfully from the ranger's face down toward the man's hand, then back to the face, and back to the hand. The large monkey blinked casually, very humanlike in his expressive gaze.

As the nights went by, I continued to put sticks in his cage.

One morning, not long after that, I was waiting to punch out. The keepers were arriving to punch in. I was just minding my own business, but one of the older keepers was throwing a fit, complaining to the zoo's curator, Don Kuenzer. I couldn't help overhearing what was being said, and I'm sure the keeper didn't have a clue as to who I was.

"Hell, I like to get the cages done real quick in the morning; it just takes a hose. I don't even have to go in, just hose them out, from the outside. But I gotta go into every cage and clean the drains, 'cause the night watchman is giving sticks to the monkeys at night."

The guy was really irritated. I felt bad.

Don said to him, "Hey, your job is to clean the cages, so clean 'em and don't worry about other people's business."

That made the guy even madder. He stormed out of the building, walking right past me in a huff. If he had realized I was the night watchman, he surely would have lit into me.

In another minute, everyone was punched in and went off to their respective stations. Only Kuenzer and I were there as I punched out. Don was working on the attendance report or something.

"Don," I said, "I'm really sorry. I just thought the monkeys would need some sticks to chew on… I only give them willow…"

"Hey," Don interrupted with a smile. "If he has to clean the drains, he has to clean the drains. That's his job."

CHAPTER SIX

It must have been after 2:00 a.m. because Matt, the junior ranger, had gone to the office to catch some zzz's. His normal routine kept him on the job until 2:00, but he could never quite handle the last two hours of his shift and I was by myself down in the lower zoo. It was a brisk night, and that invigorated me. It was football weather.

I parked the car near the Greenhouse, ditched my coat, and went on foot. I also left my bat and pellet gun in the car, taking only the Detex clock and the walkie-talkie.

It started as a perfect night to be out walking with the water lapping on the lake, the ducks and geese muttering quietly, and the moonlight fending off total darkness.

I hit the station in Wade Hall, and walked toward the Ostrich Barn, then up the back way in the direction of Kiddie Land and the Children's Farm. As I was returning near the Bird Building one of the watchdogs called out a warning. Okay, it wasn't actually a *dog*, it was a peacock, but in the park at night, they're pretty similar.

Krawwwwwwww. There it was again, and I wondered if one of them was having a bad dream. That idea ended with four or five more screams piercing the night. *Kwahhhhhh. Kwahhhhhh. Kwahhhhhh. Kwahhhhhh.*

Dick, the old Pinkerton guy once told me, "Peacocks are the best watchdogs in the world." But his praise actually went deeper. "They're better than dogs because a peacock will only scream when something ain't right."

I picked up my pace until I reached the crossroads. I was now hearing something else, voices.

I moved to the edge of the road for cover. The peafowl were also joining in the chorus of alarm. The path ahead near the Main Entrance was well lit with streetlamps, and I could still hear the voices of men talking and laughing.

Just then, four men came around the side of the refreshment stand. They struck me as being in their late twenties or early thirties, and were joking, as if on a Sunday stroll through the zoo. They were thirty feet away from me, lightly dressed in shirtsleeves.

They walked right past me, and stopped. There was another sound, the sound of pop tops. They were opening cans of beer.

I moved deeper into the trees, slipped the heavy clock off my shoulder and to the ground. I raised the walkie-talkie to my mouth and depressed the send button.

"Matt," I whispered. I pressed the face of the speaker against my stomach to muffle his reply, but it did not come. I whispered again, "Hey, Matt…" No reply. Then a third time, but the response was exactly the same, nothing. He must have zonked.

I turned off the radio and slipped it back into my pocket. I didn't want some ranger's broadcast from outside the zoo to give me away. Even driving in a patrol car, a ranger somewhere in the vast Metroparks system would take a long time to get to my position. I didn't have that kind of time.

Meanwhile, the men were slugging down some cold ones. I could see them throwing their heads back and guffawing.

"Well, let's go see the zoo," said one of them.

Those were fighting words to me. After all, I was the watchman, and the zoo was closed. As they turned to walk toward Monkey Island, I came out of cover, and yelled, "HEY."

That was enough to shock the socks off them. They yelped and took off running.

I was a lot faster than they were and was pretty sure that I could get them when it occurred to me that catching up with them probably wasn't a great plan; it was actually a four against one nightmare. Even buzz-drunk, they'd have thought, *Why are we running from one guy?*

By now, however, it was too late because I was only about five feet behind the slowest runner. Fortunately, he was more panicked than I was and instead of turning to face me, he swerved right and jumped down into the elephant yard. There weren't any elephants in there. I knew that.

He actually made a pretty good leap, jumping about ten feet onto dirt. When he hit, he stumbled forward, lost his balance, and almost fell on his face.

I saw what he had done, and thought better than to duplicate his leap. Instead, I slid down the wall lowering myself into the moat around the yard. All that, of course, slowed me down, and my quarry was now about thirty feet ahead. On the other hand, I literally had him *penned in.* As an aside, this was the first time I ever stood in the elephant yard. (That'll make more sense later.)

This guy was tall, but a bit chunky. He ran to a corner, which was pretty smart in the sense that he'd get two walls for leverage as he tried to climb out. On the other hand, his entire enterprise was pointless and stupid because this was the elephant yard. The walls were brick, and strung along the top of that brick wall and running its entire length was an electric fence, a single heavy wire charged with three thousand volts of electricity. He was having a bad day.

As he reached the top of the wall, he grabbed the steel wire. And, well, let's just say that the peacock's call had nothing on him. *Arrgghh.*

He had learned his lesson, and made sure not to touch it again. He was surprisingly agile, however, and managed to mount the wall and step over the offending wire.

I ran off to a lower part of the wall, where getting out was easier and the electric fence was strung along on some posts. I ducked under it and scrambled up the wall, jumped, and landed on my knees in soft grass.

The guy I had been chasing was just coming down from the highest part of the wall after having three thousand volts blast through him. His leap was clumsy, and about twelve feet down onto hard pavement. He landed on his feet, but then fell over, chest first. I winced when I saw it.

Up ahead in the distance, his three friends were running ahead of him. They had simply run around the elephant yard. They were now waiting for him to catch up, but I was there, too.

In that moment the three others abandoned their *no man left behind* policy and took off.

The hobbling, gimpy fellow was once again the lone straggler, limping along thirty feet behind his three friends. The lead group scrambled into the cover of some small trees, but the guy I had been chasing was dead in my sights, stumbling, bumbling, and trying to get back his momentum. I raced toward him again over the asphalt parking area at the back corner of the Pachyderm Building.

Sensing that I'd catch up with him within seconds, the heavyset man repeated his earlier mistake by taking a turn for what he thought a better exit. On his hands and knees now, he scurried off the pavement and into the bushes at the base of the hill. I suppose the good news was that he was out of *sight*, the bad news was that he was not out of *sound*. The bushes he had chosen were a prickly tangle of thorns, mostly holly.

Amid a lot of branch-crashing and grunting came a string of expletives, "ouches," "aw shits," and "ughs."

I had seen where he left the path, and was going to break off pursuit. There really was no reason to pursue. He was now staying put in one place to avoid the fate of the briar patch.

I still did not have backup, and there was certainly no need for continued radio silence. I pulled out the walkie-talkie and turned it up as loud as I could. I made the squelch make a few loud electronic buzzes, to make me sound like a policeman. *Bazzzszzz shwerrrBSSSSHHH.* I used the walkie-talkie to call Matt again in a loud official sounding voice.

"Night watchman to ranger Two-five-two. Ranger Two-five-two, come in please."

Now the zoo security would gear up into motion. Or not.

Matt was still asleep.

This wasn't good. I needed an answer to tell this guy and his three friends that they were outnumbered and outgunned. No response probably meant they were going to jump out of the bushes and beat the living crap out of me.

Time to improvise. I pretended I was getting a reply from Matt and twisted the squelch button and made some radio noises.

"I copy. Two-five-two, please read. We have a disturbance here in the zoo. Four intruders in the wooded area behind the Pachyderm Building."

I hit the squelch to release some highly over-modulated static.

"Yes, that is correct. I am armed and have the situation under control." Of course, as I'm speaking, I'm really thinking: *Matt, wake-up. Wake-up you stinking goofball.* What I actually said was, "That's right. Two-five-two, we have intruders in the zoo behind the Pachyderm Building near the back entrance. Calling Matt. Four men have entered the zoo. They are in a wooded area. This is zoo night watchman confirming transmission. Over."

Note to self: *Kill Matt.*

I made another squelch sound. Then I made some more highly

modified vocal sounds like, "That's affirmative. I have called for backup. Their estimated arrival is in two minutes. In route. Over." So it was that I pretended I was talking to lots of people, a veritable army of armed, imaginary, efficient, highly trained law enforcement officers who were awake and alert.

Of course, *Matt* was *Two-five-two*, and *Two-five-two* was asleep. As far as my listening audience was concerned, however, they might be two different people. So, pretending *Two-five-two* was already enroute, I could just keep calling *Matt* in the hopes that hearing his name might awaken him.

"Zoo night watchman to Matt. Zoo night watchman to Matt. *Two-five-two* has been advised that we have intruders in the zoo. Please respond. Please bring the .30-30 rifle to the area behind Pachy. Over."

Squelch sound.

"Watchman to *Two-five-two*. I just tried to call Matt, but he did not respond. Please stay in route, thank you. Roger wilco."

I didn't know what else to do. I knew that at least one of the intruders was hearing everything I said, but this was getting embarrassing.

"Night watchman to Matt. I know you are reading this signal, but are out of range to reply. Please advise when you are in range." From my point of view, this was my big chance at *improv* theater, but then a voice came loudly over the walkie-talkie.

"What the hell is it? I'm sleeping, man. Stop it."

"Night watchman to *Two-five-two*. There's disturbance on the channels. Please be advised that we have four intruders in the zoo at back entrance to Pachyderm Building. Over."

Matt said, "Huh. Oh? What is it?"

"That is correct." Pretending I wasn't talking to a groggy-headed dolt, I continued, "Night watchman to Matt. Night watchman to Matt. Come in, please."

Matt's powerful cave-epoch mind began working.

"This is Matt. What is it?"

"Matt, we have four male intruders here in the zoo near the back entrance to the Pachyderm Building. Please radio ranger Headquarters in Strongsville for assistance. Four intruders in the zoo behind the Pachy."

"Uh, okay. Over." At last, Matt was conscious, lucid, and, hopefully, dressed.

"*Two-five-two* is on his way."

"What?" said Matt.

"Calling Matt. Yes, I have my gun, but bring the rifle."

"That's affirmative," said Matt, finally getting with the script. "I have my rifle and will be in route." Then, like the champion of justice he was, Matt said, "I'll get dressed and be there in a minute."

Within a short time, the wonderfully noisy three-wheel Cushman came rattling down the road from Kiddie Land. Matt was wild-eyed and ready for action. His hair was as big as a pissed-off porcupine with the frizzies. He had his .22 caliber CO_2-powered rifle pellet gun, not the .30-30. He stomped in, but I gestured him aside.

"I chased these four men in the zoo, and at least one of them is there in the bushes. He's three feet inside that woods right there, and he can hear everything we say. So I think we need to make him think that..."

Matt ran over toward the bushes with his gun and yelled, "Come out of there, you f---er, or I'm going to start shooting."

A loud voice from the bushes yelled, "No, don't shoot. I give up. I give up."

The guy stood up in the middle of some tangled brush not four feet from the edge. He sighed, put his hands up, and worked his way out of the thorns.

Matt ran right up to him. The look on his face even scared me. He looked completely insane.

Matt held the rifle barrel right into the big man's stomach. It bears noting that this man was bruised and bleeding and never realized Matt was holding a pellet gun.

Matt's disheveled, *I just woke up* appearance actually added to his apparent ferocity.

"Don't move," he said, and I had a brainstorm of my own. There were several empty cages in the Baboon Building, and I had the keys.

The script came straight out of a B-movie when Matt said, "Now walk this way. And don't try anything funny."

The man wasn't really in a position to argue, but Matt was a bit over the top with his tough-guy routine. When the man complained, I suggested that Matt tone it down. The guy really *was* having a bad day.

Once inside the Baboon Building, we found a nice empty chimp cage, right in the center. Of course, there were other cages in the building, all teeming with baboons and monkeys. The smell in there was pretty toxic, but we found a nice ground floor suite, directly across from the cage where the zoo kept the dozens of screaming hamadryas baboons, including the ones who liked to look at men and masturbate.

I unlocked the brass padlock, and Matt prodded the man to get inside.

This guy was not a kid or a punk. In a different setting he would appear tall and successful. He had been neatly groomed and dressed before our chase, but here he was sitting in a cage on a urine-bleached plank. He was also wearing a gold wedding band, and knew he'd have some tall 'splaining to do.

We locked the building, and went back to the truckster where Matt had left it. Under these kind of situations, I didn't need to worry about making a hit every ten minutes. This was a special night on watchman business, and all this would go on my report. I'd write down everything... except the part about the pellet gun... and the part about Matt sleeping.

Back at the Commissary Building, Matt made contact with a *real* Metroparks ranger. I hit the Detex stations in the Commissary lobby and also the Autopsy Room, ganging the hits. After about twenty minutes, the ranger came driving in.

"So you caught a guy," he said. "Great."

I filled him in with a Reader's Digest version of the story as the ranger sat down at the desk and started sorting out some paperwork.

He said, "You're saying you have this man locked in a cage? Is he secure in there?"

"Very," I said.

"Is he in any danger?"

Matt and I looked at each other and shrugged, then I said, "I think he'll learn quickly to stay in the center of the cage and out of range of the monkeys. But he absolutely can't get out, that's for darn sure."

"Well, good," said the ranger who was now stapling some papers together. "Well, gentlemen, I have some paperwork that I need to take out to the Rocky River Reservation. Since you say this individual is secure, I believe it will be convenient for me if we just leave him in the cage for a few more hours. I'll be back." He looked at his watch. "I'll meet you back here around 5:30 a.m. Let's synchronize our watches. It's 3:10 right now."

Evidently, the ranger was going to let the guy stew in a baboon cage. He got in his car and drove away. Matt decided to stay until the ranger returned. I think he was seeing a big promotion in store, but, in the meantime, he'd get some more sleep.

I went back to my duties and continued on my rounds which is the real fate of the night watchman, visiting checkpoints every ten or fifteen minutes. Even on the nights of exceptional adventures, the Detex clocks are calling. That night, however, my mind kept going back to the poor fellow in the Baboon Building.

Eventually, the ranger returned and the man's *time-out* came to an end. At around a quarter to six, Matt hailed me on the walkie-talkie to say, "He's back. We'll meet you at that building, you know."

I opened the building and we all went inside. The guy had been there a long time and was probably glad the posse finally arrived.

"How ya doing?" the ranger asked as I opened the padlock.

The man jumped up. "What's going to happen to me?"

"You're going to jail," announced the ranger cheerfully. "That's what happens to people who break the law."

The ranger went into the cage and brought the guy out with his hands cuffed behind his back. He was led away. The baboons and monkeys were curious. They had never seen anything like this before.

A few months later the *Plain Dealer* reported on the court case. I no longer have the article, but I remember its gist. It went something like this:

> Municipal Court Judge So-and-so had a great deal of difficulty keeping order in his court on Thursday. The problem was not rowdy behavior, but laughter. The Judge had to pound his gavel on more than one occasion in an attempt to stop the uproar. Furthermore, the Judge was having a difficult time keeping a straight face himself. Appearing before the Court was John Doe, who was charged with public trespassing when he and three friends snuck into the Cleveland Zoo by climbing over a fence in the wee hours of the morning. After walking around the park for a short time, the man was captured by zoo employees. His friends escaped. The defendant persisted in the conviction that he would not reveal their names. As he related the story of his arrest, the man had the courtroom in stitches. He explained how he was chased through the zoo, jumped into an elephant exhibit where he was shocked by an electric fence, and was finally locked in a chimpanzee cage for several hours. Barely able to contain himself, the Judge ruled that the man had suffered enough and dismissed the charges amid considerable applause and laughter within the courtroom.

The wording may not be entirely accurate, but it's pretty close. Of course, the phrase *captured by zoo employees* meant Matt and me. I thought there should have been a bit more recognition, but the PR was good. The story sent a powerful message throughout the mean streets of the *Sixth City*. *Don't mess with highly trained and capable security forces of the Cleveland Metroparks*, and, while you're at it, don't mess with us, either.

CHAPTER SEVEN

My introduction to zoo work was as a summer employee, and the rest of the year was a total mystery to me. The fact is that the zoo was open every day of the year with the exception of Christmas and New Year's Day. Had I thought about it, it makes perfect sense. The animals must be fed and cared for every day of the year, not just when there are guests at the Main Gate. It was true, however, that as the temperature dropped, crowds diminished.

Cold weather brought its own set of problems. Some animals like wallabies, eagles, owls, yaks, zebras, wolves, bison, camels, beavers, otters, deer, ducks, and geese could deal with the Cleveland winter, and a chill brought little change in their routines. This was not true of other species, including the human kind.

Icy conditions in the zoo brought problems, especially for the junior rangers who were patrolling in their Cushman trucksters. In winter, that was like driving around in a freezer and the driver was a Popsicle. On ice, the three-wheeled truckster was prone to sliding sideways, catching a wheel, and tipping over. More than once, Matt or Norm would call me to help them tip their ride back upright. Eventually, Matt gave up his wheels to take shelter in the passenger seat of my Chevy wagon, and we'd make our rounds together.

Snow on the ground meant intruders were easy to follow as I made my nightly walking rounds. In general, punks and vandals rarely appeared after the thermometer went south. Evidently, they were a tropical species. Which brings me to the point: *What about the tropical and sub-tropical animals?*

By 1977, I had learned a few things about the winter housing arrangements of the animals, and one night, or rather, early one morning, I invited Matt for a tour of the basement of the Bird Building. I had to go into the building to hit the station, but I also knew, or thought I knew, what was there.

"Matt, come into this building; I want to show you something."

"Aw, shit. No, I don't wanna. It stinks in there. I'm staying in the car."

"You gotta see this. I guarantee this will completely freak you out. It's just your kind of thing."

"But when I come out, I'm gonna stink for the rest of the night," he protested.

Matt had been in the Bird Building before, but he had never entered through the basement door next to the loading dock. That was the underbelly of the out-dated 1950's era building. I was persistent and eventually Matt gave in and stepped out of the car and into the cold.

Beyond the door was an unlikely scene. This was the winter roost of every tropical bird imaginable. The cinderblock cellar was transformed into one huge cage, fifteen feet wide by forty feet long.

Areas were sectioned off with chain link barriers. There, in close proximity were two or three sarus cranes (each about six feet tall and the tallest flying bird in the world), four heavy European white storks, a dozen or so colorful cockatoos, green parrots and macaws). Mammals were also represented by five loud California sea lions, and a harbor seal. Ten to fifteen flapping pink flamingoes, a cormorant, five long-legged western crowned cranes, three sandhill cranes, two demoiselle cranes, two kori bustards (the heaviest bird capable of flight), an old lesser adjutant stork, a marabou stork, and another twenty white egrets were also housed there.

Because I had been a tour driver for years, I knew these animals by sight and where they lived during the tourist season. In one place was the wildest, noisiest, and most outrageous collection of creatures that can be imagined, but this is not what I had invited Matt to see.

Before entering, I gave him some instructions. "Here's the deal. We're only going to get one chance to see this. The door opens outward, so stand clear. I'm going to open it as quietly as possible, and we have to sneak inside. Once I turn on the lights, run in as fast as you can and turn right. Got it?"

The instructions were easy enough, though they didn't prepare Matt for what he was to see. As promised, I pulled open the door and ran pell-mell into the corridor hitting a light switch as I passed. Matt was right behind as we ran about thirty feet over the moist cement floor, only to come skidding to a halt in front of a floor-to-ceiling chain link wall.

The sea lions and birds exploded into barking and screaming and a gigantic sound of fluttering wings. Matt's reaction was as exuberant as I had anticipated. In front of him was an incredible view, but it was not of feathers.

Just in front of us, an excess of a thousand swarming gray mice were pouring out of the birds' feed dishes to become a writhing, scurrying sheet of felt-gray fur shinnying over the sides of the huge enclosure from floor to ceiling. Meanwhile, a living carpet of roving mice expanded beneath our feet on the floor. The gray stain grew like a living paint spill, blooming in every direction. The racket of the giant birds and sea lions could not mask the sounds of thousands of tiny mouse feet, which sounded like rain on pavement. It was just a short while, however, before the horde completely disappeared into the ceiling among the water pipes and ventilation shafts. Like a storm passing at sea, the high tide of vermin evaporated.

"Let's kill them," said Matt. "Let's kill them all."

CHAPTER EIGHT

Matt and I had decided to kill every mouse in the Bird Building. Was that wrong? As far as we were concerned, they were a danger to the animals, leaving feces in the food dishes of the birds. They could even spread diseases to humans so we resolved to deviate from our assigned duties and take up the battle against these rodent invaders. I suppose that we should have filled out some paperwork saying that there were mice in the Bird Building, but we had seen the response to the mouse problem before. It consisted of a few traps in the back halls, which did nothing to curb the problem.

Everyone could see the droppings, but no one could have guessed what we saw at night. The keepers would set out a little matchbox-sized pack of d-CON® to kill what they referred to as *the* mouse. Traps around the building were often not even set; they were just kind of *there* and forgotten.

In the late 1970s, one bird keeper was a fellow named Walter Wozniewicz, a fine man and an immigrant who was working in English as a second language. In fact, he spoke very little English beyond "Hello," and general niceties. Walter always greeted everyone with a broad smile and a can-do attitude of helpfulness, and he was an impeccable bird keeper.

Upstairs in the Bird Building, the exhibits were set up to be large and scenic. During these years our zoo, like most others, were struggling to move away from the old animals on display exhibits to animal surroundings that mimicked natural habitats.

Down below, where the standard was to provide shelter which could sustain the very lives of these animals, the mice had also set up their bivouac. Upstairs, the kitchen was always spotless; downstairs, the rodents were taking over the night, and I'm not sure anyone suspected what we had discovered.

Some people refer to them as *field* mice, but, more precisely, they were *deer* mice, *Peromyscus maniculatus*, near as I can tell. They live up to five years, and they do not hibernate in the winter. Their secret invasion was covered by the fact that they are nocturnal, and were not only in *hiding* during the day, they may not have even *lived* in the building. They just came in to eat after dark.

We needed a strategy. The first bit of information we required was to find out how soon they returned after our disruption sent them scurrying. Would they be back in an hour? In two hours?

Matt suggested that we come back in an hour to see if they'd returned. If they did, he thought we should shoot them with pellet guns. I suggested old-fashioned broom swatting would be safer. (I also knew there were a few we could borrow from the Pachyderm Building.)

As you might have guessed, Matt was not the patient sort. After twenty minutes he was asking, "Now? Can we go back now?"

I kept invoking lines from a popular TV show and said, "Be   patient, my young novice. The mice have not yet returned. We must wait. Wait for them to be lulled like babies into a false sense of security."

"How about now?"

"Be patient, Grasshopper."

"Hey, they're mice. How smart can they be?"

In my opinion, deer mice are very clever. When it was 3:00 a.m., the time had come.

We parked away from the back loading dock, and I set up our assault by first hitting the Detex station in the Greenhouse. If I clocked in at Birds halfway through our foray, we'd have a total about thirty minutes that would not be traceable through the paper punch record in my clunky supervisor.

The snow was coming down that night when we ran into the building, crouching like Marines up to the loading dock behind the Bird Building. Matt knew the routine by now. At 3:02 a.m., we burst in on patrol. I flicked on the lights. There was only a *small* gathering at this time, just a few hundred.

Matt let out a battle cry as he swung the broom against the chain link barrier, but on the first hit, Matt's broom shattered into three or four useless sticks. The plastic head of the broom split open. The thin, dowelled handle shattered against the metal poles. Undeterred, Matt stomped on escaping mice with his big, loose rubbery boots.

Seeing his equipment failure, I took some power off my swing, and they tumbled to the ground in heaps. More mice stampeded by at eye level, racing along the railing that supported the chain link, and I forgot myself. The baseball player came out in me, and I let loose with a full swing only to have my broom suffer the same fate as Matt's. We stomped around for a few fleeting seconds, but our window of opportunity slammed shut. The casualty count was thirty-eight; thirty-six mice and two brooms.

"Outsmarted by a bunch of dumb mice," said Matt as we began to debrief.

I used what was left of the brooms and a piece of cardboard to scoop the departed into the garbage can. I put the lid back on the can, making sure it was tightly wedged and sealed.

"There were two things wrong," I began. "Maybe three things. First, we came at them from the same place. We didn't surround them. If you had run to that end of the wall and I was at this end of the wall, we could have herded them toward each other instead of sending them all away in one direction. We need to cut off their retreat."

"And the brooms really sucked."

"Yeah, I guess we won't put them back in the Pachy," I noted.

Matt scoffed at that since he'd never actually worried about putting something back. "What's the third thing?" he asked.

"Well, we came back too soon. There weren't a tenth as many mice as before. I think we only have one chance a night."

Matt was almost inconsolable and had me drop him off at the ranger office to watch TV. He felt he'd lost to a bunch of mice. I thought we'd been more effective than the keeper's puny traps.

As we left, I tossed all the broken pieces of broom on top of part of the Bird Building. I thought I was covering our tracks, but anyone looking out the window of the kitchen could see the broken shards on the roof. That was pure, plain stupid.

On the way to the ranger office on Fulton Parkway, I stopped to tag the Detex station in Wade Hall. It was located in a janitor's closet.

"Hey, Matt," I said when I returned to the car. "I just saw some really good brooms in a janitor's closet."

CHAPTER NINE

The next night we attacked again using the brooms from Wade Hall. These were somewhat sturdier, with dark brown natural bristles. The mice hadn't been disturbed all night, and they went back to their normal routine.

As before, we opened the door and charged in, but this time, Matt moved quickly toward the front of the big cage so as to cut off their escape. We were not actually inside the cage where the birds were housed. We were in the corridor that ran along in front.

At the other end of the room, I was making my attack and trying to drive them back in Matt's direction. We were both busy. The cinderblock wall was covered with what had become a moving cushion about three inches thick, and twenty feet wide and eight feet high. They rushed for the overhead maze of pipes, conduits, joists, and ventilation shafts. My task was to stop as many as I could, and the flat of my broom was scoring at a frantic pace.

Matt was behind me, and I could hear his broom flailing at the rodents until, finally, the ranks of the enemy thinned and we could survey the damage. These were better brooms, and though they held up better, they had lost a lot of bristles. During the pitch of battle, it had been utter chaos with mice dropping on us from the ceiling when they lost their grip. Finally, it was over, and the sea lions and birds stopped their noisy soundtrack.

Again, we cleaned up the mess by sweeping the vermin into a pile. I even entered the unlocked cage to remove the fallen mice that had passed through the chain links. The sea lions and birds were remarkably calm.

We had killed hundreds of mice, and I commandeered a snow shovel to scoop them into the same garbage can as the night before. As soon as I pried off the lid, I knew my mistake. "WHEW," I breathed. The bin had not been emptied the night before and the previous haul had built up quite a stench.

This time I didn't leave the corpses to cook all day, and after cleaning up the mess, I tied off the white trash can liner and pulled it out of the bin. It weighed about twenty-five pounds, and I was afraid the bag would split before I could get it outside.

Matt was in a strangely giddy mood and discovered an ancient mousetrap in the corner of the room. He took that opportunity to leave a surprise for the keepers, by placing a dead mouse under the snap mechanism and sliding it back into its hiding place. He thought that clever, but I wondered how anyone would believe, even for a moment, that an old, unset, unbaited trap would catch a mouse.

"Well, they could," he said.

We both laughed at that, and I added, "Well, maybe if the mouse was dumber than dirt."

A lot of time had passed so I left Matt there while I walked over to check in at the Greenhouse and get another fifteen minutes on my clock. When I returned, Matt was hard at work. He had discovered more empty traps and baited them with dead mice for the keepers to find. After that, we went through the entire building and fed every trap we could find. None had been set or baited, so we were sort of leaving a calling card so that someone might get the message about what was going on with the rodent population. I drew the line, however, when we found an old trap under the kitchen sink. That was Walter's turf, and that didn't seem fair to a man who was so meticulous. On the other hand, the lunch room and Tony's and Linda's areas were all considered fair game. All in all, we placed mice in five traps upstairs.

It's pretty dramatic, and even disturbing to write about what we had done. The fact is, that this was supposed to be a safe place for the birds who took up winter residency there in the cinderblock basement. We were well aware of that, and after the fury of battle, the animals would settle down and even play up to us. Perhaps they realized that we were rescuing them from a pestilence that made a nightly visitation. In particular, Matt had made an attachment with a blue and yellow macaw.

"Hey, I love this bird," said Matt. He even had a pet name for it; I think it was *Pookie*. Pretty soon, it was up on his shoulder and walking around behind his head. Matt was just like a pirate with his parrot.

While he was playing with his new friend, I had a job to do. "Turn off all these lights up here," I said as I grabbed the two battered brooms and raced out into the winter snow. I ran over to Wade Hall to hit my station clock and return the brooms. They were a bit of a mess, so I lowered the bristle end into the lake at a spot that had not yet frozen. I swirled it to rinse it clean. Afterwards I had to keep shaking them dry before they froze in the night air.

The final step in my cleanup effort was accomplished when I loaded three white garbage bags of dead mice onto the luggage rack of the station wagon, and deposited them in a dumpster near the Commissary.

By my calculations, in two nights we had killed over three hundred mice, and we were just beginning.

CHAPTER TEN

Over the next ten nights, we continued our mission. Though it sounds like this process took us away from our jobs for a lot of time, in reality it lasted for only fifteen to twenty minutes a night. When it was over, Matt returned to the office, and I continued alone on my rounds from 4:00 to 8:00 a.m.

A lot of strange and unusual things had been happening. Of course, I probably caused half of them, but that was so much better than the John Sich plan. His version of the night watchman job was boring. He went around inspecting for trouble, but there was none because he had not found any. On the other hand, he didn't cause any, either.

When you think about it, Wolee the hippo had escaped his pen because Tim and I were in there turning on lights and agitating him. So while we were the ones who discovered the *hippo on the loose*, we had also caused the problem. Had we followed Sich's pattern, we would never have gone into the room and found the snakes uncaged. They would have just crawled around on the floor until morning and it wouldn't have mattered much.

Sometimes it was the junior ranger who created an incident, and so the nightly report was from his own missteps. There was a time, for example, when Norm had to put in a report saying that he had driven the Cushman off a cliff. Had he not been there guarding the zoo, no one would have been able to report that; then again, it wouldn't have happened.

In spite of this, I felt that I was making an overall difference. Don Kuenzer told me on more than one occasion that he endorsed my style of night watching (either that or he was being nice). I was here and there, sneaking around in the dark, unpredictable, odd, and eccentric. This made it difficult for vandals and surely made serious intrusions less likely. If someone had been studying our security system for predictable patterns, well good luck to them.

We did have our share of intruders. There were people fresh from the bars on Friday nights, and also the young punks who pestered John. The punks' primary mission was mostly focused on John, whose impeccable loyalty to the clock made him a target for pranks. So far, I had only sensed their presence a few times. One time I drove past the souvenir stand near Monkey Island and found a trash receptacle in the middle of the road. I'd been through there earlier that night, and that trash can was not there. As I put it back, I knew the punks were in the zoo and testing me to see if I'd bite.

Other things happened that I considered more serious. One bitterly cold night, for example, I noticed that the *flaming salamander*, a portable forced-air kerosene heater, had gone out in the Greenhouse. When in operation, it roars like a big loud flame thrower. The light from its combustion is not great, but enough to make the Greenhouse flicker like there were a few big candles lit in there. That glow was normal in the really cold months.

One morning, about 2:00 a.m., I noticed that it was running. Later, as I was on foot near the sea lion pool, I realized that there was no luminescence coming from the roof of the Greenhouse. I investigated and I found that the *salamander* had gone out. Had that not been discovered, the zoo would have lost many exotic plants that night. Around 3:00 a.m., I phoned the head of the Greenhouse at home and he came to the zoo, filled the tank with kerosene and fired it up. The manager's name was Bob, and he was the same guy who had helped me with my leaf collection when I was in the fifth grade. It was particularly satisfying to help him so many years later.

On another cold night, I hit the Detex station in the Lions and Tigers around 4:30 a.m., then drove to the reindeer barn. It was snowing, I   was sleepy, and a short nap seemed like a good idea. I didn't trust the exhaust system of the car, however, and made it my policy to never sit with the engine running. Instead, I drove to a stop, ran the engine for a minute to heat up the passenger compartment, then turned the car off. The car stayed warm for a little while, and worked as an alarm clock if I fell asleep. After five minutes, the cold would awaken me.

That night I drove to the reindeer barn, blasted the car's heater, then turned off the engine. I laid over onto the car seat and snoozed for a few precious minutes. Before long I was shivering like my spine was going to snap; so I started up the car, grabbed the Detex, and ran in and hit the reindeer station in the little barn while the car warmed.

I was still half asleep when I staggered back. Yawning, I put the car in gear to drive a short two-hundred feet to the sitatunga barn. I was still struggling to stay awake, and hoped that I could get the car warm enough for a second power nap. My head bobbed up and down as I fought to keep my eyes open. Suddenly, I saw something, something quite large and fast. At first I thought it might be a Great Dane. Whatever it was, it stood about five feet at the shoulder and ran right in front of the car.

I was trying to process information with a brain that was only half awake. It was tan-colored, and it was big. *Lion* crossed my mind; it was that color. But it was sort of bony (which was why I thought it a large dog.) Maybe I just dreamed the whole thing.

I turned off the car, and got out thinking, *I hope it's not a bear, but it couldn't be a bear, it was the color of a lion.*

By that time I was wide awake as my pulse quickened. I had on a couple of really heavy coats and stuff, and I felt encumbered. So I took off all my jackets and threw them on the seat. This in spite of the fact it was around 20° F. I wanted more freedom of movement , and also needed the cold to sharpen my mind. I kept a sharp eye out, looking in every direction. This was the area near the Bears' Refreshment Stand and was well-lit with street lights.

Then I saw it. It was a big male sitatunga antelope, complete with a big set of twisted, backward-pointing trophy horns that were about twenty-five inches long. Here I was in a Cleveland winter, and an African antelope had just run right past me. That ram had a grayish-brown, shaggy coat and cloven hooves. It probably weighed in at two hundred and twenty pounds and was a little bit over four feet tall at the shoulders.

The impressive animal ran right over to the edge of the exhibit area where he should have been. He was right on the edge of his own paddock, but now he was loose in the zoo. I had the key to the barn, and believed that I could get him back in.

Here were my choices regarding this large, spiral-horned, full-grown ram: (1) *Put him on report* as John had taught me. (2) Call a ranger and have him shoot the animal. (3) Telephone the keeper from that area and advise him of the situation. Or (4) Catch the sitatunga myself.

(Okay, it was a stupid idea to try and capture it on my own, but I was also one of the guys who picked up loose snakes in the Pachyderm Building.)

The animal was standing still in the shadows near the moat surrounding the exhibit. I moved toward him as he watched my approach. He was a spectacular animal, and I could see the heavy white breaths pouring out of his flared nostrils. My plan was simple and brilliant. I would run up and grab him around the chest, bulldog him to the ground, and wrestle him into the barn area of his exhibit. Had I forgotten something? No, that wouldn't work. I would first need to open the barn before doing any grabbing.

"Stay right there," I said to him pointing a finger toward him. (I was confident that he had to know that one from obedience training classes, if he had any.) "Don't move," I added.

I moved as quickly as I dared back to the station wagon, got the clock and my key ring. When I got back to the barn, the animal was still there, huffing in the chilly air. I unlatched the padlock and hasp, swinging open the squeaking, rustic wooden door. I wedged the Detex against it to hold it open, and stepped back from the barn. The calm, cud-chewing antelope hadn't moved an inch.

My plan quickly evolved. I would walk as close to him as he would let me, then if he took off, I'd chase him. I'd catch him, like a rodeo cowboy, and get my arms around his neck or chest. But maybe I wouldn't bulldog him to the ground. One of us might get hurt. I would just get a hold of him. After all, he only weighed forty-five pounds more than me. Overpowering the animal shouldn't be too tough. Sure, he had twenty-five inch horns. Sure, he could rear up on his hind legs and effectively be around ten feet tall with those pointy hooves flailing around at my eye level. If he knew how many mice I had killed, he would surely tremble. Well, of course, I didn't think about any of this stuff. I mean really, males in their twenties are impetuous. It's not our fault. It's hormonal.

I moved, step by step, toward the antelope. His eyes became a bit more anxious, but as I got closer, he didn't move. When I was within five or six feet, I began to think, *Maybe this animal is tame. I'll just lead him into the barn.*

"That's a good sitatunga. Sit-a-tongue-ga... That's a good boy..." I kept inching toward the animal, the frozen turf crunching with each step. I looked him right in his big black eyes. I was four feet away... Three feet away...

"That's a good boy. What a nice boy. All right. Cootchie cootchie. Nice, sita-tongue-ga. You're a pretty boy. You're a pretty, pretty, pretty boy."

Then he bolted, and I was close behind. We took off running.

I chased it, and it was now man versus beast. I kept coming, running up on its heels. I was running at top speed, but, unlike him, I didn't have another gear. We ran in a huge circle, all the way around the perimeter of the sitatunga enclosure. I was driving my legs, pushing myself harder and harder, deadly serious concerning the intense chase. I ran with everything I had, and didn't let up. It became a test of my mental toughness.

The night was freezing cold and crisp, but I was really heating up. My lungs were bursting, and he was probably running at about one-tenth his top speed, just putting out enough gas to stay ahead of the clumsy primate who was chasing him.

We had run a great circle and were right back where we had begun.

The antelope stopped, turned, and looked at me. I was now bent over gasping for breath. My one consolation was that the antelope was breathing heavily, too. The difference between us was that I had a plan. I would prevail. I was tougher.

"All right, you," I said gasping. "You ready? You wanna try that again? 'Cause I'm ready. Once more on the Merry-Go-Round. Let's *go*." I figured that a quick attack before he caught his breath would stand a better chance. After all, he had to be winded.

I ran at him again, and the antelope's quick response indicated that he'd had enough. *No damn way* is my human translation of his nonverbal response. He simply made a graceful leap, soaring a distance of over twenty-five feet and landing as lightly as a feather. It was like watching a scene from Peter Pan, only instead of Neverland, he softly landed back in his own exhibit area. He looked back at me, still chewing whatever he was chewing, and I realized I was a dumb-ass. This animal jumped in and out of his enclosure at will. That sitatunga ram probably grazed all over the zoo at night, enjoying the sweet clover lawns of the zoo's mall.

When daylight came, I was again waiting to punch out and the others were coming in. One of the keepers in the Bird Building was a woman named Linda. I saw her coming down the stairs to punch in.

As she passed I said, "Things are different in your building when I go in there at night. Has there been a decline in the mouse population?"

"Yes," she said proudly. "We've been trapping them. Catching a lot of them." She smiled and continued on her way.

CHAPTER ELEVEN

Early morning at the time clock was the only chance I had to interact with the daytime workers at the zoo. During that half hour or so, the employees came in one at a time. It was fun to see them arrive. Either Don Kuenzer the Curator, Joe Chery the Zoo Superintendent, or Alan Sironen the Assistant Curator would always be there, standing at the little desk to greet the keepers as they came in. Actually, this became a gathering place where people often lingered for a few minutes. It was a place for laughter and joking, and, for me, having spent my shift alone in darkness, it was a welcome experience. All around me were the loud voices of talkative and cheerful men. I just stood there against the wall, saying nothing, smiling at the antics and conversation. None of these keepers knew who I was, and I didn't really know many of them by name.

The funny thing was that these were same ones I had watched for years. As a college student, I had seen them as somewhat grotesque and alarming. Now I was seeing them differently. Many were immigrants with no college degree or any professional training that qualified them to be a zookeeper, but many came from generations of farmers in Europe. They knew and understood the animals in their care.

My earliest assessment of these men (they were nearly all *men* in those days) was that they came across like everyone's favorite funny uncle. The daily arrival sounded like the greetings of my own aunts and uncles at family reunions. The door would open, and middle-aged, paunch-bellied Perkins would walk in, and Kuenzer would announce, "There he is." To which Perkins would grin and curtsy.

Since becoming a night watchman, I now found these guys likeable, funny, and endlessly charismatic. Yes, most of these were the same keepers I had viewed as bizarre and misshapened around ten years earlier. In reality, it was I who had changed. I had seen something of the corporate world with its power games office affairs. The fact was that the keepers were a lot happier than the people in those offices whose lives, by comparison, were a mired mess.

Those older fellows were also admirable. They had aches and pains, but they worked right through them. Some had bad backs. There was one guy, who looked like Shemp Howard to me. He had that thick, Shemp Howard hair. He would walk in and limp painfully down the stairs, with a morning case of *zookeeper's back*.

"How's that back?" Don would ask.

Steve Sandusky would answer, "Oh, it'll be better after I have a cigarette." People would laugh and he'd keep going with some whimsical nonsense. "I'm gonna go lay in the hippo pool for an hour with Blackie. He can rub my back."

Bill Seman would walk in and someone would shout, "Hey, everybody, Bill's still alive."

A few days after Matt and I set out to clear the Bird Building of every single rodent, I began to hear some talk that gave me pause. Several of the bigwigs were in the area when a keeper came in to make a complaint.

"Hey, Kuenzer," he said. The keeper wasn't as angry as he was perplexed. "What's going on with all the brooms? Nobody's got any brooms. I've been talking to other people and it's not just my area. There don't seem to be any good brooms left in the zoo. We had some last week. You go to get your broom, and it's not there."

"Well," said Don. "We'll fix it. I'll have the Commissary order some and we'll get them sent to all areas. I guess it's just time for new brooms."

"Meanwhile, what am I going to do today? I ain't got no broom. I'm not talking about push brooms for the cages. I mean the regular brooms like you have at home for the keeper area."

"We'll get some," said Don. "We'll take care of it."

They were talking about us. Matt and I had disintegrated the brooms from the Pachy, basically destroyed the brooms in the janitor's closet in Wade Hall even though I had put them back. Oh, and I didn't mention that we'd smashed and demolished the brooms in the Bird Building. (They were the nearest to the action.) And, well, we also discombobulated a broom from the Greenhouse, but we put that one back. Events were catching up to us.

I was standing right there and nobody said anything to me, so, as far as I could tell, they didn't connect me with the broom problem. So people kept coming in and going out. Don was standing at his desk, reading the keeper reports from the day before. As he read, he'd take some notes before going on to the next.

Just about then, Dick Chodera from the Commissary punched in, and Kuenzer stopped him.

"I've been reading keeper reports for the last few days, and they've been having a lot of success trapping mice over at Birds. There must be a lot of them. When you're making deliveries this morning make sure that all the buildings have a supply of mousetraps? I assume we have some."

"We have plenty," said Dick, "How many to each place?"

"Five should do it. If we start finding them in the other buildings, we may have to get more." Had the conversation ended here, I would have been happy, but then Don said something that hit me right between the eyes. "I'll be at the Bird Building this morning when I make my rounds. I'll ask them what bait they've been using. It seems to be working. When I find out, we'll supply some to every area of the zoo."

Don was planning to go to Birds and ask *them* what they were setting in their traps. (What sort of answer would they give? *We don't bait or set the traps, I think the mice are suicidal and just crawl under the bail.*) I didn't want that conversation to take place. It was time to speak up.

"I can tell you," I interrupted. "They're using potatoes. I've seen the traps set in the basement and they have pieces of potato in them." (My Dad had always told me that to catch a mouse in a snap trap, a piece of raw potato was the bait of choice. So thanks, Dad.) It was a perfectly credible, yet esoteric answer. *Cheese* would not have been believable. Only in cartoons is cheese believable. Don accepted my potato answer and the matter seemed to evaporate with only the slightest echo of a near miss.

"Make sure to include a couple of white potatoes in your shipment to every area this morning."

This was an amusing turn of events, but I did feel bad about one thing which I needed to remedy. I would return in about sixteen hours to begin my shift. Before that, I'd go to Uncle Bill's on Center Ridge and buy ten assorted brooms, each matching as closely as possible the ones we had *borrowed*. That night I placed them around in all the casual, out-of-the way places *near* where they had been taken. I chose odd locations so they'd be discovered in proximity to their rightful spots. In my mind, I imagined a greenhouse worker saying, "Oh, here's the broom. It was sort of behind this wheelbarrow all the time, and I thought it was missing. Ha ha. How dumb am I? But here it is, and not only that, it's brand-new and completely different."

What actually happened was that the Commissary also delivered a good supply of new brooms to all areas, and everyone was crawling with brooms after that. I only really needed eight brooms to replace the ones we destroyed. The fact is that I bought two more of the finest industrial grade so that Matt and I could finally give up the crime of broom-napping.

CHAPTER TWELVE

People who know will say that if you see two mice, you have a lot more. The keepers never saw any during the day, and Kuenzer thought that a few more traps around the zoo would stem the tide. Matt and I had been on the front lines, however, and we knew that all the mousetraps and potatoes in northeast Ohio couldn't do the job. In spite of the odds against us, we were resolute. After all, we were Clevelanders and loyalty in the face of lost causes is our forte. We have the Cavs, the Browns, and the Indians. We were fully hardened for battle. *We'll never surrender* was our mantra.

After a break of a few days, we were back wielding the brooms in the basement of the Bird Building, and our tactics continued to evolve. First, we realized that we had to get into the cage with the sea lions and wading birds in order to get to some of the mice. That was not difficult since that cage was large and never locked.

"Ready?" I whispered outside the door. With a good grip on our new brooms, we entered, hit the lights, flipped open the gate in front of the cage, went in, then closed it behind so that no animals would escape.

The zoo animals were fine with us running in there. The birds simply eased out of our way, and we resumed our pincer tactic of cutting off every escape path.

I ran toward one end of the cage, near the pool that was there for the sea lions. Matt ran all the way toward the other end. We had about forty-five seconds before the fast mice would clear the room.

The mice had gotten used to some level of impunity if they stayed within the cage, but that security now ended. Matt and I had turned the tide in this war, but now we had reinforcements. Suddenly there were six at war against the mouse hordes.

Yes, there were *six* of us.

The four European white storks had joined us. They were into it. I was running back and forth, trying to not let mice get away, and the four big white storks were next to me, like comrades in arms. The storks were utterly fantastic. They kept a keen eye on the streams of mice running along the base of the wall. Then a stork would stab at a mouse with his long bill and snatch the mouse in his beak. The stork would then fling his head back and flip the mouse into the air. It would never return to earth, but it was caught by the bird and—gulp— it went straight into its gullet.

Mice were popping up in front of my face like lottery balls in a machine, and falling into the birds' huge throats. The four white storks were hopping around side-by-side with me in a synchronous dance.

That night we figured that we had taken out about four hundred rodents, and we might have been halfway to our goal of wiping out this infestation.

I hit the Detex station there in the basement and got out the garbage can and the snow shovel. Matt did his part by placing a dead mouse in each of the various traps in that area of the building. These traps had been recently set by the keepers, with potatoes as the bait. None of them had been triggered by a mouse. But soon every snap trap in the building was occupied by a victim.

Putting the mice in the traps was now more dangerous because they had actually been set. The first thing we had to do was spring the traps to disarm them, and then insert the mouse. Clearly, the potatoes worked like magic.

I shoveled up piles of dead mice; it was as if I were shoveling gray snow. The white storks had no interest whatsoever in mice that were dead, and therefore were useless at cleanup time. Still, they had become our allies. None of the other birds joined the Mousetoberfest. It was easy to see why the Europeans think that bird is lucky. They are good mousers.

Matt suggested that we place mice in the traps of other buildings, but I thought that it might spread disease or something. Later that night, however, I saw a trap set with a nice piece of potato in the keeper's room in the Pachy. I gave the trap a little kick with my shoe to set it snapping shut. That way, the keepers could come in and see that the bait had worked, but the trap had just missed the mouse this time.

CHAPTER THIRTEEN

"Not a creature was stirring, not even a mouse." Yes, that famous line is from a children's story, but Matt and I wanted it to be true of the winter quarters for the zoo's permanent bird population. Before we began our quest, the rodent army had been growing steadily, and was on the verge of becoming a cheap movie entitled, *The Mice that Devoured Cleveland.* The city was becoming a safer place because Matt and I had the mouse situation more and more under control with every passing night.

We continued our race into the basement for one surprise attack each night just after midnight. Eventually, we reached the point where instead of hundreds of mice, there were now only many dozens remaining. Our weapons were honed, and our alliance with the white storks was strongly cemented.

We were now targeting individual mice, not a vast swarm. Nets were employed as another weapon. They were duck nets with long wooden handles which came from the janitor's closet in Wade Hall. We were now catching live mice which we dumped into a bucket. That night after that skirmish, we inspected our haul. We had a nice catch of about twenty-five, in each of two buckets. The sides of the containers were too slippery for escape. Though we hadn't killed any mice, we had taken prisoners.

This presented a problem. As many as we had killed in battle, these were not a faceless horde. We debated as to what we should do. All the options seemed cruel (I know, I know, we'd already killed thousands, but logic doesn't always trump emotion.)

Suddenly a thought came to me. "You know, I read in Farley Mowat's book…" I could see that Matt was confused. "I read in a book once that mice are the number one natural food of wolves."

He caught my drift, if not understanding my relationship to the gray wolves who pleaded with me nightly. His mind went toward other animals which might be fed by our sudden largesse. At this point, I drew the line. The wolves would be given this one chance to let their hunting instincts return to their full force, and they did. The small horde of rodents we released in the wolf area lasted less than a minute, and while this might have seemed a cruel end, it was at least nature's way and not a battle of brooms.

The next night, we went back to the Bird Building with our brooms in hand, but how different it was then from the first night when the vermin were so numerous as to be uncountable.

We charged into the room, flicked on the lights, and only a paltry few dozen mice were there feeding. We and our stork allies made short work of all but a few. The truth is that mice, like rats, are creatures of habit. They can be found doing the same thing each night at the same time. So when we ran in and I saw a mouse escaping along a water pipe high above my head, the next night that same mouse would be taking that same escape route. We took note of the preferred exits of the final few that had escaped. Only five remained from the thousand plus that had swarmed the area just a few weeks ago.

What seemed amazing to me was that the mice would come back the folowing night to exactly the same spot. They would continue to come out to eat at this same restaurant. I mean, how dumb were they? If there's a nightclub where a thousand people go to dance, drink beer, and eat nachos, and hundreds of people are killed there right on the dance floor in front of your face, wouldn't you think you'd find another place to party? Not these five mice. They'd be back. They'd put on their mouse deodorant and platform shoes and go down to the disco one more time. And those five mice were doomed. We would not be outsmarted by a bunch of dumb mice.

The great rodent war was nearly at an end, and we went through our normal cleanup ritual, including supplying mice to continue the illusion that the traps were working. At this point, Matt got a little creative. He made a stack of five mice and set them in a single trap. It looked like they had gone after the potato bait while doing some incredible feat of mouse team gymnastics.

Next, he took six traps and set them on a single mouse, so that it looked like it had been walking along and simultaneously got caught by six traps at once. These and other creations were left for the keepers to find the next morning when they went to empty their traps.

The next night when we ran in around 12:30 a.m., we spotted so few mice, they could be counted on one hand. They were quickly dispatched, but we were not done. We went through the entire building to roust out any last holdouts. We looked in drawers and closets until we were convinced that the rodent problem was no longer a threat to the birds. Our task was finally finished.

A few days later, in the morning around 7:50, I was leaning against the wall opposite the time clock as the keepers and maintenance people came in to begin another day.

Linda, the keeper from the Bird Building, came in. She seemed to be in a pleasant mood until she saw me. Her mood suddenly changed.

"You think you're so funny. Well, you're not funny." She went off in a huff and I surmised that she was the one who found Matt's snap trap sculptures. She never spoke to me again.

As Linda walked out, I heard Don laughing. "She should be glad you killed so many mice," he said.

I tried my best to give a *I-have-no-idea-what-you're-talking-about* look, but he wasn't buying.

"Hey, I know all about it," said Don. "There's broom straws all over the building." Then he laughed some more. "It's not a bad thing, but I think you better not do it anymore. Linda's pretty upset."

"I won't," I promised. "We got them all."

CHAPTER FOURTEEN

When the zoo was up to its full complement of watchmen, there were three of us. I've concentrated on the two shifts (early and late) that were manned by Sich and me. The third watchman worked both of those shifts, John's on the weekends and mine on Wednesdays and Thursdays. This provided us with two days off. The relief watchman also doubled on the Friday early shift to provide a second patrol at the start of the weekend.

It was not an easy job, and I don't understand how anyone could adjust to the constantly shifting sleep patterns. Solitude was another thing that had to be tolerated. Not everyone is comfortable being alone anywhere, much less in a shadowy place inhabited by exotic animals and potential trespassers. So between the nature of the job and the hours, there was a lot of turnover in that third spot. In fact, whoever had the job left soon after I came on.

At first, this vacancy was a financial boon. As long as John and I were willing to works seven days a week, the time-and-a-half overtime looked good on my paycheck, and even better when a holiday was involved at double-time. (Once, John hit the jackpot when his birthday fell on a holiday and he received two times two times one-and-a-half times his normal rate.)

I was anxious to get ahead financially so I told Kuenzer, "Don't be in a hurry to hire a relief watchman. We don't mind."

"Well, that's good to know," he'd say. "It's really cheaper for the zoo to pay you overtime than to hire another person. So we won't rush it."

For awhile it went quite well, but eventually I changed my tune. Despite all the *big money*, after four months with no time off, I was ready for a relief watchman.

One guy that I liked very much was Jim Rybicki. He was a little younger than I, and we shared interests in Cleveland sports, politics, animals, history, science, and literature. Once at a party of zoo workers, Jim surprised us by bringing out his guitar and singing a song he'd written. It was a novelty song, and one line I remember went, "So I'm glad I'm not a soldier in the battle of the sexes."

Being the relief watchman wasn't his first choice. Early on he told me, "I took the job to get a foot in the door. I really want to be an animal keeper, so this is just a stepping stone. I've heard that's how it works."

Sure enough, when a keeper's position came open in the Pachyderm Building, he took the job. No one else wanted it. No one in his right mind wanted to work with the elephants and hippos; Jim was given the job despite of his lack of union seniority.

After another long span of *big money and no life*, they hired a young man named Andy. I had made Andy's acquaintance years earlier when he sold smelts at the Sea Lion Pool. I never got to know him well, and his job was, if you pardon the pun, a bit fishy.

After he was hired, Chery said, "Now you'll get a night off so you can spend all that money."

Like Jim, Andy's goal was to work for a year or two and wait for an opening for a keeper with sea lions.

Andy was a big man. He was over six feet tall, and I'd guess that he'd weigh in at around three hundred and seventy-five pounds. He came on the job in the middle of winter. The nights were intolerably cold. Joe told me that John was going to give Andy his orientation and then work the early shift over the weekend. After that, I'd finally get a couple of days off.

The promise of a day off on the way put a spring in my step. I was glad to see John and Andy waiting to punch out at *exactly* midnight. I greeted Andy, but he didn't hang around.

"Well, I broke him in," said Sich. "All trained and ready. Oh, he is a big boy, and so now I have two nights off. And you get your nights off this week. After all this time."

Andy would be on his own the very next night, and I was working out a speech in my head to tell him that it was okay to not treat the job as seriously as John made it seem.

The next night just before midnight, I pulled up into the parking area in front of the Commissary. I would be relieving Andy for the first time, but when I reached to open the door, it was locked.

That had never happened before. I couldn't get in, and was wondering what had happened. I pounded on the glass door a few times, and saw Andy's head peek around the corner wide-eyed. Seeing me, Andy hurried to the door anxiously. He turned the tumblers and unlocked it.

"Hurry. Come in," he panted, looking past me as if this were a Code Red Emergency. I looked around, too. Something must have happened.

"Hurry," he said. As soon as I stepped in, he locked the door.

"What's going on?"

"We can't stand here. We're right in front of the glass door," he said, and he hustled back to the kitchen dining area to get out of sight. I followed, looking back over my shoulder at whatever must have been wrong.

"Every time a leaf blows out there, it scares me to death."

"What? Are you kidding?"

"No. It's dark. It's terrifying. I'd didn't think this night would ever end."

I still thought he was joking.

"It's only midnight. The convenience stores are just closing."

"I don't care. I'm never coming back. This place scares me to death. Anybody could be out there in the dark."

I suddenly saw my dream of two approaching nights off sliding like ice floes over a waterfall.

"Andy, it's not dangerous. Think a second. As watchman you can sign up for any full-time job that ever becomes available. You've got it made." It was clear that my words, like my days off, were going nowhere, and I realized Andy really was scared to the bone. I offered what I could. "Would you like me to walk you to your car?"

When I unlocked the door, he made me go out first to make sure it was okay, which I did. I waved for him that it was all clear and he hustled to his car. Then he was gone.

I told Chery about it the next morning, and he said, "Yeah, his mother called me this morning and told me he didn't want to be night watchman anymore."

I didn't get a night off, and Sich was back working overtime that afternoon at 4:00 p.m.

When I saw John that night during the shift change, he said to me, "Huge man is he, like giant." He gestured with his arms. "This tall and this wide, but afraid of night."

I suppose there are times when we are all driven by ours fears. I felt bad that Andy's had closed off his dreams for the future.

Lucky for me, it only took about two weeks for them to hire a replacement. They hired a guy named Joe Sanders. He stood around five-foot-five, one hundred forty-five pounds, and in his forties. Joe was tough, and like many Clevelanders, he was of Irish descent. What I remember about Joe was that one night he caught a crook in the park. Matt and I had caught a guy goofing around and drinking with his buddies, but Joe caught a real criminal. He told me the story the next night when I was coming in, and he was waiting to punch out. We were sitting across from each other at the table in the Commissary kitchen. Joe was still pumped with adrenalin twenty-four hours after the event. The incident occurred on the 4:00 to midnight shift.

I said, "What happened?"

"Well," said Joe. "I was driving the wagon around, you know? So I was driving past the Souvenir Stand there by Monkey Island. And I saw something in the headlights. There was a little stuffed animal lying there on the road. A little panda. And I thought, hell, I know that damn thing wasn't there the last time I drove around. So I got out of the car with my flashlight. I went around the back of the souvenir stand, and the door was open in the back. Well, that's not right. And then I see out behind the building on the ground, all these boxes out there, full of stuff. Souvenirs and stuff. So I called out on my walkie-talkie and got a hold of Steve (a real ranger) and said get down here.

"I should have waited, but I took a look in with the light, stepped in, and a guy runs out to get past me. He knocks me over. A young guy, but a grown man, you know. Long hair. He ran right over me, but I got a hold of his legs and tripped him. So he got up and I got up and out comes his knife. He comes at me with a knife, and I'm fighting him with my flashlight. Then I swung the clock at him. I hit him with it pretty good in the side. So then he charged me. It really pissed me off that he was coming at me with a knife, you know? Cut me right here."

Joe held up his right hand where there was a thin open wound on the meat of his palm. He said, "That's a defensive wound. But I got the knife away from him, and it fell to the sidewalk. We started wrestling on the cement trying to get the knife, but I managed to kick it away. So he jumped up and I ran after him and kicked at the back of his legs and he fell down again. I jumped on him. We're both on the ground fighting, you know, wrestling. So then he starts punching me, and I'm punching him back. He got me right in the face, a good lick in the teeth. Right here."

Joe peeled back his upper lip to show a cut on the inside of his mouth. Then he shook his head and scowled. "That pissed me off even more. So I got a hold of this guy's hair. He had this real long, blonde hair. I pulled him down by the hair. I got on top of him and had a grip on that hair."

Looking intense, Joe demonstrated with gestures, clenching his fists tightly. "And I just beat his head into the sidewalk as hard as I could. At that point, it felt good. Every time he tried to move, I'd beat his head some more into the street, you know, till it was bloody. I told him, 'Hold still, you son of a bitch, or I'll smash your brains out.' So I just held him there until Steve drove up."

"What happened then?"

"Hey, the asshole's in jail. He's in jail right now. I gotta go to court for beating his head. It was pretty bloody." Joe grinned just slightly. "But," Joe shrugged, "I'd do it again. I'm not gonna get in trouble. You gotta do what you gotta do."

Joe went to court, and the charges against him were dropped.

The odd shifts and the nights alone, however, didn't agree with Joe. After a short while, a job opening came up in the Bird Building as a keeper. Based on the contract with the Teamsters, anyone could sign up for an open job. Whoever had the most job seniority got it. A zoo matron named Mary signed up. She had loads of seniority, but the job just didn't work for her. The only other union member on the list was Joe, and he took the job. That was how it worked in those days. People became keepers with no animal background or training at all. They became good keepers, though. Sometimes great keepers.

John and I were dreading another long tour of duty, but a day later, a replacement was hired.

This guy was Tim Pappas. (Not Tim, the junior ranger of snake fame.)

Like the others, Tim was interested in a career as a keeper. Unlike many before him, he had specialized in animal studies at college, and had a real knowledge of animals. He was also an avid hunter and outdoorsman. I remember going over to his apartment once; he and his girlfriend Val had prepared duck and venison. They were hunted, plucked, and dressed by Tim, who wore camouflage long before it became popular.

A consummate hunter and versed in survival, he could tell what mushrooms could be eaten and what berries Native Americans used for medicine. I learned a lot from him, and he was an honorable man. Everyone knew that Tim wanted to become a keeper, but positions came open and he didn't take them.

"They hired me for this job, and I'm going to do it for one year, since that's what I agreed." Both John and I were appreciative.

Technically, Tim and I were on shifts that would never overlap, but we made a bit of overlap for the sake of friendship. One winter night just before I was to clock in, Tim invited me to see traps that he had set in the zoo. He planned to come back at 1:00 a.m. to check the lines.

It sounds odd that Tim was setting traps for wild animals in the zoo. He was, in fact, trapping predatory animals that threatened the resident population. The zoo's management knew what he was doing and saw it as a necessary function.

This takes me into a more rational discussion of the kind of war that Matt and I had in the Bird Building. Zoos are great reserves of food which are left out in the open and cannot be securely locked away. Food has to be left out to feed our charges. Additionally, humans throw away a lot of calories in the form of popcorn and hot dogs. Trash cans double as food troughs for after hours feral visitors. These go unseen, just like on the streets around where you live. Most cities have hidden populations of raccoons, possums, skunks, feral domestic cats, rats, mice, and foxes.

In neighborhoods, these night visitors know the places where the bird feeders are and where pet dishes live. They know the smells of pizza boxes and French fries left in garbage cans. For the most part, this is tolerated or goes unnoticed, but if these predators were killing pets, things would change rather quickly. The fact is that for raccoons and feral domestic cats, the zoo was a rich hunting ground, especially around Waterfowl Lake. Rats and mice would steal peafowl eggs, kill and eat baby peafowl, attack nearly any zoo baby, spread disease to the animal areas, and destroy nests in all areas of the zoo. The animals on display had no defense.

Along the brushy shores of Waterfowl Lake, dedicated keepers secured nesting boxes for more than eighty species of waterfowl. Every nest was monitored, every egg counted. When a skunk or raccoon ravaged a nest, the keepers were devastated, and the breeding pair would swim aimlessly in circles near the nest.

Pappas must have approached Kuenzer and Sironen and expressed his willingness to trap these wild, local predators. Cats were another issue. Of course they are the same breeds as what we would call *house cats*, but these had never seen the inside of a house and were spawned by generations of feral ancestors; many were rabid or carried other diseases. In size, habits, and attitude, this kind of cat was more like a lynx than any cat you've seen living in someone's home. These were not the strays that should be set up for adoption. These were wild hunters, and they were fast.

Early one winter morning, I was driving the wagon past Wade Hall, and turned left to go around the lake. Just as I neared the water, a wild cat jetted past the front of my car. I saw it clear a three foot fence with no problem and then scale an eight foot fence with only two touches against the chain link. It paused for a moment then leapt down on the other side. All this took place in an instant. In its jaws was a full-grown mallard, its nightly kill from the lake. That was what Tim Pappas would try to stop.

CHAPTER FIFTEEN

The winters of the late 1970s were among the coldest winters in Ohio history. The coldest night was January 17, 1977, when the actual temperature reached minus twenty-five degrees Fahrenheit. That made my job all the more uncomfortable, but it also had its challenges for the managers who were working hard to keep the animals alive and comfortable. Kuenzer and Sironen were addressing emergency situations on a daily basis.

Emergencies ran from a frozen water main in Bears to getting hold of some type of food that couldn't be obtained because the growers' trucks weren't running. During the many blizzards, they were often on the phone, trying to find eggplants or day-old bread or some other special foodstuffs. It seemed that as the weather grew worse, Don, Alan, and Ron Seeley were arriving at work even earlier.

Once I overheard Alan on the phone with a supplier. "I need all the sweet potatoes I can get. Yeah, I know there's a blizzard going on. You think I didn't notice? We can send a truck to get them. You don't need to deliver. I'll come and get them in my own truck if I have to." (Alan had a crummy little copper-colored Chevy Luv.)

"Hey, I managed to get into the zoo, didn't I? Your trucks should be out here making deliveries. The city's not shut down. What's your problem? ... Huh? ... I don't care. We've got hungry animals here. We need sweet potatoes today, this morning. Life goes on."

Sometimes suppliers tried profiteering on the back of the zoo's need. Alan held the line on that sort of nonsense. His office was next to the time clock so I could hear how he handled it. "That's bull. It's the same price as normal. You can't charge more because you think this blizzard has made it tough on you. You were supposed to have them here yesterday." (Alan never swore, *bull* was as extreme as he would get.)

"Look," he continued, "we're sending the truck to get the potatoes. Our truck is on the way to you. If you have any hope of having the zoo or the Metroparks as a continuing customer, we're going to see those tubers outside your warehouse in a half hour."

The whole roomful of keepers had heard this, and Chery noted, "We don't have anything to do with the rest of the Metroparks as far as buying anything."

"I know that," said Alan, "but I'm guessing he doesn't."

Within a few minutes Chodera and a helper drove the zoo's truck out of the park and into the teeth of the blizzard, heading north over the Fulton Road Bridge. I watched them drive away, and by the time they reached the Parkway, I couldn't see the truck anymore. The snow was blowing too thickly.

The guys at the loading dock had it pretty rough. In ten degree weather they'd be out unloading semi truckloads of frozen mackerel. In the summer, refrigerated trucks were a treat; in winter it was just cruel, but not unusual punishment. I'd see them out there like an old fashioned bucket brigade passing boxes down the line to the next guy until all twenty of them had carried the load. That would go on for about an hour until they'd hit the last box on the last pallet.

Then the little, round keeper named Bill Seman would lift the last box and yell out, "Here it is... This is the one we were looking for." He'd hold up the box like a prize and come running out of the truck. "It was behind all those other ones." Of course it was a treasure; it meant they could all get out of the cold.

Freezing water troughs were always a problem for the animals, like the birds of prey, that stayed outdoors most of the time. The troughs were kept open by allowing the water to keep flowing through them. Hoofed animals and birds couldn't eat when their feed and hay were covered by snow, and the keepers had to provide access to food on a continual basis all day long. That meant shoveling the snow away to create a patch of bare earth and throwing down scoops of scratch and grain.

When heavy equipment such as backhoes or tractors were needed, maintenance workers and contractors would build huge wood fires around the metal treads of the machinery to melt the frozen mud and free the treads.

Locks froze and doorways were blocked by snow. Fire, propane torches, and scoop shovels were instruments which kept the zoo alive during bad weather. Seeley, Chery, and their people worked to keep the roads clear and the vehicles moving.

Keeping heat in the buildings was another essential. Matyas had to keep on top of repairs, and spent long hours replacing boiler tubes. Old boilers and old equipment meant that the maintenance folks also often had to literally build new parts by machining them themselves.

The best thing about Cleveland winters is the fact that they don't last forever.

CHAPTER SIXTEEN

I mentioned a little bit about the zoo's matron, Mary, already but such a remarkable person deserves more attention. I first met her in 1968 when I was a train driver; in fact, she was the one who suggested that I dare to sign the list for the night watchman's job.

I don't know how long she had worked at the zoo, probably from when she was a young woman. Her long-standing job in the zoo was that of *Matron*. In other words, she had the unenviable task of cleaning all the public restrooms in the park. In later years, she had two helpers, but at first she was the sole matron. I think that she really would have preferred being an animal keeper, and in a way she was. She was the one who took care of the dreaded *homo sapiens* who were known to be quite messy. She also was a mother figure to the ticket sellers, and they became quite protective of this gray-haired woman, who was overworked by a public that thought intentionally clogging toilets was a mark of genius.

I know that she would have liked to try her hand as a keeper because she applied for such a position in the Bird Building. She had far more seniority than any other applicant so the job was hers. On the first day, however, she discovered that she could not physically do the work. She was a large woman with stiff joints, not nearly limber enough to get in and out of the cages where the birds were housed. The next day, she was back as Matron, and Joe Saunders became the keeper. That had to break her heart, and it must have humiliated her, too. Mary loved animals and would have made a caring, dedicated keeper.

I learned how good she was with animals when she met me at the time clock one morning as I was getting ready to leave. "Come with me," she said. "I want you to meet a friend of mine."

She led me down the hall and into the big room to what could be called an animal holding area. It was a large, new room, always bright and clean with large cages along one wall.

Mary pointed to one cage, which was occupied by a fully grown female orangutan.

"This is the friend I wanted you to meet," exclaimed Mary. "This is Susie." With that, she reached through the bars and petted the animal's the thin reddish hairs that covered her back.

Making eye contact with the animal, Mary said, "How's my Susie?"

The orangutan responded with some friendly *euk-euks*, something I couldn't translate.

Mary hugged the animal through the wide bars and the orang's arms were long enough that she reached out and returned Mary's embrace. These two were crazy about each other. That was obvious.

"I raised Susie from when she was a baby. Didn't I, Susie? Yes, I did." Mary was speaking to me, but coo-cooing to Susie like a proud grandparent to a small child.

"Susie lived with me in my house, didn't you, Susie? And I fed her with a baby bottle because she was my baby. I never had a baby, but Susie was my baby. I even changed her diapers, didn't I, Susie? I did."

Mary turned to me and spoke like an adult. She said, "I wanted to keep her in my house always, but when she got too big they made me bring her back."

Then she turned toward Susie and smiled very sweetly.

Meanwhile, Susie was sitting right against the bars, and her big ape face was right between two of the bars with her hands on the bars like Billy the Kid in the slammer. Then Susie puckered up her lips real big. She stuck those puckered lips about four inches out into the room. You could have hung a jacket on them.

"Oh," said Mary. "Do you want a kiss? Does Susie-woozie want a kiss? Does she? Does she? She does..."

Needless to say, the kiss grossed me out, but I was not the kisser or the kissee. There was a bond between these two that was a tribute to affection.

"Go ahead, pet her," said Mary.

I slipped my hand into the cage and petted Susie on her shoulder. Her hair was sparse. But I petted her anyway, and she seemed to enjoy it. When she puckered up her lips toward me, I knew what was coming next. *(Fat chance of that happening!)* It would have had to be pretty late at the Sly Fox for something like that to happen.

"Oh, no," I said. "Not on the first date, Susie."

Fortunately, Mary intervened and everyone kept their honor when Susie accepted a handshake instead of a kiss.

After that, there was never any doubt in my mind that Mary had the compassion to care for animals. It was just sad that, when the opportunity came, she did not have the stamina.

It was already after 8:00 and I had punched out before my meeting with Susie. Everyone else had cleared the area and were busy at work, but I was taking a bus home, and the kitchen in the Commissary was a better waiting area than the corner of Fulton Parkway and Memphis Avenue.

The bus would not arrive until 8:46 so I put my head down on the table. I didn't plan on sleeping, but a short rest seemed perfect.

Suddenly someone kicked one of the legs of the chair I was sitting in, and I jolted up and found myself looking right into the face of the Zoo Director, Dr. Leonard Goss. He was dressed in a business suit, and angry as hell at me.

"What the hell are you doing? Get up, and get to work."

I didn't stand, but asked: "Do you know who I am?"

"I don't give a shit who you are. You're the goddamned laziest worker I've ever seen. Get up and get to your area."

"I'm the night watchman. I punched out at 8:00. I'm just waiting for the 8:46 bus."

"Oh," he said, and walked out of the building.

I thought it funny that he didn't thank me for taking care of our recent plague of mice. Dr. Goss retired a few years later, having served a long and otherwise distinguished career.

CHAPTER SEVENTEEN

Mary's love of animals is an example of the dedication that the zoo sought in its workers. The only exceptions that I could think of were the junior rangers, and they were not actually zoo employees; they were paid by the Metroparks system. While I recounted Matt's role in the rodent wars, the nightly forays last less than half an hour of his shift. He was weak on cleanup and I think he was more motivated out of the joy of swatting and trap sculpture than protecting the birds.

I believe the motto of the junior rangers was *What time is it?* Their two main skills were sleeping soundly in any position and getting the rabbit-ears adjusted in the ranger office so that they could pick up Channel 8 on the TV. While they were prohibited from carrying firearms, many believed that the word *ranger* in their job title gave them special permission, and they brought their own from home. They were proud when they showed it off, but always ended every conversation with "don't tell anybody."

I once asked a full-time Metroparks ranger, "Do they have junior rangers in other parts of the park system other than the zoo?"

He laughed at that. "Hell, no! What for? I don't know why they have them here."

Well, I knew why we had them. They were our backups, the eyes and ears who were a walkie-talkie click away from the watchman on patrol. They could get help in an instant. That is, if they were not fully engaged in their hobby of sleeping soundly through radio signals.

For many people, the ideal zoo day has the sun shining and the thermostat set in the comfort zone. In cliché terms, picture perfect is where the operative word is *picture*, that is, an image captured in time. The reality of a zoo is quite different. A zoo is a complex organization which revolves around animals, many of whom are in the wrong place in terms of their natural habitat. During the time I worked at the zoo, many common notions about keeping animals were changing. The Victorian era saw the formation of zoological gardens as places filled with exotic curiosities much like museums where antiquities sat on shelves in public display. People were invited to walk around and gawk at something they had never seen before. After all, what was the difference between a mountain gorilla like Timmy and the Elgin Marbles in the London Museum? The difference should be quite clear. Animals are not *things*. While this is obvious today, it was not widely perceived at the end of the nineteenth century. Humans, if an animal at all, were meant to make the rules and dominate the other planetary underlings.

In hindsight, those attitudes toward *dumb* animals have died away by the recognition that these living things are made of the same genetic stuff as humans. Exhibits are now created that show the animals in what looks like a more natural setting, at least from the public perspective. As a zoo worker, I saw these changes as addressing quality of life issues for the animals themselves. It was all about the animals and their safety. People outside the zoo family would not always appreciate how this priority affected the rules of life in the zoo. Nor can people understand the complexity of caring for wild animals. It has little in common with having a household pet.

Yes, food, water, and shelter are still basic, but it's not a matter of two bowls, table scraps, and something cushy in the corner. The wellness of the animals, the suitability of breeding pairs, and physical protection are all challenges. Here's a small, literally small, example. In 2014 the Cleveland Zoo has koalas in their Australian Adventure area. These little teddy bears exist on a diet of eucalyptus which is shipped in fresh every week at a cost of $1600 per week. Some animals eat live animals as a part of their regular diet. While this is just an obvious fact of nature, it is sometimes deemed *cruel* by certain people who bemoan that fact as they swallow down their grilled chicken sandwich.

Many people have never considered the difficulty of keeping families of animals over generations. The fact is that inbreeding is a problem in a zoo which has only a few individuals of a species. A zoo with a pride of lions may look healthy, but if the male has also sired every female of breeding age, the lion exhibit is doomed. In the old days, animals were sometimes euthanized to prevent genetic problems with future offspring. Today, things are different. Nearly every animal is marked, either with a tag or a chip under the skin. These tags, electronic or otherwise, track the parentage of each animal so that suitable mating partners can be provided. Zoos exchange animals for breeding purposes, so that captive populations preserve the full genetic viability of a species. As natural habitat is being destroyed, this practice is more and more significant for life on the planet.

As the night watchman, my job was security for the animals. In most industrial settings, this is a matter of keeping unauthorized people off the premises. At the zoo, it was not just about the human intruders. Common animals which might be tolerated in a neighborhood setting were often a threat to the wildlife under our care. Field mice, for example, seek indoor shelter and food in the winter. What's the big deal? It's their natural way. But the zoo is not a natural place, not really. It is a place where many of the animals *cannot* live year around, but they must. That makes them extremely vulnerable. They are kept in an unnatural way for the education of people, and, as has been noted, sometimes for the survival of their species as natural habitats are destroyed and breeding populations dwindle in the wild.

The modern zoo is a place of preservation as well as display. I was working at the Cleveland Zoo as these changes were coming quickly. The animals were the preoccupation of an unlikely cast of characters, such as myself, who took risks and even did dumb things. The best employees always kept their animals in mind, however. They didn't always worry about smells or propriety, but they always protected the animals in their charge. They couldn't survive in the job if they didn't.

The administration had to keep a strong public profile and nurture support from the community. I, on the other hand, could walk around with a baseball bat and look out for kids who sneaked through the hole in the fence behind Bears and pee on doorknobs as a prank.

Some of this might be thought insane, but if asked why I worked like this, all I could say is that it was one of the best times in my life. People, even the odd ones, were genuine, hard-working, compassionate, and dedicated. The ones who weren't didn't last. John Sich and I considered the pay good, but the pay was not always enough. You had to love the animals which were the zoo. The winter of 1978 is a case in point.

The great intruder at that time was the weather. The utter coldness meant that the two-legged vandals were probably home and tucked away where it was warm. This meant that the Metroparks rangers didn't patrol within the zoo at all. There was no reason for the legal firepower that they represented.

My obligation was to clock in on my rounds as usual, and look at every recess in the zoo's topography. I was provided with a car to get around, but cars do not always work in driving blizzards with two feet of snow. The short story is this, I hit all my stations during that time. The slightly longer version is that I had never been colder in my life. I had to walk through the snow, shovel sidewalks to open snow-blocked doors, and employ a Bic lighter to unfreeze padlocks so that a key would turn the tumblers.

It was January 26-27, 1978, and the Great Lakes region recorded the lowest barometric pressure ever. Readings were comparable to that in a hurricane, 28.28 mm Hg, to be exact. The temperature that night was minus ten degrees Fahrenheit with winds gusting to seventy miles per hour. Ohio's death toll that night was fifty-one, 175,000 homes lost power, and all transportation, businesses, schools, and industry were closed for two days. People still remember where they were at that time. I was in the zoo walking along rows of cages with animals to make sure there was heat, water, and food.

I couldn't keep any semblance of Sich accuracy with regard to the Detex, but I did get through my rounds. I got up to the time clock around 8:20. It felt as if I was walking in out of a Jack London novel. There was a snowplow clearing the upper parking lot already. My ears were falling off from the cold. Outside the zoo, snowplows and salt trucks rumbled up on Fulton Parkway, as I got the grain-scoop shovel out of the station wagon. Everyone was hustling around inside the Commissary Building, and no one was joking.

Ron Seeley was there that morning. "How are things down in the zoo?" he asked.

"Everything's running. Nothing's down. All the animals are okay, but the roads are pretty bad."

"We're sending the plows down now," he said.

I still had the shovel that I had lugged around all night. It now leaned against the wall. "This belongs in the Lions and Tigers," I said. "I had to use it to get through the drifts."

"I'll have the keepers take it down with them," said Ron. Their fight against the weather was a continuation of my own. It was about the animals.

The phone rang and Ron answered it. Someone was returning his call.

"I think we're going to need about eight more salamander heaters. I want two in Cats and two in Birds and two in the Pachy."

There were a lot of people running around that morning. Don Kuenzer was deep in conversation about the birds of prey. Those birds were out in the weather, in the large cages near the east side of the lake.

"Their food was all frozen solid yesterday," said Don. "We've got to get some live guineas pigs and rabbits down there this morning. If we can get some live food into them, they'll be all right."

Another blizzard hit later that day, and the battle against the weather went on for a long time. As for me, I was done. I was going home. My night had been severe, but other frozen hands were at work, and I was asleep in bed.

CHAPTER EIGHTEEN

When the snow melted in 1978, the sidewalks and roadways within Brookside Park ran black with flowing water. The ice on Waterfowl Lake faded away to nothing, and the scattershot flotillas of waterfowl enjoyed the widening expanse of dark green water once more.

Some zoo animals were returned to their summer areas; others wandered more freely, but were still kept near their barns. Once more the tan-colored elands were visible along the front edge of their paddock. The rhesus monkeys emerged from the stone tomb in the center of their island and spent time along the edge of their moat. From within the mouseless basement of the Bird Building, the storks, cranes, egrets, bustards, flamingoes, and sea lions were returned to their summer haunts.

In spring, it's a pleasure to walk around at night without all the cumbersome layers of winter clothes. Like the groundhog of Punxsutawney, Matt merged from his winter sleep fat and hairy. I wasn't so sure that Norm would ever come out of the glow of the TV set.

Tim Pappas, my inveterate hunting and trapping friend, haunted the night in search of the animals, which were a threat to the zoo. With our charges in their outdoor areas, dishes and troughs were full of food and ready to be harvested by invading critters.

He recruited me to help him find a particular raccoon, which was causing trouble. I confess that I caught up to it one night on my rounds and killed it. That action pleased Tim, but I had some difficulty and resolved never to kill anything larger than a rat. (In later years, in Knoxville, TN where I lived, I had raccoons and possums visiting my backyard. They were safe enough there. As I said earlier, neighborhoods can be treated differently than zoos.)

Tim taught me how to use my Crossman pellet gun in the lethal pursuit of rats. At night when they were active, we would go out together and shoot them when they started to overrun the exhibits.

In that regard, my world had come full circle. I recalled the times when I was a tour driver and Norm Tulodziecki (not junior ranger Norm) and John Sich used to "go up to Bears to shoot rats" at the end of the day after the zoo closed. Now I knew what that was all about. They did it at dusk, and I did it in the darkest part of night. This was not at all like killing mice in the Bird Building. There my goal was to *completely* rid the building of rodents. Rats came in a never ending supply.

CHAPTER NINETEEN

Matt was still a junior ranger. As the weather grew warmer, he came out at night more and more. He always carried his .22 CO2-powered pellet gun and joined in shooting rats up around Bears. I tried to impress on him that he couldn't just start blasting away with his repeating rifle. I tried to make him understand that one careful and well-placed shot was superior to ten shots fired willy-nilly. He never quite got the part about the stealth and making one careful shot, but he wasn't the only one whose philosophy was to just *open fire*.

One night Matt was with me during my rounds when somebody yelled at us from the brush behind the polar bears. It was the local punks who pulled so many pranks. We ran up toward the little hill, but they went quiet as we approached. So I threw a few rocks into the brush trying to get them to give away their position. I was aiming for places where I didn't think they were, but close enough to startle them.

It worked to the extent that there were now sounds of scurrying. Matt didn't get the idea that I was not trying to hit anyone, and he opened fire with his pellet gun. I grabbed the gun barrel and pulled it up.

"No. No. No," I yelled. "You'll hit 'em."

"I don't care. I don't care." (This is why Matt was not issued a .38.)

"Jeez Louise. Fire over their heads. Don't hit 'em."

By coincidence, at that moment, a *real* ranger called Matt on the radio.

"Where are you?" he asked. Evidently, he had arrived at the office and was surprised to not find Matt in his natural habitat. Matt told them that he was with me and that we had intruders in the zoo, "a little disturbance" were his exact words.

Well, those were the magic words, and the ranger also got on his radio. We could hear him calling out for other officers in the area. About fifteen minutes later, three separate squad cars showed up, pulling into the Bears area, with a total of five rangers and a lot of flashing lights.

"Some sort of trouble here?" one asked.

"We heard a couple of intruders up here in the bushes about twenty minutes ago," said Matt. "But we haven't heard anything for awhile."

These rangers all had flashlights, and so did Matt and I. The seven of us went all over the area, and even up into the ridge to the left of the

Bears Refreshment Stand. That was where the hole in the fence was. We had that area lit up pretty well, but didn't see anyone. I truly believed that the punks were still hunkered down, probably facedown in a gully somewhere, just hiding.

We didn't find them. The bunch of us ended up just standing around between the reindeer veldt and the sitatunga veldt.

"Probably just some kids, huh?" said one of the rangers.

"I'm sure of it," I said. "They won't hurt anybody."

"Well, too bad," said another. "There's nothing else going on tonight. It's duller than dirt in the whole park system."

They were just shooting the breeze with us when I pointed toward the feed dishes in the sitatunga velt. Then I said, "Hey, look over there."

All five of the full-time rangers looked, craning their heads, perplexed.

"See that trough? And that big bowl? See them? Look in the bowls."

When their eyes adjusted to the shadows, they suddenly saw a thick swarm of busy rats.

"Holy shit!" exclaimed one of the rangers.

They all jumped at that, loosened the straps on their holsters, and pulled out their service revolvers. Within seconds there was a massive hail of gun shots blasting away at the rats. The rangers emptied their pistols in rapid order, popped in another load, and started firing again. It was a blistering, ear-splitting hailstorm of firepower. They let loose about a hundred rounds in less than a minute.

It was one of the most awesome displays of shooting I'd ever seen.

I imagine that the punks laying face down in a nearby gully also got an earful. They must have been terrified. All I could hope was that it would make them rethink their priorities.

A lot of rats died that night. Matt joined in with his toy .22, but I held back. My BB gun was a single shot and hardly useful in this deluge.

After that, some of the Metroparks rangers returned to shoot rats up around the Bears. Sometimes eight or nine would arrive at once, but I never shot with them again. They would call on the walkie-talkie just to let me know they were coming in. I did, however, warn them on many occasions with words like, "Now, do you see that antelope over there? And that tortoise? And that reindeer? Don't hit any of those guys."

CHAPTER TWENTY

As my night watchman career continued into another summer, Matt and Norm were still junior rangers, and Sich, Pappas, and I were the rotating regular watchmen.

The punks whom I had glimpsed twice were back for another

summer of tormenting John. On rare occasions, they entered the zoo after midnight as well, and I was looking forward to the day I could wring their little throats, metaphorically of course.

Ever since I chased the four men and Matt and I locked one of them in the Baboon Building, I had been reevaluating what I would do if I came face to face with a serious adult intruder. What if I came face to face with a real criminal? What if I even encountered some tough guys who had just left one of the West Side bars and were looking for trouble?

I didn't want to hit a man with a baseball bat, and this became a big issue for me. The teargas gun was a dud, and John's advice to "knock them unconscious" somehow didn't seem to be the solution.

This internal debate was not purely academic. Grown men came into the zoo at night, and more often than might be thought. Most of the time I improvised, but what if my luck gave out?

Early one warm Sunday morning around 3:30 a.m., I was sitting on the long steps that went up to the Bird Building.

As I sat there, the peafowl began a commotion up in the trees near the Ostrich Barn. I left my clock on the steps and stood up. I slipped down the long stairway and headed toward the Sea Lion Pool. Then I heard a car door slam out in Parking Lot Number 1.

I saw a car in the lot. I heard three more car doors slam. I spoke into my walkie-talkie. "Night watchman to two-five-two. We have some intruders in the park, entering Parking Lot Number 1."

There was no reply, of course. The junior ranger was asleep. Through several layers of chain link fencing, dimly lit by street lamps, I saw four large men in a group heading my way. They were just outside the Main Entrance and seemed to be completely familiar with what they were doing. There wasn't any exploration about the way they were walking, nor did they hesitate. I had a feeling this wasn't the first time they had entered the zoo after hours.

I heard them talking, then I heard the clunking sounds of hands and shoes climbing up on a chain link fence. All four of them started climbing up the tall fence at once, side by side, like flies, like spiders, like crabs. There were silhouetted against the street lamps behind them. I quietly ducked into a small thicket of trees where I was confident that I would not be seen.

After scaling the fence and dropping to the ground, they came out on the pavement in front of the Sea Lion Pool. Apparently, that was where they were heading. The men spoke among themselves and were quite pleased with this adventure.

Everyone has unique gifts, or so it says in the Bible. Mine was the ability to arch my back and throw a baseball straight up and high into the air. That, by itself, wouldn't be significant if I wasn't good at being able to land the ball on a prescribed spot. When I did this, it was like incoming artillery. I was practicing that now on the four intruders. From their point of view, a rock about the size of a peach suddenly came out nowhere and hit the asphalt five feet behind them. Then I landed a second one to their other side. I kept lofting stones and they were surrounded by the fallout.

Next thing I knew they were scrambling back over the fence and that was followed by the squeal of tires leaving the zoo. I recovered a few of those stones and put them back in the pocket of my jacket. They were the perfect size, and this became one of my main tactics to repel invaders. It worked particularly well on kids looking for trouble.

Another problem was hormonal and it related to kids using the parking lot as a lovers' lane for necking. This didn't bother me much, but I thought I should tell the driver that keeping his foot on the brake while making out was a dead giveaway. The couples' vehicles would light up and make a sort of red-light district. Still, I didn't bother with them. I was more concerned with those who wanted to come over the fence into the zoo.

Matt, on the other hand, had a big problem with lovebirds. In fact, they became his obsession. He'd sit nightly in his Truckster parked near the Pachyderm Building, pellet gun loaded and waiting. Young couples in pursuit of a quiet place to make out couldn't guess that they would soon be snared in his trap.

Matt watched for cars moving slowly and bobbing over the speed bumps. When they stopped, he'd call me on the handheld radio: "Sex in the Zoo. Sex in the Zoo. Two-five-two to night watchman. Sex in the zoo."

"I'm not even headed that direction," I'd say, but he'd make a sound effect of a horse galloping. *Clop-Clop-CLOP. Clop-Clop-CLOP*, and end with a whinny. Finally he'd give his best John Sich impersonation, "We put them under arrest."

I hated this part of the job, particularly since Matt always delayed calling me until he thought the girl might have some clothing removed. This was probably the closest Matt would come to scoring, and I just thought the kids should be left alone. Matt believed that people were having large quantities of sex in the parking lot. Matt never had sex. So he wasn't really sure what sex was. He figured the best way to find out would be to run up to a parked car and shine his flashlight on a mortified couple.

We pulled up in front of the car, and the poor couple would scramble. I'd try to approach slowly enough to reallocate garments, but before I could bring the Chevy to a stop, Matt jumped out and ran toward the lovers' car. He'd shine his flashlight in the windows while repeating, "No sex in the zoo. No sex in the zoo." He was trying to get an eyeful while some poor girl was wishing she could climb into the glove compartment.

I didn't get out of the car for that type of stuff.

After the kids drove away, Matt would say something erudite like, "That girl had nice tits."

The truth is that I'd used this same lot with a girl named Cindy. We just kissed, but some of these people went a lot further.

On one occasion, Matt saw what he considered *a good one*. The couple was so traumatized that they didn't even drive off. After they just stayed, I realized that they thought that they were under arrest. Finally, I got out and walked over to the driver's side of the car.

The scared young man, now dressed, rolled down his car window. He was a small guy, around seventeen, with short light brown hair. The young dark-haired woman was leaning forward to hear what I was saying. They were a nice couple. I hope they got married and had five kids and buy this book. The young man was holding onto the steering wheel with both hands, white-knuckled.

Trying to lighten the mood, I mimicked the tone of the zoo's *Talking Storybook*. "Welcome to the Cleveland Zoo. The Cleveland Zoological Society Park is closed for the evening. For your convenience, the zoo opens again tomorrow, at 9 a.m. The zoo is open every day of the year for your family's enjoyment, except Christmas Day and New Year's Day. While you're visiting the zoo during normal zoo hours, please be on the lookout for other Talking Storybooks. Thank you, and have a great Zoo Safari."

I thought that the message was fairly clear, but these kids were in shock, so I just said, "Hey, you can go." They understood that and left.

One night after another juvenile escapade, we were pulling out of the lot when Matt noticed another parked car. This one was on a little driveway in front of a locked gate, right in front of the Zoo Administration Building. Matt was expecting the second act of his show as I pulled in right behind the other car and blocked them in.

Matt opened the door on his side of the car. I sat still in the driver's seat. The area was well lit, under a street lamp. The nose of the copper-colored Chevrolet Camaro Z28 was right up against the fence. As Matt was just about to jump out and run up to the car and shine his flashlight into the windows, something happened.

I was looking directly at the rear of the muscle car when the entire car tilted to one side and the driver side door opened. A muscular man stepped out, and the car, relieved of his great bulk, bounced back to horizontal. He rose to his full height next to the car, slammed the door shut, and began walking toward us. The man was about six-foot-three, maybe twenty-eight years old, and two hundred-thirty to two hundred-forty pounds.

Matt was no longer getting out of the car.

Then the passenger side door of the Camaro opened. The car rocked the other way on its poor shock absorbers, and an even larger man got out of that side.

"Holy shit." gasped Matt.

The second man slammed the car's passenger door shut with a *bam* and moved toward us. My guess is that they had pulled over to the side of the road to take a piss when we pulled up. I was at work, and decided to do my job.

Acting as matter-of-factly as possible, I got out of the car and walked forward to meet them. I would simply explain the situation and instruct them to not park there.

Matt did not get out of the car. He quickly closed the door on his side of the car and locked it. I closed the driver's door, and no sooner had I done so than Matt reached over and locked my door, too.

I pretended not to notice.

I walked toward the front of my car, and I met face-to-face with the two weightlifters.

"What the f--- do you want?" said the driver.

As they leaned toward me, the walkie-talkie in my pocket picked up a nearby broadcast. I was hoping it would be a Metroparks ranger indicating that he was approaching the zoo. Instead, I heard a frantic, scared voice begin a plea for help. "Two-five-two to Headquarters. Two-five-two to Headquarters. Come in ranger Headquarters…"

The two musclemen were glaring at me, and I was simply trying to act as if it were business as usual. Matt's voice on the walkie-talkie was about to beg and plead for our lives. Why bother? The nearest ranger was probably forty minutes away, and we were about to have the living crap beat out of us.

I didn't want these big men to hear Matt shrieking like a scared child, so I casually reached up with my left forefinger and thumb and turned off my walkie-talkie with a light clicking sound. I was now completely within the world of theatrics and the performing arts. I looked back at Matt who was holding the microphone of his police radio in his right hand. I couldn't hear him, but I could read his lips as he said, "We are unarmed. We are unarmed." I knew no help would be coming.

A phrase from Isaac Asimov's *The Wellsprings of Life* slowly moved sideways through my conscious mind. (It pays to be well-read.) It was something like this: "In nature, over eighty percent of all animal confrontations are decided by a bluff, with the bluffing animal victorious in eighty percent of the instances.

These two men's faces were twenty inches from mine and towered over me. I believed that they were now anticipating the slow destruction of my five-foot-eleven frame, but I held my ground.

I think the walkie-talkie sounds and my turning it off had accomplished something. I was driving a plain, old station wagon, with my official zoo shirt buried under a ragged jacket. The noise from the walkie-talkie had been the only aspect that might have contributed to the illusion that I was some sort of undercover law enforcement officer.

"Hey, guys, the zoo's closed. It's my job to tell you we don't permit parking on zoo property except during zoo hours, which is 9 to 5 every day. So I'll back up my vehicle and you two can be on your way."

The *smaller* of the two men leaned in closer to me so that his nose was two inches from mine. "Listen, here you f---ing asshole, we're going park anywhere we want and you are in serious shit right now."

I rolled my eyes, trying to look incredibly bored. I think I was more surprised than they to hear the words that came out of my mouth.

I grimaced and said, "Do you know what pisses me off?"

My question must have taken him by surprise because he seemed to go off his tough-guy script. "What?" he asked.

"Paperwork."

The man in front of me squinted and tilted his head slightly.

"I hate paperwork. I'm a pretty easy-going guy, but we got this asshole downtown and he has a rule that every time I draw my weapon I have to fill out paperwork, and I hate paperwork."

After that, I just tried to match the intensity of his stare with all the bluffing I could muster. I had to act like the only thought running through my brain was, *I'm going to blast your damn brains all over this road in about two more seconds.* He didn't flinch. He didn't blink. We just continued our stare down. Of course, all I had in my pocket was forty-three cents and my house key. No one moved.

"Let's get out of here," said the other man.

The aggressor broke eye contact, stomped over to a nearby tall tree, unzipped his fly, and took a leak. He must've really had to go because it sounded like a bathtub filling.

But he didn't attack, and they both got back in their car. I can still see them peeling off ten yards of black turf as they headed toward Fulton Parkway.

Matt and I never again bothered anyone who was merely parking on zoo property and had no intent on coming into the grounds.

CHAPTER TWENTY-ONE

Most of the memorable stories involve interactions with other people and I'm afraid it gives a rather skewed idea about how my time was spent. Mostly, I was alone among a menagerie of spottily lighted trees, animals, buildings, and shadows. There were times when all that played tricks inside my head, and I confess that if I had not been getting enough sleep during the day or enough sunlight, I could get a little paranoid. Listening to the radio didn't always help. One night, for instance, I was listening to the 3:00 a.m. rebroadcast of the Larry King Show on WGAR 1220 when his special guest was Frank Spiering, author of *Prince Jack: the True Story of Jack the Ripper.* The over-the-air descriptions of the killings and mutilations made the night seem treacherous. Especially bad was having to go into the dark buildings. I about died in the dim darkness of the Cat and Ape Building. There in the basement, out of the black shadows, came a steady voice. "Hello," somebody said.

I was certain of what I heard, but could not make out any sounds of human activity. "Hello." I was challenged again.

"Who's there?" I asked into the deep recesses of the cellar. I'm sure that the parrot who greeted me meant no harm, but it was not the time or the place. That sort of scare sticks in my memory, but never found its way into my nightly written report.

I should tell one other bit of news in terms of collaring thugs. During my rounds I found another rat-infested area in a remote corner of the zoo. It was tucked under the Fulton Road Bridge in the place where, years earlier, Whitey had his garage for working on the tour trains. That building had been torn down and the area became sort of a manure/mulch heap that was eventually discovered by the local rat scourge.

I had shown the area to Tim. He was the resident expert on trapping, and this rodent population had become settled in their new digs that came complete with catering provided. We were walking back when Tim suddenly whispered, "Shhh. There's somebody there," and he nodded toward the brush alongside the polar bears.

We stood there for a long time when I heard a twig crunch. Someone or several someones were moving our way.

"There's two of them," Tim whispered. (Maybe he was Davy Crockett reincarnated.) "There's two of them, about four feet apart. They're not very big. There's not a lot of weight to them."

I knew who they were; they were the punks who aggravated John. They were inside the zoo, but I knew where they were headed. They'd eventually be coming back toward their usual exit. They'd climb out through the hole in the chain link up behind Bears.

We picked up our pace and headed to block their exit. I ditched my clock and my Crosman in the brush on top of the concrete wall and left them there as we moved quickly and as silently as possible up toward the top of the ridge.

We sat in silence for a long time as we waited behind tree trunks in the darkness.

"Here they come," said Tim, when they were still a long ways off.

They were both clueless and still triumphing in their night's pranks. "Did you see that?" one of them chortled. "That was so cool!"

Then we lowered the boom. I had one by the shirt, and Tim had the other.

I pulled my captive's face right up against mine and yelled, "WHAT DO YOU THINK YOU'RE DOING IN HERE? WHO DO YOU THINK YOU ARE?"

Tim wasn't yelling, so I don't know what he said to his.

"YOU'RE NEVER COMING INTO MY ZOO AGAIN, ARE YOU?"

"YOU'RE NEVER COMING IN HERE AGAIN AS LONG AS YOU LIVE, ARE YOU?"

""IF YOU EVER COME IN HERE AGAIN, I'M GOING TO KILL YOUR DADDY! DO YOU UNDERSTAND ME?"

"I'M GOING TO KILL YOUR DADDY BECAUSE I DON'T KILL PUNKS! DO YOU UNDERSTAND ME!!!"

After a lot of *Yes, sirs*, the kid was bawling like the brat he was.

When I let him go, he fell to the ground.

"GET OUT OF HERE AND DON'T EVER COME BACK! EVER!"

I can still see that kid, scurrying in the blue-gray moonlight on the shiny piece of worn dirt under that fence, hustling on all fours on his belly like a lizard. The other kid crawled out behind him. They had to get right down into the dirt on their stomachs to fit through, but they were moving fast.

Actually, I wasn't angry; the whole thing was funny. I wanted to scare the crap out of these kids, and that's what happened.

The incident was never reported; every red-blooded American boy has done things like that, but that was the last time anyone heard or saw those two punks in the zoo.

CHAPTER TWENTY-TWO

The junior rangers were a real source of frustration. While they were meant to supply a life saving function, my life in particular, they did not serve much practical use. It's true that Matt was a player in helping mitigate the rodent problems, but I suspected that it mostly fed a sadistic streak and no great love of the zoo. Still, it was true that our little walkie-talkies (actually handheld VHF radios) had limited range down in our valley, and we needed the relay station of the junior ranger near a telephone.

One night, I lost my final ounce of confidence in the position and the people who were paid to occupy it. I had been on my rounds when trouble on the Fulton Parkway spilled over into the zoo. A distressed woman yelled for help. It appeared that she was being actively pursued by a man when she came onto zoo property. I radioed Norm, the junior ranger on duty, and told him to call an emergency into the local precinct. I went to the woman and explained that I could give her protection as long as she stayed on zoo property. I offered her a chance to come into the park to use the phone. She was clearly distraught, but I didn't hear or see any police cars in the area. I radioed Norm again, and he affirmed my message. The Cleveland Police had been alerted. The woman tried to get back across the street, but as she left the park, the man who had been stalking her was after her again. I followed, and doing so, stepped over the line of my jurisdiction. I was now a citizen in action. I caught up with the guy and tackled him to the ground. We fought for a moment, and the woman was yelling at me to let him go. I stayed between them; after all, the cops would arrive soon. It was then that the truth came pouring out. There was an accusation of cheating and counter-accusations. They were married, and in the end went home together to work it out. I had been sucked into a domestic dispute, and nearly injured a guy while holding him off until the police got there.

The police never arrived.

I headed back to the ranger office and found Norm and a girl named Linda in the midst of a half-naked wrestling match. They quickly readjusted the extensive wardrobe malfunctions, and introductions were made. I told the woman that she was in the park illegally and had to leave. Norm could not offer much of an argument in his defense, but he did acknowledge calling the police precinct. I specifically asked what number he had called.

Later, I checked out his story. Norm had lied about calling the cops. The dispatcher had no record of a disturbance or a call for help. That was it. Sich had started me out with a few simple rules. One of them was to *put 'em on report*. It was a mantra that referred to keepers, animals, and anything that didn't look ordinary. At that moment, I knew it applied to junior rangers as well. I guess I was in the habit of trying to work things out myself. There was a really wacko junior ranger who had been making prank calls to Sich's wife while John was on duty. That guy I cornered and threatened. He stopped, and John never knew. Fortunately, that particular creep was soon gone anyway. (Here, I use the word *creep* in the technical sense of what he actually was.)

Tim and I also had taken care of the doorknob pissers, but that, too, was off the record. With my renegade approach to watchman duties, a rift had grown between John and me; maybe it was deeper than a rift.

The next night when I came into work, John was standing by the time clock. He had been angry at me for a long time. He hadn't spoken to me in months.

When I arrived at five minutes to midnight, he grinned broadly and said, "I hear you had some trouble last night."

"There was a little trouble outside the zoo," I said, and began to relate the story. John interrupted.

"I know all about it. So, the junior ranger is not of much use, hey? Here, come in and let's talk."

We went in and sat down in the employees' kitchen. I was happy John was speaking to me again. I didn't like the uncomfortable situation that had developed. He liked to be respected; so when I spoke to him, I showed him that.

"You were right about them, the junior rangers," I began. "I finally did what you taught me to do. I put them on report."

John beamed proudly. "Well, I hear the boy is not going to be fired immediately. They will give him one more chance. But I never would trust them to be of any use for anything."

"That's for sure," I agreed.

John rolled his head back and laughed. Then he said, "When I see a problem outside the zoo, I leave the problem alone. But, when you saw a woman in such trouble, well, you did what you had to do. I would have to come to the assistance of a woman, also."

John was suddenly talkative again, and I liked that. "So how have you been? Have you found a nice girl to date?"

"No," I said.

"You go to your same church?"

"Yes," I replied. I still attended John Knox in North Olmsted, the church I had grown up in.

"Well," said John, "You will never find nice girl in this city except for accidentally. They are no good mostly, and you won't find a nice girl in disco-bars. Your church is good. It is good you have church from childhood, church of your parents. But my advice is go different church Sundays until you see good girl you like, singing in choir or teacher in church. After time, you bring her to your church. But go to other churches to meet one. I have told you, when you are old man, you need someone calling you Poppa."

We talked some more, sitting at the table.

"Hey, I don't get prank phone calls at my house anymore," I said introducing another topic. "I haven't got any for a long time. How about you?"

"Naw. Not anymore. They stopped since for long time. They were just boys. They probably sent to jail for something else." He laughed, "My wife is much happy. We have no calls for a long, long time, so that is good. I was not too worried, but my wife alone was afraid. Your calls stopped?"

"The prank calls stopped a long time ago. I think you are right. It was just high school boys who call people. They pick a number out of the phone book. I don't think the person knows who I am. I just hang up right away, you know?"

"Yes, that is the best, but it is hard time to tell my wife that. 'Just hang up the phone.' I tell her that. But she was very afraid when I was not home and they call her."

As we continued talking, John told me the construction of a new Cat and Ape Building was on schedule.

"Over three million dollars, it cost," he said. "It won't be long before the old building is knocked down, and we will be done with that."

"Maybe they'll keep it as a museum."

"No," he said. "She will be taken down. Too old. Too dangerous. I lowered down flag on the flagpole each night for twenty-eight years. I wonder where they are to put new flagpole?"

"Maybe they won't have a flagpole, since no one is proud of the flag in America anymore."

"Maybe you are right," said John.

People mocked patriotism and America quite a bit in the late 1970s. Jobs were scarce, factories were closing down, and there was double digit inflation. The Iranians could take hostages with no problem, and the burning of U.S. flags was popular at home and abroad.

Sitting at the table in the Commissary kitchen, John and I talked about different things, just like we used to. John talked about his daughter and the new job she had been fortunate to find. He talked about his lawn and his yard work. I told him that I wish I had a house and a lawn. He said that he didn't have a single dandelion in his yard, not one. The whole time, John was grinning in a knowing way, looking at me with a new sense of admiration. Whether it was from Joe Chery or a full-time ranger, I got the distinct idea that John had heard a definitely over-aggrandized version of the events of the night before.

Finally, he said, "Well, I go. My wife has the dinner for me, and I am already late."

John got up and walked out of the kitchen. As always he was dressed in the full zoo watchman's uniform, the zoo pants and the olive-colored shirt, with Metroparks patches and insignias all over it. He had key rings rattling all over his belt. I got up and followed him out. John walked to the time clock and punched out.

"I will see you tomorrow," I said.

He waved back over his shoulder and said, "Okay."

Then he left the building. It was about twenty minutes after midnight. Always fastidiously punctual, John had purposely punched out twenty minutes late. I took that to be a gesture of friendship and reconciliation. It was his way of saying that being precisely on time was perhaps not so important after all. It was not so important compared to the importance of people.

CHAPTER TWENTY-THREE

Maybe it was the talk with John, but I decided that I needed to buy a house and settle down. For that, I'd need about $10,000 for a down payment, and I'd be able to save much faster if I took a day job. I figured it would be tough, but I could raise the money in ten months if I buckled down.

The economy was pretty bad in the late seventies and the country was losing a lot of manufacturing as jobs were shipped abroad. Interest rates were high, and families were going under. On Wednesday night at church, we'd hear of people who had lost their jobs and security.

I had a job, but lending was tight and the banks were not willing to give me any sort of mortgage or even a car loan. Because of this, I drove around in old cars. Still, I was one of the very lucky ones. I had decent pay and good benefits at the zoo, thanks to the Teamsters.

In the summer of 1978, I took a full-time job in the daytime at a greenhouse called Green Circle Growers, located near Strongsville. Since it was an agricultural job, I was paid less than minimum wage, but at least I didn't have to change clothes and could come directly from the zoo.

I worked in the dirt barn, operating a big machine that mixed potting soil. I carried heavy nine cubic yard bales of wet peat moss up a ladder and dumped them in a big hopper of a machine. I was the only one who spoke English in the dirt barn, and was making about two dollars an hour. I worked like a dog with two guys named Jorge and Pepi. It was hard physical work.

One day, I hit on another plan. Cleveland was the "birthplace" and home of the cartoon strip Ziggy. When I was a driver in 1968, Linda Stojkov told me that at the American Greetings, Ziggy creator Tom Wilson had a shoebox with a slot in it taped to the door of his office. If someone had an idea for a daily cartoon panel or a Sunday feature, it could be dropped into the box. If Tom Wilson used it, he paid ten dollars. For a Sunday idea, he paid fifteen.

I was working eighty hours a week, but I sat down one evening and sketched out about twenty daily panel gags and two Sunday comic strip scripts. They were primitive. Like Ziggy had a new parrot and the tag on the cage said, *Guaranteed Talker*, but the parrot was speaking in Chinese characters. In another one Ziggy was standing helplessly with his vacuum cleaner and all his wall-to-wall carpeting had been sucked into the sweeper. In another one, Ziggy was on a ship and on the side of the ship's deck was a door. It said, *Men's room*. And the door simply opened out over the ocean. (There were lots more. I sill have my original drawings.) I drew the panels out, with crude drawings of Ziggy and his dog Fuzz. I made photocopies of all the cartoons, and mailed them to *Tom Wilson and Ziggy*, *c/o American Greetings*. I got the address out of the phone book.

The next chance I had, I wrote ideas for Hallmark greeting cards. It took me all day Saturday to do it. I was pretty excited about it when I mailed them off. The next day, I wrote and sketched twenty-eight greeting cards and mailed them out. I'd sent fifty-six greeting cards, which I had done in about twelve hours.

A week later, I received a check for five dollars. Only one of my card ideas had been accepted, and I gave up on the idea of being a writer of sappy greeting cards. I continued to wear myself out working at the zoo at night and in the greenhouse in the daytime. Eventually, I switched greenhouses and went to work for Schuster's Greenhouse on Columbia Road in Olmsted Falls. It was ten acres under glass, and again, most of the other workers were Hispanic. Schuster's Greenhouse paid a nickel more an hour.

Weeks passed and I continued to burn the candle at both ends. Then one Saturday morning after coming back from the zoo, I picked up the *Plain Dealer* and looked on the comic page. One of my Ziggys was in the paper. They had used one of my jokes, but never even communicated with me. They just used the idea, including the staging of my artwork. When I got home, there was a letter in my mailbox. It was handwritten and from Tom Wilson, himself (I still have it). With the letter was a check for $275. That was how I learned that Tom now paid twenty-five dollars for a daily idea and $35 for a Sunday. I had made two hundred and seventy-five dollars in about four hours sketching out little comic panels and jokes.

Immediately I set to writing a lot more cartoon jokes and Sunday ideas for Ziggy. This time a letter came back in two days with a check for $375. The third check I got from Tom was for $575. That was a lot of money in 1978, and I was doing something I loved.

Within about six months, between the zoo, the greenhouses, and contributing Ziggy ideas, I had saved $8,000. I walked around the zoo in the dark for $6.05 an hour doing not much. Then I worked like a dog at the greenhouse for the agricultural rate of $2.05 an hour. Then I would drag myself home and write cartoons and make $25 or $35 on a single thought. I continued to contribute Ziggy ideas to Tom Wilson for ten more years. He was a great man and a fantastic talent. He also became a good friend and mentor.

(I don't believe Tom Wilson would have a problem with my telling you this. In his autobiography he wrote, "A lot of people ask me if I do Ziggy all by myself. The fact is that I do, but I've been fortunate over the years to have many good friends who have contributed ideas to the strip from time to time." I was one of those friends.)

Working my two fulltime jobs was taking a toll, but I was determined to reach $10,000 by the end of ten months, then I could quit the back-breaking laborer's job at Schuster's. Fate smiled on me yet again. A keeper's job came open in the Lions, Tigers, and Bears. I could have signed up for that job but I didn't even consider it. That was Tim Pappas's dream job. Tim had kept his word and stuck out being a night watchman for one year. It was now winter. He had passed up other keeper's jobs so that he would keep his promise, but also because he was waiting for the Bear job to come open.

"If you want that job, you can take it," Tim reminded me. "You have seniority."

"Naw, I don't want it. The lions, tigers, and bears scare the hell out of me. That's your job."

One morning at the time clock Don Kuenzer broke the news to me that Tim had taken the position. "Good," I said. "He'll be great at that."

"We'll find another relief watchman right away," he assured me.

I hesitated a moment, and then asked, "Remember last year when Sich and I worked seven days a week for all those months? We just took the overtime for a long time."

"I remember."

"Well, from my point of view, it would be okay to do that for awhile. I don't know about John, but I wouldn't mind working seven nights a week. I'm saving to buy a house, and I could use the overtime."

"To tell you the truth," said Don, "the zoo likes that. Like I said, it's actually cheaper to pay you and John time-and-a-half than to hire a whole new person with benefits."

It turned out Sich was happy about it, too, and we went back to working without a day off. We worked seven nights a week for several months. That meant I was working an extra sixteen hours a week at time-and-a-half. The math was simple. The extra money I was making at the zoo for sixteen hours was better than my eighty-four hours, and I was back to one job, but not quite. I kept up my relationship with Ziggy.

At the end of ten months, I had over $11,000, and was able to buy a pretty little brick house on West 230th Street, close to the neighborhood where I had grown up.

CHAPTER TWENTY-FOUR

Here's a surprise. junior rangers Matt and Norm were fired for stealing a TV. One of them stole the set from the rangers' Office. Matt said Norm stole it. Norm said Matt stole it. So the Park System, with the wisdom of Solomon, fired both of them. Not only that, they completely eliminated the position of junior ranger entirely.

To replace the *junior* rangers, the Metroparks assigned *real* rangers in the park until 4:00 a.m. That was good for me in the sense that I actually had someone to call if the need arose. More than that, the rangers tended to congregate and there were sometimes two, three or even four in the little office with pizzas. They also procured another TV, and I felt a lot safer. Though they were watching John Belushi's Samurai comedy routine on *Saturday Night Live*, they could come save my life during the commercials. That actually happened once.

I stuck my head in the office and said, "Hey, guys. There's some hell-raising going on outside the fence by Parking Lot Number 2. There's a lot of vans there and I think I heard gunshots." At that time there were three rangers in the room, and they didn't take their eyes off the TV. It was Belushi doing the Samurai. Belushi brought the sword down through a countertop. I saw that part.

"We'll be down when the musical guest is on." They never came down.

With that one exception, the rangers were all business. Every full-time ranger I ever met at night was a great guy. I joke about them some, but they were professionals.

One night I got a call over the radio just as I was punching in. They were actually standing only about eighteen feet away at the time. They wanted to meet me before I started my rounds.

When I went into their office, they were all busy typing reports and tending to proper business. Theoretically, there should have only been one ranger there at that time, but apparently they were catching up on paperwork and emptying pizza boxes at the same time. Compared to their military-style neatness, I was dressed like a slob, draped in the slight aroma of manure.

"We wanted to meet you," said one of them. "If you ever need us, just give us a shout. We met the other watchman, on the shift before you."

"The older gentleman? How did that go?" I said with a slight smile.

"He was fine," one said, "but he said that we were just *okay*, not up to Pinkerton quality." With that, the three men laughed.

"He's been here twenty-eight years or so," I began. "Did he pretend to have a foreign accent? He does that to play with people's heads."

The rangers looked at each other, a bit dumbfounded.

"I'm kidding," I said. "He really is from the Old Country."

"So you're the one playing with our heads," said one of them, and everyone laughed again. The rangers all liked each other and had a strong camaraderie. I never heard one swear or say anything disrespectful about anyone. They never told dirty jokes or trashed their bosses. There was also a lot of diversity among their ranks. The only one that I remember by name, however, was a black officer named Otis.

"Actually," I said, "that other watchman is a good guy to shoot rats with when your shift begins. He knows the best spots and believe me, it's better to have him with you when you shoot rats."

"I've heard there were places to shoot rats here," said a younger fellow, "but I didn't want to just go down and start shooting."

"Yeah," I said. "I don't think anyone around here would want to hear you say, 'Wow, that was a big rat I just shot. I didn't know they had horns.'" We all laughed again, and talked awhile about the effectiveness, or lack of effectiveness, of the *Juniors*. Finally, they got to the point of the visit.

"What we really need to know," asked the ranger, "is what's safe and what's not safe down in the zoo."

"If you want to avoid dangerous animals, don't go into any buildings. The lions and bears and hippos and stuff that's dangerous are all in the buildings. In fact, if you see a lion outside, shoot it. They're not supposed to be loose at night. Please shoot it, or it will eat me." Again, the room erupted in laughter.

Outside it was snowing lightly when another patrol car drove up. When the door opened another ranger entered, I don't recall his name, but all the others knew him. For the sake of the story, I'll call him Tom. He was fifty-ish, and clearly well liked by the others. He went right to work with some papers he was carrying. "I came over here because I didn't want to work on these reports in the car," he explained.

I was on my way out the door when Tom told about his most recent adventure. It caught my attention because the place where it happened was close to my boyhood home.

"I was down patrolling in the Rocky River Reservation, near Shepherd's Hill Lane," he began.

My friends and I used to ride our bikes to the end of Clague Road, cross over on Mastick to get to Shepherd's Hill Lane. That led down into a park that Westsiders called *The Valley*.

"I needed to use the facilities," he continued, "so I parked and walked to the pit latrine that's there. You know the one."

I knew the exact outhouse he was talking about. How could anyone forget? On a summer day, it was major stinko inside. When necessity called, however, it was a matter of hold my breath, run in, make it happen, run out, and breathe again.

"Anyway," Tom continued, "I went in there and sat down, and I put my walkie-talkie down right next to me on the... the... the board there, in case I got a call, so I could run back to the car and answer it." He acted out the motion of carefully setting the heavy walkie-talkie down on the plank next to him.

"Was there a full moon?" said one of the other guys and everyone laughed. Of course, in those outhouses, there was only a narrow section of wood between one big oval hole and another.

"I finished my business and was using the toilet paper when I bumped the radio with my elbow and it fell into the latrine right into the next hole." Again, everyone broke up laughing.

"I looked down in there with my flashlight, and I didn't even see it. Well, there was no way I was going to go fishing in that mess, so I just wrote that it's *missing for unknown reasons*. I'm going to claim that either someone took it off the seat of my vehicle or it was incorrectly inventoried as to being in my possession. Does that sound official enough?"

They offered me pizza, but I had to get going on my rounds. I liked those guys, but this wouldn't be the end of Tom's story.

The next morning I saw Tim Pappas come bouncing in. This was the first time I'd seen him since he'd become a keeper, and he told me to stop at Bears after I punched out. When I got there, he was hard at work. He'd only been a keeper two days, but he had the routine down and he worked steadily as he chatted. He had to get a meal ready for all his charges and that meant chopping meat and thawing frozen mackerel.

I had almost forgotten how invigorating daytime work was at the zoo and suddenly felt a little left out by being on the night shift. Tim had a friend with him; it was a big raccoon that he had befriended when he worked nights. It lived up around the Baboon Building, but now it was up here at Bears and following Tim wherever he went.

"As soon as I became keeper," he said, "I told the other keeper, Jackie, about the raccoon that was down in Baboons. I suggested that we bring it up here as a pet, and now he has the run of the place. He's having a blast. We don't ever lock him up."

Tim playfully wrestled with the huge raccoon, rubbing its enormous pelt of soft fur. The raccoon stood up on its hind legs and wrestled right back at him. "Now look at this," he said.

He pulled the heavy metal gate of a cage aside, and a tiger cub came leaping out and jumped up to greet Tim, who jostled the fur on the side of her face back and forth.

"This is Lucy," said Tim. "She has the run of the place a lot of the time, too."

"How is she with the raccoon?"

"They play together. They're just fine."

Lucy was around five months old and was already pretty big. She bounced away, running all over the room and Tim squirted the hose at her. Tigers love water, and Lucy attacked the water spray and *bit at the spray* just the way some dogs do when you turn a nozzle toward them. Tim was walking around his area like Dr. Dolittle or something. I figured I'd better get out of there before he let a bear loose.

"So what do you think?" asked Tim. "If you have this tiger running around with you as a juvenile, when she's full-grown, do you think that she'll still be running around loose in here? Will she be tame?"

I didn't know what to say to that, but he beat me to it. "I guess we're going to find out."

I walked outside, and he came out to say goodbye. It was a winter's day, with snow on the ground, but the sun was shining, and we were standing right in front of the wolf exhibit. I had seen their sadness so often, and I turned expecting to see it now. This was different, they seemed like they were anticipating something.

"How are you getting along with these wolves?" I asked.

"They're great, and having a blast, too." He approached them and they sat up and pranced back and forth like happy dogs. Their tails came up, practically wagging. I had never seen this before.

To my surprise, Tim reached through the bars, and lightly patted one of the wolves on the top of its head. He was remarkable with animals.

"You know they eat mice in the wild," I said.

"If I catch some, they're going to get them."

Plenty of things were changing in the zoo. There were now rangers in the park during the midnight to 4:00 shift. Tim was taking to his job in Bears like nobody's business. And there was also some bigger news. The new Cat and Ape Building at the upper level of the zoo would be opening in a matter of weeks. All the monkeys, apes, panthers, cheetahs, leopards, baboons, and the mandrill would be moved to a new facility. Timmy the lowland gorilla would be moved out of his small cage and moved to a brand new space. It was a sunny day in the winter, and the whole world felt bright.

CHAPTER TWENTY-FIVE

When I arrived the next night, I was once again summoned by the rangers. I wondered what emergency we might be in progress.

"We just were wondering," asked the one of them, "if there's a soda machine in this building?"

"There's one just down the hall in the kitchen."

"After your warning we weren't sure we should go into that part of the building. We're a little worried about the animals." I led two of them around the outside of the building. I pointed out the alligators and suggested that they avoid that place. Then, I took them into the central area and showed them Susie, the orangutan. Susie stuck her hand out, wanting to shake. (I had fallen for this once, and found out she could really squeeze and wasn't a big fan of letting go.)

"This is a serious warning," I said. "Never go near her. Don't kiss her and *do not* shake her hand."

"Huh?"

"She'll pucker up to kiss. Don't do it. After that, she'll offer to shake your hand."

"Are you kidding...?"

With a lip-smacking sound, Susie puckered up like a split cantaloupe. Her wormy lips protruded out through the bars.

"No," I said sternly, keeping my distance. "See what she does?? It probably looks tempting if you are very, very lonely, but *do not* shake her hand."

"Buddy," said Otis, "I'm never coming in here unless you're with me."

We went to the kitchen, and they bought some sodas and I took them back to their office. Now that they knew where the soda machine was, they didn't need me.

Just after midnight, Tom came back to straighten out some paperwork. He had more to tell about the walkie-talkie down-the-hole incident in *The Valley*.

"I told you guys about dropping my walkie-talkie into the latrine last night." He was not as lighthearted as he had been the night before. "I turned in a report saying that the radio was stolen, and the Captain said that didn't make any difference. You need to remember this; the regulations say you're responsible for all equipment, even if lost or stolen. So I have to replace it. Wanna guess how much it's going to cost? Just guess."

"I don't know," said Otis.

"Seven-hundred-fifty bucks!" Tom bellowed. (In 1978, that was a huge chunk of cash.) "They're going to take it out of my pay over the next two pay periods; that's my whole check for two pay periods. Anyway, I said, 'Hold it, for now, it might turn up.' Since it was lost, I had a few thoughts about where it might be. It could be stolen, or I might have just misplaced it on patrol. That's what I told him.

"I can't lose two paychecks. My wife would go out of her mind, and that's a short journey. Looks like I'm going to have to go fishing out at the Rocky River Reservation after all."

"That'll be an adventure," said Otis. Most of the guys were trying not to laugh.

"I've got my flashlight and my fishing rod's in the car. I'm thinking I can loop the line at the end of the rod, and then get the loop around the radio and reel the line tight. That is, if I can see it down there at all. I guess I'll have to dig down there until I find it. I brought along a broom handle with a garden cultivator claw taped to the end of it... Jeez, I gotta locate it first... I mean, last night when it fell down in there, I couldn't see it at all in all the mess. I'll just keep digging down in there, until it turns up..."

Pursing his lips tightly shut and trying earnestly to keep a straight face, Otis maintained a supportive and positive attitude. "Well, it's winter," he began, "probably not too many people have... you know... since last night... so it might be right on top... unless... it... sunk... I don't know, really... everything's probably pretty frozen."

Tom opened the door and a chilling wind greeted him as he made his way back to the car.

"I thought about offering to help him," said another. "I know that's what he was waiting for, but I had to think of my duty. Nope. I'm needed right here." And he popped open his soft drink.

I never did learn how the fishing trip went.

CHAPTER TWENTY-SIX

John Sich's words about finding the right girl kept haunting me, and I thought how great it would be to meet the right person. There was a very pretty young woman who worked at the Seven/Eleven on West 117th Street. It was a good place for me to stop on the way to work, and I thought that I might someday be able to strike up a conversation that might lead to a date.

We'd had some nice conversations in the past, and I liked her more and more. She was probably twenty-five and seemed both funny and hardworking. She had a great smile, and paid a lot of attention to me when I bought a shrink-wrapped egg salad sandwich and a half-pint of milk. I figured that I had a lot going for me. I had a nice little house, a pretty good job, and one day I'd get off the nightshift. I was all geared up to ask her out, and her wonderful smile gave me hope.

It was Saturday, December 23rd, 1978, at fifteen minutes to midnight, and I was heading to work. There was no one else in the store. Outside a light snow was falling. When I entered the store, she brightened up and said, "Hi."

I headed back toward the coolers and gathered what would be my lunch at 4:00 a.m. There was a carton of chocolate milk, a ham sandwich, and a Hostess apple pie. As I stepped up to the register, I noticed a stack of the Sunday *Plain Dealer*. As usual, the comic section was folded on top, and Cleveland's own Ziggy covered the upper half of the front page. It was one of my ideas; in fact, I had drawn the pencils for it. It was the one in which Ziggy meets a bearded old man and the reader knows that the man is really Santa. It was one of the best Ziggys I had worked on up to that time. Tom Wilson's artwork was fabulous. He was an artistic genius. The colors were done up in rich gold and browns, autumnal and marvelous.

I couldn't resist this unexpected opportunity to try and make a good impression. As she put the pie, sandwich, and carton of milk in a brown sack, I pointed at the Sunday strip. "I wrote this."

"What?" she said, looking confused. "What do you mean?"

"This comic strip right here. I write Ziggy jokes and sell them. This is one I wrote.."

"Wait a second," she said. "You say you wrote this, but it's almost midnight on Saturday night, and you're going to work right now? That's stupid. You would be rich if you wrote this. You wouldn't be going to work dressed the way you are. You work outside, don't you? In the middle of winter at night? You've got on a snow suit and ten shirts. And you're telling me that you did this cartoon?"

"Yeah, I get paid for each cartoon, but I still have a full-time job."

"So what do you do? What do you do for a living?"

"Well," I said, looking down at the adorable face of old Saint Nick, "I write Ziggy cartoons as a freelance writer, and I'm the night watchman at the Cleveland Zoo."

Icy is too soft a word to describe her changed expression. "I've met some bullshitters in my life, but you take the cake." That was the last time I shopped in that store.

CHAPTER TWENTY-SEVEN

January is one of the coldest months, and when the zoo is in the deep chill, outside invaders are rare. For survival, a watchman has to find warm places to hunker down while waiting to hit the next Detex station. I liked the Greenhouse. It was warm and homey.

The lobby of the Administration Building was another good place, domestic compared to a chilly barn, and the rooms felt like they still had some echoes of laughter left over from the day crowd. The place, when empty, also had a great reverberating echo, and, though I'm a terrible singer, I'd let loose with a song.

Surprising as it may seem, I also learned to love the Pachyderm Building, which became a place of refuge for me, a place of *hearth and home*. In spite of the overpowering rancid manure stench of the animal spaces, the cozy little keeper room in the Pachy was about the most *homelike* place in the zoo. There were two easy chairs, a space heater, a coffee maker, and a toaster oven. Even though cold winds blew up and down the back halls in the building, the tiny keeper room was snug. The noisy little space heater could even bring the temperature up to what I'd call toasty, and I decided to stay there as much as possible on the nights when the winter was the most discouraging. Over time, the smells I thought repulsive seemed more like the smells of nature and of life itself, which, of course, they were.

In the keeper room, I'd take off my mechanic's suit and my winter jacket, make myself a cup of instant coffee, and sit in one of the two cheap, creaky green vinyl stuffed chairs. In the adjacent area, I might hear the sounds of an elephant stirring, but mostly, the animals were quiet. I worried that suddenly Wolee would charge into the room and attack me, but he never came. And eventually, the Nile hippos ceased their discontented moaning and all was still.

When I sat quietly, the ever present rodents would start their rounds. Once a small brown mouse was sticking his nose into a pack of saltines that had been left on the table, and two others got into some Lorna Doones. I think the mouse was more surprised than I was to find that it was not alone. I left a note for the keepers. *Don't eat these cookies. Mice were in the package. -Night watchman.*

After that, I was back out in the snow. I checked in at the Ostrich Building, then went back to Pachys. Then it was time to hit the Kiddie Farm. Each time, I'd strap on my Detex and grab up my keys. After each security check, I'd return to the Pachyderm Building to warm up for the next foray.

After the Children's Farm, it was into the Chevy for a drive to my next oasis, the Greenhouse. From there, I could visit the Bird Building and Wade Hall. Overall I was in there for up to an hour. Eventually, it was time to leave the area as well. My next stop was Lions, Tigers, and Bears.

From this new central location, I could make quick runs to the Reindeer and Sitatunga Barns. The cold weather made my fear of lions, tigers, and bears seem trivial; after all, the big room where the lions and tigers were caged was warm and modern. I never saw a mouse or a rat in there. Never. Like the Commissary, it was a new area and vermin-proof as far as I could tell.

To pass the time, I had a blue racquetball, and I could stand in the center of the room and aim for the strike zone on the far wall. After awhile, I noticed that I was being watched by the tigers who were mesmerized by the bouncing ball. I bounced the ball right past their swiveling heads for ten minutes. Then I made a Detex hit in the building and returned to the same spot. The tigers were lounging on their bellies, quite content to have me amuse them.

Emboldened, I tried another game. I knelt down in front of their cage and flipped the leather strap of the watchman's clock under the bottom of the bars. It was like playing with a friendly housecat that happened to weigh eight hundred pounds. The tigers tried to trap the strap before I pulled it away. When they did, they were content to immediately release it so that the game could continue. Of all the big cats, only the Siberians seemed willing to interact.

I used these comfort zones to stage my shift and protect myself from the brutal weather outside, but no matter what the temperature, there was no cozy place to stay inside the Old Cat and Ape. To visit the areas around there, I'd stay in the car even though it got cold quickly after killing the engine. Nevertheless, the Chevy felt better than the haunted soon-to-be-demolished Ape House.

CHAPTER TWENTY-EIGHT

In an already icy, frigid winter, there was one day and night in particular that was hideously cold. It was on that night when John Sich met me as I clocked in.

"Tonight is new hit. Is big night. You hit new building, new Cats and Ape."

The three million dollar Cat and Ape Building was finished. That's what John was saying, and it came out of nowhere as far as I was concerned because I hadn't expected the construction was so close to being complete. I also couldn't imagine the animals being moved under these weather conditions. I thought they'd wait for milder temps.

"So should I hit the clock in the old building *and* the new building?" I asked for clarification.

"No, no. Old building finished for animals. All animals new building starting now."

All the animals had been moved, all the apes, monkeys, leopards, jaguars, the mandrill, and Timmy the gorilla. They had emptied not only the old Cat and Ape Building, but also the old Baboon Building.

So it was, that with no fanfare, the original zoo building of Brookside Park was closed after seventy years. I never set foot in that building again. Just like that, it was out of my life. I didn't even have to go there to raise the flag in the morning.

"Where should I go in?"

"Any door," said John grinning. "We got animals in exhibit top floor of building, ground level. You need to get to basement. Boilers in basement and there you hit clock."

John held up the watchman's key ring and singled out a brass key. "This is new master key to new building. Opens any door. Go in any door and get to basement and hit 'er."

I needed a close look at that key or I'd never find it among the dozens of others. It was a Wilson Bohannan with the same make and shape as the key that opened the park gates and the all-weather padlocks on the barns.

The new building would not be my first hit for the night. I figured it would be around 2:00 a.m. before I'd be in that part of the zoo.

Outside, a blizzard was forming, and I started my winter survival regime by keeping out of the deeper drifts. The Chevy's tires were now equipped with chains so I hoped to have the traction that I'd need to make my rounds.

The main roads had been plowed earlier in the day, but by 2:00 a.m. they were covered with a half foot of new snow. I was grateful for the noisy cascading steel-chains on the tires that kept me moving.

Finally it was time for me to make my first hit ever in the all-new Cat and Ape Building. I turned right onto the drive that led toward that building, but was stuck after going two feet. Bad idea. I put the car in reverse, and was able to back out to the main utility road. I left the car running right next to Fulton Parkway. I would walk the remaining two hundred feet through the blizzard rather than chance getting stuck.

Under foot, the pathway was treacherous and made more difficult by the bulk of the heavy Detex-Newman watchman's clock. The snow was deep here, and each step required lifting my legs straight up and down rather than moving at a normal pace. I couldn't walk in a straight line on account of drifts, some of which measured six feet. I had to finds the low paths around each drift where the snow was not deep. At times *not so deep* meant three feet, and I was snow covered up to my thighs.

In spite of the bitter cold, I was working up a sweat under all the layers of sweatshirts and coats, but there was a warm building just ahead.

Of course, that was mostly a matter of blind faith, blind because the swirling snow made me lose sight of it as I continued to walk ahead.

Finally, I burst through one final powdery drift and made it into the cover of the west side of the building. My legs felt like lead as I stomped as much snow off myself as possible. Thankfully, there was an overhang of roof at the big glass doors of the main entrance, and pavement that was nearly clear of snow. I made it into this darkened place, that was sheltered from the wind, and caught my breath for a few moments. The actual temperature that night was measured at around minus twenty degrees Fahrenheit with wind gusts at twenty miles an hour which put the wind chill at minus forty-eight.

I pulled off my gloves and fumbled to find the new keys. I remember peering through the glass doors and wondering what was in there. It was completely dark inside. I didn't know the layout, but would be soon walking around in the dark.

My cold fingers were nearly useless. I found the shiny new key and slipped it into the tumblers of the door lock. I twisted the key clockwise, then counterclockwise, but it wasn't turning the lock. I didn't dare take a chance at breaking the key. Thinking the tumblers might be frozen, I blew breath after breath into the cold metal before inserting the key again. I wasn't about to use a *flick of the Bic* on a pristine lock. I gave up on that entrance and looked for another door.

I cleaned off my frozen glasses as best I could and used the sheltered doorway to get ready to set out again. I moved clockwise along the outer wall of the big building, keeping my head down as I went. I came upon another entrance, but this one was exposed to the storm, and I had no luck with the lock. I knew I was using the right key, but it just wouldn't open the doors, and figured that John must have gotten in before the tumblers all froze.

I continued around the building. The north side was bearing the brunt of the weather, and I was staggering through big drifts. I was now away from the public entrances, and found a small landing with an access door. The key fit the lock, but just as before, the door would not open. A smarter guy might have given up, but I continued around to the back and slid down a steep hillside. This area was well-lit, and I saw an entrance lower down which must have opened directly into the basement. I sledded down the steep slope on my butt. When I got to the bottom, I was covered in white.

The door was all-metal and, thankfully, the key turned easily in the lock. I pulled the door open, plowing against the five inches of snow in front of it. I slipped in as a rush of warm air and mechanical sounds greeted me. I stomped my feet, and tried to get a sense of direction. I didn't have the first idea where I was or where I needed to go, and had no feeling in my face or fingers.

I felt around along the wall next to me to the right of the door and found a panel of light switches and flicked two switches. A single light bulb came on overhead and to my right. Of course, with the sudden temperature swing, my glasses fogged completely, and I was dripping as I began to thaw.

There were no animal smells to give anything away. Everything smelled like fresh paint and concrete. I was in the basement, however, and John had said the Detex station was next to the boilers. Theoretically I was in the right place. I just had to find the boilers, which were nowhere in sight. I began exploring. It would have been good to have a flashlight, but I didn't.

Between the sweat and the snow melt, I felt like I weighed three hundred pounds. I was already dreading the fact that when I went back out into the blizzard, I'd freeze up like a Popsicle.

Up ahead, I could dimly see that the wall ended and that the chamber I was in would turn to the left, in a L-shape. I walked around ten more feet where I entered an area that seemed like a rain forest. Overhead, the new plumbing was throwing off condensation, and I was adding *raindrops* to my already soggy self. I moved out of the better light to avoid the dripping. The farther I walked into the basement, the darker it became. The single light bulb was now sixty feet behind me, and hidden by struts in the ceiling.

In the far corner of the basement, I finally caught a glimpse of the building's massive hot water boilers. To me, they looked splendid in their mint-fresh coat of light brown paint. Each had a small maintenance lamp on top of them, and that was the only light in the large chamber. All was quiet. I was utterly alone deep in the bottom of a brand-new building at 2:30 in the morning.

Suddenly, *BWAM!*

I jumped out of my skin. Just behind me there had been a bone-rattling crash of monstrous flesh slamming into a wall of vibrating metal. The noise hit me like a blow to the chest that knocked the wind out of me. Exploding from behind me was a huge sound, right up against my back, inches away. I felt air move. It all happened in an instant, and I leapt into the air and away from the noise, or at least that's what I thought.

The sound echoed, but I had misjudged its direction and turned the wrong way. A heavy hand grabbed at me. Again, I launched myself away. Something struck my left shoulder with a hard, glancing blow. I twisted my body away from the grasping hand. I dropped my left shoulder down by moving my hips to my right. My attacker was lost his grip.

I was now about ten feet away from that grip. I had my watchman's clock, but had yet to see my assailant. I gripped the straps of the clock as tightly as possible in my fist and swung the clock until it was orbiting around me.

In the dim light, I could now make out something that I had missed earlier. About twelve feet away were the white-silver bars of aluminum. It was a cage. Though as new as the building itself, the bars were already bent and distorted. They were spaced about eight inches apart, and I knew my attacker. It was Timmy, the five hundred pound western lowland silverback gorilla, and he was quiet again.

It was an animal cage, right in the center of the basement, strange and out of place. I had walked within two feet of the front of that cage, just at Timmy's fingertips. The fact is that I would have walked even closer to it, if the cold drops of water from the ceiling hadn't made me change my route as I turned around the corner. I slowed the swing of my clock and pulled it back to my side.

This all had happened quckly, and I was trying to process the situation. Timmy was still in his cage, and nothing was loose in the basement. I was okay. Outside were the still howling blizzard winds, and the splattering of the new plumbing sounded suddenly comforting.

My throat was dry as I walked toward the new boilers. They were in the back corner of the basement. Next to them, the Detex station box was bolted to the pristine cinderblock wall. I took the key out of the box. Pulling the key to the full length of its stainless steel chain, I inserted it into the L-shaped slot on the clock and twisted the key clockwise a quarter turn to make the hit. I had encoded onto a paper disk the exact moment I was there. I had made it to that moment alive.

Timmy had scared the living wits out of me. Of course, that was his goal and he succeeded. He just loved to scare people to death, whenever he could. Had he tried to grab me? Or did he simply mean to say, *Tag. You're it?*

I had to walk past him on the way out. I looked into the cage as I passed, but saw nothing. Just as I reached the door and pushed it open, there was another crash behind me. Once more, the big ape had run with all his speed and might and slammed into the bars of his new cage. He was sending me a message. *I'm here, and you are terrified of me.* He was right.

Sweaty and tired, I froze my butt off making it back to the car in the sub-zero blizzard. Within two minutes from the time I made it back to the car, I was standing naked in a shower in the Commissary Building. There were clean towels straight from the linen service, and they smelled great. I took a long, hot shower for about an hour. It was the only time I ever took a shower as night watchman. I even sat down on the floor in the shower and just let the steamy water pelt me, forever.

There were two Detex stations in the building. So every fifteen minutes or so, I just put a towel around myself and ran up and down the halls dripping wet to make my hits. Then I went back to the shower. I could have stayed in there for hours, but a single hour would have to do. I was sure that no one else would be out on a night like this. Besides, I was just glad they didn't come in the next morning and find me ripped to pieces by a gorilla.

The next morning I saw Dick Darenzo seated in the lobby. He was the old Pinkerton watchman, who had become a keeper over in Apes.

"Well," I said, "I hit the clock in the new building last night for the first time. Twice actually."

"Wha'd ya think of that?"

"I only went into the basement, but I saw your friend Timmy down there. Why is he there? I don't get it. Why isn't he in an exhibit?"

"That's just his night cell," he explained. "He's up in the exhibit during the day, and we lower him down there into the basement at night. The cage you saw him in goes up and down like an elevator. We put him in up top and lower the whole thing. It's actually a leopard cage."

"The bars aren't very heavy. Do you think he'll ever bust out of there?"

Dick laughed, "We'll find out."

The other people nearby also laughed. He was just joking. It was a leopard cage, but they expected that it would hold Timmy. I wasn't so sure.

Dick said, "But if it doesn't hold him, the only people who go down there are the watchmen."

Boy, this guy was hilarious. Everybody laughed again. "If we bring Timmy up in the morning and he's wearing a watchman's shirt, we'll know he got out."

The room rocked with laughter. Dick was holding court now, and everyone was amused. I was his straight man.

"So last night was the first night Timmy was ever in that cage," I said. "That means the cage is brand new, right?"

"Yeah," said Dick as if agreeing to the obvious. He took a drag off a cigarette.

"Well," I said, "Last night by two o'clock, Timmy had bent out most of the bars in the cage. The front of the cage is bent out of shape. I mean, he has some of those aluminum bars hammered out about three inches."

"Well, that's Timmy. He'll enjoy testing the bars. Aluminum's pretty ductile. It will be interesting to see just how far he can bend them. Like I said, the cage is really designed for smaller cats."

A ninety pound leopard was a small cat to those guys. A lion or tiger was big.

From then on, I had to fear that twice a night I went into a basement where a five hundred pound gorilla was *testing* the bendable bars, just to see if they would hold his considerable strength. Before long Timmy had the whole front of the cage bent out like a contact lens. Whenever I was down there, Timmy repeatedly slammed his big shoulder into the bars, just to remind me how puny I was and how mighty he was.

As watchman, I never went in any door except that back door when I entered the New Ape Building. John was right that the key opened any door. Even though locks were just frozen on the first night, I kept going in the back door.

One morning as I walked to the time clock, Dick from Apes came over to speak with me. I was still carrying my baseball bat, and I saw that he had a twinkle of mischief in his eyes. Knowing full well where I had just been, he asked where I came from.

"I just hit the station in the New Ape."

He nodded toward my dark-blue Easton and asked, "What's the bat for?"

"I carry it in case there's a chimp loose or something."

"If there's ever a chimp loose in that building, the bat won't do you any good." A lot of men laughed knowingly. "That chimp would grab that bat out of your hands before you can blink. You'll have no chance. An eighty pound chimp will rip a bat out of the hands of the strongest man on the earth."

He took a long drag from his Chesterfield. Then he said, "On the other hand, the chimp will be glad that you brought him a bat so that he'd have something to beat you to death with." The keepers erupted in laughter.

After that, I didn't carry the bat into the New Ape building.

I expected kidding from the keepers. What I had not expected was that John Sich sent me into the new building without a word of warning. Timmy nearly ripped my head off, and John never mentioned anything about the gorilla being there. Maybe he didn't know. After all, I found Timmy by going through the back door into the basement. John always went in through the public entrance. From there, he went down some stairs to check the boilers and hit the station. I started to worry that one day he might make a misstep and walk around the corner past the bars of Timmy's cage the way I had.

One night, when John was punching out and I was punching in, I asked straight out, "Are you careful when you go into the basement of the new building? You don't walk around down there, do you?"

"I go down stepses, hit 'er, and come up stepses. That's it," he answered.

"Good," I said. "You shouldn't walk around down there. Just do what you've been doing. It's dangerous in that basement. Just hit 'er and get out."

"I do," said John. "Why do you say this?"

"Well, I just think that if you spend any time down there, it could... anger the gorilla. He might try to grab you or... smash the bars. It's best to not explore down in there. Just get in and get out."

John looked at me like I was speaking a language he didn't understand. "Gorilla? What gorilla are you talking about?"

"I probably shouldn't have said anything," I said. "But I think it's smart that you just go in and get right out."

We had different ways of doing our jobs, and he didn't need my advice. I didn't try to give John any more advice after that. As things worked out, I really didn't have to worry about Timmy for long. I wouldn't be a night watchman much longer.

CHAPTER TWENTY-NINE

The winter had been brutal, but I now had a home of my own. I owned the mortgage of a little brick house on West 230th just off Clifford Road. At that time I also made the final payment on the little Capri I was driving. In accordance with Murphy's Law, the car immediately broke down and had to be taken to the shop for a long period of rehab. The result was that I had no car for quite some time.

It was spring, and so my fall-back position was a Huffy Strider ten-speed bike.

The distance from my house to the zoo was around eleven miles, and, with a little effort, I could make the trip in twenty-five minutes. Driving in my car actually had taken longer, about thirty-five minutes. (The difference was that I didn't stop at traffic lights.)

During that bike riding period there was one particular night that I remember as being normal and uneventful, at least on the surface. There had been no incidents when I made rounds in the station wagon. The only thing I recalled about that night seemed pretty inconsequential. I saw a car parked outside the zoo near the Children's Farm. It was on the lawn across Brookside Park Drive. When I walked along the fence, I saw the license plate and made a note for my nightly report. The car, a Pontiac Bonneville, was parked at a cockeyed angle across the road so I was looking at the rear bumper.

In the morning, at the end of my shift, I filed my report and rode my bike home. After puttering around the yard for awhile, I went to bed.

About 2:00 p.m. my phone rang. It was one of the rangers calling. He asked if I could come down to the office immediately. Of course that meant another bike ride, and I was in their office in about forty-five minutes. Their were several officers in the room, and all seemed busy preparing weapons. Some had donned bulletproof vests. The mood was different; there was neither joking nor pizza. No one seemed very friendly as I walked in.

The detective who interviewed me was standing behind the desk, and his first order of business was to make sure who I was, and that I had been the watchman on duty the night before.

"Adam, there was an incident here in the zoo last night. As near as we can determine, this incident occurred around 3 a.m." (I was glad he had called me by my first name. That made me believe that I wasn't in some sort of trouble myself.)

"Someone entered the zoo last night, and it was during your shift." He looked at a report on his desk, probably to make sure of the name of an animal. "Around 3 a.m. last night, as nearly as we can determine in regards to the time, someone entered the zoo, probably from the Brookside Drive direction. Once on the zoo grounds, this individual climbed over the concrete barrier and dropped to the ground inside the exhibit of the barasingha deer. This individual used a high-power crossbow to kill a large male deer with two or three arrows, with at least one shot piercing the heart and one shot in the animal's neck. Afterward, he proceeded to butcher the animal near the fence on the north end of the enclosure. Using a hunter's knife which had a blade of approximately four inches in length, over a period of around one-half hour, he removed approximately sixty pounds of meat from the carcass, packing it into bags and then exited the area, while dragging the bags. He left the zoo's grounds by climbing over the fence leading to Brookside Drive. We were able to follow a trail of blood drops and human footsteps leading out of the zoo, and presumably he gained entry along a similar path."

I was in shock, as he continued. "I want you to come with me down to the zoo."

Well, we drove down to where the barasingha deer were housed. The barasingha is a large deer. I saw several of them in the very back of the enclosure, but the biggest buck with the largest rack of antlers was not there. That individual had been the outstanding feature of the exhibit for years, even before I started driving tour trains. Obviously, the area had been cleaned up before the zoo opened to the public.

"Now, Adam," said the detective with great seriousness, "I want you to go to the spot where you were able to identify the license plate on the vehicle you noted in your keeper report."

I pointed out where I was standing and the location of the car.

"All right, Adam," he said, swallowing hard with an impending sense of drama, "I'm going to ask you a question and I cannot prompt your answer in any way. Once I ask the question, you must answer it, and I cannot ask it again, or contribute any information to your answer. Tell me the exact position that car was in. How was it situated there across the road?"

I did the best I could to report every detail including the odd angle of the vehicle.

The detective was pleased with my answer, and wrote everything down on his notepad. "Excellent," he said when I finished. "We have already taken plaster tire tracks of the car. The ground over there is very soft. We concluded which tire tracks were the freshest, but I had to make sure that you were able to identify the position of the car without my prompting. All right. Those tracks are from a late model GM car, and that matches the vehicle registered to the license plate you provided. This is excellent."

When we got back to his office, he gave the order: "All right, men, we have a go." It was then that I realized exactly what I had seen earlier. They were preparing a SWAT team. In fact, it was fairly clear that they had memorized every aspect of the next sequence of events. They had drawings of a building, and men had been assigned positions and doors. He said, "Okay. We're going in. We all got the address, right? Is everyone is familiar with the objective?"

The other men nodded, but the plan was reviewed once again. Finally, the strategy meeting was over and the man in charge gave his last warning: "Watch out for each other," he added, "this guy's not worth the first hair on any of our heads. Ready? Let's go."

With that they left the room *en masse*. As he was leaving, the detective turned to me and said, "Hey, Smith. If this works out and we get the guy, we rangers are going to take you to the *Top of the Town* and you'll have the biggest steak dinner you've ever seen in your life." He wasn't smiling.

I closed the door behind me, and rode my bike home taking the long way on side streets.

CHAPTER THIRTY

At that time, *The Top of the Town* was one of the most popular restaurants in Cleveland. It was on the thirty-eighth floor of the Erieview Tower, which was Cleveland's newest landmark that provided views over the city and the lake. In my mind, I was envisioning this as a great adventure and wondering if I could bring a date.

I had been to the building itself before, but never to the restaurant. My dad had an office there, in fact. He was a supervising engineer with Ohio Bell, and they leased a good many stories of this East 9th Street, modern glass building.

John Sich was interested in the whole story when I arrived to punch in.

"Well, it could not be on my shift that it happens. That is what I notice. It was for your shift," he said baiting me. "Things such as this will not happen on my watch. Your shift is when this was."

He was rubbing it in, and that was a little annoying. The point was that given his style, he would have never captured the deer killer in the park. To be caught by John, the guy would have had to kill the deer in the backseat of the Chevelle. Still, John's comments hurt. I was already disappointed with myself that I had not seen the killer when he was in the act. I had a lot of ego invested in the fact that my patterns of patrolling brought more security to the zoo. My guilt feelings came from the fact that on the night in question, I had stayed in the car listening to music and Larry King. I was angry with myself. I thought I had my finger on the nighttime pulse of the zoo, but now that little foolish house of cards tumbled.

"How did you not notice such thing?" John wasn't letting go, and what hurt most was that he was correct. I had failed as watchman.

I could wager that when the man came into the zoo, the peafowl in the Children's Farm area made a terrific ruckus, and I was probably rocking to ELO's, *Can't Get It Out of My Head.*

Whatever I was singing, as that happened, the hunter's knife was slicing into that poor deer, and I was a useless idiot exhibiting just the kind of behavior I had ridiculed so often in others. More horrifying was the fact that I must've driven right past the murderer as he was butchering the deer, and he must have heard my car and the radio.

Hundreds of times on the tour trains, I had said, "You can see our herd of barasingha, or swamp deer. Notice especially the large male deer with the large rack of antlers. He is one of the most magnificent animals in the zoo."

In another world of singing, I had been of no use at all. The killer herded the deer into one corner, and the large male was easily singled out from the others. There is a pure and marvelous intelligence in all animals, unknowable and indescribable to humans. As soon as the killer thought to that the big buck was the one he wanted, the lesser deer knew they could slip away.

It was, at best, a cowardly act on the part of a hunter who was not hunting at all. The unknown assailant was living a cliché, shooting his fish in a barrel. No doubt, he'd serve up a feast for his friends and tell them of a great hunt, and not the great thieving truth.

I was the stupid fool who would feel a burden of guilt over my failure. I would have to live with that reality for decades to follow, unless, "Well, you know I did record the license plate of a vehicle. Have you heard anything about this? The rangers were going to arrest the man today." I thought this would corral John's assault.

"No, they would have told me first if such thing happened," he said. "No arrest is made at all. But, there is ranger here right now. You should ask him. He will know."

Within a nanosecond of the stroke of midnight, John shoved his time card down into the top of the Simplex Time Clock and left. It was true that my phone did not ring all afternoon. If there had been an arrest, it was still hush-hush.

I walked down the narrow corridor to the office. A tired-looking ranger was sitting at the desk, and it was clear he hadn't shaven or gone home since I had seen him last. In front of him on the desk were piles of papers. There were headshots and reams of wet paper faxes. The detective barely looked up at me.

"How did things go today? You know, about the…"

Without looking up, he said, "We went there…" His voice trailing off. Then he mumbled, "That car was owned by the father of a teen-age boy who'd gone out on a date that night. He and his girl friend were just parking when you saw the car there. He wasn't the one."

I thought I noticed a faint smile, and then he added, "It was kind of funny when we showed up, with all the guns and everything. The father was pretty shocked when the SWAT team blasted in." The quirky smile vanished, and he added, "It wasted hours of my time. The fact is, I'm nowhere on solving who did this."

As he spoke, I felt resentment aimed at me. In the light in the small room, he rubbed his exhausted face and resumed sifting through the piles of documents. "I've started over," he said. "I've got it all here. Lists of the members of Ohio archery clubs, hunters with criminal records, men with criminal backgrounds who've bought crossbows in the last ten years, lists of former zoo employees. I've been on the phone all over the country, trying to see if there's been any kind of case that's similar. I'm sending out information packets tomorrow. They're bringing me a better copy machine so I can copy these Polaroids. Maybe someone can tell me what kind of boots he was wearing from these photos I took of his footprints."

He kept talking, but not to me. I guessed that he'd been talking to himself all night, and he was just going over it again.

"There has to be some reason this happened. Did he want the meat? I guess that's possible. Who would do that for the meat? Was he starving? Was he that desperate? Is he a nut? A survivalist? Some guy who thinks he's Daniel Boone or something? Then, somehow I think to myself maybe this guy has some connection to the zoo. He really knew what he was doing. I can't find the first indication that he was in any other areas. Why didn't he kill a camel? Why didn't he kill a polar bear if he just wanted a thrill? Why did he kill that deer? They are rare, but did he know that? Is he an anti-environmentalist or something? Does he hate the people in India or what? He just came in and did it. I mean, he didn't wander around the zoo looking for something to kill. He was efficient, like he knew every step ahead of time. How could anybody know that? But then I think, *it's a zoo, a public place.* Anyone can come in and walk around to become familiar and make a plan. He could have been here a hundred days in a row to scope out the particulars."

I could feel both his frustration and my own burden of guilt. I said something lame like, "Well, good luck."

The detective looked up at me at last, and said with determination, "I'm never going to stop. He has no idea what he's up against. If it takes me a year, or ten years, or the duration of my entire career, I'm going to get this guy."

Then he went back to working just as if I weren't there at all. I just quietly backed out the door and went off to begin my shift. But the nature of my job as night watchman had been altered forever. Everything was different now.

CHAPTER THIRTY-ONE

It's said ad nauseam, *A criminal always returns to the scene of the crime.* Now, I wondered if that were true. I hoped so. It was the only thing I could hold onto in the light of my own failure. At night, the killer might revisit the site of his conquest. For about two weeks after the incident with the deer, I changed my routine.

The zoo had just completed a wooden walkway that went from behind the new Cat and Ape Building down through the woods to the lower level. Each night I'd begin my shift by walking from the upper level about halfway down the walkway which had a number of switchbacks that crisscrossed down the steep wooded hillside. The trees were still bare enough that I could see inside the dimly lit exhibit of the barasingha deer.

I could extend my observation times by zipping over to Ape or to the administrative offices, make a hit, and run back. It was futile.

During those weeks, I never drove the station wagon. I walked everywhere, often staying among the shadows. Because of the incident with the deer, a ranger was stationed in the zoo until 4:00.

I had plenty of time to think about what I would do if I saw the killer return. I made up my mind I would call the ranger on the walkie-talkie. Then I'd stay out of sight and follow the person's every move. If he left the zoo, I'd follow him to see the vehicle he got into. If I saw that he was about to shoot a deer, I'd utilize my rock throwing defensive maneuver and drop a projectile near him. Of course, these vigils were all for nothing. Good advice is captured over generations through proverbs. Wisdom is knowing which one is true in a particular instance. Yes, it is said that *the criminal always returns*, but it's also said that *it's no good locking the barn door after the horse has escaped.*

One morning, I was waiting to punch out and heavyset Dick Darenzo, the old Pinkerton watchman who now worked at Ape, cornered me.

"You're still dwelling on that night the guy killed the deer. Let me ask you something. If you were driving along that road and you caught a glimpse of that man just as he disappeared over the wall, what would you do?"

That was a rhetorical question. Dick didn't have conversations. He gave sermons. He continued, "I know what you would do. You'd stop the car and get out. You'd run to the wall, and if you saw the guy in there, you'd be chasing him in two seconds, ready to take him on. So let's think about that. If you had seen this person that night, you would have ran right at him, an armed hunter with a loaded crossbow."

"I guess so," I said.

"I know so," said Dick. "I would have done the same thing when I was younger. So you see, you've been cursing yourself because you didn't see the guy, and that's wrong. You should be thanking your lucky stars you didn't see him. There could have been a lot more than a deer laying dead in that pen. I know how you feel about it. I'd feel the same way, and believe me, things like this happened to me when I was a watchman. But at my age my advice to you is to keep three things in mind. One, it's not your job to fight anyone or take him out. It's your job to call the cops. Two, it's over and done. That's two. But the third aspect of it is what I believe, and a lot of people think so. The way it happened was good, not bad. Best thing for you would have been that you were home sick in bed when it happened. The farther away you were, the better. It's not that important, believe me. So learn from it and forget about it."

What he said didn't make me feel any different at the time. The slaying bummed me out and made me feel like a failure. I lost heart for the job after that. That was added to the fact that I was getting sick of working at night. Suddenly, it became like a phobia or something. I needed sunshine and normal hours. For years, working in the dark alone had been different and exciting. I'd even had a surprising amount of fun hanging out with Matt, Tim Pappas, and Norm. Those guys were gone, and the entire eight hours were solitary.

Each night as I wandered the dark zoo, I kept a constant watch on the sky above. I felt relief when I could see the stars fading and a faint light beginning to appear. The shooting stars stopped, and the first waking birds let me know that, in their opinion, it was safe to be moving about once again. The earth itself breathed, and the oppressive part of the darkness melted like a dying vampire in a horror movie.

I longed to return to the life of the ordinary. I wanted to get up in the morning and walk around in the daylight, with other people around me, like a normal guy. I decided the next time a daytime job opening came around, I'd take it. Any daytime job would be fine. I would have even liked a job where I had to stand outside on a hot day and shovel big piles of dripping wet manure into a wheelbarrow. That sounded pretty good to me. I was more than ready.

CHAPTER THIRTY-TWO

Finally, my car was functional again, and I was on the road. Next to the time clock was a new position, posted according to the union regs. It was just like every job sign-up sheet I had ever seen, and had words to this effect:

> According to the contract of Teamsters Local 507, all full-time job openings shall be posted for a period of two weeks for applicants to consider, restricted to current full-time zoo employees only. This is a notice that there is an opening for a full-time position within the Cleveland Metroparks Zoo. Per the contract between the Cleveland Metroparks Zoo and the officers of Teamsters Local 507, the position shall be awarded solely based on seniority. If you are interested in the following position, sign your name on one of the lines provided. Please be advised that there is an opening now as
> _____."

On the line, someone had written in hand, "Keeper. Pachyderm Building." Underneath that were lines numbers one to twenty-five. The notice had been posted now for fifteen hours, and it was still blank.

Of course, whoever had the most seniority would get the job, and ninety percent had more seniority than I did. I had more than Tim Pappas, Jim Rybicki, Joe Saunders, and maybe a couple of maintenance men, but that was about it.

I looked at the blank sheet for a long time. I wondered why no one else had signed it. What was the deal with this job that no one wanted? I thought about that all night, and looked again at the sheet after everyone in the day shift had punched in. There were still no takers, and I began to think, for the first time, that I could actually get this job if I wanted. I had let Pappas, Saunders, and Rybicki step in front of me in line to take a keeper's job. Now it was my turn.

Just then a guy named Jerry Studiak walked in from down the hall. He was the custodian in the Commissary Building. I'm not sure what his job was, but I'd seen him sweeping the floors in there and scrubbing the kitchen sink a couple of times. He was around thirty-five, pleasant enough, with sandy blonde hair that hung down over his forehead. Always outspoken, he sometimes rankled people the wrong way.

Jerry didn't just let anything go. He wasn't shy about his opinion and always seemed to have an issue with something or another. Actually, he was smart. Though he spent his days pushing dust around with a push broom, everyone knew him as a somewhat unsociable, but an educated and moody genius.

As I was looking at the blank sign-up sheet, Jerry shuffled into the room. He was emptying the big round, sand-filled barrel which sat next to the time clock. He had a little sifter to clean the butts out of the sand. The *Plain Dealer* was sitting there on the desk. Jerry picked it up and took it to read later. As he was leaving, he suddenly spoke.

"Thinking about the elephant job?"

"Yeah."

"Well, *don't*," he said brusquely. Then he went off toward the kitchen area to read the paper. After staring at the sheet a few more minutes with a sinking feeling in my stomach, I went into the kitchen where Jerry sat at one the tables. I took a seat opposite him.

"Let me show you where I got mine." As he said this, he leaned back in his chair and pulled up the front of his shirt to reveal a long, thick, mangled scar about sixteen inches long angling down his right rib cage, starting near his armpit and ending at the bottom of his ribs. Above and below the twisted scar tissue were thinner white scars and the signs of healed stitches. One thin scar went up toward Jerry's throat. The lower thin scar ran down across his large belly. The entire landscape of destruction showed where an initial impact had ripped into his body and where the surgeons had opened him up even wider to go inside.

"Simba got me one day," he said, lowering his shirts and tucking them in. "She missed my heart by four inches. I was lucky. Have Sandusky show you his arm." I knew he meant Steve Sandusky, the keeper and not his brother Frank, the train driver who promoted *beaver shots*.

"How'd that happen?" I asked.

"She's nuts," said Jerry, avoiding specifics. "That's it. She's just fine for a long time, but then she goes nuts. Donnie had a run in with her, too. She nearly killed him. She busted every bone in his body. Do you know

Donnie? Donnie Tresise? Simba took him for quite a ride. He won't go near her now. Ask Tresise to tell you his story sometime. Ask Pacerak why he won't go near that elephant anymore. Simba's put plenty of men in the hospital. Do you know Vince Rimedio?"

"I know who he is, but I don't know him well."

"He's that keeper in the Ostrich Barn. Talk to him about Simba sometime. He can tell you about all the men she put in the hospital, guys I've never even heard of, lots of guys. You know Perkins, don't ya?"

"Yeah, he's a nice guy."

Perkins was a soft-spoken older keeper with a lot of mischief in his eyes. His hair was always combed perfectly, and that made him look like a well-groomed gentleman. On the other hand, he was one of the major participants in the goose-somebody-in-the-balls competition. That was how I knew him. He was always sneaking up on Bill Seman or Vince to goose one of them in the balls. Other than that, Perkins was a gracious and harmless man. It was hard to imagine even an elephant having an issue with him.

"Yeah, Perkins was the relief keeper. He worked with Simba a long time ago. There's a lot of guys who *used* to work with her, who won't go near her now. They don't put elephants in the insane asylum, but if they did, she'd be at the head of the class. She knocked Perkins down one day. I saw it. He was just shoveling out her cage, not doing anything. Suddenly, she pulled his legs right out from under him, knocked him on his ass. He tried to crawl away. It would break your heart to see it. It was pathetic. He was a little younger then, but still in his fifties. She caught him by the leg and lifted him up, and held him up in the air. Then she threw him down like she was spiking a football. She's quick. She got over him and he curled into a ball. She poked him with her tusks, like sticking him with a fork, but didn't gore him. She just tormented him. Every time he tried to crawl away, she'd let him go, then grab his leg and drag him back. That was sick. She pulled him back and just tortured him. Then she pinned his head down to the concrete floor with her foot. His head was on the floor and she was stepping right on the side of his head. The look in his eyes was just awful. She kept his head pinned. He couldn't move. She just kept pushing and pushing his skull into the floor, rolling her foot back and forth over it. He said later when she pressed down, he could feel it popping. But she didn't kill him. She just pressed his head down, right down into the shit, and kept rolling his head back and forth like a ball of dough under her foot. Like Silly Putty. She held him like that for a half hour. She just kept a little pressure on him sometimes, and sometimes she pressed hard, like she was going to pop his head at anytime. Then, she let him go. She just let go and turned around like it was nothing. Ask Perkins about the job opening.

"Then there was Kuenzer. He was in her pen one day. There was a keeper with him, and the vet. Kuenzer tried to walk around her, going under her tusks. That pissed her off, just that little thing. She slammed him into the wall and caught him. Then she pressed her head against his head and held his skull against the cement wall. She had her forehead right against his forehead, with the back of his head shoved into the concrete wall. That's what she does. She tortures people. Sometimes she gores 'em like me or Sandusky, and sometimes she just tortures them 'cause she's sick in the head. We all just stood there while she held Kuenzer's head against the wall, putting on the pressure like she was going to pop it. She held him there for ten minutes."

"Well, what happened to him?"

"You mean Kuenzer? She let the pressure off a little bit, and he slipped down under her tusks and snuck away. He said, 'She was just *playing*.' That Kuenzer's nuts, too. She wasn't playing with me or Sandusky. There were other guys gored by her before I even got here. I don't even know about them. You have to ask one of the older keepers. Ask Vince."

He was seething, bubbling with anger.

"Tara was all right," Jerry said, "but she's dead now, and Simba's a time bomb. Now they've got that new little elephant down there. She's not trained, still wild, and they don't know what to do with her. What's going to happen when she gets big? That little elephant is way out of control already. They got that girl Ellen down there, and her ideas about how to train an elephant are crazy. Then they've got Rybicki there with her. Who's he? I think six months ago, he was an accountant, never an elephant trainer. He's just doing whatever Ellen tells him. You got a screwy woman with crazy ideas running the show, trying to do a man's job. I think Tara helped to calm Simba down some, but she's gone. They're all idiots down there, so don't go running into a situation where you've got a bunch of crazy people who don't know what they're doing."

He opened up a brown bag and took out a sandwich. "Just forget about that job. Trust me on this one. Why the hell do you think that sheet's blank? You got people in this zoo who could get another $1.50 an hour by signing the sheet, but they won't do it. Don't be stupid. Stay where you are. That's me telling you."

I had no reason to doubt Jerry or the scars he showed me. On the other hand, Rybicki had left his watchman position to work in the Pachy. He came bouncing in every morning with a cheerful attitude and didn't seem to be having any problems. The pretty woman, Ellen, was an elephant keeper, and she didn't seem to be in and out of the hospital all the time.

I went home without signing the sheet, but my mind was not at rest.

For some stupid reason, I felt like I had to take the job, or I wouldn't be able to live with myself.

Next midnight, I found myself standing again in front of the blank sheet. The next morning, the page was still pristine. Feigning excitement, Seman yelled, "Look. The elephant job is still open." Everyone   laughed. "Gimme a pen. Gimme a pen." exclaimed Bill.

Perkins played, too. He turned to Kuenzer and meekly asked, "Mr. Donald, is it too late to sign up for the Pachy job? I've had my heart set on it?" Everyone laughed and even Kuenzer cracked a smile.

After that, somebody asked Perkins to do his impression of Steve Sandusky. That was a popular suggestion and Perkins immediately starting limping as if his back were killing him.

Any impersonation of Steve required a cigarette hanging loosely from the mouth, so Perkins rearranged his own to mimic Sandusky's style.

Turning around like an ancient, bent-over gnome, he moved as slowly as a slug. It took him forty-five seconds just to get a foot up on one step. He kept raising and lowering his foot and missing the step. It was funny. Then he staggered backwards, until he was five feet in the opposite direction, losing all the progress he'd made. Everyone split a gut.

With his whole body shaking, Perkins moaned, "Arrrrrr. Here I am, old Steve. Yes, sir. Here I go off to my job in the Pachyderm Building. Hope I get there by lunch time. I gotta get there by halfway through the day so I can turn around in time to get back and punch out. I'm off to take care of old Blackie the hippo. Hope he doesn't shit on my pants today..."

Perkins announced, "If I get hippo shit all over my pants... Everyone will think I did it."

The room erupted with a huge blast of laughter as the master comic did his shtick. The funny part was that he captured the essence of poor, stoop-backed Steve.

"I'm so old. I'm Steve Sandusky. I remember when I was six feet tall like it was yesterday," croaked Perkins, who was surrounded by guffaws. He had his back turned to the audience now. That was his big mistake. Out of nowhere, Vince zoomed up the stairs and grabbed Perkins' balls from behind with a quick squeeze. It had all been a setup.

"Gotcha." And the show was over.

Just as the room emptied and I was leaving, Tim came in the door. He was wearing a yellow vinyl raincoat as he bounded lightly down the stairs.

Tim saw me, and said, "Adam, remember when you asked me if Lucy the baby tiger would grow up tame, and whether or not I'd be able to let her loose even when she's an adult?"

"Yeah," I said.

"I think I know the answer to your question." He turned his back to me and I saw that the back of his coat was shredded to bits. "I let Lucy out in the hall with me yesterday when I was hosing out the work area. She came up behind me and jumped on my back and did this. I'm guessing we're not going to be letting her out in the future. She was just playing, but that's the end of that experiment."

Again, I was alone with the Pachyderm sign-up sheet. The outside door to the lobby opened with a noisy screech, and Ellen Leach came bouncing cheerfully down the three concrete steps. I hardly knew her, but she was one of the keepers in the elephant building.

"Hi, there," she said, reaching for her time card and punching in as fast as she could. She was already late. *Keeper* had always been a *man's job*, but *the times, they were a'changin* and she was one of two women who held the position. In fact, she was Cleveland Zoo's first ever, and the second was Linda in Birds.

"Well, the job's still open," Ellen announced humorously, as if the empty room were full of people. Then she said to me, "You oughta sign up."

"I might," I said. "I was just here thinking about it."

She bounded up the concrete stairs on her way out. Then, almost shyly, she looked back over her shoulder and said, "Well, just don't let any of the 'horror stories' influence you. It's all right, really." Then she was gone.

I was a bit stunned, wondering how She knew people had been telling me stuff. It made me feel a little odd, like I was in a bottle with people looking in. Jerry must have told someone that he had warned me to not to sign the sheet, and someone probably said to her, *"Hey, you'll never get a new keeper. Loud-mouth Studiak's been scaring off the night watchman."*

The zoo was always rife with gossip. Yes, the stories and scars were horrible, but she and Jim seemed happy being down there. Her attitude and those few words overtook Jerry's long-winded and ominous warning. I signed the sheet.

I spent only one more night as a night watchman. At the beginning of my last shift, I said goodbye to John. He smiled broadly, as he always did. Then we briefly hugged each other with a warm feeling of mutual affection. As the hug broke off, John patted me on the back with his rough, meaty hand, and said, "You be careful with that big elephant. You watch for her tricks."

"I will," I said. "Goodbye."

"Naw. We will see each other again more. I am sure of it. The zoo is not so big as that."

BOOK III: THE ANIMAL KEEPER YEARS

To Vincent Rimedio,
easily the greatest animal
expert I have ever known.

CHAPTER ONE

The word pachyderm literally means *thick-skinned*, and generally refers to elephants, hippos, and rhinos. In September of 1979 I began working days as a pachyderm keeper. It was a welcome change. Now I would assume sleep patterns that followed the sun, and would be arriving at work at a *normal* time. I was a real person again.

That first morning, I punched in around 7:00 and headed for the Pachyderm Building, unlocked the back door, and sat down in the keeper room waiting for the others to arrive.

I was still wearing the uniform I had been issued as a night watchman. I was uncertain what footwear would be best for here in the Pachy. Should I now wear heavy steel-toed work boots to protect my feet, or lightweight shoes so that I could run like hell if necessary? I wore tennis shoes.

The job I had just taken had come open when Brent Sanchez left to become an auto mechanic in the maintenance department. That sort of switch was only possible on the seniority system. A person could be a janitor one day and be feeding raw meat to a lion the next. After everything I had heard about the elephants, I wondered why Brent had moved on. I felt a little better when I learned that he had recently married. I figured his wife decided it would be great if he didn't smell like crap all the time. That was one of the less than desirable perks of my new job.

I was there only a few minutes when Jim Rybicki arrived. His first task was to put on a pot of coffee. After that, he went into the exhibit area to unchain the elephants. As he worked, he spoke commands to the great animals.

"Get in line," he'd shout, to which the lumbering Simba and an energetic three-year-old elephant named Tiani quickly obeyed. They knew that if they stood in line and were good, they would soon get breakfast. In fact, they seemed to be acting like the family dog who knows exactly what comes next when its owner gets out the can opener. Tiani was actually more like a nine hundred pound puppy.

"Steady," boomed Jim. He was now removing the chains from the feet of Simba. "Foot," he said, and the great beast raised its leg balancing on three feet as the links were disconnected from the bracelet that was permanently attached.

After Simba, it was the young elephant's turn. Tiani's journey to the zoo began when she had been orphaned in the grasslands of Africa only a few months earlier. When the youngster started to lose focus, Jim yelled the first command, "Get in line," and she was back to her proper spot. She was excited as Jim moved toward her. Her excitement caused her to wander and stray. She gradually spun around, a little bit skittish, and soon she was nearly turned sideways.

Jim spoke again, "GET IN LINE."

Little Tiani hopped back into place, facing straight ahead, having been scolded. She held as still as possible, eyes wide in anticipation of what would happen next. Jim walked over and stood next to her right front leg. He said, "Foot," and Tiani lifted her front leg off the ground.

She had not fully mastered the three legged stance, but her unsteady cuteness didn't stop the keeper from getting the first chain removed. The *little* animal seemed anxious to please, and raised her other leg in anticipation of the next command.

"No, no," he scolded, and this was my first exposure to the danger of an elephant, even a cooperative one, who moved before the handler was ready.

"Get in line."

She hopped back to her spot and once more stood as still as possible. But before Jim said anything else, Tiani eagerly raised her rear left leg, also. She was once again ahead of the sequence of commands.

"No. No." Tiani went back to standing as Jim walked behind her. "Foot," he said, and this time he unhooked the chain. Though free to move, it was essential that the keeper maintain control. "Get in line, get in line." They obeyed, and they heard the words they had been waiting for, "All right."

It was as if the drill sergeant had given the *at ease*, and Tiani began to roam and feed from the fresh hay that had been set out nearby. Simba, however, sniffed the younger elephant all over, checking to see that she was okay.

"Every morning the first thing we do is unchain the elephants," Jim was beginning my orientation. "The first keeper here is to do that. At the end of the day, the chains are the very last thing we do. That way, they spend the least amount of time chained. It wasn't always that way, but that's what Ellen and I do.

"One question you'll hear over and over is: 'Why are the elephants chained?' They are only chained at night, but people sometimes see us getting them settled and think it's cruel. You need to be able to explain why it's necessary. Basically the chains keep the elephants apart and restrict them to a somewhat confined area to keep them out of trouble when a keeper is not around. It also prevents them from urinating in their feed hay. Once the feed is fouled, they'd have nothing to eat all night. We can be sure one elephant is not keeping the other from its food. There have been cases in other zoos where a larger elephant would actually gore a smaller one. Simba's protective at this point, but it could happen. It's also a part of their training. Without discipline, these big guys would be uncontrollable. The daily rituals provide security for the animals at night and a margin of safety for the keepers."

Jerry Studinak's description of Rybicki as *an accountant* who didn't know anything about elephants suddenly seemed ludicrous. I was now experiencing another version of the story.

"Before Ellen started here, a keeper might read the paper and leave the elephants chained until ten. In a hurry to check out, they might be chained as early as three. That's pretty lousy for the elephants. That's why the first to arrive releases them; one of us is usually here until six. In the summer, we also get them outside as quickly as possible and bring them in as late as possible."

(I was beginning to see why Ellen had been late to punch in. She knew the elephants were already out, and that she would be staying late to give them a bit more freedom.)

We sat down in the keeper room and had coffee. "Ellen will probably have you working at the hippo end of the building," he explained. "That's how she started me. I worked exclusively with hippos for several months before I was trained with elephants." When coffee was over, Jim showed me how to prepare the elephants' breakfast.

A short time earlier, truck drivers from the Commissary delivered several large plastic containers loaded with fresh fruits and vegetables. They also left two red coolers full of thawed smelts and mackerels for the keeper over at Sea Lions. Jim dragged the fish inside and left them where Little Johnny would pick them up when he came in. Then I helped him lug containers full of bananas and apples inside to a food preparation table along the back wall of the building. This was the daily allotment, and everything looked as fresh as you'd find at the grocery store.

The metal food preparation table had a nine-inch butcher knife chained to it. This was a replacement knife. A previous one was stolen by a junior ranger, which accounted for addition of a chain.

Jim continued to talk as he hacked away at the fruit. "You have to watch your fingers," he said, ramming the glinting blade all the way through a heavy sweet potato. Soon he had two galvanized buckets filled with big chunks of fruit and vegetables. After that, the discussion was about the Cavs and how cool Joe Tait was, and what a great game Bingo Smith had the night before.

He filled other buckets with dark-green alfalfa pellets and a few scoops of a molasses coat called *sweet feed*. He mixed the pellets and the sweet feed with his bare hands. After four buckets were filled, we walked back out toward the elephants.

"Get in line," he called, as we approached the cage. Both Simba and Tiani hurried back to their spots as Jim slipped between the bars and set the buckets down. The two elephants stood patiently waiting, and I could appreciate their disciplined training. I've seen dogs who almost knocked their owners over to get to a dish as it was being lowered to the floor. How much worse it would be to face a hungry leviathan.

Food was first set in front of Simba and then Tiani whose excitement released a sudden flow of urine onto the concrete floor behind her. She twisted and turned and wandered off her spot like a skittish puppy, her trunk snapping back and forth like a whip.

"Get in line," and Tiani jumped back into her place as best she could.

Nearby, Simba was waiting patiently, rocking back and forth with her meal in front of her. She knew the drill. Tiani was still a jumpy bundle of expectation, but she too waited until Jim gave permission.

"Steady," he said, and Tiani went still for just a few seconds before resuming a fidget.

"STEADY!" shouted Jim. Ten seconds passed before, "All right." and the animals both dug into their provender.

As I watched the animals eating, and saw the discipline that had preceded the meal, I wondered how this obedient and serene Simba could be the same animal who had put so many men in the hospital. Jim put fresh Timothy hay in their cage. This was food that they'd work at all day.

It was still a little before 8:00 a.m. when Steve Sandusky himself hobbled in. I knew about this guy, and had seen Perkins imitation, but this was the first time I'd actually met him. He extended a calloused and slightly arthritic hand, and we shook.

"Adam's the new keeper," said Rybicki, "he's taking Brent's place. We'll have to teach him everything that Brent knows which should take half an hour, don't you think?"

Sandusky laughed at the predictable banter.

For some reason, I took a liking to Steve immediately. Maybe because he looked like he fell off the same tree as my Uncle Ollie or my Dad. He also looked and sounded a great deal like his brother Frank, a train driver I had known ten years earlier. Frank was a nice enough guy, but not much of a conversationalist. Steve, on the other hand, was a real kidder, so much like my Uncle Ollie, who would bend over pretending to tie his shoe and then yell back under his chair saying, "Hey, Ollie, have a beer." Then he'd sit up and pretend that the voice had come from some other part of the room. "Okay, thanks," he'd say. Then he'd get a beer.

Perkins' imitation of Steve highlighted a bad back. The fact was that he really was crippled over with pain, some days worse than others. Doing the work of a keeper was an ordeal, but he was only a few years from his retirement.

This was Ellen Leach's day off so I chatted with Sandusky until Sanchez came in. He was the keeper who I had awakened on the night of the pygmy chase. Now, I would be working with Wolee, too.

Brent's first mission was a cup of coffee, and I wondered if he'd also get into the Lorna Doone's that I saw being shared by a mouse when I was on watch. Before heading for the java, he explained the drill.

"After this, I'm going to break you in on one end of the hippos, real quick. Then I can get up to the garage and get started up there. They need me already. So... see ya in about twenty minutes. No, a half hour."

It was then that I realized that Steve and Brent were hippo keepers and stayed clear of the legendary Simba. Jim and Ellen worked the elephants.

As Brent settled in with a mug and the newspaper, Jim went off to shovel the loose olive-green crap out of the giraffe cages. Steve disappeared into the main hippo hall. I walked out into the public area to wait until Brent was ready.

I looked into the first hippo stall where a pygmy was standing quite still. This was not Wolee. It was a young female, backed up against the left wall, looking dismal. As I moved toward her for a better look, she grew tense and edged away from the wall.

Littered around the floor of her stall were various clumps of soiled alfalfa hay and several wide puddles of rancid yellow urine. The sides of the enclosure were painted a glossy gold with areas where the old layers of pink paint were showing through. The entire enclosure was speckled with a brown spray of dried droplets of feces. The stall was filthy from a long night of repeated defecations. Even the concrete tub of drinking water, which was being fed by a slowly running stream of tap water, was clearly a place where the hippo had done her business.

The five hundred pound animal had her head down, angry and scowling. Pygmies, as may be surmised, are not known for their pleasant personalities. They can be far more aggressive than their Nile cousins. This one's mouth was drawn back in a snarl, and under those lips were the feared razor sharp tusks that are the chief weapon of that species. Their upper tusks are indeed two-inch wide double-serrated fangs, as sharp as a butcher's knife and could be employed with great jaw strength.

In reaction to my presence, she stretched out her neck, thrusting her head forward to create the illusion that she was growing taller before my eyes. In time, I realized that this was nothing personal; her anger at humanity was general and almost universal.

What in the world am I doing here?

I remembered what Les Mertus had said so long ago as we looked at the wolves in their cage at the Old Main Zoo Building and how he knew that he wouldn't be able to look at their forlorn faces every day.

My trance was broken by the sound of a heavy door's metallic groan. It was Sandusky coming into the keeper area. He was whistling and pushing a big green wheelbarrow with a tarnished coal shovel and a scrubbing broom laid across the top.

As if greeting his favorite pet, he smiled broadly and said, "Hey, there, Mushka. Here's your old Steve. Here I am, baby."

To my surprise, the pygmy came to life, prancing excitedly from side to side. She opened her huge mouth, and she began to work her jaw open and shut as if chewing gum. Her top and bottom ivory tusks gleamed against the pink fleshiness of her mouth and tongue.

"How's my Mushka today?" He looked at her directly and smiled quite naturally. "That's my baby. That's my pretty Mooshkie. Soooo pretty, pretty, pretty."

Clearly, he was as delighted as she. His face beamed as she pranced toward him, skittering from side to side and bobbing up and down. Even her butt was twitching back and forth with joy. With each bounce and prance came more wet slaps on the cement.

Steve tugged hard to drag a good length of the hose into the stall, and started blasting the muck off the walls of the enclosure. Perhaps what I had seen as a total hatred of humanity was, in fact, a pouting pup anxiously waiting for her master to return.

When Mushka saw Steve, another sunny day had begun for her.

This is going to be ok, I thought.

CHAPTER TWO

Brent Sanchez walked down the little incline out of the keeper room and down toward the public area where I stood. "Are you ready?"

I was, but I also knew he was a man in a hurry to move on to a new job.

"I'm going to break you in on one end of the hippos, and show you the morning routine. Most of the work takes place in the morning. Then I'm going to leave and come back around 3:00 to teach you the afternoon schedule, which is essentially the same as the morning's, so that will be easy. None of this is complicated."

Brent opened the first gate that sealed off the entire back hippo hall, and the lecture began. "Rule One: This Gate must *always* be closed. You open it and go through it, then you close it behind you. There's nothing else I'm going to tell you today that is even close to being this important. This outer gate is *never-ever* to be left open."

After my first encounter with Wolee, I understood completely. I took a folded paper from my pocket and wrote down what he had said: *Never leave outer gate open.* I underlined it twice.

"What? Do you gotta write that down?" Brent asked. (Obviously, he didn't go to the John Sich school.)

"Well, I thought I'd write down some of the big stuff."

"If you need to, but I'd think you could remember it. Don't let the stinking animals loose." He continued with his one-sided conversation.

"Basically, in the Pachyderm Building there are three job descriptions…"

I wrote that down.

"Oh, come on. You don't need to write down everything I say. This will take forever. I'll tell you when there's something you need to write down."

I put the pen and paper in my back pocket.

Shaking his head, he started again, "Basically, in the Pachyderm Building there are three job descriptions…" He paused, "Are you in the Union?"

"Oh, yeah, sure. I've been in the Union since…"

"Okay. In the Pachyderm Building there are three job descriptions. Two jobs on the hippo side and the elephant-giraffe job. You may or may not eventually work the elephants. I don't know, and I don't care. We're not going to think about that now. You can train for elephants eventually if you choose. Personally, you're crazy if you do, but that's your decision. On the hippo side, there are two jobs, two areas designated by the current Teamsters' contract as full-time positions.

"Every day two keepers work the hippo end. We have a total of five hippos. One day you might work one end of the hippos, and another day you might work the other."

The phrases *hippo end* and *other end* of the hippos struck me as comical, but I kept a straight face.

"Today Steve is working Area One. He is taking care of Mushka the pygmy in stall one; big Blackie, the Nile is in stall two. That also means that today he is responsible for cleaning the big hippo pool in the central area because Blackie was in there last night. You'll find out that cleaning that pool is a hell of a job. You have to haul all that wet shit up out of the pool in a wheelbarrow. It's a long way up out of that pool, and there's a lot of heavy loads of shit. Today, as keeper of Area One, Steve is also is responsible for the tortoises in the Bull Room."

I wanted to write down what he was saying, but I didn't dare.

"Now pay attention." He gestured with both arms toward the far end of the hall, looking like a football referee waving to show which team had possession after a fumble. "Hippo Area Number 2 at that end of the building consists of Wolee the pygmy hippo, Red the Nile hippopotamus, and Bomi, another pygmy. Red and Blackie *alternate* spending the night in the big pool. Blackie had the pool last night, and Red will have the pool tonight, and so forth. They alternate. Okay?

"If Red is in the big pool at night and you are taking care of Area Two the next day, then you will clean it in the morning. Whichever keeper cleans the *big pool* in the morning does *not* have to clean the public areas of the Pachyderm Building. Whoever *doesn't* clean the big pool sweeps the entire floor in the public area before the building opens; this includes the lobbies where the people come in, and also emptying the trash containers, and cleaning the glass doors in the lobby. That means that we have to do that today, but I gotta go real soon. Any idiot can do it so I don't need to show you how. Steve will show you where all the stuff is and you can do it. I'm sure you know how to dry mop a floor and empty trash containers and clean glass with Windex and a rag. What's the most important thing?"

"The first gate is always kept closed."

"Right. That gate is always closed. No exceptions ever."

Just then Steve opened the heavy barricade-gate that sealed off the back hall. Wearing big rubber red-topped boots that came up to his knees, he moved haltingly through the open gate, dragging a heavy pressurized fire hose. Steve didn't close the hall barricade behind him.

"Okay," said Brent, a little uneasily. "He'll close it in a minute after he hoses out that stall. It has to be closed at all times. Really."

Whistling, Steve hauled the hose through the back door of the stall that housed Blackie. The door was open just wide enough for a man to slip in. He cleared the entrance by moving sideways through the opening. Soon the hose was engaged and the whole room felt damp.

"Now pay attention," continued Brent. "If this was a nice summer day, the first thing we'd do is put all the hippos outside. The elephants and giraffes, too, for that matter. Then cleaning the stalls and cages is a piece of cake, but it's too cold right now. In another couple of months it'll be different. So to clean their stalls this time of year, we have to move them all around. That makes it more dangerous."

Brent explained the specifics of cleaning the stalls and feeding the three hippos in his area. The three were Red the Nile, and two of the three pygmies, Wolee and Bomi (pronounced, *Boh-me*).

"Now maybe this is the second most important thing," he said. "For your own preservation it might be the most important thing. It's about Red." As he was speaking, he fit a metal crank into a mechanism at the back door of a hippo stall. Turning it with some effort, he opened the door a mere four inches.

Bursting into view through the narrow opening was the sweat-drenched, snorting muzzle of an enormous Nile hippopotamus. This was Red. She immediately charged the door's opening, hitting it forcefully.

BAM. The air around me moved as hard droplets sprayed off her body and flew at me through the narrow crack; it wasn't water. She had been *dry-docked* all night, but was wet from animal fluids oozing like thin oil from her pores.

She snorted in deep, throaty grunts, *Whuh, whuh.*

The air around us shook so that my eardrums felt as if they'd been smacked. As big liquid-spewing snorts blew out of the thirty-five hundred pound animal's flared nostrils, hot blasts from her mouth hit my face. Through the small opening in the door, I could see part of her snout, then her cheek, then one big dark eye. Only her left nostril appeared in the opening, and she blew out more blasts. I was terrified. I had been warned off about an elephant named Simba, but I forgot about that. Who was that? *Simba? Simba who?* I had just been introduced to Red. She was the true monster of the Pachyderm Building.

Each time she slammed into the big metal door, it shook and popped towards us, away from the wall. I was afraid she would hit it so hard, it would fall off its track. Brent cranked the unwieldy door closed which only seemed to embolden the animal. As the door settled heavily into its final position, she attacked it harder, slamming into it with one last charge, her final comment on the encounter. Then all was silent.

"You don't want to mess with Red," said Brent, and I felt no need to write that down. "Don't go in with her. Don't put your arm into her stall. Don't try to make friends with her. Don't have anything to do with her. You've just met the meanest, damn son-of-a-bitch animal in the whole zoo, period. This animal will kill you and is always lying in wait for that opportunity. Once she has you in her sights, you will have no chance whatsoever. She can run faster than you. Given a chance, a Nile hippo will *eat* a human being. They kill more people than any other animal in Africa. This is the most dangerous animal in the zoo. I'll bet if a grizzly got loose, it'd run to the woods. If Red gets loose, someone is going to die. Red doesn't have good days and bad days, like Simba. She doesn't have good days and bad days like you and me. Every day is a bad day. Every living thing on this earth is her enemy. If you threw that bear in with her, that grizzly bear is going to be chewed up and spit out. I'd bet you money on that. It is your job, and the job of everyone in this building and everyone in this zoo to make sure that *this animal* never gets loose from this stall and this area. Trust me on that one."

"Hey, you're preaching to the converted."

My comment may have thrown him because he just shook his head and said, "Whatever." Then he picked up where he had left off. "The only thing we'll do with Red right now is throw in a sheaf of Timothy hay from the front of her pen so she'll have a snack to hold her over. It will be awhile before we'll be ready to feed her this morning. Other than throwing that in, we don't do *anything* with Red right now. Steve needs to clean the big pool. That will probably be done by around ten o'clock, the way he moves. When the pool is clean and refilled, then we have some place to put Red; she'll come in for that. Then, you'll *close the door between the stall she's in now and the pool.* That's very important. That's probably Number Three. You better be damn sure another door out of the stall or pool isn't opened. Once she's secure, then, and only then, can you go into her stall to clean it. That will happen around 10:00 a.m. I won't be here. They need me up in the garage. But I'm going to show you how to clean the pygmy stalls. You can clean Red's yourself. It's the same general idea, except the shit is bigger. If you have any questions about how to shovel hippo shit into a wheelbarrow, ask Sandusky. He's an expert.

"We're going to clean Wolee's pen and feed him. He gets mad when he doesn't have his breakfast by nine." Brent looked at his wristwatch. "Go to the tool area and get a wheelbarrow, a coal shovel, a rake, and a scrub brush. Bring it here. I gotta go take a coffee piss, and I'll throw a sheaf in for Red from the front. I'll be back in five minutes."

Brent headed off toward the keeper room, closing the barricade behind him.

I went to the tool area and started to gather the requisite stuff. Before loading up, however, I pulled the pen and paper and hastily wrote: "Red and Black alternate nights in big pool. Whoever doesn't clean big hippo pool... cleans public floors. Windex glass doors. Empty trash cans. 10:00 a.m. Move Red into big pool before cleaning her stall on alternate. Close door between pool and Red stall. Avoid Red."

I got back to the start before Brent came down the hall. He took a final drag on his cigarette and threw the butt into a water drain.

"Steve and I smoke all over the building," he said. "But I don't take a cigarette into the pens. I just don't want a cigarette butt to end up in there."

"An animal might pick up the habit, huh?"

"Whatever."

Red was still drying out in the other stall until the pool was open. Meanwhile, it was time for us attend to the needs of Wolee, who I had met several years earlier. "Okay," I said, "I already know this animal is dangerous."

Brent's head popped up at that. "Wolee? Are you crazy? He's a sweetheart. He's my baby."

He swung open the gate that led toward the stall. "Wolee's a pet. He's a house pet." The enclosure was different from the others in that it was split into two by a four-foot-high steel barrier running right up the center. We stepped into the empty half-stall next to the animal. A gate in the middle of the barrier gave access between the two sections.

"Wolee was found as an orphan by a couple that lived in Africa,"

Brent explained. "They were missionaries in Liberia or somewhere, and they raised him. They had him in a bathtub for awhile. They bottle fed him and when he got bigger, they kept him in their swimming pool. When he got too big for that, they donated him to the zoo."

Then he opened the dividing gate and, very matter-of-factly, stepped in next to Wolee. The hippo came up out of the dirty pool at his approach. The rubbery animal seemed as harmless as an inflated beach toy.

"As you can see, there are two sides to this stall. So we move Wolee back and forth every day. This side is dirty so we'll move him over to the clean side through the gate and leave him there today. Then we'll clean this side.

"Now," said Brent. "Some guys simply like to let Wolee down into that other pool over there when they're cleaning his stall."

Brent was referring to the other larger pool in the Pachyderm Building's display area. It was fairly large, and right next to Wolee's stall. The animal could be let in through an electric door. He preferred not to do that because the drains were clogged in that area. As he spoke, the five hundred pound pygmy with the razor-sharp tusks was anxiously awaiting for the talking to stop.

Eventually, Brent moved toward Wolee, and the hippo waddled up to meet him. "Where's my Wolee? That's a *good* Wolee."

Wolee excitedly slapped his wide, webbed feet on the floor like he was about to shit out diamonds. "There's my Wolee. Wolee. Wolee Booger. Come to Daddy. You're my Wolee Booger. You're my Wolee Booger. I wuv my Wolee. Does Wolee wuv Brent? Does he wuz he? Does he wuzzy wuzzy?"

That's what the man said. Then in a more human voice, he said, "Okay, now watch this."

I thought maybe he was going to pull a six pack of beer out of his ass, but he didn't. Instead, he reached into his pocket and pulled out a crumpled box of candy root beer barrels. With great anticipation, Wolee pranced and skittered about like a five hundred pound Doberman hearing the can opener turning.

"I'm Wolee's Daddy. I taught him this," said Brent like the proud father he was. "Watch this." He held a single root beer barrel above the hippo's head, and sternly said, "Wolee, sit."

Like a shot, the hippo sat down on his big haunches. "Good boy, Wolee." Praise gushed from the keeper. "That's a good Wolee."

He placed a root beer barrel right between the very ends of the hippo's lips, right between the upper and lower lip.

"Wait. Wait. No," he said to his *little* friend. It was like watching a trained dog who was balancing a biscuit on his nose waiting for the order to chomp.

"All right," exclaimed Brent, and the animal popped the candy back into his mouth and actually savored the sweetness.

Hokey Smoke, I thought. This hippo was not only *not* dangerous, he was a marvel. Nothing like I'd seen in the middle of the night.

"I taught Wolee to sit," said Brent proudly. "It took me about three weeks. I hope you'll get him some root beer barrels, because he's going to miss his Daddy, aren't you, Wolee?"

Wolee stood back up and bounced around a little.

Brent said, "Sit. Sit," and Wolee sat again. This time, he held the root beer barrel up high over the sitting animal's head. Wolee opened his mouth wide, like a funnel, and Sanchez dropped the candy right down into his throat. Then, as Wolee was chewing and savoring it, Brent petted him right on the top of his head.

"Let me tell you something about pygmy hippos," said Brent. "They like to be petted on the top of the head, but do *not* touch their ears. They do *not* like having their ears touched."

"Do you mind if I write that down?" I asked

"Okay, go ahead."

Buy root beer barrels. Don't touch pygmy hippos' ears.

Brent began cleaning the dirty stall with the hippo at his side. Every once in a while he'd give the command to sit and followed that with a piece of candy. Finally, Brent came back over to my side of the stall and closed and latched the gate.

"Now," he said, "We'll drain the pool and clean this side of the stall. So today, Wolee will stay on that side of the gate. Then, tomorrow morning, that side will be dirty, and you'll move him back to this side. But like I said, if you want to you can just put him in the other pool while you're cleaning."

Zoo work is very educational. For example, Nile and pygmy scat differs greatly. They have different modes of delivery as well, again, maybe this is too indelicate. On the other hand, working with animals is always a bit messy.

Brent showed me the great valve which drained the pool; I opened it and would soon be up to my ankles in poop. Everything needed to be washed down with a pressurized hose. As a way of marking territory, pygmies back into the walls when they defecate. The result is higher pressure between wall and hippo, which creates an outward spray that, in a short amount of time, covers the entire pen. Niles, on the other hand, drop drier globs of manure, more like an elephant or a horse, but I was in a pygmy stall.

Brent and I sprayed the walls and then used long-handled brushes to scrub the caramel-colored goo from the enclosure. It actually hardens into a lacquer, so soaking and rescrubbing was a part of the routine.

I thought I had finished the stall when Brent came back to say that the pool itself had drained. The finishing touch on the stalls, however, was to hose everything down one more time using the water pressure to force all the residue toward the front and down into the pool. From the pool, all the liquids would disappear down the drain, so he showed me how to minimize the bulkiest material using the water pressure to pulverize as much of the crud as possible. The remainder would have to be scooped up and carted away.

In honor of my first day, I was allowed to do most of the shoveling, though Brent did add a final scoop. All the while, Wolee was next door on the clean side of the stall, and already marking it so that it would feel more homey. I had to admit that the jets of spray he created were both impressive and effective, that is, if you're a hippo.

Brent reached the hose over the wall and washed off these early deposits and then turned the water onto Wolee's butt. Not only did this clean the animal, but he liked having it done. This was my third lesson in hippo's delight. The second had been the root beer candy, and the first, just plain beer. Brent explained what had become obvious, that is, hose the stuff when it's fresh and save a lot of work later. It also made the scene better for zoo visitors.

When it came to refilling the now clean pool, Brent's instructions were very precise, and my past memories underscored the lesson.

"This is vital for you to understand. For all the pygmies *except* Wolee, you fill the pool to the top, that's for the females, Mushka and Bomi. It doesn't even matter if you let it overflow. But in Wolee's case *never* fill it all the way. Fill it only halfway. If you add more water, he'll come out of there like a rocket. Again, *never* fill his pool more than half, if you do, he'll be on the loose." That explained a lot, and brought back less than fond memories.

"Feeding is last, always last," said Brent. "It's the reward for cooperation while you're cleaning. The routine has to be consistent, and the *end* of the routine is getting fed."

Food for all three hippos in our charge was prepared at one time. At this point, Brent encouraged me to take notes. I had already seen how Jim had chopped up the elephants' grub, and this process was similar with a major exception. That exception was eggplants. Evidently, they are the fourth pleasure on any hippo top ten.

Dietary needs were worthy of extra note-taking. Niles liked alfalfa hay added to their Timothy mix, but more than about one twentieth of a bale and it's diarrhea city. A keeper has to watch for mold in the hay. He told me how to identify mold versus normal dust. I was never to use moldy hay. Sometimes a whole shipment was moldy and that created real problems.

The hay mixture was topped with alfalfa pellets and a bucket of cut fruits and veggies. The food for a single Nile was about a quarter of the animal's size, but it would be eaten in twenty minutes. Pygmies would polish theirs off in ten.

When we fed Wolee, we just walked straight into his area. I broke up the hay bundles, but it was clear that he was waiting for the toppings of the fresh stuff.

Brent turned and said, "Wolee, sit." Again, to my astonishment, he listened. Sanchez poured the bucket of alfalfa pellets down into the small pile of hay.

"Steady. Steady," he commanded as he poured out the load of fresh fruits and vegetables.

"Okay," and that was the command that initiated the feast, and he had plenty of eating to do. We moved back out through the gate and slipped the deadbolt home.

One down, two to go.

CHAPTER THREE

Wolee, as it turned out, was a pushover. The learning curve was going to get steeper as we approached Bomi's stall. This female pygmy was actually the mother of Mushka, who I had seen with Sandusky. Brent seemed apprehensive.

"Don't mess with Bomi," he said. I learned that posture spoke volumes. Pygmies lower their heads and tighten up when they are angry. Bomi was showing us rage.

"She's not as scary as Red," said Sanchez, "but she's still a mean old bitch. Keepers used to go into the stall with her until one was attacked. She took a couple of bites out of a guy, and was lucky he wasn't killed. He hit her in the face with a shovel to get her off; that's how she lost an eye. It was quite a battle."

We climbed in through the empty side of Wolee's pen to get into the space behind Bomi. We set her food on the concrete floor and went back behind a metal barricade, the last one in the hall. Brent turned a crank to open the way for the pygmy to get back to where we had placed her dinner. I heard wet, slapping footsteps and saw a dark form glide in as I peered over the five-foot barricade. She was still in her threatening pose as Sanchez turned the crank in the other direction to seal in the animal. I thought she'd head for her meal, but there were no sounds of chomping.

"She'll eat when we're gone," said Brent. "She doesn't like people."

We cut back through the public area to get back to the stall that had been vacated. We set to work cleaning the area so that the pygmy could be moved back once cleaning and feeding were complete.

My instructions were to clean everything, refill the pool, and vacate the area. After that, I would crank the gate open again, and Bomi would come back into her stall.

"When Bomi's done eating she'll come back, so close her in. She'll get in the pool when she's ready. The water filling the pools is ice cold, so all the hippos will wait for it to warm up to room temperature."

After that, Brent left to not return until the afternoon. My next task was to clean Red's stall, but that couldn't be done until Sandusky cleaned the large pool. Brent said that Steve would explain the mechanics of moving the big Nile from the holding area to the stall where she could eat.

By the time I had Bomi's stall clean, she was already finished eating. She had to wait a little longer, however, until her pool filled. Once done, I opened the gate and she was back in the correct spot. I then went to find the other hippo keeper.

Steve was in the stall with Blackie, the zoo's male Nile. These animals can weight up to six thousand pounds, but Blackie, who was over twenty-three years-old, was a not-so-slender five thousand. Both he and Red had been at the zoo since 1955.

Unlike Red, however, this male was gentle and good-natured. He seemed to have a perpetual smile, but that may just have been his natural hippo good looks.

Steve looked up from his scrubbing when he saw my approach. "How ya doin'?"

"Good," I said. "The big pool's cleaned and filled; I suppose it's okay to move Red."

He agreed, and went back to his work. "I've got this pool draining now," he said, "I'm almost done in here."

I couldn't believe the difference between Blackie and Red. This big, black rubbery creature was lying in the stall where Sandusky was scrubbing. Steve noticed my gaze. "He's a sweetheart," he said, "Old Black is as nice a fellow as you'd want to meet. Aren't you, big Blackie?" The Nile opened one eye, then closed it.

"Watch this," said Steve. "Tomorrow, I'll bring my camera and you can snap a picture. Brent would never do that for me, but I'll bet you would."

He set his brush down on the floor, and jostled the great animal until the sleepy bulk stirred and rose up on its skinny legs. He then hopped, butt first and scooted up onto Blackie's back, sitting on him as if sitting on the tailgate of a truck. He swung his legs back and forth, like a kid on a swing.

"Will you help me get a picture of this?" he laughed. I saw no reason not to get this in the archives. He slid down from the beast and winced slightly as his feet touched the ground. His *zookeeper's back* was not a joke.

Now that the hippo's stall was clean, I went and got a second shovel to help Steve muck out the pool. I did my best to anticipate what needed to be done so that I could deal with moving the wheelbarrow as it got heavier, and it did get heavy. The soggy manure held a lot of water. I was wearing cloth tennis shoes, and he had on Galeton steel-toed rubber work boots that came up almost to his knees. By now, those boots looked pretty good.

"This shit's heavy," I said, adding another dripping load to the wheelbarrow.

Steve grinned and chuckled at that and continued shoveling.

"Hey, if I fell over forward right now," I said, "I'd be shit-faced."

"You're a nut."

He stopped to wipe his forehead, and I kept shoveling. The odd thing to me was that there was very little of what I would call a foul odor. It turns out that the Niles fully digest their food. The result is, in spite of the great bulk, it's much less noxious than the stools of a dog or cat.

I suppose that I wanted to prove myself, and I quickly filled and maybe overfilled the large barrow. Steve didn't say anything, but he had a mischievous look about him. I didn't understand what he must have been thinking. I hadn't made the load any larger that what I was used to hauling at Schuster's Greenhouse. That, however, was on flat ground.

"You gonna push that up those steps?" asked Steve.

Actually, I *thought* I was, but my thinking didn't square with the reality that I couldn't get up the first step. The thing probably weighed two hundred pounds, so I dumped out about fifty pounds of crap and tried it again.

Okay, I can do this, I thought after I'd achieved the first step.

"It would help if there were some air in the tire," I said.

"Hey, you're doing great," said Steve, "I usually take about half that much in a load."

In my mind every sort of disaster was taking place. I imagined it getting out of balance and careening sideways releasing a river to slosh back down into the pool. Finally, I reached the top and none of the worst scenarios had happened.

"You took too much," said Steve. "I didn't think you could push that up there, but you did. You're strong like I used to be."

"Couldn't you just train Blackie to shit up here?" I thought *that* the best suggestion.

"I'll get the next one," Steve said. Youthfulness and stupidity kicked in and I offered to do it. After all, Steve was sixty-four, had a bad back, and an arm that had been gored by an elephant.

"I'll push 'em up," I said, "but I won't try to carry so much."

"I tell you what," said Steve. "You wheel the loads out, and I'll dry mop the public floor later."

That was our first real deal, and I took out five loads. With all the sloshing, my pants were pretty wet and I understood why the keeper uniforms had brown pants.

Steve was true to his word about mopping the floor, and I Windexed the lobby doors. The zoo was now open to guests, but it was February and we had the day pretty much to ourselves.

When the large pool was half full, we went to deal with Red. The doors that isolated her from the pond were driven by an electrical motor rather than cranked by hand. The control lever was a small toggle switch.

"Now, use the switch to nurse the door along. If you keep holding it, the door will get moving too fast, hit the end, and come off the track. So just sort of goose it a little, then a little more. Just nurse it. Especially when it gets close to the end. Never open it all the way or close it all the way by just holding the switch the whole time. Take it slow and easy."

"Have the doors ever flown off?" I asked. That idea was terrifying. It would mean Red would be on the loose.

"It's happened," he said, "but not too often. Maintenance has to come down and put it back. It takes a lot of men to lift."

Sandusky *goosed* the switch and the door began to open. I looked through the slot and saw the looming shape of Red moving through the door into the pool area.

"You got to be careful that the animal goes all the way through," said Steve. "Make sure she isn't just standing in the doorway when you start to close the door."

When he was sure that the hippo had cleared the entrance, he inched the door shut again. Red was now safely out of her stall, and it would be safe to enter her domain.

Steve and I cleaned out her area in about three minutes. The Nile didn't make a big mess because she always went in one spot. We then set out her meal of Timothy, alfalfa, pellets, fruits, and vegetables. Red was eyeing us the entire time. We could see her through a barred opening on the upper half of the door. Her name was well deserved as the red and tan hippo sweat flowed over her neck, face, and back. It was the color of cedar.

"So Red's a mean one?" I said, breaking the silence.

He shrugged, "I'm not going to be sitting on her back. Don't ever trust her, and don't ever go in a stall or a yard with her. I get along with her okay only because I stay out of her way. She won't be friendly to you. She'll kill anyone who sets foot inside her cage, that's for sure. I don't agitate her, and she doesn't agitate me. Some people have agitated her, and that's not right. She's been tormented in her day. No one should do that."

"What do you mean?"

"Oh, just... things... mostly yelled at and prodded through the bars."

We stepped out of the back of the stall, and I cranked the back door shut in preparation for opening the big door which would invite Red back. The hippo could be viewed through a peephole. This time, I would operate the mechanism.

"Pull it toward you," said Steve.

The big door began moving with an echoing clamor and the rolling of chains. I nursed it along, in spurts, as I had been told. I could see the thirty-five-hundred pound female glide through the door. Unlike Blackie who waddled in ponderous jerks, Red moved smoothly, almost gracefully.

Yesterday, the pool was Blackie's domain. Today, Red would have access to the big pond.

"What would happen if Blackie and Red were in the same stall together?" I asked.

"They could be," exclaimed Steve. "They were together most of their lives. They've had a lot of babies. I don't think they want them breeding anymore. Otherwise, they'd get along fine. Ask Vince, he could tell you better."

I knew Vince Rimedio was a keeper in the Ostrich Barn, and a rock star in the sport of goosing at the time clock.

Steve and I went back to the keeper room and had some coffee. It was noon and our first real break. For the next few hours there was not much to do so I brought my notes up-to-date. About 3:00 Brent showed up to ask how things were going.

"Perfect," said Steve, smiling. "I think we've got it under control."

"Good. I'm going back up to the garage. We've got an engine completely apart." After that, I never saw him in the Pachyderm Building again. I understood why. When you break an animal's heart, you don't come back on a careless whim just to break it again. When it's over, it's over. Brent had said goodbye to Wolee, in his own way. I knew it when he told me that Wolee liked root beer barrels and showed me how to make him sit. It was the way he said to me, "And *that's* how you feed Wolee." Brent wasn't a warm and sentimental guy, but I knew that teaching me was his plea to me to take care of his baby. I can understand what Brent was thinking, but who knew what was going on in the mind of the sharp-tusked, powerful young pachyderm?

CHAPTER FOUR

The next day I was feeling comfortable with what I had to face that day. Steve remembered his camera and wanted me to snap his picture while he was seated on Blackie. We went to the stall where Sandusky quickly combed his hair, and I snapped one photo, and then a second for good measure. The keeper was really pleased and couldn't wait to show his friends, who met him at a local bar.

The morning routine began, and I was flying solo. Red was in the big pool so I closed the barrier and cleaned her stall. When that was complete, it was simply a matter of opening the gate, and, with the lure of food, isolate her from the pool. The pool would be Blackie's all day, and Red would have to be *dry-docked*.

I prepared the pygmy's food and fed Bomi with added caution which was based on Brent's stern warning. Wolee was next.

I had taken a detour on the way to work in order to pick up my new supplies; of course I'm referring to a box of root beer barrels. I was totally prepared to perform my very best imitation of a doting Sanchez.

I was actually looking forward to adopting *Wolee booger* as my personal pet. I cleaned the pool and got ready to move the animal.

"Who's a Wolee booger? Wolee. Wolee. Wolee." I had two buckets of his favorite mixture. "Hey, Wolee, Wolee, Wolee."

As naïve as a first grader on the first day of school, I opened the dead bolt, and walked into his side of the pen. I was about two strides into Wolee's pen when he charged me.

I was only eight feet from him and he would be on me at the blink of an eye, but I saw him. I stumbled backwards through the gate, hitting my right hip against the metal wall. The two buckets were on the ground and the grain pellets and fruit and vegetable mix was all around me.

I didn't get much of a grip on the gate, and though I tried, I wasn't quick enough to pull it closed. Through the gap in the opening, I saw the chomping mouth approaching at light speed. Then, bam. The hippo crashed head first into the steel gate and drove it home. My hopefulness, however, was short lived. It bounced open about twenty inches, and Wolee's hog-shaped body poured through the opening.

I was now running to the front of the stall and took a flying broad jump over the pool. I cleared it and was now in the space between the front wall of the pool and the brick railed wall. Fortunately, I landed on my feet and brought my momentum under control. Whirling around to see the pursuit, I saw the last thing I expected. Wolee was *back to normal* just as if nothing had happened. He was standing at the open gate and gobbling pieces of sweet potato.

In the course of his grazing, he wandered back to his side of the divided stall. The door swung shut of its own accord. It was not, however, latched. This was my best chance, I jumped across the pool and slid the deadbolt before the animal was aware.

I scooped the pellets and cut produce back into the buckets as Wolee continued chowing down on the food like a greedy monster. I dumped the pails over the wall and the load came right down on Wolee's head which was now covered in alfalfa dust and lettuce leaves.

"F--- you," I yelled and stormed out of the stall, my heart still racing. Of course, my shout had exploded through the entire building.

Steve had to have heard me. It was my first day on my own, and I was already yelling profanities at the animals. He, on the other hand, was in the stall with his Mushka.

"How ya doing?" he asked calmly.

"Well, I just went into Wolee's pen and he charged me."

"Oh, God no!" exclaimed Steve, "don't ever go in with Wolee."

CHAPTER FIVE

Jim Rybicki was an unusual keeper. What made him unusual was the fact that he was always reading something literary, books by Dostoevsky or Hemingway, for example. Mertus used to read plays when he was at the zoo; Rybicki read literary novels.

He spent a lot of time working with Tiani. It was a job which required great patience with a lot of repetition. I watched him for some time on my second day. He was working on the *leg command*. The command would be given, and then the keeper would touch the animal to indicate lifting a specific leg. These were not circus tricks. This command, for example, was needed when the animal needed to have her feet worked on, and to be chained or unchained. *Trunk up* had the elephant lift her trunk and open her mouth.

I knew that I didn't have the patience for that sort of thing, but Jim worked tirelessly with Tiani. Everything he did was part of a training regimen he'd developed with Ellen. The list of commands was long, a testimony to the intelligence of these giants. *Stretch, turn, kneel, get in line, steady, back, move up, spin*, and more were an important part of a vocabulary which provided safety, both for the animals and keepers.

During these training sessions, Tiani was hard at work, and Simba was always watching her progress. She seemed to be thinking, *I'm glad I know all that stuff already. Where's my treat?* Every once in awhile Jim would reward Simba's patience with a treat. The older elephant understood every word of command, and I was seeing it in her expressions. It was dawning on me that these lumbering creatures were extremely intelligent in their own right.

Learning the words of commands was not Tiani's only difficulty. She was being physically challenged as well. With the balance of a toddler, she tried to obey Jim's commands, but her wobbly legs wouldn't cooperate.

"No. No," Jim would say patiently, and they'd try again. She really wanted to please her kind keeper.

The persistence of the man and the beast made me glad Jim and Ellen were training the little elephant and not me. I would have sucked at that. For me, it was a lot simpler to go shovel out a stall full of hippo dung.

By mid-morning Blackie was in the big pool, and Steve invited me to see another of what he considered comical wonders.

Sandusky walked to the edge of the central pool and slapped the front of the wall. On cue, the huge Nile rose majestically out of the water, placing his massive head on the railing. Steve reached over and affectionately petted Black's upper muzzle.

"He wants a treat," said Steve. "I don't ever make him exert himself like this unless I have a treat for him." At this, he pulled an apple from his pocket. "This is really comical," he said. (*Comical* was one of his favorite words.)

Steve dropped the apple into Blackie's mouth, and the great maw closed. The hippo chewed and chewed. You'd think his mouth had a bushel full of fruit in there. Finally, he popped his big mouth open again, ready for another apple. The only problem was that the apple in his mouth was still whole, not even a mark on it. Steve reached in and recovered the saliva-covered fruit.

"The Black can't chew an apple if it's in one piece," he said. "You gotta break it in half." As he said this, he gave the apple a firm twist and it split open. This time, Blackie swallowed it.

The hippo opened wide for seconds, but instead, Steve reached into the mouth and started pulling bits of hay out from between gigantic rear molars.

"He appreciates it when I clean the straw out from between his teeth. Go ahead, try it."

I hadn't expected this, but I obeyed. I grabbed a wet clump of hay wedged tightly between two teeth.

"Tug hard, he'll hold still."

Yeah, and Wolee is a sweetheart who'll do anything for a root beer barrel. I did what I was asked, however, and it was true. Even with both of us tugging on a stubborn clump of hay, Blackie remained stoic.

To further demonstrate the animal's awareness. He said, "Watch this. When I pull my arm out of his mouth, he starts to close it. When I put it back, he opens right up. Blackie knows when you have your hands in his mouth. He's the sweetest animal I've ever met, but that's nothing. Watch this."

With this, Steve leaned over and put his neatly combed head right in between front Blackie's huge upper and lower tusks. No sooner did he do this than the Nile opened wide, and the keeper stuck his whole head deeply into the wet cavern. He continued to speak from inside the hippo.

"He'll never in a million years close his mouth on my head 'cause he's so gentle. If I start to pull my head out, he starts to close, but if I change directions, he'll open up again."

As he told me this, he demonstrated and the animal was true to his words. Fortunately, Blackie did not have bad breath.

As all this happened, I could see that the hippo's big left eye cocked toward us. He was watching every motion. The Black's eyes were soft with sensitivity and radiated a calm intelligence. After the *all clear*, Steve thanked the animal, and the mouth closed with a wet clomp.

"You've solved a mystery," I offered.

"I have?"

"Blackie and Red are each in this pool on alternate nights; if Blackie's in the pool and you slap the sides, he comes up, like he's doing now. When I was night watchman, one of the junior rangers tried to show me that. It was about 3:00 in the morning, and he bent over the pool and slapped the sides, but no hippo came up."

Steve grinned knowingly, and said, "Red must have been in the pool that night. Is that guy still living?"

"I think so," I said.

Steve chuckled, "Yeah, you don't want to be looking down into this pool when Red's in there. That was a lucky fellow."

"That's all for now, Blackie. That's all," said the old keeper, and Blackie lurched away from the wall and dropped down into the pool with a wallop that sent six-inch waves racing away from his body.

After that, many was the time that I plucked hay out from between Blackie's teeth and split apples in half for him. Everyone loved Blackie. He was the wise and loving gentle giant of the Pachyderm Building in those days.

Much of the day was spent hosing down the stalls as they were being marked by the animals. Mushka, in particular, seemed to have an artistic flare for spatter painting. Goodness, that girl could paint. Huge areas. Dynamic.

Wolee was equally prolific, but only left smudges when compared to Mushka's skill at pointillism. I was working along the long line of stalls, and finally reached old, dangerous one-eyed Bomi. She was in her pool at the time, and surprised me when she suddenly bobbed up to the surface. She quickly came out of the water, but not at all like Wolee. Bomi was excited and squirming like a giant puppy. It was as if she'd been waiting for me to get there.

Her head was two feet from me, and I could see where her left eye should have been, there was a bare socket. This was the scar that remained from a life and death battle with a keeper. I felt sorry for this old fighter, who was giving me a friendly greeting. Her mouth hung open, much like the way I had seen Mushka and Wolee greeting Steve and Brent.

Ignoring Brent's advice to fear her, I stepped in closer. After all, he had been way wrong about Wolee. Soon, I was actually leaning over Bomi, as she bobbed like a black cork in her pool. As I leaned over her, she kept her head in a natural position and looked up at me. We were alone in the far end of the building, and I had the sudden feeling of déjà vu. I even remembering dreaming it. It came into my mind that I had dreamed Bomi was friendly to me.

"Well, what are you doing? Are you a good Bomi? You are good girl, aren't you? Yes, you are... Such a good Bomi. That's a good girl."

She responded to my offering of mush, and moved back and forth in the water, sending up bright splashes. Her mouth was wide open. She wasn't chewing the air like a hippo who's begging. She was just grinning essentially, and arching her neck way back to look at me as clearly as possible.

"Who's a Bomi? That's my good Bomi Womi."

I reached my right hand out and held it high above her head, holding my hand still for a few seconds so that she could see it there and get used to it. Then, slowly and cautiously, I brought my hand down.

"That's a good girl," I said softly.

Without making any sudden movements, gradually I placed my hand down right on top of her head. I sensed that this was an action she had once been used to. Nothing had a sense of reality. Easily and softly, being careful not to touch her ears, I petted her on the top of her head, slowly, like petting a kitten. Her head rolled back and her mouth stayed wide in its grin.

"That's a good Bomi. That's my Bomi."

I petted her whole back, giving her a back rub all over the big rubbery hide. As I rather briskly rubbed her hide, I felt slippery mucus sliding off her back, oozing between my fingers. It felt like the huge bobbing watermelon was covered with slimy moisturizer. She seemed to accept my attention, but I stayed ready to pull my hand out of the water and jump back. Maybe this was really a stupid thing to do. But somehow, she had told me what she wanted.

She was an old, battled-scarred lady, quite a bit on the gruesome side to tell the truth. This time, when her mouth opened wide, she began chewing the air as if begging for food. Again, she twisted her head oddly in order to watch me with her right eye.

"Bomi Womi. Do you want a root beer barrel? Do you? You do."

Of course, she did, and the candy was conveniently in a flattened box that lived in my pocket. I dropped the little barrel-shaped piece of candy directly on her tongue. She didn't close her mouth until my hand was safely pulled away. She was one happy hippo as she submerged beneath the rolling surface of the water.

I had made friends with the *deadly* Bomi. More precisely, she had made friends with me. After that, Bomi never went into exile in the back hallway while I cleaned her stall. She stayed with me when I came into her area. She followed me around like a faithful pet.

Bomi was truly a dangerous animal, but not to me. My relationship with her was really no different than Sandusky and Mushka or Sanchez and Wolee. They were dangerous to me. Each pygmy had his or her well-established territory, and that territory included a human being. Understanding these animals was complex. There was a lot more going on than most people would ever perceive.

CHAPTER SIX

On Saturday, Ellen Leach returned to Pachy after her two days off. She was working with the elephants and invited me to tag along. "I'm taking Tiani for a walk through the zoo. Wanna come?

"We have to go right now," she said, "before the zoo opens. I don't want her out there when people are in the park."

The dew was still heavy on the lawns as Ellen, Tiani, and I walked out into the air of the morning. We moved around the perimeter of the elephant pen and past the refreshment stand. The young African moved along like an obedient puppy.

As much as the elephant was enjoying this, so was I. It seemed like forever since I had been in the zoo in the daylight. The birds were singing as we walked past the Sea Lion Pool and across the open mall. The grass was soaking wet.

"This is really good for Tiani," she explained. "I'd like to bring Simba out, but I haven't worked up the courage to do that. There's really no reason not to, but it's never been done. I'm thinking that if we keep doing this with Tiani while she's small, we can simply keep it up when she's grown."

My shoes were now soaking wet, and we were nearing the rhesus colony on Monkey Island. Tiani was getting friskier now, even ripping off clumps of lawn and shoving them in her mouth. I keep saying that she was still small, but she probably weighed nine hundred pounds and was leaving an impression on the soft ground. Suddenly she trumpeted loudly and took off running west across the mall.

"No. No. Stop!" yelled Ellen. She ran after the elephant, but Tiani was widening the gap. I was running next to Ellen.

"I think I can catch her," I offered.

"Do it," she said. I took off, but could still hear Ellen's voice from behind. "Just grab the top of her ear and hold on to it. Then yell, *NO!*"

It was a sprint, and Tiani looked back to gauge my progress. This was a game for her, and we were in a race. After about sixty yards, we were running side-by-side. I reached out and grabbed on to the fuzzy top of her big flapping ear. "NO!"

Tiani hit the brakes, turning up big divots as she slid across the wet lawn. She then gave me a look as if saying, *That was awesome.* I'd swear she was grinning as steamy heat rose from her body.

Ellen came up and took hold of Tiani's ear. "Thanks," she said. "I hope nobody saw that. If they did, we'll never hear the end of it."

I'd already heard rumors in the zoo about Ellen and the *out-of-control* elephants. So I agreed with Ellen when she suggested getting Tiani back in the barn before something else happened. We turned around and made our way back toward the Pachyderm Building. A couple of maintenance workers saw us walking along with everything *completely* under control. We had dodged a bullet.

In my opinion, Ellen was a completely modern woman. She had a tiny piercing in her nose, with a diamond stud in it. This was long before it was a fashion rage. She endured criticism with equanimity, and kept a clear focus. She was always well-kempt, and considering she shoveled shit all day, that was a remarkable feat. She was the whole package. A competent, attractive woman whose feminist views weren't always accepted by some of the older guys. Everyone who worked with her and knew her, however, really liked her and I truly believe she liked everybody.

She ate differently than the rest of her staff. We mostly ate fast food, but she was a vegetarian who prepared spinach quiche, vegetarian lasagna, and an oxymoronic dish called vegetarian *meatloaf.*

She was, at that time, an oddity in the male-dominated world of the Cleveland Zoo. Prior to her arrival, the zoo was pretty much an all-male world. She was the first woman keeper ever, and there were some who balked when she was hired. Then Linda started in Birds. She was the second woman keeper and never forgave me for the mice that were left in her traps.

Ellen was clever at adapting to the rigors of being a keeper. While she couldn't lift a sixty-pound bale of hay or a hundred-pound grain sack, she'd rig something to do the job. She might move the grain sack on a cart, or drag the hay bale with a hook. Since she advocated equality among genders in the workplace, I never heard her say to a male worker, "Oh, would you get me a bale of hay? It's too heavy for me." She was adamant about figuring a way to do everything herself.

Ellen was *all* about animals, especially African elephants. You could tell that in her conversations. Guys shoveling manure would say something like, "What did you think of Brian Sipe last night?" or "My wife is really excited about our new car."

Ellen was completely different. She talked about elephants, their diet, habits, vanishing habitat, skin care, training, Asians versus Africans. In my eyes, she was quite an extraordinary person. Everything she said was interesting and useful. Her lessons were a direct rebuttal to the other keepers who thought she knew little about elephants.

"I've been reading some studies on zoo elephants," she said to me one day. "One report theorizes that in a zoo the elephants begin to regard their keepers as other elephants, as members of the herd. That means that the keepers are part of the hierarchy, with rank and position within the group. A lot of times the keepers are unaware of this, but it totally affects the way the animal looks at them. Isn't that interesting? The elephants give their various keepers a rank and position among the elephant herd, which then consists of keepers as elephant surrogates and the elephants. If they're right, the animals begin to think of the keeper as the dominant elephant. That makes sense to me, since anyone who becomes the elephant keeper has to go through a trial period and establish dominance over the other elephants. That's why they are obedient to the keeper. If the elephants never accept the keeper into the herd as one of them, their obedience is withheld, and there is not a comfortable resolution to the order of the herd. That makes a lot of sense to me, actually."

She was very concerned about skin care for the elephants. She wrote to keepers all over the country to see what they were doing to combat dry skin. "One keeper told me that the secret is peanuts," she said. "There, they make sure each elephant eats ten pounds a day, for the oil. But in the summer Simba eats tons of peanuts that the people throw her and still her skin is dry. It's just about the biggest mystery I'd like to solve. Some people say that they rub Neat's Foot Oil on their skin. But that's not the solution I'm looking for. I want to know how they can have perfect skin internally, from diet. The skin on the outside is dead cells, anyway, so just oiling it isn't a solution. That's just cosmetic."

She was constantly on guard to see that all the keepers used exactly the same vocabulary. "We all must give commands in the same way with the same words and inflections," she said. "Jim and I have spent a lot of time getting on the same page about that. If I say, *I told you to get in line* one time and then *will you get in line* another, and Jim says, *Simba, get into line,* that's not good for anyone. Inconsistency of commands among dozens of keepers over the years could be one factor that irritated Simba and caused some communication breakdowns between keeper and elephant. We can't put extra phrases at the beginnings of commands. For example, we say, *Get in line*, then if the command is repeated, we shouldn't say, *I said, get in line*. When the vet comes he uses different commands, and that's not good. I've talked to Don and Alan about this. I told them that only *keepers* should give commands to the elephants, and that hasn't made me popular. I've heard the vet say, *Give me your foot* and he expects Simba to raise her foot, but we taught her to respond to *foot*. The *keeper* should give the command. Simba's not really obeying the vet anyway. She's only obeying because there's a keeper in the cage. If he says, *Trunk up* to Simba and I'm standing there, she looks like she obeys him, but if I weren't there in the cage, she'd probably attack him. Yet he lives with this illusion that he's giving commands to an elephant. The whole subject of the vet or the curators walking around like the *hi-de-ho*, showing off and giving commands to the elephants is a sore point with me."

Initially, the zoo had a problem with the fact that Ellen was keeping the elephant exhibit open on Sunday nights until 7:00. All the other keepers would be gone by then, and the management were worried that a woman alone might be vulnerable to be attacked by some pervert.

Her defense was simple and to the point, "If attacked, I'll just run and get between Simba's legs. If a man wants to try and attack me, he can go for it. That's the safest place on earth for me. Then they said, 'Well, what if you're alone in the building and the man has a gun?' I said, 'Well, what if a male keeper is alone in the building and the man has a gun?'"

She had her run-ins with the zoo's vet. He'd decide that an elephant needed an injection of some vitamin and expect the keepers to administer the shot. She protested that if he was going to have the elephant mad at somebody, better the vet who came twice a year than a keeper who's there nearly every day. When Ellen put her foot down and insisted that *if* there was going to be an injection, it would be done by the vet. It then turned out that Simba didn't really need a shot *that much*. "I'm not going to stick a needle in Simba one day and then be shoveling around her the next day," she said.

Ellen explained to me that Simba wouldn't wade in the outdoor pool, even though she had when she was younger (at least that's what the older keepers had reported). She surmised that the elephant had had a bad experience in the water. Maybe the pool was struck by lightning while she was in it. Ellen encouraged the animal, even waded into the water up to her waist to try and coax her in. This was an important goal for her. Wading would provide a means of rinsing Simba's feet and legs after a night of standing in one spot which was fouled by urine. She really cared about these animals and would lose sleep over the their health and comfort.

"People come around and they want to see Simba stand up on her hind legs like a circus elephant," she said. "I explain that Africans can't do that. Only Asians can. The African's center of gravity is just so different. They can't stand on their heads or sit up like a dog and raise their front legs like a circus animal. They can't get over a wall that's only three feet high, either. It doesn't take a very high wall to pen in an elephant. So if Simba's attacking you and you see a low wall, climb over it."

As I mentioned earlier, Ellen was the zoo's first female keeper in a time when gender discrimination had just been added into civil rights law. She was not in her position by accident or seniority. She was a rare keeper, who actually had a degree in her field. When one of the interviewers announced, *We're not going to hire you because you're a woman,* she interrupted with "Excuse me, but that's sexist and this is the 1970s the last time I looked." She knew the law was on her side, but didn't want to completely offend her potential bosses. "You need to base your decision on my qualifications, my work history, and my performance in this interview. According to law, you can't refuse to hire a person based on race or gender." They argued that hiring her would not be fair to the men, there were no separate bathrooms, and the work was too physical. She countered by saying that separate restrooms were not a problem and that she already knew that some of the older male keepers managed the work with physical limitations. From her descriptions, I knew that she had fought for this job, and now she was fighting for the animals.

"I think it would be great if we had some Asians here, too. Then the public could see the difference between them and Africans. They are a different species and can't interbreed, but they can coexist and form a herd. Side by side, people could see the differences. The Africans have two fingers, opposing, on the end of their trunk and the Asians have one. Of course, the difference everyone notices is the size of the ears. The Asian's ears are so much smaller and their heads are round at the top. Like a lot of people, I think the Africans are more beautiful, but that's just me. I've heard Asians are really sweet, and I'd love it if we had one here. A lot of circuses have Asians that become too old to perform, and we could really help an animal out. I read about certain ones that are available for free. Some people are trying to give them away. When I hear about one that needs adopted, I put in the suggestion, but so far they don't seem to think too much of my suggestions."

Differences in training techniques with Asian and African elephants were a curiosity for her. One she wanted to unravel. She once told me about an article she had read. It was written by a former trainer with Ringling Brothers who claimed that whereas Africans should be trained with rewards, Asians by punishment. She was not so sure about this distinction and believed that Asians might do well with positive reinforcement. It was certainly true that Africans like Simba would eventually rebel against a punishment model. She had never worked with Asian elephants, but was anxious to try.

I was fascinated by the way both Ellen and Jim approached animal training. My respect for them only grew as time went on. The odd part was that the career I had left behind was involved with editing primary school books. Now, the philosophy of elephant training that I was learning was eerily similar to what educators were trying to use in elementary schools. Both were about consistency, positive reinforcement, praise, and tactile learning. It all came together, and was something that occupied my thoughts on a daily basis.

Ellen talked to me in the keeper room and in the back halls about elephants, but I did *not* go into the elephants' cage with her at anytime during those early weeks. Something was going on between Simba and me. She would charge anytime I went near the front of her cage. It was unnerving, and I suspected that she remembered me as a night watchman. I was someone who did not belong in her territory.

All I had to do was go out into the public area and Simba would storm to the front of the enclosure growling with a deep rumble, flapping her massive ears. Her outrage was directed specifically at me, and I recognized the look in her big, dark eye, her right eye which was always glaring my way.

If I was dry mopping the floor near her, she'd bellow and charge. Other people, even visitors, could walk by and she paid no attention to them. Keepers from other areas could accompany Ellen or Jim into the cage itself, and Simba would remain calm and cool, chewing on hay. This vision haunted my fears, especially when she shoved her two-foot-long ivory tusks through the bars at me rasping them along the steel. It sounded like twin sabers being honed. Then her gigantic forehead would slam into the bars. *WHAM.*

Ellen laughed it off, "Oh, she's just playing with your head."

If that was so, she was doing a fine job. Incredible as it seems, Simba also knew that at some point in the future I was the next guy who was going to become an elephant keeper. She knew I was next to have a confrontation with her. The war had already begun; Ellen instructed me not to enter the cage until I was ready to confront the beast and take my place in the herd. Until that time, I would just be with the hippos.

I was scared to death, but also completely determined to do it.

CHAPTER SEVEN

Animals are creatures of habit. They do the same thing every day, and if the routine varies, then something's wrong. On days he didn't have access to a pool, Blackie always laid down in the same place in his stall, right next to the wall. When Steve or I put his meal down, he stood up and ate it. Then he returned to his spot. He was as predictable as gravity. On the days he had access to the pool, he immediately went down to it when he was done eating. That was his routine.

Well, all of a sudden he wasn't doing any of that. Steve was a mess; he was sure Blackie was going to die. He didn't eat. He didn't go in the pool. He just laid there for about three days. Sandusky phoned in on his days off to ask about him. This was February of 1980.

It was so clear to us that Blackie was sick. He just lay there like a stuffed whale, even when Steve pleaded with him to get up. The old keeper was walking around with tears in his eyes. Once I found him crying inconsolably as he sat next to the great Nile.

Each day, both of us documented Blackie's condition in our daily reports. Finally, on the fourth day the vets made a visit. Steve was at lunch, and two vets were accompanied by the zoo's Director himself. They were in suits, ties, and dress shoes. Of course, I was wearing my brown zookeeper's uniform.

"Where's this sick hippo?" the head vet asked.

"It's Blackie," I said. "We can go in with him."

We walked down the back hall and cranked open the door to the stall. Blackie was still in the same place, not even attempting to go into the pool which was open to him that day. He loved the pool, normally.

Annoyed, the vet asked, "What's the matter with him? He looks fine to me." I explained about his listlessness and his not going into the pool. "Oh, nonsense," scoffed the learned veterinarian. "That doesn't mean anything. What do you know about it?"

I was surprised he said such a rude thing.

Apologetically, I said, "Well, you know… it's just that… well, we work with him every day, and I guess we're just so familiar with his normal routine. Blackie never lays there like that for so long. Every day he gets up around 3:00 in the afternoon and eats and then goes into the pool. Something's wrong."

"There's nothing wrong with this animal. He's old and might die anytime. I'd say he'll probably die within the next year or two, but I can't predict that. But there's nothing specifically wrong with him that requires my attention. There's nothing I can do about the fact that he's getting old. Now listen, we were heading out to a big luncheon and you have us down here for nothing, and I don't appreciate that."

I hadn't even requested that they come to the building and didn't know why they were there at that moment. I could tell that all three were annoyed with me.

Looking back, I think that Blackie must have had a major blockage, and maybe the visit from these strangers stirred up his internal processes because suddenly the animal wheezed and struggled to his feet. It was not easy as he tried to get some of his great bulk moving forward.

This only underscored the diagnosis. "See, there's absolutely nothing wrong with this animal. He's fine, as is evidenced by the fact that he just stood up. I know you're one of his keepers... I know you people can become emotionally attached to these animals, and I appreciate that, but you're not the expert, we are."

Blackie took a few clumsy steps forward, rotated his body and began to back into the corner where he always defecated.

The Director and the veterinarians went into a little huddle which excluded me. They turned to look back at the Nile, "Look at that. He's got good energy."

I was behind them all. I could see the broad backs of three nice wool jackets, flecked with fibers of gold and brown. All I knew was that Blackie was now earnestly backing up toward the wall. It was a sure sign, with absolutely zero doubt, that he was about to dump a load.

I shouted out the most direct warning that I could. "Okay, I know I don't know anything, but we all need to get out of this stall *immediately*."

The lead vet assumed that I was trying to suggest that the animal was about to become dangerous. He knew better. "Oh, nonsense."

I had tried, and was the only one who heeded my warning by ducking through the open back gate and tucking into a spot out of the line of fire.

Blackie's muscular tail smacked the cold concrete wall. After about eighteen loud slaps, he was ready to claim his territorial rights by unleashing an enormous pelting storm of green-brown hippo dung.

It was too late for the dignitaries whose feeble retreat could not outrun Blackie as he opened fire. Their heads and nicely pressed dress suits were soaked and speckled with flying manure. Meanwhile, I was safely protected.

They hurried out into the back hall to a cadence of *Jesus Christ.*

I'd tried to warn them, but what did I know? On the other hand, I think their visit had really helped the patient. I think that big shit helped him a lot.

CHAPTER EIGHT

There were a great many duties that went with my new job. For example, at Red's end of the building there lived a squawking collection of Egyptian geese outside in the yard. They stayed outside all year around, even in the coldest Cleveland winters. There were about nine of them. There were one mated pair and seven individuals who hung out in a group like a street gang, muttering all the time. They were simple to care for. All I did was throw out lettuce and a few scoops of feed for them twice a day. Twice a day I supplied them with fresh water as well.

We also cared for the zoo's three huge elephant tortoises during the winter months. These were kept in one of the unused pens. Unlike the pygmies these hardly ever tried to charge me, or anyone for that matter.

Dealing with hay shipments was heavy work. When we took delivery, keepers from all over the zoo would gather to unload and stack the fresh-cut bales. The older keepers were exempt from handling the bales as they came from the back of an eighteen wheeler and along a conveyor belt to where we'd lift and stack. It took hours, but gave me a chance to see people from the other parts of the zoo. People like Steve Gove, Tad Schoffner, Tim Pappas, and Ken Pekarek. Rybicki and I rounded out the crew. Oh, there was one other. Ellen pulled her weight by using a bale hook to position the great stack.

It's funny how my point of view had changed. As a watchman, I liked roaming over the entire zoo. Now, I stayed close to home, and my home was the Pachyderm Building. Pappas bantered that we hadn't had a chance to talk in awhile and told me to come up to Bears sometime. All I could think was, why? Those bears stink. (Not at all like elephants and hippos.) It was a different perspective, but the atmosphere during hay loading was one of laughter and friendship.

My first encounter with clogged drains was also a learning experience. I discovered one when I tried to drain Wolee's pool to hose it out from the front, but the drain was clogged causing a backup. It was so full of gruesome brown liquids that the pygmy wouldn't even go in.

"That happens all the time," said Sandusky. "We'll move him out of the stall for tonight, turn in a request to maintenance, and they'll come in around 7:00 in the morning and snake out the drain."

"What are we going to do with Wolee?"

"I'll help you move him down into the stall next to Blackie," he said. "By the time you're in here tomorrow, they'll have his drain cleared and you can move him back."

We used Monkey Chow to make a trail for Wolee to follow, and so we lured him along, opening and closing gates as we went.

When we were done, Steve said that we needed to write all this down because it was *out of the ordinary*. He made a sign and taped it to the steel door. It read, *Warning. Wolee is in this pen.*

"I'm taking a sick day tomorrow," said Steve. "So you'll have a relief keeper in here. I don't want anyone opening this door not knowing Wolee's in there."

"I hate that he'll have to spend the whole night without some sort of pool," I said.

"He'll be all right," said Steve. "They'll unclog his drain before dawn in the morning, real early, and he'll be all right. You can let him back down the hall when you get here."

CHAPTER NINE

The *relief* keepers at the Cleveland Zoo were a breed apart. Some were specifically hired to do this, like Bob Perkins, Tad Schoffner, Steve Gove, and Donnie Tresise. Others were keepers in other areas who just wanted some overtime. Bill Seman and Kenny Pekarek used to do this.

The relief keeper often had no idea where he'd be working on any given day, or even if he would be working at all. When they were called on, it would often begin with a last minute phone call.

Full-time relief keepers like Tad, Steve, Perkins, and Donnie were like nomads, rogues, vagabonds, shovels for hire. They worked in different places in the zoo on different days. Sometimes they'd be in one place for a few weeks if a keeper was on vacation, or just a day or two in the case of an illness.

A relief keeper could fill any position with the exception of elephants. The needs for these fill-ins also covered the fifteen *sick days* that were guaranteed by the Teamster contract. It was a great benefit to those who were fighting the flu, and extra vacation days for those who made sure that every day was used in a given year. (In all my years, I only missed a single day, and didn't feel right using them if I wasn't actually sick. On the other hand, when I left the zoo, I received ¼ pay for all the days I had accrued.)

The day after Sandusky and I had temporarily moved Wolee, Don met Tad Schoffner at the time clock and assigned him to cover for Steve.

I was already down in the building because I knew I had to move Wolee back to his regular stall. When I pulled up and parked my car, Joe Matyas from maintenance was inside the building. I found him and his helper behind Wolee's pen winding the long metal cable onto the rotating hub of the electric sewer snake.

"We snaked out your drain. The clog wasn't very deep so it wasn't tough. You guys got any coffee?"

I said that we only had instant, but that was evidently good enough, and I made the trip back to the keeper room to run water through the coffee maker.

It was not long before Ellen arrived, cheerful and prompt as usual. It was probably twenty minutes until 8:00 and I turned on the lights as Ellen went back to release the elephants, which was always her first order of business.

I went to check on Wolee and was shocked by his appearance. He was covered with frothy dried sweat, and, from his stance, really pissed off; every muscle in his body was tense.

"I'm sorry, Wolee Booger," I said. "I'm so sorry, big boy. It's time for your pool." With that I ran to get the water flowing in the newly repaired pool.

After saying goodbye to the maintenance crew, I opened a path for Wolee to get to the water, and sealed everything else off before pulling Sandusky's note down off the door. Figuring that Wolee would go like a shot right to his pool, I didn't use any Monkey Chow as bait.

I heard the back door open and Schoffner, the relief keeper, came in.

"I guess I'm working hippos with you today," he said cheerfully.

Tad was probably more experienced than I with regard to the routine, and asked which side of the hall I wanted him to work. I offered to take Red, but first we had to move Wolee.

To my surprise, the pygmy had not moved closer to the water. He was still locked in position where I had seen him, and his attitude had not changed. Ted questioned why all the barricades had been raised when people could just go in when working around this particular hippo. Brent had, but I would not dare it again. Not today, not ever.

"I've worked with Wolee a lot," he said, "I always just go in with him."

"That may be," I said, "but he was dry-docked all night. He hasn't been in water since yesterday. He's really angry. I don't think we should go in with him. Maybe we can lure him down the hall."

"Seriously," said Tad, "I just go in with him. I can start him going down the hall."

One look at the hippo said our going in wasn't the best idea.

"Well," said the other keeper, "we should hose him off, and maybe that would make him relax a bit. Then we could lure him down the hall with some fruit. I'll get the hose and we'll do that."

By now, Ellen was approaching and wondering why we seemed so serious.

Tad said, "We're trying to figure out how to get Wolee back to his pen."

Ellen said, "Why don't you just go in and shoo him?""

Tad said, "We think he's in too bad a mood."

"Oh. Don't be silly," said Ellen, smiling.

She reached out and grabbed the deadbolt on the metal barricade. Just as she uttered the word silly, she pulled open the door, and stepped into the back hall. She made a gentle shooing motion with her arms, the way a person might shoo a gaggle of geese.

There was a blur of motion and horrible sounds, like scuffling and grunts. Wolee was at Ellen and savagely mauling her. She doubled over when he hit her, and she was in his jaws. The hippo spun around and the slender woman was thrown to the ground. It happened like the sudden clap of hands. He picked her up and now had her around the waist.

I don't remember how I got there, but in a moment, I was in there. I didn't feel like I had any presence of mind, but I must have run and grabbed a pitchfork from a nearby tool rack. I swung it at the beast, but it was a wimpy glance off the side of his head. Odd as it sounds, I didn't want to hurt him. I thought about Bomi's eye. I thought of a billion things in a fraction of a second, but above all things, I was terrified.

I was not aware of any sound until hearing Ellen moaning "no... no..." She was curled into a ball and Wolee was whirling around, dancing all over her. Blood was beginning to flow over the sandy gray cement floor. In the distortion of time and space, I felt that Wolee and Ellen were far, far away.

He was now crushing her with his weight, stepping onto Ellen's chest, back, and stomach. Wolee didn't care at all about attacking me or Tad. It was just Ellen.

After I hit Wolee one weak time with the pitchfork and nothing happened, I was defeated. Two feet away from Tad was a grain scoop shovel.

"Tad. Pick up the shovel." He saw what I had seen.

"HIT HIM. HIT HIM. HIT HIM ON TOP OF THE HEAD...."

Tad stood over Wolee, who was mauling Ellen, and believe or not he said, "I don't want to hurt him." What could I say, I felt the same way. But the fact remained that she was being mauled to death by a five hundred pound monster, and her protectors were two kind, gentle men.

Beneath the flurry of Wolee's attack, Ellen lay quite lifeless, eyes closed. I saw the red stains spreading on her brown shirt, which was torn, raglike. Everything had happened in such a short amount of time. Was it twenty seconds total? Maybe.

Tad took a new strategy. He covered Ellen's body with the shovel. He placed the broad wide scoop right across her body over the part of her torso Wolee was biting. But Wolee kept biting. Deftly, Tad moved the shovel to whichever area of her form Wolee attacked.

Tad's ploy was working. Wolee chomped down hard one more time. With the full force of his powerful jaws he closed his mouth like a vice, but he bit right into the unforgiving steel face of the shovel. He bit so hard he hurt himself. If he were a dog, he would have yelped in pain. But the pain ripped through his head. I could see him wince, stunned and in shock. In a blink, he ran. Wolee didn't know how he had been hurt. He didn't know where the stab of pain had come from. He ran right back into Stall 2.

Finally, I was worth something. I ran toward the crank on the stall and cranked it shut.

Ellen was not dead. She was even conscious, though groggy and a little incoherent. She was laying on her back.

Tad leaned down close to her face and said, "Ellen. Ellen. Stay awake. Don't go to sleep. Ellen, stay awake."

Most of the blood seemed to be coming out of her back, with rivulets trailing away from under her body.

"Ellen. Don't sleep. Stay awake. Do you know where you are?" Tad kept talking to her.

"I'm in the zoo."

"Ellen, stay awake. You have to stay awake." When she mentally grasped what he meant, she held on to it with a force of will.

Smiling as if she were just tipsy, she said, "I'll stay awake. I'll stay awake."

I ran to the keeper's room and came back with anything I could to keep her warm, jackets and towels. I covered her and carefully slipped a clean white towel under the back of her head.

"You stay with her," said Tad. "I'll call the office."

I kept talking to Ellen, who was groggy and yet smiling. "I just closed my eyes and knew I was going to die. It was very peaceful. It was really just, really very peaceful."

Ellen sighed dreamily, as if willing to slip back into that wonderful place of enveloping peace. Her eyes closed as her head nodded off to the left.

I said, "But you're awake now, right? You're staying awake?"

A moment passed. Then she said, "Yes."

"Are you cold? Do you feel cold?"

"No, I don't feel cold."

It seemed like only a minute passed. Then the back door opened, and Alan Sironen came in. He was there very, very quickly.

"Oh, hi, Alan," said Ellen.

She recognized him; that was a good sign. But on the other hand, she said *hi* as if it were totally out of context. It was as if she were walking down the hall in high school.

Alan spoke softly, but urgently. "Adam, we need to check her back. This blood is coming out of her back. If she's bleeding, we need to apply pressure to the arteries or she'll bleed to death before they get here."

I reached around Ellen and lifted her up off the floor, pulling her toward me as Alan quickly scanned her back. Her shirt was pretty much torn away.

He looked her over quickly. He had a lot of medical training. "She's not losing a lot of blood now. There isn't a major artery severed. Let's lay her back down."

"Put that towel under her?" I said pointing to one I had carried from the keeper's room.

I felt like I was setting an infant in a crib. Her torso was now fully exposed, and Alan took off his own coat and laid it over her body, tucking it up under her chin. Together Alan and I put everything we had on top of her, to try and keep her warm.

"I'm going out to direct the ambulance this way," he said.

"They'll be here soon," I reassured her.

"I'm hot... I'm so hot..." she said.

"Ellen, we need to keep you warm. We need to keep you covered."

After what seemed like a long silence, she said, "Okay..." and seemed to drift off.

"Ellen, you're staying awake, right?"

"Yes." Her eyes opened, "I'm awake. I don't feel any pain. I don't feel anything..."

"Just stay with me."

"I'm sorry," she said. "You're so new on the job, and now this happens to you. It must be awful."

"Just stay with me. The ambulance is coming."

After several seconds, she smiled and said, "Thank you for being so sweet."

CHAPTER TEN

I don't remember much about the ambulance or the paramedics. I just know they came and took her. They had her on the gurney and gone in about four seconds from the time they got there.

All morning people from other areas came down to see if there was anything they could do. Matyas came back and stayed a long time. Tony from Birds, Vince, Perkins, and Little Johnny came in.

The elephants, still unfed, also seemed dazed. I don't have any doubt that Simba was fully conscious that her beloved keeper had been attacked and carried away. She stood near the front center of the cage making little nervous picks with her tusks, otherwise, hardly moving. Leach had changed Simba's life for the better, and the animal knew something was very wrong.

I wasn't much different, and found myself pacing in the public area. The world seemed dark, until suddenly, a crew from one of the TV stations was in my face. I don't even know how they got in the building, but they were shining a bright light in my eyes and some pushy guy was asking questions. I wasn't smart like Tad who told them directly to go away. I spoke to them like a zombie caught in the headlamps of a truck. It was awful.

"Did you save her life?"

"No, not at all. Tad Schoffner was at the business end of the hippo. I was really quite useless. Tad worked a shovel into the hippo's mouth and the hippo bit it and that hurt him. So he stopped the attack. It just happened so fast..."

"Was this a life or death situation? If you and the other keeper hadn't been there, would she have been killed? Can you say that in a statement?"

I didn't know what he meant. I thought he meant a statement like in a court of law. What he meant was, "Give me a short sound bite."

"I guess so. I think she would have definitely been killed."

"Are you a hero?"

"That's enough questions. Leave me alone."

The team then ran over to Mushka's stall and began taping her.

"Well, that's not the right hippo," I said and pointed to Wolee. So they went and took some video there.

My impression was that they were rude and insensitive. To top it off they edited it by cutting from *Did you save her life?"* to me saying, *I think she definitely would have been killed.*

Jim Rybicki was called in to tend to the elephants that day, and he worked seven days a week for a long time thereafter.

Throughout the zoo, people were shocked and hushed. When Jim gave commands to the elephants, he practically whispered them. Simba obeyed in a sullen and low-key manner. Sironen went around to all the areas frequently and gave people updates on Ellen's condition. Ellen had severe cuts, much like long knife wounds, mostly on her back. These gashes were ten to fifteen inches long. She had required a massive number of stitches. She had numerous bruises and a collapsed lung. One of her arms had been pierced in several places, by repeated bites. But the prognosis was good, Alan said.

Tad, who had visited her, said, "Ellen told me to thank you for being there, and she thanked me. She's in good spirits, and she said she's coming back. She'll have a lot of scars, on her back mostly, but not on her face. They say she'll be in the hospital for a week. She said, 'I knew I was going to die, so I just closed my eyes and accepted it.' And she said, 'When Wolee had me in his mouth and was shaking me, I felt just like a little rag doll, like I was nothing.'"

Ellen's life was saved by the fact that Wolee had bitten down hard on a steel shovel that Tad was holding over her as a shield.

Of course, the story of the hippo attack was also covered in the *Plain Dealer*. The attack occurred in February of 1980. By then, the new zoo Director was Michael Vitantonio; he was interviewed for the article.

When Tad and I read it in the keeper room, we laughed. The story indicated that Ellen had been *bumped* a few times by Wolee.

"Where did they get this? Did anyone ask you what happened?" I said to Tad.

"Nope."

"Me, neither. They must have talked with Ellen." Whatever the reason, the paper had downplayed the whole attack. As for me, I began having nightmares about Wolee the very first night after the incident.

I was tormented by what I felt was my cowardice. The nightmare was always the same. Suddenly and out of nowhere, Wolee's open maw was running toward me and then I'd awaken with a start. I tossed and turned, filled with regret. I hated the fact that I hadn't done something. I should have bulled into Wolee and rammed the pitchfork handle down his throat. I should have stabbed it into his eyes. I wished I had just been brutal to him. Why didn't I just run up and kick him in the side of the head?

I knew the answer to that question. I was afraid he'd turn on me.

Night after night, as I fell into the *Theta state*, half between waking and sleeping, the little dream roared at me. Wolee's open jaws charged toward me. His maw was right about the same level as my head. Once awake, I would just lay there thinking. I thought about how a person in such a crisis simply has to be totally brutal. I shouldn't have had the first worry about hurting Wolee. Second, I understood why police and firefighters go through training. I realized that the whole incident simply had no preparation. Many times before the incident with Wolee and Ellen, I had thought that if an animal got loose I would run to the tool rack for a weapon. When it happened, I did that without hesitating, but that was as far as my plan went; after that I froze. I suppose that's why police have shooting ranges with targets in human shapes. A response has to be practiced. Without any training or forethought, I froze. Understanding that was a big epiphany for me, and it came only after hours of tortured thought.

Mercy toward Wolee nearly killed Ellen, but I resolved to eliminate the moment of indecision. I wanted trained and practiced behavior to be my first instinct. I did it because I felt horrible at my failure to help Ellen.

She later told me, "You were new, just starting. Don't feel bad about it."

But I didn't ever want to live with the regret of another cowardly failure. No matter how foolhardy my actions were, I would not freeze the next time. The incident with Wolee changed me.

CHAPTER ELEVEN

After a month or so, Ellen returned. We all knew that she carried long scars on her back, but the scrapes on her face had completely healed.

The spring was beautiful that year, and with the warming weather, the animals were outside for the majority of the day. All the doors and windows were open so that the natural light and air flow felt more like an outdoor pavilion.

Cleaning the indoor stalls was much easier when we could let the animals outside. Between the indoor and outdoor pools, it was hippo heaven; each one occupied by what looked like a floating bulbous manatee.

One sunny Saturday, Ellen and I were working hippos. Jim was working elephants. I was cleaning out Red's stall while the Nile was outside. Don Kuenzer came into the building around 10:00 a.m. and asked me how everything was going.

"Mostly, fine," I said, "but there is one thing. The hippos aren't eating very well. The pygmies are eating about half their food. Blackie's eating the most normally. But Red hardly ate a thing yesterday."

Don knew what I was going to say before I said it. "Well, that's because it's spring. You've got so many doors and windows open, and it's beautiful outside. The hippos can smell the grass growing, and it puts them off their feed."

"Would it be okay to give them some of the wild grass?"

"You might give them a handful, but just a little with their food. Too much, and they'll get diarrhea."

You'd think that the animals would simply graze in their outdoor pens, but the fact was that they had packed down the soil so much that nothing would grow there. I resolved to get Red a taste of grass since her appetite seemed to be the most affected.

Just then, Ellen appeared and saw me talking to Don. "Adam and I are going to have an adventure today," she said. "I'll be showing him how to clean the big outdoor pool."

Don looked at me and broke into a wide grin. "Oh, that'll be loads of fun."

There was some sort of joking going on here, but I wasn't privy to it. "How is it different from cleaning the indoor pool?"

Don mischievously glanced sideways at Ellen, then said, "Well, it's a problem of volume. Indoors you haul out the feces from one Nile who's been in the water for sixteen hours. Outside, you'll be cleaning out the feces from two after an entire week."

"It'll take us a couple of hours," said Ellen.

I moved Red indoors, and we began draining the pond. She showed me the valve which needed to be opened to drain the pool. This was accomplished by inserting a large t-shaped key to twist it open. Once opened, the soil beneath our feet actually vibrated with the surging of the drains beneath us.

It took fifteen minutes to drain. In the meantime, we gathered the equipment that we needed. When we returned, I saw an entire landscape of wet hippo dung and digested hay rising like mountain peaks out of a foamy brown sea. This was the most difficult work I had ever done at the zoo. It was extremely physical, but satisfying to accomplish, and we carted load after load away in wheelbarrows.

Each loaded wheelbarrow was taken through the back door and into the long back hallway, then out the open garage door to the little Heidi Shit Barn.

"The first loads are easy," said Ellen. "You just dump them onto the floor of the barn." I didn't fully take her meaning until the Shit Barn started to reach capacity. The pile in there was chest high, and eventually, we had to dump the loads onto the walkway in front of the barn. Then we had to re-shovel all the waste and throw it high onto the pile, one shovelful at a time. Therefore, a lot of the stuff had to be shoveled twice, and when the morning crew came with a truck, they'd have to shovel it a third time.

"Ellen," I suggested, "we need a waste barn that's high up off the ground so that a truck could back under it. They could load the, err... *waste* like a railroad gondola car."

"Oh, just call it *shit*," said Ellen. "I figured out a long time ago that everybody just calls it what it is." Anyway, that was how Ellen taught me how to clean the big hippo pool.

Later that afternoon, I kept my promise and went out on the little hillside behind the Pachyderm Building and gathered some nice thick clumps of grass for Red. I cranked open the back door to her stall where she was standing next to her untouched meal. I only opened the door a crack, the way Brent had shown me and there she was, snorting and angry. As before, she charged, but then stopped suddenly when she smelled the grass I was offering.

"Hey, there, Red. Hey, girl. Look what I got for ya. Look at this."

The behemoth peered at me through the little crack as I cautiously brought the fresh green grass, folded in half, near her whiskered muzzle.

She snorted again, backing away from me as a snotty burst came out of her flared nostrils. From the bottom of her chin, long drools of saliva were hanging like liquid stalactites. I slipped the cord of grass further in through the opening in the door and shook it in front of Red's face.

"Hey, old girl, here ya go. You want this? Come on, big Red. I'm not gonna hurt you."

The reddish mammal's huge feet slapped against the concrete as she retreated out of the doorway. I peeked in through the crack, and she was far away, near the front of her stall. Red was standing in profile, looking at me sideways. It suddenly dawned on me that I was doing what both Brent and Steve warned me not to do. I was messing with Red.

She paced around a bit at the front of the stall, wheezing from the back of her throat. I gave up on the idea that she might eat out of my hand. At a moment when I was sure she was far enough away, I tossed the grass into her pen with a quick flick of the wrist. Then I closed the door.

I went through the empty side of Wolee's double stall and climbed out over the pool into the public area where I could peek around the corner and see the Nile. She was eating the grass. I could hear her chewing; afterwards she ate everything that I had put in her dish.

On Monday Steve was back at work, and I told him that Ellen and I had cleaned the outdoor pool.

"How did you do that?" he asked.

I thought that an odd question from a man who had to have done it before. I went over the process of draining and carting and told him that it took three hours.

"Oh, God, no," said Steve. "You didn't have to do that. Later this week I'll show you how to clean the outdoor hippo pool."

CHAPTER TWELVE

There are people who subscribe to the theory that everything, even seemingly trivial and unrelated things, can have long-term significance in our lives. I never put much stock in this, but, every once in a while, I become a believer.

When I attended Westminster College, I had student employment in the dining hall to pay for my room and board and earn money toward tuition. Mostly, I'd run the big Hobart dishwasher, lug the stainless steel beverage containers, or set out the salad dressing, ketchup, mustard, and mayonnaise. Pot washer and condiment man was my primary job description.

Standing side-by-side with me in this venture was a Japanese student named Yoshio. His ambition was to become an interpreter at the UN, and we talked all the time as we scrubbed pots.

Once I asked him if he could teach me some Japanese while we were working. The first word in his lesson plan was *konnichiwa*.

After I had repeated it aloud a few times, he said, "That is *greeting*. It doesn't exactly mean *hello*. It is for greeting used when saying hello or goodbye. It is to say good afternoon or good day."

"Kind of like *aloha*," I suggested.

"Um, something like that, but it is only used in the daytime. In the afternoon. At night, the greeting is not *konnichiwa*, it is *konbanwa*."

"Okay, but that's too much to remember. I will remember *konichiwa*. What else? How do you say, *How are you?*"

"*Ogenki desu ka.*"

I butchered that several times before my master let me continue through the phrase vocabulary. When I said it passably, we moved on to *I am fine* or, in this case, *hai, genki desu.*

All this dialogue was just too predictable, so I asked him to teach me something really crazy and different. Out of the clear blue, I asked, "How do you say *fat hippopotamus?*"

Yoshio was surprised by my selection, but then he said, "*Kabba dubu.*"

This is my complete and total knowledge of Japanese: *Good afternoon, How are you? I am fine, fat hippopotamus.*

Fast forward ten years and I am standing out front, hosing the drains in front of Blackie's stall. A nice looking Japanese family walks in on an otherwise slow day. Most of the animals are outside in the open areas, so they are mostly seeing empty giraffe pens and elephant cages. There are four of them: Mom, Dad, teenage daughter, and eight-year-old son.

I hear them speaking Japanese as they approach Blackie's stall. The hippo was lying on the concrete apron of his pen doing his best imitation of sixty-five hundred pounds of blubber, and snoring lightly.

I bowed my head slightly. "*Konnichiwa.*"

I think I surprised them and the man smiled and whispered something to his wife. "*Konnichiwa*," he answered.

The eight-year-old's eyes suddenly turned to Blackie. I was still involved in the niceties and called his *Konnichiwa* and raised him one *Ogenki desu ka.*

Smiling, the man said, "*Hai, genki desu.*"

I raised my right arm and gestured with a flourish toward Blackie, "*Kabba dubu.*"

It took a second for the man to decipher my bad accent. "Ah. *Kabba dubu.* Ah, yes, very good."

The whole family laughed and a chatter of light conversation raced back and forth among them. It was a very special moment. I could sense that every life has a real destiny and is not so random as we might believe.

CHAPTER THIRTEEN

People often complained about the smell in the Pachyderm Building even though we were fastidious about cleaning all the animal areas, human and otherwise. Hoses were one of our main weapons in the battle, and Don Kuenzer promised he'd order fire hoses for our fight. Before too many days, the maintenance department delivered three more fifty-foot lengths, and we could reach areas that had been immune from our high-powered water assaults.

I began using the fire hoses instead of the push broom to clean the public walkways in the exhibit areas. In the mornings I used towering blasts of water to clean the walls, the ceilings, the windows, and everything else. Roaches that were up on the ceiling, once safe, were now annihilated and fell fifty feet to the floor to be swept away in the maelstrom, down into the drain in the front center of the indoor Nile pool.

The result was that the Pachyderm Building was a lot cleaner than it had ever been. But I knew that somewhere, lurking out of sight, were dozens of rats, hundreds of mice, and thousands of industrial-size roaches.

Realistically, it still smelled like a fragrant barn, mostly because that's what it was. At some point a visitor who must have had some clout had an idea that some shit didn't actually have to stink. The idea was to hang fragrant eucalyptus leaves in the building. The zoo's artist hung little pots with dark burgundy eucalyptus branches sticking out of green Styrofoam on the wall opposite the Nile pool. The whole building was steaming from hundreds of pounds of elephant and hippo crap, but this was supposed to take care of the smell. We thought this made a pretty good joke, one that was funnier than the leaves were efficient at masking anything.

Steve Sandusky's method of how to clean the big outdoor pool was quite a bit different than Ellen's. One Wednesday afternoon, as promised, he showed me an easier way.

From the tool rack, Steve retrieved a beat-up snow shovel, the kind that is pushed rather than lifted. "This is all we need," said Steve.

We started to drain the pool, but did not wait until it emptied. As soon as the water level dropped a couple of feet, it was time to swing into action.

Steve was wearing waders, but I just had sneakers on. When the pool was drained down to around chest high, I walked out into the floating vat of feces. I couldn't see into the water at all. It was as brown as coffee.

Steve didn't come into the pool right away. The water was still far deeper than his boots.

"If you weren't helping me, I'd just wade in over my boots," he said, "but since you don't seem to mind wading in there, I'll stay dry this time."

He told me use my feet to feel for a grated manhole cover in the center of the pool. (As the pool drained, the suction was compacting the feces over the grate so that my job was not as *easy* as someone might think.) Once I located it, he continued my education.

"Use your feet to scrape off the top of the grate so that it's not clogged. Bust all that... material off. You need to be able to pull the cover away. If the openings in the grate are clogged, the suction on the lid will be too strong."

I kicked furiously against the seemingly unmovable collection of twisted hay and waste.

"You might have to reach down and pull it clear with your hands," said Steve. He was getting more insistent. "You have to get the drain cover off pretty soon. There has to be several feet of water in the pool for this to work. If all the water escapes, we'll be back to wheelbarrows."

As fast as I kicked the lid clear, new feces were drawn in. Steve began to wade into the water. He was now boot deep; I was up to my waist.

"The water level's dropping," said Steve with some nervous urgency. "You need to get the top of the lid clear so you can lift it. The water's gonna be too low in about a minute. You'll have to pull the waste off the grate with your hands."

I reached down into the cold brown soup as far as I could, my face just barely above the water. I turned my head sideways to keep my face from being submerged. I grabbed firmly onto a large clutch of wet hay and filth and ripped it off the grate, creating a nice flow. I felt a faster, wilder current whooshing around me, and I grabbed the cast-iron cover by slipping my fingers through its broad, metal mesh. It came free.

The fast swirling water made me a little fearful that I might actually be sucked down, but I managed to lug the grate over to the edge of the pool. Sandusky scrambled out and came back with the old snow pusher which he used to agitate the strange soup. "We need to turn the whole pool into a giant whirlpool. Everything needs to be swirling in the water, otherwise it will settle to the bottom and we'll have to shovel it out. Watch this."

He began walking counterclockwise around the perimeter of the pool. He was rapidly pushing the shovel ahead of him, vigorously scraping along the pool's pebbled-concrete bottom. He moved as quickly as he could until the brown water was orbiting in rolling waves. As the water drained, his circles grew smaller and smaller.

"You have to know where the hole is," he warned. "You don't want to step into the manhole. Notice that I stay away from the whirlpool."

When the last bit had been drained, there was one final *whoosh*, and all the brown water was gone. The entire pool was empty, and clean. All the feces and hay, as well as twigs and leaves, had vanished down the big drain. We hadn't even used the hose. Steve had just *flushed the toilet*.

"That's great," I said.

Triumphant, Steve sat down on the side of the pool and lit a cigarette. Steve didn't care that the seat of his pants were wet. I was soaked from head to toe, but we had bypassed hours of drudgery.

"I'll tell you a story," said Steve, relaxing in the middle of the bright afternoon. "Everybody knows it, except the young people, so don't repeat it, but it's important for *you* to know.

"I told you to be careful when you drain the pool that way. *Do not* step into the drain, it will suck you down. It happened to me once.

"The manhole is only six inches, so you can't really go down the pipe, but if you step on the wrong spot, you can get sucked down into the manhole trap. One time I was pushing the snow shovel and I stepped over the opening. Vince was with me that day. He was watching and, well, all of a sudden, I was gone. Vince saw that and ran over, but he couldn't find me at first. The suction was awful. It took all my strength to get my head up to get a breath of air. God, I was scared I'd drown. Vince got hold of my arm. He pulled and I struggled and then I finally came up. But when I did I was missing my upper plate. Boy, that was embarrassing.

"There was a young guy who worked here in the zoo, down in maintenance, and Vince must have called him about my teeth. He came around, and climbed down into the sewer's holding tank in the basement and looked around for my plate for a long time. He eventually found them. I learned a lesson the hard way. Be careful not to walk over the open drain. It will suck you right down. I could have drowned."

Just about every day, I went outside of the Pachy area and found a nice handful of fresh grass. And every day I opened the back door of Red's stall just a crack and held the grass toward her, trying to get her to take it out of my hand. She snorted and rebelled against me. I wondered if she would ever stop being so angry all the time.

Sometimes Sandusky saw me at the back of Red's stall, holding the grass toward her through the slight opening. Steve didn't like that.

He shook his head and said, "Oh, don't do that. I know you want to make friends with her, but you don't know what might happen."

Steve's words made me more careful, but I continued offering Red a handful of grass in the afternoons. I folded it into a long, twisted cord, like a bent licorice stick. She'd bring her face to within ten inches of it, but wouldn't take it, so I'd just toss it into the stall. I knew I was giving her the *reward* without really training her. I wasn't trying to train her. I was only trying to give her a little bit of kindness. Her life seemed so miserable; she festered in isolation. Red was extremely vicious, but I had the sense that it was because she was afraid. She was afraid of everyone who came near her so she lashed out. It had been going on that way for over twenty-three years, since around 1955, as far as I knew.

CHAPTER FOURTEEN

Months passed and Simba kept playing with my head. Every time I went anywhere near the bars she growled and moved toward me aggressively. She huffed and she puffed, and she made me tremble, but I knew the time was fast approaching when I needed to learn how to work the elephants.

Kuenzer tried to relieve my apprehension, cutting me some slack. He told me that there were quite a few people who wanted nothing to do with Simba, and he'd completely understand if I just wanted to stay on the hippo side of the building. Besides, Jim and Ellen seemed to be working them fine by themselves.

He knew that Simba frightened me plenty. It would have been easy for me to agree and say that I'd just as soon stay in hippos, but Simba was a fear I felt I needed to face.

That night, I made a promise to myself. I swore to God that I would not back down from learning how to manage elephants. In preparation for this, I spent almost all my spare time with Ellen. She was a great teacher and intellect. I tried to take in everything she said.

My fears of Simba were well grounded. Don Tresise, a keeper, had been brutally attacked. He wouldn't go near her. Experienced relief keepers like Schoffner and Gove had already passed on learning this part of the business, and no one blamed them or expected them to. Kenny Pekarek had been an elephant keeper, but now refused to even go into the cage with her. Steve had been gored, and acted like the other side of the building didn't exist. It was the Dark Side which he avoided. Vince Rimedio, the Ostrich Barn keeper, was sent to the hospital more than once thanks to the beast, and, of course, Jerry Studiak, Perkins, and Don Kuenzer had all been brutalized one way or another. Dick Darenzo, Bill Seman, and Little Johnny had all quit elephants, deciding they would live a whole lot longer without going into Simba's cage.

Ellen and Jim were Simba's only advocates, but they readily admitted she represented a true and unpredictable danger. They always measured the animal's mood, and simply left her alone when she was growling or her ears were flapping. Sometimes Simba charged around in her cage, trumpeting and even careening into the bars, as if she was not quite mentally stable. When one of Simba's angry fits commenced, Ellen got out of the cage as quickly as she could. The fits usually lasted around twenty minutes. Ellen recognized the danger, and was always trying to figure out what triggered the episodes.

When my orientation began, Ellen was my mentor.

"The first step for you is to come into the cage with me. Simba will be okay as long as I'm with you. Come in right now and help me clean the cage. That'll be the best way to start. Just do normal activities with me, and that will help Simba accept the idea."

The first moment that I passed through the front bars is etched in my memory. Simba immediately charged forward, emitting a rumbling growl. My heart was pounding.

"Simba. Oh, stop it, you big lunkhead," said Ellen with a lightness in her voice. To my surprise, the animal backed down, and I helped her shovel out the area.

"She's a bully," said Ellen. "Act unafraid and she'll stop pushing you."

As we mucked out the cage, I told her what I had heard from one of the previous keepers. "Vince says Simba's calmed down. She's not as mean as she was years ago."

Ellen rolled her eyes and smiled slightly. "Well, it's very complicated, but here's the circumstances, in a nutshell, well, as briefly as I can manage. This whole topic really goes back to the 1940s here at the zoo. At that time they had an Indian elephant named Frieda. She was over by the Old Main Building, and *this* building hadn't been built yet. All the elephant goads and cattle prods and hooks that you see around here in the closets are really from that time. In those days, there was only one keeper here who knew what he was doing, but his background was with Indian elephants in the circus. I think he was from Ringling Brothers. Well, the handling of an elephant in a circus and in a zoo are quite different disciplines, but that's what they had. This keeper came in with all that circus training on Indian elephants (that's what they called the Asians in those days). *Training* simply meant you punished the animal until she got it right. As time went on, that one keeper taught everyone who had anything to do with elephants how to work with them. If he was a monster, he trained other keepers to be monsters. That meant that the elephants were beaten if they deemed it necessary. So within the zoo, his methods were established and passed on. Things like cattle prods, hooks, and physical punishment were how Indian elephants were trained, and that goes back to the 19th Century circuses and, gosh, back into ancient history, I'm sure. So that was the method in this zoo, and really in every zoo in the United States during that era. But again, they were working with Asians.

"In the 1950s, along comes baby Simba, Tara, and a bull from Africa. No one said, 'Hey, these are Africans and this is a zoo. Should we learn how to do this right?' They just went on with the same methods. Since then, we've witnessed the evolution of elephant treatment in zoos, but that didn't get here in time for some of the old guys.

"You just don't treat an African in a zoo the way circuses treat an Asian. I'm saying it's wrong to simply beat any elephant, Asian or African, under any circumstances, but those guys got away with it with Frieda and their so-called Indian elephants. Simba and the bull were a completely different story. Tara was always sweet. She probably didn't get many beatings because she was obedient, but Simba was a hard case and the long war began.

"I don't really like to say bad things about anyone, but it's not fair for you to think badly of Simba at this point. I just can't let it go by without comments. You take a keeper like Jerry Studinak. Simba gored him in the chest and nearly killed him, so does that make her evil? I'm going to tell you right now, Jerry used the shock prod on Simba on a regular basis. Sometimes he would command her to kneel. When she kneeled, you know, stretched, he'd grab hold of her eyelashes and yank them out. That hurt her, and he shocked her with the prod while she was kneeling to keep her stretched. Jerry had some heavy leather gloves he used with Simba. While she knelt, he would punch her in the eyes with those leather gloves on his fists. He'd just punch her, right in the eyes. I filled out a million reports about that, and that's why he's not here anymore. We had awful fights. And God knows, if I were Simba, I would have gored him, too. She didn't kill him, and she could have. I don't think anyone in his right mind can blame Simba for that or anything she's done, but people do. Some of the early keepers were mean, and some of them just were ignorant. They did what they were taught. But their entire *modus operandi* was about shock prods, leather gloves, and beating her with the *ankus*. They'd hit her in sensitive places, like her trunk. No one should hit an elephant there, even when the elephant is being disciplined. If you hit an elephant in there, you can paralyze her trunk permanently. It's all nerve endings, like a spine. When she's being struck with a goad in the trunk, what recourse does she have? Of the keepers who mistreated her, I won't defend any of them, but I will defend her *against* them. On the whole, I'm on Simbolina's side. That's my name for her."

Ellen laughed, and suddenly the big elephant wrapped her trunk around Ellen's waist. Ellen said, "I don't know how I started calling her that. Right, Simbolina?"

Old, leathery Simba rumbled and began rocking as if she had been listening. One suspected Simba had the gist of the whole conversation.

"What about Donnie Tresise?" I asked.

"Oh, that was completely different. Donnie was never mean toward Simba or Tara in the least. Same with Kuenzer. He never did anything to Simba to cause her to pin his head against the wall. Donnie never raised a hand toward the elephants or even yelled at them. But one day, Maintenance drove a backhoe into the back hall when Donnie was in the cage, and Simba went insane. So he was in the wrong place at the wrong time. That's why now, Maintenance can't bring any equipment with an internal combustion engine into this building or this area without first letting us know."

"What about Perkins?"

Ellen laughed. "I guess you heard how she stepped on his head. I really can't imagine he was ever cruel to her, either. But I don't know. He worked with her before my time."

I was glad to hear that about the fun-loving and friendly Bob Perkins. It would be impossible to believe that Perkins could ever be cruel to any living thing.

CHAPTER FIFTEEN

I decided to bring a little class to the Pachy by installing a system where a phone caller could hear music if I put them on hold. Actually, we had a very antiquated system (maybe the word *system* is too grand). We had an old bulky, black Bakelite phone that was usually encrusted by whatever muck was on the last keeper's hand.

What I actually did was bring in my boom box and set it next to the phone. I'd set the radio WCLV, the fine arts station that played classical music. When I answered the call, I would use my best public radio announcer's voice and say: "Cleveland Zoo. Pachyderm Building. Please Hold." I'd set the phone next to the radio and click it on. I'd let whoever it was have around forty-five seconds of music, while I was just sitting there. Then I'd click off the radio and say, "Thank you for holding. How may we help you?"

"Uh… is Jim there…?"

"One moment please. Thank you."

So I'd put them back on hold and try not to laugh as I went to get Rybicki.

The whole shtick seemed harmless enough until one day as I was standing near the time clock I overheard Bill Seman talking to Don Kuenzer.

"Hey, I been meaning to ask you. They have on-hold music in the Pachyderm Building. How come we don't have that in Apes? Apes is newer."

Don saw me out of the corner of his eye, and I think he instantly figured it out. He just shook his head, "I don't know anything about that, or if it's even possible." I left the building and went down to start my day's work.

This was during my *elephant-breaking-in time*, and I worked with Ellen or Jim every day, mostly Ellen. Together we'd work quickly to take care of the hippos, and then spend the rest of the time working elephants.

After a time, I was able to do everything. I chained and unchained the elephants, cleaned the stall, bathed them with the hose, let them in and out. When I gave Simba or Tiani a command, she obeyed me. There was just one little catch. Every time I gave them a command, Ellen was standing next to me. They weren't really obeying me. They were only obeying because Ellen was standing with me in the cage. This meant that the drama had not yet begun.

"If I weren't in the cage with you," Ellen had warned, "Simba would not obey you. In fact, she would attack you. We'll do this for a couple more weeks, and then you'll have the big moment." The words were ominous, but she spoke them cheerfully.

"Tomorrow is the day," she said after the two weeks had passed. "Tomorrow, we'll start you working elephants by yourself. Just be aware that the first time you give a command to Simba, she'll challenge you. She might charge you and try to drive you out of the cage. It's hard to say. It could be that nothing will happen, but I doubt it. More likely, you will have a confrontation with her. What will happen is simply that you and she will battle for dominance. It will be a one-time event. Whoever comes out on top will remain dominant, and except for little spats now and then, the order of dominance will remain stable after that. You need to establish yourself as having a higher rank within the little herd we have here."

"It's like with wolves in a pack," I said. "They fight to establish dominance, but once the order is established, they don't fight again."

"Yes, I suppose," she said, "although I really don't know much about wolves, but that's certainly true of elephants. Well, there's no other way to say it. Tomorrow, you and Simba will have a fight. It's probably better if we call it a *confrontation*," Ellen said, smiling. "Once done, it'll be done, and she will obey your commands thereafter. But, if she is able to drive you out, or somehow you lose the battle to her, you really won't be able to be an elephant keeper. You'll have to go in by yourself; Jim and I can't be anywhere in sight. It needs to happen tomorrow. Simba knows the time has come, and if we wait, she'll view that as her victory. But you don't have to do it. It's never too late to just stay with the hippos. No one will think less of you."

"No, I'm going to do it. I'm ready."

Later that afternoon, Jim was in the keeper room, reading the paper. He really hadn't said much to me about Simba when Ellen was taking the lead, but I wanted to hear about *his* confrontation.

"Well, like you, I had heard all the stories," he began. "Ellen told me what to expect. I just made up my mind that no matter what happened, I wouldn't run. Personally, I also didn't feel comfortable in duking it out with Simba. I knew that in anything physical, I would be easily outmatched. Ellen told me Simba would charge me, and she did. I thought, if she's going to gore me or run me over, it's going to happen, but I'm absolutely not going to run. She charged, and I just stood there with my hands at my side and didn't move. She ran right up to within a few feet of me, and then she just stopped. And that was it. There was never anything else. I gave her a command, and she obeyed it. I can't recommend that strategy to you. What you want to do is up to you. You may feel better defending yourself with an *ankus*. I'm not going to tell you what to do, but that's what happened to me."

"Did you have the ankus with you in the cage?"

"No. I left it outside the front of the cage. I leaned it against the wall in front of Simba, so that she could see that I wasn't bringing it in with me. I was laying down my weapon. I decided that I would take an approach like Gandhi, and make myself just completely non-threatening to her."

Jim's story was fascinating, but I didn't think I had the guts to do that.

The next morning came soon enough. The plan was that the moment of truth would come when I gave Simba a bath. To do so, I'd need to give commands and establish a good level of control. Ellen thought the bath scenario would be to my benefit. She wanted to force the confrontation in what would appear to be a routine situation rather than wait for it to happen at random.

We began the morning chores as usual with Ellen and I working together. Then it was time for her final instructions. "I can't be in sight of Simba. So I'll stay here in the hallway. If I hear anything that sounds really bad, I'll run out. You know how to give Simba a bath, so begin the routine just as you've done it before. When you tell her to *get in line*, I think she'll do that without a problem. That won't be the time she gives you any trouble. Then, she'll probably let you hose off her one side. She likes being hosed. I don't think Simba will pick her battle over that. But to hose off her other side, you will naturally have to command her to *turn*.

"When you say, *turn*, I think that's when the challenge will come. You'll have your back to the bars near the front of the cage. You won't be pinned into a corner, and you'll have a way out. Once you say *turn*, she'll most likely come after you with her tusks. That's kind of what we're hoping for. If she swings at you with her trunk, she'll knock you over. If you're down, that would be the time to yell for help.

"Now, what do you want to have in the cage with you? I use the hook, but you may feel more comfortable with your baseball bat."

"I'd rather have the bat. I'm used to the feel of it."

"Okay, you can use the bat. Now, Simba is going to either charge you or get her tusks in your face or try to knock you down, but you should stand your ground. If you let her drive you out of the cage, that's it for your elephant career. Whatever happens, you need to discipline her for her disobedience. After all, you gave her a command. You'll need to hit her with the bat to set her straight. You gave an order. She didn't obey. She needs punished. Then you can both move on with your relationship, and everything will be all right."

"Where should I hit her?"

Ellen grinned at that. "I'm glad you asked because I nearly forgot. Well, I can tell you first where *not* to hit her. No matter what happens, you cannot hit her in the trunk. That's hard to avoid because if she charges, her trunk is going to be right in your face. Ideally, to punish her, you would hit her in the rump, right up on the fat part, like a spanking. If for any reason that becomes possible, that would be best. But… that's not too likely. She's not going to turn her rump toward you. You can't hit her in the trunk. Don't hit her near her eyes. Don't hit her in the kidneys. I've been thinking about this day and night, and I would suggest that it could happen that the only place you can hit her to defend yourself and not hurt her would be to hit her in the forehead.

"If you take aim at her forehead, you have to hit it. She'll be moving, so we'll see how good you are with the bat. She has that big hump up there, and that's one of the thickest bones in her body. After all, elephants knock over trees with their foreheads. Ideally, hit her in the rump. But… it's not going to happen. So, those are just some thoughts even though I suppose it's really unpredictable."

With that, she wished me luck and disappeared around the corner.

For the first time ever, I stepped inside the cage with Simba alone. I went right through the center of the cage and out the door at the back to get the hose for the bath. I walked between Simba and Tiani. As I did, Simba growled and turned her tusks toward me, but she didn't attack.

When I returned, I was dragging the hose while squeezing my aluminum bat under my left arm.

"Simba, get in line."

She did, and I began hosing her off. She was rocking back and forth with a lot of latent energy. Periodically, she turned an eye to me as if to tell me that she knew I was alone. On the positive side, everything was taking place exactly as Ellen had foreseen.

"TURN."

The moment I said the word, tusks were coming toward me. The yellow-ivory sabers whooshed past my ears, on each side of my head, and I reacted immediately to her disobedience. The fact was that if Simba had meant to do me harm, she would not have missed me. This was a warning.

Ellen had prepared me well for that moment, and Simba's disobedience was followed instantly with a bat to the head. I didn't threaten, I clubbed her immediately.

WHAM. It was a blow in the dead center of her massive forehead with my arms fully extended in an overhead swing. In baseball terms, it was also a *stinger*, and my whole body came up off the floor.

"I said *turn.*"

Simba turned so quickly, that she over-rotated and made a complete circle.

"*Turn,*" I said again. This time, she did her usual one-eighty, and the bath continued as usual with *stretch, kneel, turn.* She obeyed every command. I hated what I had just done, but my heart was also pounding.

Ellen met me immediately and told me that now I needed to reward the elephant with fruit and by spending time with her in the cage.

I cut up several apples and bananas, and stuck them in my pockets out of convenience. Then, I took a page out of Jim's book of elephant handling. I leaned my bat against the wall far outside the cage where Simba could see that I didn't have it.

"Good girl. That's my good girl. *Trunk up.*" She knew she was going to get a treat, and I put the apples directly into her open mouth. At one point, her trunk moved to sniff out the fruit in my pockets.

"You're a good girl, Simbolina. You are so good."

By now, Ellen had joined me. "If you really want to make friends with her, you'll learn how to pet her tongue. All elephants love that."

"Are you serious?" She *was*, and I rubbed hard against what can only be described as hot and slathering.

Ellen left the cage to allow Simba and me time to bond. That was the first of many, many times that I actually hugged that elephant. It's really quite simple, just hug the trunk. And Simba gently hugged back. Her sounds now were more purr than growl, and after that, she was never the first one to break off from even a long hug.

CHAPTER SIXTEEN

It was not long before I was working in all areas of the Pachy. I worked elephants two days a week and hippos the rest of the time, and it was clear that all the keepers in our building had become protective of the animals. As a result, we were happy when Joe Matyas made good on a promise to find a way to fix the boiler that heated water for the indoor pools.

It was not an easy promise to keep. The boiler was so antiquated that

Joe literally had to track down parts from all over the world, and those he couldn't find, he fabricated. When the time came to actually do the rebuild, he spent two weeks in the basement of our building.

Early one morning he came up out of that tomb, filthy from burnt fuel oil, and said to me, "You now have hot water." That was a great victory for him and the animals.

It was only 8:30 in the morning, and I had a box of doughnuts with me. There were plenty to share so Joe stayed for coffee as the team arrived. Lori Entsminger, the new keeper over at sea lions, also stopped over.

When Ellen came in, she threw the morning's *Plain Dealer* down on the little table.

"So this is how my day started," she said. "Can you believe this? I got up this morning, and find my picture is in the paper, and it's the worst picture of me imaginable. Look at this."

Inside the paper was a photograph of her and our Tiani. It didn't seem to be part of any article; it was just used as a filler and carried a caption which began something like this: *(Cleveland, AP.) Trouble by the tail.* The caption also identified Ellen by name, and she did look a little bit ridiculous.

"I *never* pull on her tail," said Ellen. "If ever in my life I've pulled her tail, it was just so that she would know I was there. But they have a picture with my name and make it look like I'm really tugging."

We passed the newspaper around the room. Tad, Joe and, by that time, even Lori looked at it. It was a low-quality print, a typical low-rez half-tone common to that era. In real life, Ellen was a very attractive woman, and in that photo she looked kind of stupid. She was right about that.

"Where was the photo taken?" I asked.

"Sometimes I walk Tiani over to the coal scales at the foundry down on Brookside. They let me weigh her there. One day a photographer was there and took some pictures. But, that's not the worst part." Ellen now sounded lighthearted. "This photograph was picked up as an Associated Press wire photo. It's in every newspaper in the world."

Tad laughed, "It's not that bad."

"It's awful," said Ellen. "But, I suppose, twenty years from now it will be forgotten."

(Actually, that wasn't quite true. Twenty-seven years later, I bought the original glossy print off eBay.)

Ellen left the paper on the table and went out to work. Matyas was still enjoying a well deserved doughnut when he changed the topic.

"Did you know they caught your deer killer?"

I never expected this.

"You were the watchman the night that guy murdered the deer, weren't you?" Of course I was, and that night was etched in my brain. "The Ranger Department caught him. He's going to prison for a long time."

I remembered the oath that the detective had sworn to me that he would find the killer. "Was it one of the detectives who figured it out?" I asked.

"I don't know who solved it; it could have been a detective. They offered a $1,000 reward for information leading to his identification. The reward was out there for several months. Finally, someone called and turned him in. He'll be in prison for twenty-six years."

That seemed like a long sentence, but Joe explained further. "He was on parole when he killed the deer so he was also a parole violator. The twenty-six years is the time left on his previous conviction, and they added something like six months for killing the deer. He's a former zoo employee, a maintenance man. That's how he knew what he was doing and the watchman's routine."

"Somebody must have turned him in then?"

"His ex-wife. She knew he did it. She knew the moment she heard about what happened. But she was afraid of him. She didn't say anything for a long time. The rangers assured her they could protect her, and that the guy would go away from a long time. I guess she finally decided that $1,000 made it worth it. He can't be paroled now. He'll be in prison for the whole twenty-six and a half years.

"I'd say you're lucky you didn't run into the guy that night. He's a hardened criminal."

I thanked Joe again for what he had done with the water heater. It meant that the hippos would be able to be back soaking much sooner than when they were waiting on the cold water to get near room temperature. In time I learned that the pygmies liked their water even warmer. Somewhere around 101 degrees Fahrenheit, a good deal higher than the 56 degree winter tap water temps.

One day Alan Sironen came to the building and couldn't contain his excitement. He had written a lot of letters and received many replies from zoos around the world. What he had managed to do was compile a list of North American tree species that would be fine for elephants to eat. He also explained that the large grove of white willows next to the railroad tracks could be used to supplement the diets.

After that, I brought a tree saw from home, and kept it at the zoo. On late afternoons, I'd climb over the chain link barrier to cut off some of the flowing branches. Ellen was the first to make me aware of the fact that our normal feed was really unnatural for elephants. "We feed them hay, fruit, and grain," she said, "but in the wild, African elephants eat trees.

The main ingredient of their diet is wood."

It also bothered me that the elephants really didn't have a fresh supply of water at night. We'd fill their troughs, but we'd often find them fouled the next morning. I discovered a way to handle the problem. On the back of the elephant's pen was a peep hole so that a keeper could look in on the animals without disturbing them. The hole was about the same diameter as a common garden hose. As an experiment, I jammed the brass threads through the opening and turned on a tiny trickle of water that drained into the cage. The hose took a while to fill to the point where anything actually came out the other end, but Simba could smell it.

She could put the end of her trunk over the nozzle and suck out the entire contents of the hundred foot hose. Then she'd blow all the water out of her trunk into her mouth. Tiani saw what the older elephant was doing and picked up the skill. It worked perfectly. The elephants couldn't defecate in this water supply. And every thirty seconds or so, the supply was replenished. For the first time since 1955, Simba had clean water all night.

My feeling was that there was a great camaraderie, not just among the employees, but between the humans and animals as well. The humans laughed, and the elephants fed on fresh branches. The well-fed hippos were lounging in their saunas. Well, the only animal that was both disconnected and discontented was Red. Her anger and fear were constant.

CHAPTER SEVENTEEN

The outdoor hippo pen at the far end of the building had quite a colony of fully-grown Egyptian geese. Over time, I watched them, almost on a daily basis. Like many of the exotic birds, each had one wing clipped to prevent it from flying away. These nine geese were bivouacked within the concrete walls of Bomi's outdoor yard. There was a pool in that area, but for some reason, the geese never went in the water. In my first spring, I observed the mating habits of the Egyptian goose firsthand.

The nine geese had a self-regulated order in their gaggle. There was one dominant male who mated for life with a single female. They were the only mating pair. The remaining seven didn't pair off or mate as long as there was one mated pair.

Vince explained this to me. "Only this pair will nest and breed. If there were a thousand Egyptian geese in this yard, out of them all, only one pair would mate."

Since it was my job to feed them, I got to know who they were. The mating pair set up their territory just outside the door. Those who had taken a vow of chastity stayed far away.

When I walked near the seven vestal virgins, they were docile and simply moved out of the way. King Goose in the Royal Corner, however, would invariably attack me. He would spread his wings and come right at me with his head low and menacing, honking like a delivery truck. It was about ninety-eight percent bluster; when he got about two feet away, he'd veer off. After I passed by, he would often attack again with a rear assault. Sometimes he would actually grab hold of my pants cuff, and I'd simply shake him off.

Tad was working there one day when he was attacked. Like me, he thought the entire thing hilarious, and I suppose our laughter probably infuriated the feathered warrior, but even in his most frenzied state he could not rise above the image of a Baby Huey cartoon. It was Tad who gave him the nickname, *Poppy*. After that, the mating pair were named Poppy and Moms, because she chattered with a rasp like *Moms Mabley*.

Vince seemed more concerned than amused. "You'll need to give her stuff to build her nest with. Some trash and debris might drift in here but you can give her better stuff. Bring branches, grass, and leaves for her, and put them in the corner where the pair likes to stay. She has nothing in there to build a nest."

After that, I brought in grass, branches, leaves, sticks and scattered them. Vince was right; within a few days, Moms built a nest and started to sit on it.

Vince said, "She's not laying yet. She's just sitting on the nest to form it into a nice shape. She's working it like a potter. That's all."

The nest itself was fairly large, over a foot in diameter. "After they've mated," said Vince, "she'll start laying eggs. She'll lay only one egg a day until she's got about ten to fourteen eggs. She won't start incubating any of them until she's done. After that, she'll sit on them for thirty-five days until they hatch. For a lot of geese it's thirty days, but with the Egyptians, it's a little longer. You can mark it on your calendar when those eggs will hatch, set your watch by it if you've paid attention. Those eggs will hatch probably around 10:00 a.m. thirty-five days from the day she lays the last egg.

I was impressed by what Vince knew about these birds, and he was right about everything. The eggs stayed dormant until she began to incubate them. The effect was that eggs laid days apart would hatch around the same time. Actually, what he said was, "The last egg she lays will be the very first one to hatch." He also explained that during the time she'd be on the nest, she wouldn't eat or drink.

Vince also warned us, saying, "And the moment those babies are hatched, they'll be hungrier than hell."

I wanted to know what I should feed them.

"They'll eat just about anything they can find, bugs mostly. The rest of their whole life, they won't eat meat, but right after they hatch out, they're starving, ready for anything. Another thing: the morning they hatch, you'll want to have the hippo pool full of water. The babies will be looking for a place to swim to clean themselves off. So when the time is getting close, keep the pool filled and clean."

The next night, she indeed laid an egg in the big soft nest that she built. She laid it during the night. She covered it up but didn't stay on the nest much. She stayed close to the nest and so did the fierce Poppy, her protector. Of course, when I walked near the nest, he attacked. He charged with his head down and his feet flying everywhere in a fast and furious manner, honking at me like a spastic with a party horn.

The next night Moms laid a second egg. It was there when I came in the next morning. Every day I reached into the nest and felt under the dry grass for the eggs and kept a running count. They were smooth and beautiful, a lot bigger than the largest chicken egg. Of course, when I did that, Poppy hissed and muttered all around me, even jabbed at my sleeves and pants.

I make fun of him, but both geese were diligent and fiercely loyal to their nesting area. Most likely, in the wee hours of the night, he was fending off skunks, rats, and raccoons as best he could.

After two days and two eggs, I followed more of Vince's recommendations, and took a large cardboard box, cut a goose-sized opening and air holes. I then covered it with heavy plastic from a bail of peat moss. It was a sort of sturdy cave which provided protection from night predators. I wasn't sure Moms would like it much, however, but again, Vince was right. She took to it right away.

On the ninth day when I came in, she was nesting. She was stuck onto the nest like a fixture. So I knew she was done laying.

I asked Vince, "So she won't eat at all in the next month?"

"Aw...she might come off for a bite or a drink sometimes. But not much. She'll be all right."

Of course, I placed another concrete-and-metal drinking dish near the nest so that she could get a drink (which she did). And I put food near her, also. Every day as Poppy nipped at my legs, I ripped up lettuce and placed it right at the edge of the nest. Moms stuck out her neck and gobbled it up. She ate and drank while sitting on the eggs.

On day thirty-five, I made sure that the hippo pool was cleaned and filled. At around 9:30 in the morning, Ellen came in from Bomi's yard saying, "The geese are hatching."

Ellen, Lori, and I went out into the yard, and the little egg-white soaked chicks were breaking out of the shells. That was going to take a while so I took a mattock from the tool rack and dug earthworms on the ridge near the Children's Farm. I brought them back and the zippy little brown goslings scarfed them up in an instant. The babies raced into the pool and swam around like crazy for about forty-five seconds. They swum under water, rocketing beneath the surface to clean themselves off. It all seemed so amazing.

It was then I asked a fateful question. "If there are baby geese born here every year, what happens to them all? Do they take them somewhere or ship them to other zoos?"

Matter-of-factly, Ellen said, "Over time the predators get them at night. One by one, the wild cats and raccoons will pick them off."

The hell they will, I thought. Unlike many keepers, I knew what went on in the zoo at night. I figured I might have to sleep out in the yard next to the baby geese with my Crosman 1377. That is until Kuenzer came around on his usual morning rounds, and I showed him the new goslings.

"Ellen says they're pretty vulnerable to predators as this age."

Without hesitation, Don said, "What I would recommend is that you simply bring them in at night. Then, let them back out each morning."

Don had so much experience; he knew exactly what to do. Now it was up to me to make it more complicated.

I found a big cardboard box and cut down the sides so that the box was about two feet deep. It was a large box, around four feet square. I set the box down on the floor at the far end of the hippo hall, right inside the big door that led to Bomi's outside pen.

Then I cut a front door, leaving part of the cardboard intact as a hinge. The plan was that I'd open the door to herd the babies and Moms into the box. Once they were in, I'd be able to close the flap of the cardboard door and tape it shut. I put a bed of hay and grass in the box, as well as a concrete water dish and a tray of goose feed and cut-up lettuce.

Next, I collected several massive armloads of shop rags out of the utility room. After the geese were inside, I planned to stuff the rags around the edges of the big metal door, so that a cat couldn't squeeze in, under, or around the sides of the door.

It occurred to me that rats in the building might also attack the goslings. The rats had burrows outside the building, but nothing I could do would prevent them from getting in at night. There was also certainly the possibility that a raccoon, cat, or skunk could find another way into the building.

So, I cut up boxes to make big, wide cardboard sheets. I laid these three-foot-wide strips of cardboard all around the goose's pen to form a moat of flat cardboard. In our arsenal of odds and ends in the utility room behind the giraffe pens, we had several gallons of what we called *rat goop* or *rat glue*. It was thick like axle grease, but super sticky. We used it to make traps that would become a barrier to rodents.

Just before closing, Ellen, Tad, and Lori helped me herd the baby geese into the building and into their new box. First, I moved all the rat glue traps down the hall, carrying them away carefully. We herded Moms and the babies in from the yard and into the little cardboard pen. In a few moments it was clear that Moms wanted no part of the building, not at all. She didn't seem to care a bit that her babies were no longer in her charge.

"She's seems okay with this," said Ellen. "We'll just leave her outside."

With the goslings in the box pen, I closed the flap door and taped it shut. Then I carefully moved all the glue traps, placing them around the box. I taped them down, also. I didn't want some predator to get stuck in a trap and move the trap out of place as it struggled. That would create a hole in the barrier for the next predator. Finally, I stuffed the rags all around the big metal door that led outside. The baby geese, without their mother, were secure in their fortress of rat goop and cardboard.

We did that every afternoon for weeks. That plan worked perfectly, and all nine goslings were raised to maturity, but no predator ever stepped into the goo, either. We let the babies out in the daytime and moved them inside every night until they were about three-quarters grown. Within a month, there were eighteen Egyptian geese in the yard, and the new arrivals blended in with the other seven at the far end of the yard. Poppy and Moms remained the only mating pair, but they wouldn't mate again until the following spring.

I told Vince about what we were doing. "Kuenzer's done just about everything in this zoo," he said. "He's a good guy to ask about anything."

"Well, you know plenty about animals, too," I said. "You were right about everything. The geese hatched exactly on time and were starving. Really, you have as much knowledge about animals as anyone."

Vince seemed melancholy and preoccupied before he spoke. "Well, I don't have any education. I only graduated the eighth grade, you know, and I had to go back to school to do that."

"But that isn't unusual for a person of your generation," I said. "My Uncle Adam only went through the eighth grade, and he became a Captain in Patton's Third Army."

"I suppose," said Vince.

At that moment, a small bird crashed into one of the darkened, sloped glass windows on that side of the building. Vince immediately stepped off the walkway and picked up the stunned bird. I think it was a towhee.

The poor animal struggled in Vince's cupped hands. "This bird won't make it. His neck's broken. It's a male, pretty young."

Quietly and lost in thought, Vince said, "It will take hours for him to die, and he'll die slowly. I'll put him to rest."

He rolled the bird softly over onto its back, still holding it in both hands with both the bird's feet up in the air. Vince worked his thumbs up toward the tiny breast of the bird.

Vince said, "This won't be painful to him. He'll just go to sleep. I'm just going to close his heart shut with my thumbs. I'll squeeze it flat."

Very tenderly and expertly, Vince's thumbs wiggled into the bird's plumage, into its ribcage, until the very tips of his thumbs were buried in feathers. Looking down at the dark bird in his cupped hands, Vince was solemn and reverent. Standing close to him, looking over his shoulder, I could see that within the bird's bosom Vince's thumbs were coming together in a tender pinch. Instantly the bird's whole body drooped, and he was utterly limp.

"He's dead," said Vince. "That's how you do it. He just went to sleep."

I probably would have thrown the bird's body into the brush or into the nearby trash receptacle. There were plenty of them around, but instead, he pulled open his left shirt pocket and eased in the tiny bird. He laid him down into the pocket so that the feathers were smoothed. "I'll take care of it, " he said.

I don't know what he meant to do. But it was clear he wouldn't simply throw it in the trash.

Vince continued talking, opening up his life.

"About the eighth grade, education wasn't even a possibility for me. I had to work for my family, even when I was a boy. That's how I learned what I know about animals. From the age of six, my father raised canaries in our house, and I had to help him every day. He learned the trade from his grandfather. He had another job, a good career. Then the Depression hit. But he knew how to raise canaries from when he was a boy, so he had some birds shipped to him from California and that's how we survived.

"We had over three thousand canaries in our basement at different times. I stayed out of school for a long time to work with him. We raised them right here in Cleveland. That's not an easy business. Canaries are sensitive to exact temperatures and even the amount of light they receive. And they're picky about their diet, if you expect to breed them successfully. Everything we did had to do with thermometers. The room's temperature. The temperature of their drinking water. Everything. And you have to pair them to breed them, match them up out of hundreds of birds, and move them around until they're happy. They're choosy about their mates. My father knew every one of those birds, as an individual. I didn't; I was just a kid. I couldn't tell them apart. He had pet names for a lot of them. I just fed them all and cleaned their cages. My father taught me everything I know about birds.

"There was a time in Cleveland when, if you went to any of the downtown department stores, all the canaries there, at Higbee's, Halle's, Sears, and the May Company, it didn't matter... they all came from our house. Every store. Just before the war, our canaries contracted canary pox. We couldn't stop it. My father killed hundreds and hundreds of sick birds and burned them in our coal furnace. He cried when he did it, but killing them and burning the bodies didn't help. The next day more birds were sick, and he would kill them. He killed them just the way I killed that bird just now. He cried like a baby, my father did. He said prayers in Latin. But you can't stop canary pox once it gets going. It would have been brought in by other birds we had shipped to us. It went right through our house, killed every single bird.

"We had nothing, no way to live. I was around fourteen when that happened, and so I went to work. But my father never recovered from that. He was never the same. He loved those birds, and they were the support of his whole family, even helping to support his parents in Europe.

"Well, that's good about the geese..." said Vince softly. "You did a good job. I better get back to work."

That was one of the few times I saw Vince Rimedio that he wasn't upbeat and outlandish. Most of the time he was a ball of fire, full of piss and vinegar.

CHAPTER EIGHTEEN

Though not pachyderms, giraffes were also housed in our building at that time. Ours were Masai giraffes (also called the Kilimanjaro giraffe). They are the largest of all giraffes and were probably brought to the zoo from the 1955 Cleveland Zoo Expedition. From what I'd been told, that was the same expedition that procured Red, Blackie, a black rhino, Simba, Tara, and a bull African. The giraffes I took care of weren't the animals captured in 1955; they were the offspring of the offspring, and probably in danger of being too inbred. The original Masai giraffes had dozens of births over the years.

The zoo had three giraffes. Two females, called Lulu and Patches, and a male, Bert. They were all big. It was estimated that the neck alone weighed five hundred pounds. They had to be strong just to be able to swing their necks around with ease. Their black hooves were around ten inches wide and their eighteen inch black tongues were constantly snaking out of their mouths.

With their heads towering so high above, I felt that they lived in an entirely different dimension. This made contact with them seem less personal. Their heads were up there somewhere, on the second floor of the building, but for the most part, the giraffes were docile and harmless. We all walked right into their stalls, and they always shied away when humans approached.

These two thousand pound giants move with a sort of mental remoteness and seem almost other-worldly. Adding to the eerie quality of being near them was the fact that they are mute.

The giraffe stall was divided into halves. It was designed for elephants, but modified to accommodate giraffes, and all three were housed together. Every morning a keeper herded them from one side of the cage to another, then cleaned the empty side. As a result, they alternated between the right and left side of the enclosure. In the summer, they were herded outside for the day, and the pens could be cleaned. Their food, which was green alfalfa hay and alfalfa pellets, was kept in feed baskets and troughs which were eighteen feet off the floor. To put food in the feeders, we mounted a spiral staircase to a balcony overseeing the stalls.

Mucking out these stalls meant getting out the shovel and the wheelbarrow and carting dung to the Heidi Shit Barn. There was little need for caution when doing this. Though the hall behind their cages was large, open, and full of miscellaneous stuff, they never seemed interested in exploring. The food was in their pen, and that's pretty much where they wanted to be.

Early on, I opened the door to the hall so the giraffes could pass through on their way to the out-of-doors. After ten minutes, I realized the giraffes hadn't moved. I looked down the back elephant hall, and the giraffes simply weren't willing to budge. There were three long necks and three heads peering into the building, looking all around. It looked like three orange octopus tentacles squirming in and out of the door way.

Ellen later explained, "They won't come because something's different in the back hall. They think it's a trap." What she meant by *something different* is that these creatures were absolutely aware of every detail of a place. They might have remembered seeing a rake leaning against a wall, and now it was gone. That's their level of hypersensitivity. If one thing was different, they would be wary.

So then a game of deduction began. Ellen would ask, "Where was the wheelbarrow this morning when they went out?" or, "I think that bucket is out of place."

We'd move the bucket and they still wouldn't move. "Well, that wasn't it."

"I think the rake was laying sideways on the tool rack this morning," I suggested, "and there were a couple of buckets on top of the hay bales."

We'd put things back, and sure enough the giraffes would come in. That was interesting, but more often exasperating. Because of this quirk, the back hall behind the giraffes was kept as simple and uncluttered as possible. It wasn't that they were afraid of dangerous things, *per se*. You could put boxes of poison and land mines in there in the morning, and if nothing was moved, they'd come inside. If you left a bucket out of place, however, they'd crane their necks around and think, *That looks dangerous. I think it's a trap.* I suppose that's not unlike some people who fear change more than adjusting to new realities.

I hadn't been working in the building long before a giraffe gave birth. The actual event took place at 3:00 in the morning, but Ellen was there. She was still there when I arrived in the morning. Actually, I came in at 6:30 to check on the mother when I found Ellen sitting on a folded chair in the stall.

"Were you here all night?"

"I went home to eat, but I came back at 10:00. The birth took several hours, but here he is."

"When I drove a tour train, I told people that mother giraffes gave birth standing up and the baby drops six feet. Is it true?"

"Yes. I thought I'd put down some hay to soften the fall... I guess I got carried away."

I laughed because Ellen had laid down a bed about twenty-four inches thick across the entire pen. "It didn't seem to me that falling six feet and landing on earth would be the same as falling six feet and landing on cement. I'll leave it for awhile. It's getting stomped down already."

That day and for a few days to come, the birth was big news in the zoo. People came around to see it including the curators and the private veterinarian who also served as the zoo's vet.

When Kuenzer came, I told him that I had thought of a great name for the calf. Don said that the wife of one of the Board members had an idea, too, and that it would likely be the odds-on choice.

My idea was *Kareem Abdul-Giraffe.* Don liked that and said he'd pass along the idea. A few days later we were told that the new baby's name was *Lyle.*

Lyle (I still liked my idea better) grew quickly, and was taller than a big NBA center. In no time, he grew to be about ten feet tall, and the vet decided he needed to get some blood samples.

This was important, and zoos across the country were cooperating in giraffe breeding programs. The fact was that Lyle was a bit inbred, both of his parents being from the same herd. Blood samples could be useful for managing the breeding of the Masai subspecies.

Ellen wasn't too crazy about the idea of anyone taking samples of Lyle's blood, the reason being that the vet wanted to use tranquilizers in order to get the sample.

"I just hate it when they even suggest that," she said. "These larger animals have so much mass that they can suffocate when they're under. With the Nile hippos and the elephants, we surely don't ever want to knock them down. Their weight is so great, their breathing may stop when they're unconscious. I don't know how much of an issue that will be with Lyle, but it's a risk. I'm having nothing to do with it. All I know is Lyle is about to be greatly stressed. I don't like it. You'd think they could take a sample by surrounding the animal. Get ten keepers to move in on him from all sides, the way they do with horses. He's not that big yet. I doubt that he even weighs five hundred pounds."

When the vets arrived they went into the pen and were deaf to Ellen's misgivings. That kind of stuff always makes zookeepers feel a bit disenfranchised. The keepers work with the animals, and then for an isolated incident, there are strangers in the cage, stressing the animal and running the show.

Ellen and I watched from behind the rail in the public area.

She said, "They offered to let me help, but I don't want anything to do with this. Firing a dart is a totally inexact science. It's not like giving an animal a shot with a measured injection. Tranquillizing Lyle is completely unnecessary, and there's no way to know how much of the tranquilizer will actually get injected when the dart hits. They expect it to be ineffective so they always overload the syringe. All that says to me is that if the shot hits so that it fully drains, he could be overdosed."

The older vet, a thin man with white hair, had a gas-powered dart gun. A younger vet was also in the cage. Next to them was a large aluminum gun case lying open with an array of darts and hypodermic syringes and bottles of tranquilizer potion. Lyle had been isolated in this pen, with the three adult giraffes in the other stall.

The gun was not the vet's first choice, and he suggested trying an injection. When Lyle saw the needle coming, that was something different and the ten-foot tall juvenile bolted. He galloped around, slapping hard hooves against the cement. The vet backed off.

"We'll have to use the gun."

It took the two a long time to figure out how to load the syringe into the rifle. The darts were fired one at a time, and the discharge of the gun made an ear-splitting explosion.

BAM.

With the sound came a frozen puff of gas, and the dart struck Lyle in the neck, just above the shoulders. He lurched into a frenzied gallop, whirling in circles. Now wide-eyed, he opened his mouth and let out an ear-piercing scream.

"I thought they were mute," I said, leaning over to Ellen. The screams sounded like a four hundred pound goose honking in long continuous notes or those aerosol horns people blow at a Browns' game.

The panicked animal kept running and screaming for about three minutes before the vets realized that whatever amount of medication got into the giraffe was not having much of an effect.

"I think maybe the serum wasn't properly discharged from the dart into his bloodstream," said the doctor. "Let's load up another one."

"This is the problem I was telling you about," said Ellen. "Now, who knows how much of the drug is getting into the animal?"

One dart was already hanging from Lyle's neck, bobbing around like a pendant.

BAM.

The second dart slammed into Lyle's spotted neck near the shoulder, sticking into a muscular section of flesh, and it only inspired a renewed burst of terror.

"That ought to do it," said one of the doctors.

Evidently, Lyle had not read the paper insert that came with the drug because he wasn't getting sleepy or slowing down at all. Four minutes later, a third shot echoed through the cavernous building, followed by more ear-splitting screams, and Lyle had three darts hanging from his neck, and his eyes were lit up like he'd just drank a fifty gallon barrel of coffee with extra sugar.

"Well, this isn't working. We'll forgo the blood sample for now. We don't want to stress the animal."

The other vet agreed, and packed away their arsenal.

"I'll recover those darts when they fall out, and get them back to you," Ellen said respectfully.

"That would be fine," he said without looking at her. They didn't get any blood samples on that day. I don't think they ever did.

CHAPTER NINETEEN

I liked working in the Pachy, but from time to time, I roamed around the zoo and frequented familiar places to see how things had changed.

The new Cat and Ape Building was vastly superior to the old one. The public areas were carpeted, but I had really come to see Timmy. The massive silverback was more glorious than ever. In the old building, it had been difficult to get a good look at him as he was always cowering in the damp corners. Now he was brightly lit. There wasn't any doubt that Timmy's new surroundings were now better than his previous damp and chilly dungeon. His improvement in conditions were the most marked in winter. I don't know how he didn't freeze to death in the old Main Building. His cage was icy cold, without a blade of straw or anything. In the new building, his area was always warm and sheltered. The new gorilla exhibit was enormous, with a lot of fake concrete trees and boughs. He was also markedly less moody, and actually seemed more sociable than threatening. If he slammed his hand against the glass, it was to get someone's attention rather than scare the bejeebers out of them.

While I was disappointed that the new Goss Cat and Ape Building didn't feature outdoor enclosures, Timmy was in a new and better world. [Editor's note: Currently, the zoo does have an outdoor venue for the great apes.]

About this time, I became aware that the Teamsters' contract with the zoo was expiring. The overall economy was bad, and people didn't expect much of a raise. Actually, we were more afraid of pay cuts or no contract at all. Like a lot of people, I was just afraid that we'd all end up working for minimum wage.

In a few weeks, we heard that the zoo had put a new three-year contract on the table, and there was going to be a big meeting down at the Teamsters headquarters. Zoo management would also be at the meeting, represented by the new director, Mike Vitantonio. He would explain the offer, and the workers would vote whether or not to accept.

I ran into Jerry Studiak in the Commissary kitchen and we talked about the upcoming meeting. I asked if he was going.

"Hell, no. I have better things to do with my time."

Naturally, he was a Union member and paid his dues. But he was extremely skeptical about it. I asked if he thought we'd get a raise. He didn't trust any of them and figured everyone was in cahoots, and this was just a dance to entertain the membership.

"Here's what's going to happen at that meeting," he said. "Write this down. Vitantonio will stand up and tell you how broke the zoo is and that they can't afford to give anyone an increase. Then Jackie Presser from the Union will stand up. He'll called Vitantonio every curse word in the book. He'll curse him up and down for about ten minutes. He'll say the new contract is an insult and a disgrace. But, he'll say, we have to take it because we're lucky to even have jobs in this economy. Vitantonio and Presser will have met and have all that worked out. It's just a bunch of bullshit."

I was very pro-Teamsters. Our decent pay was due to them. The union dues were around $600 a year, but they got us our living wage.

"Let me tell you what that $600 gets you," Jerry said. "For that $600 you get a free frozen turkey at Christmas."

I countered by saying that I was just scraping by from paycheck to paycheck, but without the union, I'd have to go back into advertising or the book business.

"Hey, the union used to be good," he admitted. "They got us that money in the past. But nowadays, the deals are sealed behind closed doors. Like I said."

I went to the public hearing and sat next to Bill Seman. Everyone was there, except for Jerry. Our union steward Vern, who thought the f-bomb was a form of proper punctuation, spoke first. This may have been the first time I thought he was completely sober, but he was nervous enough to probably want a quick snort. It took an enormous force of will to get through his part without swearing. The result was a halting and painful delivery. He took many pauses, and I realized that the pauses were the places where I think the written script might have reminded him: *Do not* insert an expletive here.

Next, Zoo Director Mike Vitantonio talked for some time. He didn't go to the podium. He just sat in a folding chair near the front. His talk was very brief. He said the zoo was losing a lot of money, and could give a five cent per hour raise each year of the three-year contract, which was the best I'd hoped for.

Then Jackie Presser gave a speech. He also didn't go to the podium, either. But he stood up. He was a great speaker, very charismatic. He made broad gestures and paced the floor. Unlike Vern, he didn't pause or stumble for words. He also didn't delete any expletives. He called Vitantonio every name in the sailor's handbook, and the zoo director seemed vaguely amused at this.

Then, with no connection to his five minute rant, Presser concluded by saying, "But now let's look at the other side of the issue. The economy is down. The Metroparks didn't have a good year. They lost a lot of money. So, considering those circumstances, the new contract is about all you could hope for, and my recommendation is that you accept it."

Vern rose to call for the vote. Emboldened by Presser's colorful language, he released a series of cluster f-bombs, before asking us to vote by show of hands.

Every worker in the room raised his hand, and the new contract was ratified. I was very glad to have three more years of decent pay. It could have been a lot worse. Studiak had been right on target about the meeting. He must have seen the script in advance.

CHAPTER TWENTY

I had my first bout with *zookeeper's back* when I went skateboarding. Technically, there were no skateboards involved, and I was not the one on wheels. Let me start again.

I had just opened the valves to begin draining all the hippo pools when Steve Gove popped his head through the doorway and said, "Adam, Tad and Kenny Pekarek are here. Can you help us move the giant tortoises?"

These guys were all young and strong, but they needed an additional recruit to help lift the tortoises.

It was summer, and there was no longer any danger of cold nights. So it was time to move the three reptiles to the outdoor sitatunga exhibit up near Bears. The move was made by first lifting, then setting each tortoise onto a wheeled cart.

So it was, on that day, that I went from coffee and donuts while water was draining to doing some quick stretching exercises. From there I became part of a circle of men holding onto the bone-hard shell of an elephant tortoise.

"One, two, three... *lift*," said Steve. He should have said, "One, two, three... *hurt yourself*."

It was really lift, shuffle sideways, lower onto the dolly. It would have been easier if we were moving something lighter such as an upright piano, but the smallest of the males weighed four hundred and seventy-five pounds. We all tried to lift properly, using our legs rather than our backs, but this particular task required legs and back and every other connected body part.

During the ride, the tortoise withdrew into his shell.

The next step was to wheel the cart across the zoo while balancing our carapaced friend on his wild ride. This part was fun. On the downhill stretches, the skateboarding reptile could really travel and we had to run to keep up. That is until a sudden bump, and the load was shifting off-center. That required braking power and load readjustment. Finally, there was the unloading and the walk back pulling the heavy dolly behind us.

"Well, that's one," said Steve. I suppose the little guy that we had just unloaded was to loosen us up because number two was five hundred and twenty-five pounds.

"All right, Ladies and Germs," said our boss. "One, two, three... *lift*."

This was the lift I would feel in exactly forty-eight hours, and that's how you get *zookeeper's back*.

The big guy was a slow, hard push. It wasn't that he couldn't be a speedster like his predecessor, it was because his feet were not always withdrawn into his shell and we feared abrasion if one leg scraped along the ground.

Our last passenger, a svelte, four hundred pound female was a different story. She was all about speed, hot and spicy. On that final journey, she went at a breakneck speed as we bent over and pushed with our legs. She didn't shrink into her shell. Instead, she rode with her neck out and her head facing into the wind. She held her legs out and back like she was a plane in flight.

Tad Schoffner gave her the nickname, *Slick*.

We pushed the cart at top speed, and Slick stretched her neck forward contorting herself into an arrow imitation. As we went faster and faster, Slick opened her mouth and gulped down the breeze. She liked speed. She liked the fast lane. She craved excitement and risk. What did it mean?

When we reached the end of the final straightaway, Tad said, "Well, this is the end of the ride, old Slick."

That's when Steve said, "Oh, what the heck, let's run her back and forth a few times. She only gets this twice a year."

We all agreed, and Slick's excitement continued. As far as I know, she still holds the land-speed record for giant tortoises.

Two days later I woke up with *zookeeper's back*, and really had a hard time straightening up. I don't think it created any lasting damage, but I hobbled around for a few days.

One more note must be added to protect the daring macho image of one of the guys who was with us that day. As it turned out, Slick, our speedster, was later discovered to be a male. Since 1955 *she* had been thought a female because of her size and other characteristics. Her official name was *Mary*, but I think we had it right with *Slick*.

CHAPTER TWENTY-ONE

As the summer grew warmer, Red became moodier. When I opened the door a crack, she would charge the door, slamming against it with her shoulder, and sealing the argument with a snort. She turned her nose up at hay as long as she could smell the lush vegetation growing on the nearby hillsides.

Elsewhere in the zoo, the whole world was lounging in lazy warmth. The outdoor hoofed animals were in their summer heaven, grazing in nearly natural veldts. Simba and little Tiani moved calmly and leisurely in the Cleveland sunshine. The little one often played liked a grade-school child in the outdoor pool. Both elephants could grab a clump of some green weeds, in addition to the willow branches I brought them on many days.

Blackie spent hours snoozing in the sun when he was outside, and inside, he bobbed like a big cork in his heated pool. His appetite never waned. He devoured the mountain of hay and grain that was set before him twice each day. But the fasting Red became more discontented as the pretty summer days lengthened. She ate the fruit off the top and left the rest untouched. She sulked and paced and was continuously agitated. When I walked past the front of her exhibit, she snorted and huffed. She also seemed jittery. One day as I stood watching her, Vince came by.

"She's off her feed from the smells of grass and trees," he began, "but right now, I'd also say she's coming into heat. See how she's sweating? Being in heat with no… uh, culmination will also make her moody. She's talking to Blackie. Haven't you been hearing him snorting? It's all language, all words. He's way over there behind two doors, and she's over here. The big Black, he can take it, but it's driving her nuts when she's in heat."

As we talked, Red was standing sideways, looking at us. I looked at her closely as Vince pointed out every distinct feature that displayed her current mood and condition. Red had hippo sweat pouring out of her neck and face. The foamy red mucus was streaming down from around her ears, appearing very bloodlike. The flow was so copious, it dripped onto the floor around her front legs.

Vince said, "And see that? Look at her chest under her neck. She's red as hell, boiling. She's flushed. Hear her wheezing? Her heart rate is sky high. She's off her feed and she's in heat. Look how she's up on her toes. Antsy. You've seen it. She's as skittish as a beehive. Just be really careful to steer clear of her. She'll be out of heat in a week. She's just coming into it now. As far as the feeding, she'll get back to normal at some point."

It became more and more of a challenge to get her back in the building. Food was not going to entice her out of the pool where she wallowed all day. She didn't care about food. One day I could not get her back into the building until after 6:00.

I told Vince, and he gave me some advice. His tone was serious. I knew what he was suggesting would be dangerous.

"What you gotta do is get the pool draining with her in it. Once she hears the water draining out beneath her, she'll get out of the water. She doesn't like being in the pool when it's draining."

"I'm sure you see the tricky part in that, don't you? The drain valve to the pool is right next to the edge. Who the hell was the idiot who thought of that, I don't know. To start the water draining, you have to go right to the edge of the pool while Red's in there. So be careful. She can come out of that water faster than a croc, a hell of a lot faster. Here's how you get that valve open. Red will get agitated when she knows you're trying to let the water out of the pool under her. When she's agitated, she'll start swimming in circles, like a roving shark. Always counterclockwise. You want to run out there and get the drain valve turned while she's swimming away from you. You'll be right on the water's edge when you open the drain. But that's how you do it. Get her agitated so she starts swimming in circles. Once the pool starts draining, she'll come inside. She doesn't like being exposed out in the yard." As he spoke, he gestured with dramatic arm movements. He said, "Watch her. She'll come out of that water like a shot." On the word *shot*, Vince smacked his hands together.

"Listen," he said. "Out in the Nile yard there are those big logs, like telephone poles, stuck in the ground to make a barrier. You know what I mean?"

I knew what he was talking about. Within the area was a small patch of ground surrounded by four-foot high poles spaced about two feet apart. They were a safety zone near the concrete walls of the enclosure.

Vince said, "That little zone next to the fence is not far from the drain valve. That's what it's for. If Red charges out of the water, you can slip between the poles into that spot. You don't have time to make it all the way back to the building. She'll catch you before you go ten feet. So go into the zone behind the poles instead. Then get the hell out of there. Climb out over the wall. I wouldn't put it past Red to take out one of those poles if she started hammering them. You can get up on top of the wall at your age."

The stout concrete wall that surrounded the entire outdoor Nile pen was around eight feet high. But I was pretty sure I could pull myself over with a running leap. I had done it before as a short cut between the two pens.

"Just remember," Vince was pressing his point, "if she charges up out of the water, don't try to run to the building. You might think you can make it, but you can't."

From Vince, I now knew how I could get Red out of the pool, and I used that method many times as the weeks went by. It worked fine with no problems, usually.

CHAPTER TWENTY-TWO

With vacation and sick days to burn, Steve Sandusky was gone for all July and half of August that year. Steve Gove was the relief keeper assigned and he worked almost exclusively in hippos. He was a funny and somewhat eccentric person, with short blonde hair and a reddish-blonde beard. We got along fine and hung around together a lot during those times. When things were really slow, we'd kick footballs in the back halls or play catch with a softball in the public area. More than once a ball bounced into a hippo pool, and I'd retrieve it as quickly as it was safe.

Steve was also the manager of the zoo's baseball team. There were teams throughout the Metroparks system, and games were set up as *friendly* competition. One game in particular was against the downtown office. They apparently had done some pre-game trash talk about dealing with the stinky zookeepers. It was probably true that most of us, coming straight from work, were on the aromatic side, but we were tougher than their talk. The score ended six to zip in favor of the doo-doo covered brown shirts.

One night Steve and I were recruiting our roster for the next game and, as a consequence, I was running late. Everyone else had left, but I was still waiting for Red who was still outside in her pool. I could have used Vince's trick earlier, but I wanted her to take what comfort she could by staying out. My plan was to bring her in at the very last minute. Her meal was already in her pen, with the back door open and all barricades in place. She could come in anytime she wanted, but she chose not to, so I busied myself by straightening up the tool rack.

Just then, Ellen surprised me by walking back into the keeper room. She appeared to be exasperated by something.

"Okay, I have to come in here and tell you that I admit defeat. I have a flat tire, and I can't get the old tire off of my car."

This was the first time I'd ever seen her throw in the towel. She was always proud of her independence, but tonight, she had been out in the parking lot for twenty minutes attempting to change a flat tire. Had she succeeded, I never would have known about it.

"Every time I've had a flat before, I've always changed it myself," she said. "I have the car jacked up; I simply don't have the strength to get the lug nuts off. When I bought these tires, they used one of those hydraulic wrenches and put the wheels on super tight. I hate that I have to ask, but can you help me change my tire?"

Knowing Ellen, those words must have come hard. "Not a problem," I said. "I haven't even brought in Red. She'll love staying out there while we work on the tire."

We went out to the car and I lowered the jack until the tire made solid contact with the ground so that the wheel would hold against my efforts to crack the lug nuts.

Ellen was right about how tightly the guys at the tire store had ratcheted them. Once the nuts were loosened, however, the job went back to her. While she was doing that, I went on an errand of my own.

"I'll be right back. I'm going to go get you a present."

I went back in the building and found a two-foot length of steel pipe, around two inches in diameter. I took it to Ellen, who was tightening the lug nuts on the spare.

"You probably could have used this and done it yourself." I slid the pipe over one of the arms on the lug wrench and she understood that by extending the length of the tire iron, she'd have a lot more torque. "Keep this pipe in the trunk, and you can loosen any lug nut like a piece of cake."

She thanked me and asked if I was done for the day.

"I'm just going to move Red and then I'll be going home. I'll see you tomorrow."

I went to see if the hippo had stirred from the pond, but she had not, and it looked like I'd have to open the drain to get her to come inside.

I got the valve key that I'd need to open the drain. It was a seven foot long steel rod with a *T* at one end and a two inch square socket at the other. It weighed twenty-five pounds. I closed down the barricade door until it was open about fifteen inches so that Red could not enter, but I could slip through if necessary. As I was doing all this, I suspected that only two people were now in the zoo, John Sich and myself.

Red's big, round body bobbed just beneath the foamy surface of the pool, and I simply walked out into her yard, carrying the valve key. This was somewhat risky, but I kept an eye on the pool to see if there was any water movement. I would have to react quickly if the monster burst out of the foam and charged me. I knew that I could not outrun her. In spite of this, I had to go near the edge of the pool to insert the key and open the drainage system.

I stayed to the left and headed directly into the safety zone which was defined by the sawn timbers near the wall of the enclosure. That was my base of operation, and was ten feet away from the pool itself. As usual, my plan was to make quick forays out into the open to perform several small tasks, one at a time, in order to start the pool draining.

Step One was to remove the small lid over the valve so that I could insert the key when the time was right. Red, of course, knew I was in the yard, and I could tell she was angry because she began swimming in counterclockwise circles, churning up the water.

I didn't mind that she was agitated; I wanted her to keep moving. I yelled out to her, "Hey, hey, hey," and the rolling waves told me exactly where she was in the brown water.

The moment she turned past me to take another revolution, I ran out to uncover the valve. I didn't look at the valve cover itself, I kept both eyes on the pond. I had one chance to flip it open, and could not afford to fumble. If it didn't come off at the first try, I still had to get back to the safety zone.

I missed, and immediately pedaled back to safety. The waves were now larger, and I knew Red was swimming faster. I let her circle a couple of times to feel her rhythm.

I ran out again. This time, without looking, I reached down and caught the metal cover perfectly with my two index fingers. I flipped it off the hole with a dull, metallic clang. Red reacted, moving more furiously. As my fingers were flipping the cover aside, I was already retreating back to the creosote-soaked poles.

Red knew this little cat-and-mouse game by now, and was anticipating the day when she could stop it from being played. The next step was simple enough. I would insert the key in the hole and run back like hell. This also had to happen smoothly with no delays.

Red continued circling. In the past, she would have come out of the water at this point, but she didn't. I continued to watch from behind the barrier. I knew that the moment she turned away from me, she would actually be closest to me, but her forward momentum would be in the opposite direction. If I waited for her turn at the far end, she would have a straight shot to accelerate toward me.

She began a new loop. When all her momentum was going away, I raced forward holding the heavy valve key in front like a pole vaulter. I threw the socket end down into the hole with a loud rattle and raced away backwards. I kept both eyes on Red's movement below the dark froth.

Red broke the surface of the water and snorted, sucking in a huge breath through her flared nostrils. Then she disappeared beneath the churning surface, and continued her volatile swirling in an elongated counterclockwise pattern. The vise was closing in on her now. I only had two more steps before she would hear the rush of water in the drain below.

I composed myself with a few deep breaths. I was still not ready to actually turn the key, however. On my next scamper, I had to seat the socket on the valve. Once this was completed, I simply had to turn it, but one thing at a time. First, the socket had to be properly placed.

To this point, everything was tense, but normal.

Vince often warned me, "Watch her. You can bet your ass she's playing with your head."

I didn't want to bet my ass and lose it. So I edged slowly out from behind the poles, moving like a base runner about to steal second.

Red suddenly burst up through the surface of the pool, snorting. She blew wet flares up out of her nostrils, then again slipped out of sight. When she was swirling away from me, I ran forward. But beneath the surface, Red had doubled back to catch me. She had reversed direction underwater.

I thought I had been watching her, but my eyes had been following a mass of moving water.

With a blast, she exploded into view right in front of me. Sheets of water cascaded off her shoulders, back, and sides as she ran toward me right past the valve key.

Fortunately, for me, she jumped before I was near the valve, and I immediately backpedaled into the safety zone while, in front of me, a wall of red flesh and water rose like a tidal wave out of the pool.

Vince had warned me about the scenario of having only poles as cover. He had said, "*get out!*" and that made perfect sense as I turned with a leap to scale the concrete wall behind me.

In quick order, I was standing up on the top of the wall, high above the enclosure. I held onto the sparse branches of a tree to steady myself. The tree was actually growing up out of the next pen, in Mushka's yard, and my head was now fourteen feet above the enclosure.

Below, Red looked small and far away. She knew I had escaped this time and trotted in a straight line back to the pool. With a whoosh, she disappeared beneath the cloudy surface and disappeared.

I slid down off the wall and back into her enclosure, but I saw no water movement in the pool.

"HEY, HEY, HEY!" I called again, and slapped the sides of one of the posts.

Once more she began swimming in rolling counterclockwise circles. I watched her movements while taking a few careful steps toward the valve key that was still sticking up out of the ground. As Red turned to head away, I ran straight toward the valve key and turned it counterclockwise. Half-turn, half-turn, and then one last half-turn. I could hear water roaring beneath the earth.

The game was over, and the big hippo came out of the pool again, but this time, she was on the far end of the pool. The drain was open, and the water was roaring out of the pool. I was done. Without thinking, I just acted. Without a bit of hesitation, I ran back toward the building as fast I could possibly run. This was exactly what Vince had told me not to do. Red and I were suddenly in a foot race.

I had a head start. I started running first, about three seconds before she did. I had to run thirty-five feet in a straight shot on flat, solid ground. Red's starting point was down in the bottom of a pool around five feet deep. She had to shoulder aside hundreds of pounds of water and run up steps set at a forty-five degree incline just to get out of the water. As the race began, Red was running *away* from the finish line, and she would have to turn around to get a straight shot at me. She also had to run around the pool. I was confident about my head start, and the fact that she had to run a hundred feet to my thirty-five.

I had the jets on full blast as I ran toward the fifteen-inch wide opening, but when I was still ten feet from the door, I could hear the big wet paws of Red galloping behind. I could hear where she was, just a few yards behind me. Adrenaline was my friend, and I could not afford slowing to slip through the door. I just kept going top speed, and right at the last instant I turned my whole body sideways. My shoulders were parallel to the opening as I flew through the narrow slot.

I landed hard with a loud *bam*, that came, not from me, but from the sound of Red hitting the steel door. Slowly I got up and pulled the heavy barricades into place. I then cranked open the outside door and let her into the building.

"C'mon, Red. Eat something. You'll feel better."

Red moved into her indoor pen. I closed the back door to the stall. I could see her as the door slid shut. She was plowing into her meal. For the first time in a long time, she had her appetite. With every bite, she probably thought about me.

Incidents like this happen all the time in zoos.

CHAPTER TWENTY-THREE

In 1980 Christmas fell on a Thursday. My days off were Wednesday and Thursday so I was scheduled to be off on Christmas. Additionally, the union contract provided that these were paid holidays for all employees, and the zoo was closed to the public.

Still, the animals needed to be cared for, and the zoo operated with a skeleton crew. People who worked that day were paid for the holiday plus double time and were permitted to leave as soon as their necessary work was done. Generally, one keeper in each area came for part of the day.

I had worked out a deal with Ellen. I worked the holidays in exchange for regular time off. She wanted to be sure that I didn't mind this, but I really didn't have family within driving distance anymore and was happy to do it.

Ellen also thought that whoever was in the building should do a thorough cleaning on Christmas since it was not often that the public was excluded from our operations. New Year's Day was exempt from the thorough cleaning seeing as how it was only a week later.

When Ellen said "clean the whole building," I knew she was thinking about my using traditional cleaning methods, buckets, wet mops, dry mops, Windex, brooms, squeegees, etc, but I had something else in mind.

Then she added another proviso. "I won't trade days with you unless you promise one other thing. I want you to work the whole day. I don't want the elephants to be left alone for so many hours."

I assured her that I would, especially after she explained why. Before Ellen and Jim arrived in their lives, the elephants usually remained shackled all day during the holidays. Of course, this only fed Simba's violent streak. From the late 1950s through the middle 1970s, the keeper on duty that day would rush into the building around 10:00, shovel the old hay and feces out the back of the cage and leave it there. Then, the keeper would hurriedly put out feed and new hay without unchaining the elephants at all. In twenty minutes he would be done and gone. The animals, however, remained chained to one spot for forty-one consecutive hours. A week later, it would happen again.

That no longer happened when Ellen was on duty. She'd spend the entire day with the animals, and before she'd switch with me, I had to promise to do the same.

The evening before Christmas, I went to the Kroger at the corner of

Clague Road and Lorain and bought eggplants, apples, and eight jumbo bags of unsalted peanuts. I came to the zoo early, around 6:00 a.m.

As soon as I turned on the lights at Pachy, Simba began to let me know she was waiting with a rattle of her chains. The hippos had their own form of greeting. Whenever they realized that the keeper had arrived, they'd stand in hopeful expectation that a shipment of fruits and veggies would soon arrive from the Commissary.

It was Christmas, and I'm sure the animals knew. I'm not referring to the idea that they were counting down the days, but to the fact that they understood a lot of human speech patterns. Simba would have heard keepers leaving with the words *Merry Christmas* or *Happy Holidays*. She would know that the most dreaded days of the year were soon to come. Ellen and Jim changed all that beginning in the mid-1970s.

The *first* thing I did that morning was unchain the elephants. I then opened two large sacks of peanuts and scattered them over the front of the cage, which was still dry and clean. In the hippo area, I started cleaning all the stalls. I went through the entire building mucking clean the floors, hosing, and scrubbing the walls. After that, I prepared the morning meals which included the food I'd bought at Kroger, eggplants for the pygmies, apples for the Niles and the elephants. I also put aside some for the afternoon.

I had split the treats unevenly between Simba and Tiani. After all, the elder was four times larger. Even so, the elephants were respectful of each other's portions and did not try to eat out of the other's larder.

It was now time to clean the entire building, and my plan went into effect. Thanks to Don Kuenzer, we now had enough hose to reach every part of the building. In all, I put together a three hundred and fifty foot length. No one else in the zoo was running water that day so the pressure was fantastic.

My strategy was based on the fact that the design of the building was ideal for being hosed down. It was just a massive shower stall constructed with glass, painted steel girders, brick, concrete, and cement covings at the base of the walls. This was how the building was meant to be cleaned, a giant toilet that I could simply flush. All the water flowed into concrete gutters and drain. Very few things in the building could be harmed by water.

Dust, spider webs, dead flies on high window sills were all vulnerable to the blast from the hose. The hippos and elephants must have thought we were having a party when the water started dripping from the ceiling like refreshing rain. When the cold water accidentally hit a hot light bulb it exploded, and shards of thin glass joined the rain that fell around me.

Wolee chewed at the air as he took in the odd nature of the smells and molds. His back was covered with a gray spew. I drilled the fire hose at him to hose him off. As always, he turned his back. He liked the powerful spray but not in his face. The other hippos were frolicking (can that word be used for hippos?) in the rain. The elephants were trumpeting and extending their trunks through the bars of their cages to catch some of the water that was rushing in the gutter past their stalls.

I had to avoid the ceilings in the giraffe area since they were tiled, but that was one of the few areas off limits to the onslaught. On the other hand, the Masai loved the spray that came in from the front.

Sometimes, I can get carried away, but Ellen had asked me to clean the entire building and I thought it made a fun challenge.

I turned my attention now to the hay loft. I knew quite a bit about the nesting and feeding habits of mice, and my guess was that the bales of hay were a regular mouse hotel.

A hose would not work on hay, so I set out to move the entire stack, one bale at a time. I'd pick up a bale, shake it, and let it drop to the floor. If mice were there, I was going to roust them out. I spent the next hour moving the mountain, and very few mice appeared.

After moving perhaps sixty bales of Timothy hay, I was down to the last five. The second to the last bale contained the mother load. As I lifted it up, mice began to bail out. This batch went out into the snow, and those who had jumped had nowhere else to go except outside as well. Those in need of encouragement were incentivized by the nearby hose.

What surprised me most was how few mice I had found. We were always fighting mice and roaches, and I had assumed that they'd be in the hayloft, but not so much. This was a mystery yet to be solved.

By the end of the day, I had cleaned the whole building, and it was a great adventure. I didn't chain the elephants until 8:00 that night. That's how I spent several Christmases in the early 80s. It's really not a bad way to spend a holiday. I made good money on Christmas. How many people can say that?

CHAPTER TWENTY-FOUR

As winter increased in severity, I spent a lot of time stuffing rags and fiberglass insulation in the cracks around the doors to keep out the chill and the blowing snow.

January 4, 1981 was a downright awful day. On the list of that day's calamities is the fact that the Raiders beat the Browns 14-12 in the Divisional Playoff at old Municipal Stadium. The temperature on the field only reached four degrees above zero and was the coldest NFL game since the Ice Bowl of 1967. I brought in a thirteen inch black-and-white TV to watch in the keeper's room.

The next day, it hit minus five degrees Fahrenheit and the snow was getting deeper. The piles left by the plows were now towering at intersections and parking lots.

The Egyptian geese were still outside, and I'd go out to them several times a day to scrape away a patch of ground to keep it free of snow and to give them their feed. I also carried out buckets of hot steamy water which they gulped down like it was *mmm mmm good* soup. Meanwhile, the hippos were happy since they now had heated pools, thanks to Joe Matyas.

My two days off were coming to an end, and I woke up to go back to work. I was looking forward to it. I had been housebound the whole time, and the company of the Pachy was calling.

I looked out the window and saw that another foot of new snow had fallen as I slept during the night. Just getting to the zoo would be an accomplishment. It was around 6:00 a.m. and still dark. Cleveland was blanketed, but the salt trucks and snow plows were out and about.

Kuenzer was already at the zoo and thanked me for making it in that morning. He was really scrambling. In addition to employees stranded on unplowed streets, there was a lot of sickness going around, and there were gaps to fill.

"We may be running a little lean today," he said. "Steve Sandusky called and said he can't make it, and I'm not sure I can get a relief keeper for you. So it may be just you and Ellen. She hasn't called to say she wasn't coming. If that's no good, I can keep calling people."

"We don't need a third person, Ellen and I can handle it."

"Good. Tad said he could make it, but I need to send him to Bears. So far, Pappas is the only one I can count on for bears. Jackie's snowbound out in the boondocks."

The guy was scrambling to cover all the bases. "Even if Ellen calls and says she can't make it, I can work the whole building, I did it on Christmas."

The zoo was buried under mountains of swirling drifts so I left my car near the Commissary and went down to the lower level on foot. I trusted that maintenance would have the roads cleared before my shift ended.

As I approached the building, however, I saw that Ellen's car was parked there. In fact, her old tan Chrysler had been there for awhile since it was under a foot of new snow. From what Don had said, he must not have known that she was in the zoo, and had never made it out the night before.

I was relieved to find her half asleep in a chair in the keeper room. She was fighting to wake up and a bit disoriented.

"Simba's coming down with something," she said when she saw me.

"I think it's more than a cold. I stayed here last night, so excuse my appearance. What time is it?"

"It's almost 8:00."

"I better check her. She didn't eat a thing yesterday or the day before. She has some sort of infection, but I don't think it's the elephant equivalent of a cold or flu. It's worse, maybe something lymphatic. She's having a pus discharge from her nipples. It's dripping all over the cage. Her lungs and sinuses are bad. She's wheezing. I was in her cage and came in here for some tea around 6:00. I didn't mean to leave her for so long."

"Did you eat anything last night?"

"Oh, I had some crackers. God, I think these were Brent's old crackers from years ago. They've had mice all over them, but they were wrapped in cellophane, and well, there wasn't much choice. I wasn't sure anyone would be in this morning."

An elephant's illness can come out of nowhere fast. Sometimes an elephant can appear fine, but then be dead two hours later. When we walked through the bars and into the cage, I could see why Ellen was so concerned. Simba was teetering like a nauseated drunkard, eyes closed. I hadn't seen her for over two days, but she looked gaunt. Even her skin color was changed; she was jaundiced.

"I kept Tiani chained," said Ellen. "I want to keep her away from Simba who's been staying in line even without the shackles." I looked at poor Tiani whose gaze never left the older elephant. She was clearly subdued.

Simba didn't seem aware that I was now in her area. As Ellen had stated, there were new traces of oily yellow-green pus coming from her nipples and pooling on the floor.

"Hey, Simba. Hi, angel," I said as I tried to raise her spirits.

She staggered a bit, straying off her spot. It was clear that she was completely congested, and her mind was swirling in groggy discomfort. Every once in awhile, her back legs would suddenly buckle. When that happened, it was dramatic. Her whole body recoiled in agony, she'd shudder and more oozing discharge would drip from her nipples.

Ellen used a mop to try and stay ahead of the foul flow.

We briefly debated over calling the zoo vet, but dismissed the idea. They would have trouble getting through the storm, and would be limited to giving her a shot of vitamin C or putting something in her feed. That wouldn't be of much use since she was refusing to eat. The biggest threat, from Ellen's point of view, was that they would want to knock her down. In the end, we decided to just stay the course.

Ellen knew that the real crisis was yet to come. "At some point," she said, "the fever will break, and we'll have to help her through it. We have to keep her on her feet. If she lies down, she'll never get up. Elephants have to stay on their feet when they're sick. I think she's still conscious right now, believe it or not; she's just not sociable. She hears us and knows we're here, but she's too sick to care. At this point, she's still with us."

The fact was that we had an entire building with animals who were still waiting in the dark for lights to be called to life.

"I'll clean and feed the hippos and the giraffes," I said. "Then I'll feed Tiani. The Commissary is up and running, and that should be business as usual."

"I'm going to sleep on this folding chair next to Simba for about an hour. What are the roads like?"

"Bad, but the plows are out. We should be able to go anywhere in a couple of hours. My car's at the top of the hill."

"After I have a nap, I'll go home and get a clean shirt and bring back something to eat. Then I'll check to see how things are in an hour or two."

"After I take care of the hippos and giraffes," I said, "I'm going to dig your car out of the snow, and that's simply the way it's going to be." I said this firmly because I knew she would likely protest. It was a testimony to her fatigue that she didn't. Instead, she slumped down into the light brown folding chair, just a few feet away from Simba.

"She knows I'm here," having said that, she was asleep.

I have to admit that my cleaning was cursory and minimal that morning, but pools were drained and filled and the animals, geese included, were fed. I moved the giraffes over to the clean side of their pen and fed them, but mucking out the dirty side would have to wait. There were piles of filth left to be carted away, but none in an animal's area.

When I returned to Simba, Ellen was more alert.

"Here's what I think will happen," she began. "I've been monitoring her temps, and she has a fever right now, but it was normal several hours ago. It's rising, again. Last night, she was shaking with chills when her temperature was still up. Eventually, the fever is going to break. When that happens, her temperature will drop suddenly. That could even send her into shock. We're going to have a difficult time keeping her on her feet, but it's utterly essential that we do. Hopefully, I'm being overly dramatic about everything, and all this is nothing more than a bad cold, and that pus is not what I think it is. At some point she will feel better, and then we have to get her to accept food and fluids. She won't take anything right now, but it would be really smart if we had about a hundred oranges here. If she improves, that might be the best thing to have ready."

I trusted Ellen's knowledge and intuition, but there was something I could contribute as well. "I'm going to clean the snow off your car. Give me your keys, I'll get it out of the drift, and have it running by the back door. Go home and do what you have to do, but I'll feel a lot better when you get back."

She made a quick promise, "I won't even stop to take a shower; I'll be right back."

"As soon as you do, I'll go up to the A&P on Memphis Avenue and buy as many oranges as I can. Then you can sleep in Simba's cage or in the keeper's room."

Ellen said, "I really feel fine now. I'm completely awake. I'd say in the last four hours I slept for three of them."

That's what we did, and by noon that day, Ellen was back and I had a half dozen or so bags of oranges in the back hall. Simba was about the same, and Ellen took occasional catnaps in her chair.

No visitors came to the zoo that day, so I took Tiani for little walks up and down the back hall. Her mood was still low key and sullen.

Simba was barely conscious. Her eyes were closed and swollen. She had a lot of mucus discharge from her trunk. Even oranges could not tempt her.

The day seemed endless, and I went back to shovel out the mess that I had left with my hasty cleaning. In the meantime, Ellen cleaned the whole elephant pen, moving all around Simba.

"It's good, having something to do," she confessed as she mucked out the stall. She didn't use the hose, however.

It had been ten hours since I came in, and we tried to bed down the building. We did everything we could to keep busy. Waiting was the worst.

Around 6:00 p.m., I went out and got something to eat at the Convenient Food Mart on Memphis. I ate dry sandwiches in the car on the way back, but that probably wasn't the best idea. The discharges in Simba's cage smelled toxic, and she, herself, was like death warmed over. Every time her body convulsed in pain, the discharge erupted. Suddenly, I became nauseated. It poured over me, and I told Ellen I had to go check on a hippo pool. I went down to the far end of the hippo hall to pull myself together. As soon as I returned, I knew I was about to be ill.

"I better go give the geese some hot water," I said, and it *could* have been true.

I went outside into the dark and breathed in gulps of fresh, cold air. I got down on all fours and lowered my face down toward the fresh snow. It wasn't emotional. It was just physical. I was breathing something in Simba's cage that bothered my system. I felt like I had motion sickness. Pretty soon, I was bending down into the snow and puking in the yard. I went back to the keeper's room and rinsed out my mouth. Then I went and got some buckets of hot water for the geese. I stayed out in their yard for about ten minutes until I felt ready to go back.

It was approaching 11:00 p.m. when Simba's crisis began. Her whole body convulsed, and she contorted like something was bending her in half. She shuddered then staggered sideways, losing balance.

As she teetered, she moved toward her left. That seemed to be the way she would fall. I followed Ellen's lead, as she impulsively ran to the elephant's left side. In a heartbeat, we were both standing next to Simba, with our hands pressed against her.

"This is it," she said.

The big elephant was like a prize fighter who just had his bell rung. She staggered to her right as all four of her legs buckled. Then she staggered back the other way to her left. As she swooned left, I had to lean back to avoid her left tusk as it brushed past my stomach. At one point her hind legs nearly collapsed and her head went up, rising far above us. Her expression was grotesque, tortured, and macabre.

"Don't let her fall. Don't let her fall. She can't go down, or she's dead."

Simba continued staggering in unsteady circles, swooning and fainting. She was fighting to stay up. I sensed that she was losing the battle.

"Simba. SIMBA. UP. UP. UP," Ellen was giving the commands that the elephant knew so well.

All of a sudden, from my perspective, the lights dimmed. I realized that Simba's left legs were collapsing. She was falling; it was her massive bulk that had brought a shadow over me from above.

Simba was falling on us, but we ran in even closer and pushed as if we could hold up the monstrous form. We pushed with all our strength against the leathery gray hide.

"SIMBA. NO. NO. NO." Ellen was calling her to consciousness.

Simba staggered to her left, delaying the topple. I pushed up against her rough, wide shoulder with all my might. My face was pressed against her body, and I saw Ellen pushing against Simba's belly with all the force she could muster in her one hundred thirty pound frame. The African came down on my right shoulder, but we pushed and fought to keep her up, and she kept falling toward us, driving us back. She staggered to the left as we backpedaled.

Ellen continued to shout, "NO."

I think I also yelled, "NO, SIMBA. NO," but I'm not sure.

Simba weighed around five tons. Of course, we couldn't hold her up. If Simba was conscious at all, it was just barely. Now her eyes were wide open with no glint of awareness. She was finished. To me, it felt like she had surrendered. She had just let go of her suffering, and she was past caring. It's my belief that only one thought remained alive in Simba's brain. It was a small germ of an idea. She remembered that there were two puny people pushing her from her side. She had used that great weight to intimidate and injure people before, but she was not going to do that now. If she fell, Ellen and Adam would be dead. Ellen was commanding her not to fall. Those commands were far away and small. Adam was a small twig poking up into her left cheek. She wanted to fall, to escape forever. Drowsy, she toppled, collapsing, weak and finished. That meager, last thought glimmered in her mind like a far-off star nearly smothered in dark, passing clouds. "*If* I fall…"

Simba would not fall.

Simba's left front leg was caving in on me when suddenly it came alive and stepped down hard onto the cement. She caught herself. She righted herself. Simba pushed with that huge left leg and straightened herself up as Ellen and I kept pushing into her side, as if we had done it.

Ellen screamed, "Good girl. Good, Simba. Good."

The elephant took a deep breath, then several more breaths. She flicked her trunk about for the first time all day. I was near the left side of her face, and she was looking at me. Her eye closed again, then reopened. She rocked back and forth ever so slightly as she reasserted herself up to full height.

"She's shaking. Can you feel it?" Ellen shouted. "She's shaking like a leaf."

The crisis came in a clearly defined moment that had now passed. Simba rumbled.

"Adam, I think you should see if she'll eat some oranges now."

I ran into the back hall, and cut some up. I had four buckets of halves when I came back.

"Trunk up," I commanded.

She was so weak that she could barely open her mouth. I grabbed a piece of fruit and worked my hand into her mouth. She didn't seem interested.

Ellen was washing Simba's side off with wet cloths. "Squeeze the juice onto her tongue."

She wasn't opening up so I slid my whole forearm into her mouth. It was a tight fit, like pulling on a boot that's too small. Simba's mouth was practically closed, and there was a lot of bony pressure on my arm.

I felt around in that tight space until I found her big tongue, and crushed the orange. Weakly, I felt her tongue arch toward my fingers. I pulled out my arm and threw that rind aside and picked up another one. Over and over again, we kept the fruit going and her mouth gradually widened. Before long, she had her trunk up, curled back onto her forehead. I felt a great deal of relief as the drama of the day dissipated.

As I was acting like the human juicer, Ellen continued swabbing the elephant's body with warm, wet cloths. I went to the back hall and cut more oranges. Returning, I realized that Tiani has been watching all this, and smelling the fruit. I threw her a good treat before returning to Simba.

"She made it," said Ellen.

I asked Ellen if she was going to go home, but she was not yet ready for that. "She's doing just fine, but I can't leave her. You go home. I'll sit with her for awhile. I'll sleep in the keeper's room."

It was funny how that dumb little keeper room could sometimes be so much like home. The room was only around ten feet square.

CHAPTER TWENTY-FIVE

Later that winter, a position as keeper opened in the Bird Building and Rybicki took the job. He never made any secret of the fact that he eventually wanted to be in Birds, and saw Pachy as an interim post.

It seemed to me that Jim was moving to a less dangerous environment until Tad Schoffner told me what happened to one of the keepers in birds. The fellow's name was Tony, and he was good friends with Lori, Ellen, Tad, and Jim. He stopped down to our building one day when Tad was working.

After he left, Tad turned to Rybicki, "Did you see his face? It looks good."

"If a person didn't know, he really couldn't tell," answered Jim.

I was confused. "What are you talking about?"

"Tony has undergone quite a bit of plastic surgery on his face. You can tell if you look really close. He was attacked by a macaw. It really lit into him. Ripped his face open."

I was shocked to hear that.

I said, "I'm a little familiar with the three macaws over there, from when I was watchman. Which bird was it?"

I knew there was a green-winged Macaw, a scarlet Macaw, and the feisty blue and yellow one.

Tad said, "It was the blue and yellow."

I didn't say so, but that was the bird that junior ranger Matt had adopted those weeks we were mousing in the basement. He called it *Pookie* and let it walk over his shoulders, and now I found that it had ripped someone's face off, literally. Animal psyches are complex, and they're always territorial.

So the musical chairs of keeper jobs had begun again. When the Pachy position was posted, once again no one was interested. Normally, when a job opened up in the zoo, the people bounced around like steel balls in a pinball machine. Everyone called it *Musical Jobs*. But nobody jumped to our building because no one wanted anything to do with Simba.

After the time required for advertising, the zoo hired from outside. Mike Lamb had never been a keeper before; in fact, he had never had a job in his life. He lived with his parents in Lakewood. He had just finished graduate school with a degree in Chinese language studies. At that time, there wasn't much of a job market for Mandarin Chinese speakers so he applied at the zoo, and they hired him.

The way he explained it was that he and his girlfriend, Jill, had an agreement. His was to apply for an average of four jobs every week for three months. If he didn't get a job in that time, Jill and he would go ahead and get married, but she'd support them both by teaching while he went back to school to get a degree in something other than Chinese studies. They had visited the zoo one Wednesday, and filling out an application seemed like a good idea.

Somewhere in that explanation there must have been some hidden logic, but I didn't see it. Mike, however, became one of my best friends in the zoo. The animals responded to him because he was calm and peaceful. He never raised his voice above a mild level of conversation, and he never got overly excited about anything.

In this respect, he was like Ellen. She was always reasonable and peaceful, and the animals were content around her. I, on the other hand, would jump around the corner and try to shock Steve Gove with a Monty Python yell: *"NOBODY expects the Spanish Inquisition. Our chief weapon is surprise. Surprise and fear. Fear and surprise."*

Mike never made any sudden movements or had any temper at all. He was as calm as George Gobel. Mushka especially took to Mike's gentle attitude. She came out of the water to be near him when he cleaned her enclosure. Mushka bonded with Mike, the way Bomi bonded with me. On the other hand, when I went into Mushka's pen she charged me so I stayed out.

By the time Mike started to work with the elephants, Simba's transformation into an appreciative and generally loving animal was complete. I was the last person to have a confrontation with Simba. Ellen broke Mike in on elephants without incident.

He was an eager learner who learned how to be an good animal keeper very quickly. If a guy can learn Chinese, I suppose he can learn how to turn a hose nozzle off and on. Mike listened to me and Ellen.

Ellen said, "Always double check the feed hay to make sure there's no twine cords in it."

I told him, "No matter what you hear from anyone, never ever, *never* go into the pen with Wolee. If people tell you they kiss Wolee on the lips, don't you do it."

CHAPTER TWENTY-SIX

Steve Sandusky's retirement was looming, and one day he pulled me aside.

"I need to talk with you today, Buddy. This afternoon when all the work is done. Do you think we can sit down and talk?"

This struck me as rather odd, since our communication was open and we'd say whatever we had to say while working in proximity. About 3:30, we met in the keeper's room. He seemed more serious than usual and a bit edgy.

Wondering how to begin, he just began. "I've been working here in the zoo for thirty-five years. I'm near the end of that now... And there's a couple of stories... things that happened to me that..."

His voice trailed off.

Then with a sudden emphasis, he leaned forward and exclaimed, "I need to tell you some of these stories because someday you're going to write a book about this place and I'm going to be in it."

It had never once crossed my mind to write a book about my zoo career, but he seemed to think I would.

That afternoon, there in the keeper room, Steve told me stories, and I suspected that before the end of the tale, he was going to show me his arm. I wasn't sure I wanted to see it. Studiak had told me to look at it before I signed up for the job in Pachy.

"I got injured one time really bad at the zoo here. I'll tell you what happened..."

I thought to myself *Here comes the story of Simba*, but it began quite differently.

"One afternoon I was working up in Bears... This was in the old place. We had an old polar bear named Silver, and she was a mean son of a bitch. Everybody hated her. Me and her were always fighting. Those cages had bars. That was an outdoor cage where she was during the daytime. One afternoon she was really mad at me. I dunno, she just had that temper. She was agitating me from the other side of the bars. It just got my adrenalin going. I picked up the coal shovel and started beating it against the bars.

"But I just got too close; I was... careless. She was closer than I thought. And I didn't think she could, could fit her mouth through the bars so far. Silver got hold of my arm in her mouth. Right here."

Steve squeezed his right upper arm with his left hand like he was biting it. But he reached his hand around under his arm to grab it from the triceps side, like his left hand was the jaws of the bear.

He said, "She had her snout through the bars and had her teeth tight around my upper arm. Oh, it hurt like hell, and I couldn't get loose. I just was pulled into the bars and I hit them with my whole body. I hit my side. She lifted me right up off the ground. The pain was awful. I could hear my arm crushing. She tried to pull me toward her, she had the force to do that... but..."

Steve's eyes searched the air.

Then he said, "Of course, that couldn't happen 'cause I couldn't fit between the bars, not alive anyway. So she just tried to rip my arm off and get that. She was tugging on it, shaking her head back and forth like a dog with a rag. She had a good grip on it and tried to just rip off my whole arm, at the shoulder. I felt it dislocating. She jerked her head back and... my arm..."

Steve became silent, lost for words. He sat with his head down for several seconds. Then he found the thoughts and continued, acting out the whole drama, holding his arm out horizontally.

"She just ripped all the flesh off... She pulled too hard and her teeth slipped off the bone and pulled off all the flesh. Ripped my upper arm wide open. I could see the bone in my arm just right out in the sunshine, with the flesh just hanging down... it was all wide open...hanging... like the meat off a cooked chicken leg... that's how I got loose...

"Well, I was screaming like hell, and the other bear guy heard me. They came in the ambulance and got me and took me to Lutheran Hospital. I was in there for a long time. For about three weeks. They sewed my arm all back up until it looked like a roast tied up with string. The doctors put it back together, but it was a mess, all black stitches and bandaged up. They had me laying there.

"Above the bed was one of those– what do you call it? IV, intravenous. A clear glass bottle hanging from a rack with a drip going into my arm with a needle. The arm was all bandaged up. That was some new kind of medicine they had, some antibiotic dripping into my arm night and day... through a tube. It was brand new back then, whatever it was. One night after about three days a nurse came in, and she comes right by my bed. I was asleep, but I woke up when she came in. It was dark in the room. I looked up and she turned the drip off... at the, the, you know... the... the... stopcock. She turns the stopcock and shuts off the drip. I said to her, 'What are you doing?' She said, 'Oh, Mr. Sandusky, I'm turning off this IV because this medicine is expensive.' I said, 'You turn that back on right now... I don't give a shit how expensive it is.' And I made her turn it on. Then I said, 'Now get the hell out of here and don't you come back.' I had a different nurse after that. They kept that stuff dripping into my arm the whole three weeks.

"After a couple of months at home, I came back to the zoo to work.

But I said, 'I don't want bears no more. I'm through with bears.' So they juggled the jobs around for me. They were real nice about that. And I came to work here in the Pachy with the guys here. That was Vince and Perkins and those guys. Billy Seman, too. Yeah, Bill used to work elephants, but Simba drove him off.

"So I worked the elephants for awhile. We had three African elephants, Tara, the bull, and Simba. The bull was a handful... awful, but predictable. You knew what to expect with the bull. But Simba was out of her mind in those days. Tara, she was a sweetheart, but not Simba. It was always battles all the time. I don't know if she's changed like Vince says or what you guys do, but that's just the way it was back then. She was a killer in those days, and that's all that can be said about it. She attacked anyone who worked with her eventually. Lots of guys, all the time.

"One day I was in the cage, shoveling it out, and I was having a big fight with Simba. I had it cleaned pretty good and she starts throwing the shit around after I had it in a pile. She starts kicking it everywhere, all over the cage. That made me mad, and I yelled at her. That's the kind of thing she did. I was yelling at her, and she was trumpeting, you know? She flapped her ears out and was throwing shit all over the place. Then she came at me like she was going to charge, but she backed off. I was sick of it and all her attitude. I picked up that coal shovel..."

Old stooped-over Steve stood up, and spread his feet wide, showing how he had braced himself so many years earlier. He showed how he had defiantly held the handle of the grain scoop shovel horizontally in both hands down near his waist.

"So I held the shovel like this, and I yelled, 'Come on, you big son of a bitch...'"

After a dramatic pause, Steve sat down and exclaimed, "Well, she came on. She was just so quick. I couldn't do anything. She gored me. She stabbed me with her right tusk, right here."

Steve violently poked his upper right arm with his left index finger. He said, "She got me right in the same place that the bear had injured me."

Then Steve wrapped his left hand around his upper right arm and held it as if still in pain.

"So then I'm back in the same room in the same hospital with the same IV back in my arm. All over again. For a long time. When I came back here, I said, 'I'm just working rhinos and hippos. No more elephants.' A lot of others came to the same conclusion. Perkins, me, Vince, Tresise, Dick, Billy, Little Johnny, Studinak. Lots of other guys you don't know. We all just said *to hell with Simba*. She's just a time bomb. That's what everyone found out. Then that Ellen came in, and she took it over. We all thought she wouldn't last long at that. That was a joke. I mean, we had some pretty tough guys working with Simba. Then suddenly there's this hundred pound woman working elephants. Everyone figured they'd carry her out of here in a week. People wanted Ellen to fail. I won't say who, but they did. I'm the only one from the old days who's seen her working here, you know, every day. I still hear some of the old guys with their opinions about it. But when people say something bad about Ellen, I tell them she knows what she's doing better than we did."

I asked, "What was the story with Perkins?" His telling only reaffirmed what others had said, that Simba was proving a point, not trying to kill. The same was true with Don Kuenzer who had never done anything to provoke an attack. Kuenzer had blown it off, "She's just playing," he said.

Steve also told me things that happened outside the zoo, like a bar fight where he'd thought he'd killed a guy.

CHAPTER TWENTY-SEVEN

A few weeks later Diane, the zoo's matron, spoke to me at the time clock. "I'm organizing a retirement party for Steve Sandusky," she said. "It's gonna be two weeks from this Friday, and I was wondering if you'd give a speech at the party. Not serious, more like a comedy routine, maybe like a roast. I thought of you since you work with Steve."

They were planning to have chips, hot dogs, and kielbasa, a real party complete with music, thanks to a boom box. The whole thing was her idea even though she didn't know Steve. She had asked the administration if they were giving some sort of recognition, and when she found that they weren't, she took it on herself. I asked if we should buy a gift.

"I don't know," she said. "He's been a keeper for thirty-five years. He gets a pension, you know."

Later, I went to the Westgate Mall and found a kiosk where they'd engrave plaques. I swallowed hard when I found out it was going to set me back forty-five bucks, but I ordered one for Sandusky.

When I told Diane the next day, she asked who was going to pay for it. She was okay with the fact that it would come out of my pocket, but then added a bit of *new* information.

"This is also a party for Frank Maro. He's retiring, too."

Durn, now I'd need two, unless Maro had not worked at the zoo a long time.

"Twenty-eight years," she said.

Double-durn. I went back to Westgate and ordered another.

They would have a microphone at the party, and I had to think of some jokes. I came up with around eight and practiced them a couple of times.

Sandusky's last day at the zoo arrived, and it was pretty much like any other day, with the exception that Steve was usually out of the building by around 3:30. On his last day, Steve was still in the building at 5:45. I found him in Blackie's stall, scrubbing the walls.

"Well, I'm taking off," I said. "Don't forget there's a party up in the Administration Building in fifteen minutes. They got food up there and beer."

"I'm not interested in any parties."

This was a crisis. "I'm not supposed to tell you this, but the party is for you and Frank Maro. Everyone's going to be waiting for you to come. You're the guest of honor. So, why don't you join us?"

"Yeah, all right."

I went up to the party, and was there for about thirty minutes. Still, no Steve.

Diane asked me to go down and see if I could get him moving in the right direction. In the meantime, I was having second thoughts about my comedy routine.

"That's okay," she said. "Just see if you can find him. Frank's not here yet either, but he phoned and said he's on the way. Steve might be ducking out on us."

It was now 6:30 and Steve was still in Blackie's area. The big door to the back of the stall was open, and I'm sure Steve didn't know I was nearby. He was sitting at the edge of the pool with his bent-over back towards me. He was talking to Blackie, who was listening from the water. I could tell I was coming in at the middle of a conversation.

"I guess I'll never see you anymore. You're a good boy. I've been here in this zoo a long time, and you're the best animal I ever knew in thirty-five years. You're very special to me, but I don't think I'll ever be coming back here ever, even to visit. You be a good boy, and I know you will, 'cause all you've ever been is good."

With his whole body pointed toward Steve, Blackie was bobbing up and down in the crystal-clear water. He looked at Steve and blinked, totally attentive. Every once in awhile, Blackie's head dipped under the water and came back up with a snort as his ears flicked away the wetness.

I retraced my steps and waited outside for several minutes. When I went back in, I kicked the door open to let him know I was coming.

"Hey, there you are," I said as I approached. "Everybody's waitin' for you at the party."

"Aw, I don't want to see any of those people."

I sat down next to him on the top step of the pool.

"Do you want to have a cigarette with me?" he asked. I didn't usually smoke, but I had taken lessons from the refreshment stand girls.

He gave me a Marlboro and lit it, and lit another one for himself.

"Come up to the party. You know there's no one up there except maintenance guys, keepers, and the two matrons. There aren't any administrators or big shots. It's just the working guys. And even some of the keepers aren't there. It's really amazing. Everyone who's an asshole isn't there. They've got beer and Polish sausage, and Diane made potato salad. She cooked all kinds of food, went to a lot of trouble. They're just waiting for you, Jackie, Pappas, Vince, Seman, Tresise, Tad, Alex, Tony, Linda, Mary the matron, and Sanchez. Even Walter came back for the party and so did Johnny Ranallo, and Perkins, Steve Gove, and Dick Darenzo. If you don't get there soon, the Crusher is going to eat everything. Oh, I forgot the guys from maintenance, Joe Matyas and Ray from the garage."

He stared straight ahead. "I'm not going to go. I've seen enough of all those guys... I'm just going to sit here with Blackie."

"Steve, will you go if *I* ask you?"

He looked right at me and seemed relieved. "All right. I'll do it for you."

I put my arm around his shoulders and gave him a sideways hug for about five seconds, with my head against his. Then I stood up and said, "I'll tell them you're on the way."

Steve said, "I'll be up in a little bit. I'll be there."

I went back to the party and told Diane that Steve was coming. People were getting a bit antsy. She handed me the microphone and told me to tell everyone that he was on the way. Suddenly, I was onstage. People were getting grumpy, so I reconsidered my comedy routine. We needed something to keep them there until Steve arrived.

There was an echo in the room that made everything sound like a Bill Cosby routine.

As I looked at the people there, they were all out of uniform in white socks, cuffed pants, and twenty-year-old, open-collar shirts, all neatly ironed.

A lot of those guys had their hair neatly combed and parted off to the side, slicked down with Brylcreem. They were the same crowd of working men I had seen a dozen years earlier when I drove the trams.

They were now looking expectantly toward me, relaxed and happy, waiting to see what I would say. At one time, they had all repulsed me with their missing teeth and ball-grabbing pranks. Now I knew each and everyone and loved them all.

Of course, I was one of them.

I hadn't changed and was still dressed in my smelly, dirty brown uniform. In the back of my mind were the discarded jokes.

"Some of you may be interested in a little history about Steve

Sandusky. I'm not saying Steve is old, but his first job here in the Cleveland Zoo was head keeper in the Dinosaur Building."

I sat down for a minute, then stood again at the mike. "While we're waiting for Steve to arrive, I can read you some telegrams from people who could not be here in person tonight."

I took a piece of paper out of my pocket and fumbled it open.

"Here is a telegram marking the occasion from a former Director of the Zoo, Dr. Leonard Goss. I will now read the telegram in its entirety: *Steve WHO?*

"Here's another telegram, this one from Blackie the hippopotamus: *Dear Steve. Sorry I couldn't be at your party. But thank you for all the wonderful sex.*"

Things were going well, so I kept going. "Ostrich Barn relief keeper Frank Maro will be here tonight to accept his award. Frank has been a keeper at the zoo for twenty-eight years. You've probably noticed we only have one ostrich in the zoo at the present time. We used to have, oh gosh, six or seven, but now it's just that one. Well, let me explain why Frank's late tonight, it takes a long time to rotisserie an ostrich."

When Steve came in, he had showered and changed out of his uniform. He was wearing a green knit shirt and slacks, and his thick hair was perfectly combed. Then Frank came in dressed up in a nice yellow polo and slacks. We gave them their awards. Steve and then Frank each said, "Thank you very much," into the microphone. As Sandusky spoke, I noticed a tear rolling down his right cheek. That was the last time I saw him.

CHAPTER TWENTY-EIGHT

One afternoon I was out front of the hippo stalls, and a man walked by. I recognized him. It was Rich Kemper, a tour train driver from the late sixties.

The last time I'd seen Rich he was working toward his degree in Business. In the mid-1970s, he'd finally gotten his Masters and was working toward his PhD.

So when I saw him that afternoon in the early 1980s, I asked, "Well, did you ever get your doctorate?"

"Yes. In fact, I have two doctorates now."

"So, are you working for some company? Or teaching at a university?"

"Hell, no. I'm a fireman."

CHAPTER TWENY-NINE

For two weeks they posted the job on the bulletin board. Of course, everyone in the zoo was too much of a wimp to want to work in the Pachy. Mike Lamb commented on the unsigned list saying, "I guess we can tell who the *real* men are in this zoo. You, me, and Ellen."

The zoo finally hired a person right out of college. She had studied animal husbandry at Ohio State. Her name was Donna Miller, and she was only nineteen.

I showed her around the building and warned her about the fact that Wolee's pool must never be filled to full, or he'd be able to launch himself into the keeper's area. "It's important that you learn and remember the 'Too Full Pool Rule.' Wolee's dangerous," I said from experience. "I'd even call him cruel. If the pool's too full, he'll come right out and kill us all. If cruel Wolee's pool becomes too full, as a rule we drain the pool. To do that we have this tool, which is a valve key."

She liked plays on words, so I told her that the valve key was technically called a *Too Full Pool Rule Tool*, and that people who are too stupid to learn how to use the tool on cruel Wolee's pool were promptly told, *We'll have to send you to Too Full Pool Rule Tool School, Fool*.

This woman was very smart, but I wondered how she'd do long-term in the filthy world of feces, smelly barns, crude men, and mundane work. It turned out that Donna was completely into shoveling big wheelbarrows full of shit and eating cheeseburgers in a barn.

Donna broke in on the elephants faster than anyone in history. I don't know why Simba never gave anyone any trouble after I hit her in the forehead with a baseball bat, but she didn't. Donna really took to being an elephant keeper. In fact, within a few weeks, tall, pretty Donna was riding around the elephant yard and inside the elephant cage on Simba's back. No one had ever done that, and once more, the dramatic evolution of Simba's life continued. She'd gone from the era of tough men who she gored to having a nineteen-year-old woman riding around on her back.

Donna was what would be called an *animal person*. In fact, Donna loved animals to the extreme in some ways. She loved rats, mice, and roaches, too. When I stomped on a mouse, Donna objected.

"Donna, it's all right. There are thousands of them. They're vermin."

"But they're so cute," she said.

As you know, I had already killed a squillion mice in my life. One morning I cornered three mice in the keeper's room back in the toilet stall, but Donna intervened, so I told her that I would release them outside. Of course, she caught on to my act, and I actually had to do it. I put some grass in the box and sealed it off. Then I poked air holes in it and put the box in my car with the window cracked a little bit. Holy cow. They were wild fricking mice, and I was taking care of them, but a promise was a promise. After work that evening, I took them back to North Olmsted and let them loose beside the Kroger at the corner of Clague and Lorain.

Fortunately, it only took a few days for Donna to be convinced that mice, roaches, and rats are a major problem for zoos in general and the animals under our care in particular.

Her conversion came suddenly one day when Ellen, Lori, Donna, and I were talking in the keeper room. I noticed a really bad smell.

Lori burst out laughing. "We're in a *barn*."

"No, no," I said. "It's a different smell in here today. Awful; there's something different, really close by."

I sniffed around the corner from where I'd been sitting. I followed my nose to two decomposing mice in the bottom of a locker.

"That's it. I'm going to clean the whole room and see what else is here." There were some old wading boots in the corner. I dumped out the boots and found a dead mouse in the bottom of one of them. This dead mouse was as flat as a stick of gum. People had been wearing those boots with a dead mouse in them.

I found two more dead mice in lockers. I found a dead mouse inside the electronics of the toaster oven, and another back in the corner hidden by the little table. I swept all seven of these mice into a pile in the center of the room. They made quite a stench. We had been literally stepping on them in our stocking feet and cooking things in the toaster oven with a dead mouse rotting in it.

Disgusted by this, Donna said, "You have my permission to get rid of mice in this building."

A couple of days later, Donna came into the keeper's room and exclaimed, "My God. I just saw a rat running right over Blackie's back. Right in his stall. Right on his back."

After that, I had permission to kill rats and roaches, too. In fact, Donna and I worked side-by-side in setting up traps with the famous, but ineffective, *Rat Glue*.

Ellen said, "What we have here now are *Super Rats*. If a rat is immune to poison or has the inborn inclination to avoid it, that rat lives and reproduces. Those are the genetic traits we're engineering. Over time, we may have poisoned some rats, but all that's been accomplished is we've bred *Super Rats*."

Eventually, we resorted to our secret weapon in the war against feral invaders. His name was Tim Pappas. I called him at Bears saying, "Tim, we've been seeing more rats than usual. Any ideas?"

Tim had a wonderful intuition about dealing with this sort of problem; the reality was that he could think like a rat. In the end, we enlisted an army and rooted out the nests and breeding grounds, which were the major sources of the zoo's infestation. At this point, I want to state very clearly that every zoo, landfill, farm, food storage facility, barn, feed store, baseball stadium, and any area near fast food restaurants has rats. I don't want readers to say that the Cleveland Zoo had a lot of rats. I want people to know what I believe: our zoo exterminated rats more successfully than any other in the history of the world.

So, exactly how good were we at dealing with feral rats?

One day Pappas was in the Pachyderm Building. We were standing in front of Blackie's stall when a man came walking in. The guy was around thirty, with a goatee and disheveled hair. He had on a long-sleeved flannel shirt. He was somewhat interested in the pachyderms, but more interested in rats.

He introduced himself as a professor at the School of Medicine at Case Western Reserve. He wondered if we had ever seen an infestation of feral rats in the zoo.

"It's been known to happen," said Tim.

The professor continued, "I'd love to study them in the lab. It would be very interesting to determine their genetic traits and how they are differentiated from domestic rats. But no one can get me any for research. We have lab rats. I once thought I'd love to perform some blood work on wild rats, but I've given up on that. Years ago, I called nearly every professional exterminator in Cleveland, asking them how I can get some wild rats. *Live* wild rats. They said they can get dead ones, rats that have been poisoned. That's no good. All they can come up with is dead ones. I need live feral rats, uninjured, but no one can get any. It's just impossible."

I turned back to him and said, "How many do you want?"

"What?"

"We can get you all the live, feral rats you want. How many do you want?"

"Thirty would be great," he exclaimed, "no, make it forty."

On Saturday morning, the eccentric professor arrived in an old, flatbed truck. It looked like a truck out of *The Grapes of Wrath*. He backed it up to the garage door on the northeast side of the Pachy. On the truck's wooden bed was a homemade cage.

We had our own cage of rats we had netted the day before. Without any trouble we sealed the two cage doors together, then slid open the doors and dumped all the rats down into the professor's cage.

"Thanks," he said. At that moment, I think he was in rat heaven.

CHAPTER THIRTY

Moving animals was an adventure, sometimes, one to be avoided. Once, Alan had the maintenance department build some heavy wooden shields out of plywood. They had handles on the backs of them and were about four feet wide and five feet tall. He called them *Grizzly Bear Shields.*

He tried to recruit Tad and me to help the guys in Bears to move a grizzly from one cage to another. The principle was simple enough. Five men would go into the cage and use these plywood shields to move the bear along a path into another cage. I suppose we'd be like shielded warriors marching in a phalanx to the battle of Troy.

I didn't even have to think about that one. There was no way I was going to trust a sheet of plywood against the claws of a grizzly. Tad was completely with me on that.

I never heard anything more about it, but if anyone had actually tried, I would have heard of it when news of the disaster broke in on Channel 5.

The shields did, however, get used but not against a particularly aggressive animal. Lyle, our baby Masai giraffe, was moving on to the national stage, the National Zoo, that is in Washington D.C. The fact was that our *baby* was now tipping the scales at twenty-two hundred pounds, and sixteen feet tall. The real problem was genetics and inbreeding. The giraffe needed to become part of a larger gene pool so that the subspecies, *Giraffa camelopardalis tippelskirchi,* could survive and remain healthy in captivity. Anyway, it fell to us to put Lyle in a shipping crate, and we had two months to do it.

Ellen came up with some design ideas; Matyas would build it. I had no idea how we'd ever manage to gift wrap a giraffe, but Ellen did.

"We'll simply need to train him to go into the crate of his own free will. That will be a long process, and there's not as much time as I'd like, but we'll have to get it done. The worst thing a zoo can do to an animal is physically force it into a cage or crate. If we train Lyle to go in, it will be a lot less stressful. It's like when you have a travel cage for your family dog. Some dogs actually feel secure in the cage. I don't think we have time for that. We should have started six months ago. But hopefully, we can train Lyle to enter the crate and instill in him a certain familiarity with it. Ideally, the crate can be a comfort zone when he's traveling. To simply force a giraffe into a crate and truck it a long distance is extremely stressful. The odds of Lyle surviving a twenty-four hour journey under those conditions are slim. We need to help him avoid that shock. The truck will stop overnight, so we're talking about a two-day trip. That's a long time for an animal to be stressed. Stress is what kills large animals.

"Here's what we need to do. First, we need to make him comfortable with having the crate in his stall. Once he's used to its smells, he'll get over fearing it. After that, we'll make food available in the crate as well as outside the crate. I'd like him to get used to eating both outside and inside. If we can get him to walk in and out of the crate in a normal manner, that will be a huge victory. Then, when he's comfortable with that, we'll only put food inside the crate.

"That's about the best we can hope to accomplish by the day the truck gets here. I can't imagine we'll have time to lock him in the crate for periods of time so that he accepts that. That would be the ideal situation, but it would take more time. Of course, there is going to be that moment when we shut that crate door and lock Lyle in there. He'll freak out when that happens."

The crate was designed so that Lyle's head and neck stuck out of its top, a bit like an illustration you might see in a children's book.

Joe said, "The crate will be eight feet high and open at the top. That's convenient, since the three-quarter inch plywood comes in four-by-eight sheets. But I'll build a space below the floor of the crate so that it can be picked up with a forklift. How long will the crate be and how wide?"

We figured out that it needed to be around six feet wide. In its final form, it was ten feet tall, six feet wide, and sixteen feet long. When it was assembled within the giraffe pen, it was as sturdy as a tank.

I thought that it was really overbuilt. After all, it was for a giraffe, not an elephant. The flooring itself was over two and a half inches thick. The crate alone weighed over a thousand pounds. We had five weeks to get him inside.

The next morning, we began the process of separating Lyle from the other three giraffes so that he could be placed in a different cage with the crate. Sironen organized that effort, and it went well. We started early in the morning.

"All right," said Alan. "We can use the *Grizzly Bear Shields* for this. I've got them outside in my truck."

We wouldn't need to actually push Lyle. We'd just form a moving barrier, and he'd move away from it. They say that an adult giraffe can crush a lion's skull with a single kick, which is their primary defense. We were in the cage and started to move our *wall* forward toward the big male giraffe who aimed a kick at my plywood shield. The force almost knocked me over. Fortunately, the shield held, but not without splintering the outer plies. Our goal was to separate Lyle from the others, but they were all busy kicking away at us.

"Hold the shields up. Protect your faces," said Alan.

I pondered that advice for a few seconds, but ultimately I preferred to find a happy medium whereby both my face and my nuts had a modicum of protection. Soon several layers of my plywood shield were splintered with shards of wood hanging loose. But overall, against giraffes, the shields worked.

Alan was very much the leader in this. Ultimately, we cordoned Lyle away from the others and forced him into the empty side of the giraffe pens. Once moved, none of the giraffes seemed to care about the new arrangement.

The first part of Ellen's plan was underway. Lyle would spend several days in the stall with the shipping crate to get used to its presence. All his usual sources of water and feed were set outside the crate, but additional food and water were placed inside as well. At first, he stayed as far away from that enclosure as possible.

Getting the giant animal into a crate would be a monumental task, but, as always, Ellen seemed to have the answer. She had envisioned each step of the process, and I wasn't too worried that she could guide us through Lyle's training period.

A few days after Lyle was isolated, Ellen made an announcement. "I just need to tell all you guys that I'll probably be leaving the zoo soon. It's pretty likely to happen so you guys will be on your own as far as training Lyle and putting him in that crate. Good luck."

CHAPTER THIRTY-ONE

In one of the American Association of Zoo Keepers newsletters, Ellen had seen a job opening as elephant keeper in the Seattle Woodland Park Zoo. Her interview was over the phone, and Mike and I were tempted to sabotage her chances by yelling in the background, *Oh, my God! They're loose! The elephants are all loose! Run! Oh, my God! The giraffes! They're all dead! Ellen, what did you feed them?* But we stayed clear.

Naturally, Ellen did well in those interviews and took the offer. She was excited to start a new chapter in her life, but we were going to miss her. All too soon, she was gone. A few months later, she was back in town to collect her furniture, and she stopped in at the Commissary.

"Everyone says I should go down to the Pachy and visit Simba," she said. "But I don't want to go anywhere near her. If she thinks I'm back, it could just break her heart all over again. I'd love to see her, but I simply can't. Things have to stay the way they are."

I gave her a final hug along with everyone else, and she was out of my life, too.

Meanwhile, Mike, Donna, and I were left trying to remember everything Ellen had told us. After a few days, Lyle was not the least bit concerned about the big wooden creation that took up nearly half the cage. One morning, Donna carried a ladder into the crate. She hung a black rubber water pail and a net full of alfalfa hay in the top rear of the big crate. A few days later, we cut off his other food. Now he had to go into the cage if he wanted to eat. Several days passed. The food was untouched.

Then one morning, Mike and I were in the keeper room. Donna came in saying, "Lyle's in the crate."

Quietly, we snuck down the back hall to peer around the corner, but Lyle heard us coming and got out before we could catch a glimpse. The sounds of heavy giraffe hooves gave him away, and telltale blades of alfalfa strewn over the wooden floor was the final bit of proof.

CHAPTER THIRTY-TWO

Within a few weeks, Lyle was moving in and out of the big crate to eat, but didn't want us around when he was inside.

Alan came in on a Thursday to say that the truck was arriving on Saturday, and it was time to finish the job.

A relief keeper named Kenny Pekarek was working so I thought I'd get him to help me close the crate door with Lyle inside. Kenny normally worked in Bears with Pappas, and Mike was off on Thursdays. I thought it would work because Pekarek was a strong guy.

Donna, Kenny, and I worked out a plan. We'd all hide in the back hall until Lyle went deep into the crate to eat. On a signal, Kenny and I would run in and close the door on the crate. Donna would close and pin the latch. It was direct, simple, and pure stupidity.

Lyle was in the crate, eating. We heard him walk in with his heavy hooves clomping, and we heard him shredding mouthfuls of hay from the feeder. The trap was set.

I was Moe (which made the others Larry and Curly). "Now," I whispered. And in we ran.

The big giraffe whirled around within the crate. His side and shoulder slammed hard into the side wall as he turned. The force of his chest immediately made the thousand pound crate rock sideways. It contorted, bending out of shape as if made of rubber. Lyle's long neck swung around. I was halfway to the crate and his face seemed already to be only four feet away from me, towering overhead. He charged forward with amazing quickness. One loping stride was all it took for him to be inches from the open end of the crate. Chest first, he came. His vast, ribbed torso leaned forward toward me, and I ran straight toward it. I saw Lyle's dark eyes opened wide. He was two feet away from the open end of the crate, but Kenny and I were also quick. We pulled hard and slammed the door right into the oncoming chest of the sixteen foot tall mammal. The door was within three inches of being closed when Lyle burst into it with his full force. Out of the corner of my eye, in the blur of action, I saw Donna absolutely ready to slide that pin down into the latch. All Kenny and I needed to do was hold the door shut against the gigantic animal as he rammed against it.

He didn't actually ram it. *Ramming* would require hitting an immoveable object. He just ran through it with zero impedance. The door swung like a flyswatter; Kenny and I were the flies. We were simply swatted into the air, launched straight backwards.

Donna was screaming as she jumped to the right to get out of Lyle's path. What Donna did next seemed physically impossible. She ran around behind me in a huge arc and climbed up my back.

When the world came to a stop, she laughed, "Did you see that?"

I said, "Yes. Get down."

"Sorry," she said, and climbed down as if coming out of a tree.

CHAPTER THIRTY-THREE

It was Friday, and Lyle was not ready to travel. Matyas came by to have some doughnuts, and I asked him if he could put latches on the door so that it would snap shut without having to insert a pin. After I explained what had happened, he went out and looked at the crate. It had been twisted cockeyed when the giraffe threw us across the room.

"I think it needs reinforcing," said Joe. "He might be able to kick it apart once he's trapped in there. How long did it take him to do all this damage?"

"About two seconds."

Joe knew he could fabricate the latches I had described, and he put on two, one at the top and one near the bottom. When we slammed the door shut, it was locked in place.

"What time are you going to try it?" asked Matyas. "I want to be here with my crew. I'm guessing that giraffe will kick this crate to pieces once he's in there. We'll bring a lot of lumber, hammers, and nails. Once the he's inside, we'll rebuild the crate around him. We'll completely close it around with another structure of some sort. Otherwise, by Saturday he'll kick his way out. Once in Washington, they can figure out how to get it open. That'll be their problem."

After he left, I took a length of nylon rope and attached it to two screw eyelets that I put on the bottom of each door. I fed out enough line to run the rope all the way out to the public area. The exposed rope was then covered with hay so that Lyle wouldn't see it. I hoped that when I gave the rope a hard, sharp tug, it would pull the door shut from over forty feet away and around a corner. Joe's new latches would do the rest.

At 3:00 Joe, Mike, and John Robb came in with a stack of boards. Donna was our lookout from a remote spot just outside the keeper's room. When Lyle was busy eating, Donna would raise her right hand up to her chin.

I waited a long time before I heard a heavy footstep on concrete and knew he was on the move. Finally, she touched her chin, and I yanked the rope as hard as I could. Then came the sound I wanted to hear, a loud slap of wood against wood, like a crack of a tree falling. The sharp noise echoed through the building, and then all hell broke loose.

We had caught a giraffe, but the huge crate was rocking, bending and twisting into peculiar shapes amid the horrible sound of nails being pulled free. Suddenly, that sturdy crate seemed flimsy and cheap as the giraffe rammed and kicked it into submission. Lyle was kicking his way out of the big wooden box.

The fury of the animal was met by a rush of hammering sounds. Nails were being driven to seal the door, nailing it to the frame of the crate. Two-by-fours were slapped up to become hasty braces. Working like maniacs, Joe's crew grabbed more lumber and nailed pieces at every stress point, diagonally, vertically, and horizontally. The men hurriedly rebuilt the crate as fast as the giraffe dismantled it. By the end of the war, the men were nailing on more boards and the giraffe's big hooves went silent as he accepted his fate. Littered around the crate were splinters of wood that had actually flown out of the crate as Lyle fought to break out. He had kicked great chunks out of the plywood, and that's not easy to do.

"Well," said Joe, "I took a lot of pride in the aesthetic quality of this crate when we built it. Now it looks like it was built by idiots, but I think it will hold. I have no idea how I'd get him out of there, but that's not my problem."

Not long after that, Lyle calmed down and even resumed eating.

Saturday and Sunday were my days off so I wasn't there when they came for the giraffe. On Monday, Alan came 'round and told us that he made the trip okay.

"He's in D.C., but they're going to rename him. They're going to have a Name-the-Giraffe Contest at the National Zoo. I figured that just about any name they came up with would be better than Lyle."

CHAPTER THIRTY-FOUR

I had heard almost all the Simba stories except one. Before the elephant's incredible reformation, she had been the nemesis of many keepers. When I was being warned off from the job in Pachy, Studinak told his horrors and said, "Ask Tresise to tell you his story sometime."

When I asked Sandusky about it, he just passed by saying "You'd want to ask him about that." The fact was that I didn't know Donnie very well. Gove knew him better and described him as *the best athlete in the Metroparks, and maybe the city of Cleveland.*

Donnie wasn't particularly large and imposing, but one day we convinced him to join us for touch football during lunch. I was on his team so I saw his athleticism in action; he could outrun everyone else. The fact was he did so in uniform and wearing hard shoes. He could also catch a pass.

Every year the Metroparks had a park-wide golf tournament, and every year Donnie won. Still, if he was placed in a lineup, no one would pick him out as a great athlete. Donnie was about twenty-eight years old. He wasn't in any kind of athletic shape. I mean, he was in animal keeper shape, but he wasn't training like an athlete would.

One evening we were playing softball in the Rocky River Reservation during a Metroparks league game. Before the game, Tresise and a summer worker named Suprunenko started getting into a discussion. Suprunenko was enrolled at Ohio State, and he was being hyped as a future star in the hundred yard dash. Donnie said that he might be fast *for college,* but that older men are faster. Racing, however, could settle that dispute, so someone paced off a hundred yards, and I had a really good view of Tresise as he crossed the finish line about ten inches in front of the Big Ten track star.

I once asked him to sub in a bowling league. "I haven't bowled in years," he said.

His first game was a two thirty-five, and that must have warmed him up because after that he rolled somewhere around two-fifty, and finished with a two eighty-three.

I had a chance to talk that night on the lanes. He was troubled by the fact that he had just come back from the doctor's office.

"I've had a lot of pain in my joints," he said. "I went to the doctor today and he diagnosed me with rheumatoid arthritis."

That perked my ears up. "What did he prescribe? Prednisone?"

"Yeah, that's one of them. And something else. They're both anti-inflammatories. Somebody in the zoo said you had the same diagnosis some years ago."

"Yeah, I took prednisone and Azolid and another drug. Your health is your business, but let me ask you a question. What do you eat? Like what did you have for dinner tonight?"

"Burger King, I pretty much go to Burger King every night after work."

"Donnie, I don't like butting into someone else's life, but I know what happened to me. All I can say is– this is what I'd do, if I were you. Eat real meals, meals like you probably ate when you were a kid, beef, baked chicken, salads, peas, corn, green beans, you know. When's the last time you ate like that?"

Donnie laughed and said, "When I moved out of my mother's house nine years ago."

"There are a few restaurants around town where you can get a real meal, like at home. Change your diet, that's the first thing I'd do. The second is… when I got home tonight, if I were you, I'd take every one of those damn pills and flush them down the toilet."

He said he'd do that, and I don't doubt that he did.

It was not long after that that he came into the Pachyderm Building as a relief keeper for the hippos, but I still had not heard his take on Simba. All I knew about the incident was that Simba had attacked when a backhoe came roaring into the back hall. I felt I knew him well enough to ask.

"Everyone says I should ask you about that life-or-death incident you had."

He began by answering a question that I was not aware that I had asked. He told me about being in a car that went off the road. He was riding in the back seat. There were four of them on Pearl Road. Anyway, they must have slammed into a telephone pole. The car twisted and flipped, and the four were thrown everywhere inside the car. When everything stopped, he was underneath the others, and they were all dead. He wandered around for awhile. When the cops came, they asked if he had seen what happened, and he told them that he had been in the car. The fact was that he didn't look hurt, and when the paramedics asked if he needed to go to the hospital, he said, "I don't think so. I don't think there's anything wrong with me." After that, he told them what he knew, walked three miles home, and took a shower.

As incredible as that was, it wasn't a Simba tale so I was more specific this time.

He took a deep breath. "I can tell you that story, I guess.

"Some guys did some shit to her, but I never did anything to Simba. She goes nuts though when she hears a gasoline engine.

"One afternoon I was in the cage, cleaning up; we were getting along fine. Then all of a sudden, these guys from maintenance decided to bring a new log for the elephants into the building. We didn't know it was coming. I was in the elephant cage when, all of sudden, the crew comes with a backhoe dragging a log. It was so loud, I jumped, and Simba went fricking nuts. She just went crazy, running all around and screaming. Tara was in the cage, too, and she was trying to get out of Simba's way just like I was. But I couldn't get out.

"She just zeroed in on me, charging. I ran backwards until I felt my back was against the corner. She raced into me to gore. She rammed her tusks right at me, but they hit against the wall. I was lucky to be small enough to fit between them, so when she pulled back, I jumped down. I couldn't get around her, though, and she charged again, and the same thing happened. I tried to get past her toward the front, but she's so quick. She was like trying to swat a fly. She tried to gore me again, and I was right against the flat wall and she drove into me.

"Since I couldn't get away from her, I ran toward her. I just jumped up into her face. I leapt up and figured the only place I can find protection was between her tusks. I grabbed hold and stayed as close to her trunk as I could. I mean, I was off the ground. I just held onto her tusks, and she shook her head all around and ran around the cage. And I just held on with everything I had. She rammed into the wall a couple times, but I was between her tusks and she couldn't quite crush me. She swung her head around and tried to fling me off. I was way up in the air, but wouldn't let go. She ran all around the cage, just out of her mind, and I was holding on.

"Then she had the idea she could ram me into one of the bars. She's that smart. So she did. She ran toward the front bars and drove me into them. But when she rammed me into the bars, instead of crushing me into one bar, I went in between two of them, and I was stuck between them—wedged tight. I was up in the air between the bars. I couldn't get loose. I was squeezed in too tight.

"Simba backed up and ran forward to hit me, to finish me off. When she did, she rammed and just popped me right out the front of the cage like a cork out of a bottle. I was launched into the air. You know where the wall is out front of the elephant cage, the brick wall with the rail? That wall is at least twenty feet out in front of the cage. When she hit me and I popped loose, I flew so far into the air that I hit that wall. I landed really hard right against it. And I jumped up, and I was pissed. Simba was storming around and screaming at me from the cage. I tried to run back into the cage to fight her, but by then the other keepers were there with some of the maintenance guys. It was about four or five guys by then. They all grabbed me and said, 'No! No! Donnie.' I was trying to get loose, but they all had hold of me. They held me back. I just wanted to go in and fight her. I had so much adrenalin. Vince was screaming at me, but I was just so mad I couldn't understand him. Finally, he got through to me and said, 'Donnie, we're not letting you go until you tell me you're calm.' Finally, I said, 'Okay, I'm all right. I won't go in the cage.' They walked me into the keeper room, and I sat down right in that chair where you are now."

I was sitting in the green chair right next to the lockers.

Donnie continued, "Everybody asked, 'Are you all right?' Lots of people were here. And someone said, 'Hey, Donnie, do you want a cup of coffee?' I said, 'Okay,' so they made me a cup of coffee, and I drank that. After I finished that coffee, I sat there for about twenty minutes. Guys kept asking, 'How are you? How are you?' I said, 'I'm okay.' Lots of people left to go back to work. After twenty minutes, I thought, *Well, I'm going to get up.* And I tried to get up, but I couldn't move. I couldn't move a muscle. I said, 'I think I need to go to the hospital.' The ambulance came, and they took me and x-rayed everywhere. And I was in the hospital room, and my mother was there and my sister. They gave me something for pain. After awhile the doctor came back. He said, 'Young man, just about every bone in your body is broken, and the bones that aren't broken have stress fractures.' I was out for about six months."

I was glad that I hadn't heard that story earlier. The eerie part was that it was time for me to go into Simba's cage to check on the elephants and do some housekeeping. I shoveled up some of the waste and dumped it out the back door into the wheelbarrow. As I worked, I walked in between Simba and Tiani, moving right between their bodies. There had been times when they had accidentally squeezed me between them. The great gray wall of Simba's side, rough with sparse, coarse hairs, pressed up against me. Tiani, who was larger now, suddenly stumbled against me as she turned. I was caught between the tonnage of two elephants.

"Hey. Hey," I said loudly.

Simba eased away, being very careful that I wasn't being harmed. Attentive to where I was, she hurriedly slid out of the way when she realized I was in a pinch point. I knew that the Simba I was working with was greatly changed, but I now also knew that an internal combustion engine could cause instant regression, and it would.

CHAPTER THIRTY-FIVE

We began to house some new animals in our area, among them were Brazilian tapirs. Of course, tapirs aren't pachyderms, but we were charged with their care. We put them in Bomi's stall at the far end of the building, and reloaded her into the stall between Mushka and Blackie. Old one-eyed Bomi was actually Mushka's mother, and now they were side by side in stalls separated by a block wall. It wasn't like a tender reunion or anything. The two seemed indifferent to one another.

Tapirs are pretty much like you'd expect from a breed of hog-horse-pig-moose-Labrador with dark gray, short soft hair, and ears like a deer. Ours weighed about four hundred and fifty pounds each. They were the most harmless and friendliest animals in the building. Their feet were broad paws with toes, actually quite a bit like the feet of a pygmy hippo. We just went in with them when we cleaned the stall and even waded in the outdoor pool with them.

When they got really excited, they were like brainless, but friendly big dogs, and the most danger they presented was accidentally stepping on someone's feet. In fact, this finally convinced me to go out and buy some steel-toed work boots.

They didn't seem to mind anything about captivity or confinement by humans, even though the train driver's speech indicated that *South American natives use the tapir as a major source of food.* The biggest curiosity for me was their teeth. They looked like an oversized set of perfectly straight human choppers. That made them look like a cartoon.

The second thing about the tapirs that was funny was that the male tapir sort of started his day off with a big erection. This provided endless amusement for keepers, who watched families with children and guys on dates hurry past the exhibit.

Another animal that was new to us was Amelia the aardvark, who bunked in the Bull Room. She wasn't on exhibit, but our building was her winter home. She was tan and perhaps three and a half feet long from her sniffing, hairy snout to the end of her long, thick pointed tail. She had huge, thick claws for digging. Amelia smelled like old yeast and dandruff.

In my opinion, aardvarks are adorable, and being nocturnal, she slept almost all day. We'd sometimes have trouble waking her up to get her to eat before her food dried out. We'd steer her to the bowl, and sometimes she'd fall asleep while eating.

By this time the Director of the zoo was Michael Vitantonio. People liked him, and he made a great deal of effort to get to know the keepers. On the other hand, he knew almost nothing about animals. This was quite a contrast to Don who had the knowledge, but no formal credentials. Vitantonio had the necessary degrees, and he got the appointment. He was very approachable, however, and people just called him *Vitantonio* or *Vit.*

One day I was in the back hall when he came in. He was just being friendly and I was cleaning Amelia's winter home in the Bull Room. He asked how everything was going, then nodded toward the sleeping anteater. "How's the tapir doing?" he asked.

"Well, actually, that's an aardvark."

I really couldn't fault the guy. On one of my first days driving the tram I had told a lot of visitors that the prairie dogs were otters. On the other hand, they didn't make me the director of the zoo, either.

With the tapirs in an outdoor pen, and Amelia in the Bull Room, we were overflowing with animals. I tried to think of configurations which might work better. For instance, there was one hippo to each stall, and most of the time, that hippo was submerged and out of sight. I thought that grouping hippos into herds or families might be more interesting and more efficient. Surely, they existed together in the wild. And what about Blackie and Red? Why were they separated? They'd had many babies together. Wouldn't it be a more interesting exhibit if a hippo family were on display?

One day when Kuenzer came around on his morning visit, I asked, "What would happen if Bomi and Mushka were put together in the same exhibit?"

"I don't know," said Don. "I've thought about that, too."

"Well, they are mother and daughter. Do you think they might just coexist?"

Don said, "It would be a great thing if we could consolidate the exhibits in this building. That would open up a lot of possibilities."

"Yeah, suppose all three pygmies were in the same enclosure. And then there's Red and Blackie. What do you think about putting them together again?"

"They haven't been together for years," he said, "but, if you guys want to put them together, I don't have an objection. I don't know how the pygmies will react, but I'd say Blackie and Red would be fine."

"Do you think they'd breed?"

"I guess so," said Don. "Red still comes into heat, doesn't she?"

I remembered my adventures with trying to get her indoors for the night. "Oh, yeah."

"Let's start with seeing how Bomi and Mushka get along in one pen," he suggested. "I'll come around at 10:00 this Tuesday, and we'll give it a try."

"Great. And I'm going to try to see if I can get some grass growing in these yards."

"Good luck with that," said Don. "The ground's so hard no one's been able to grow grass in the hippo yards. The maintenance crews have tried it before."

I set out on a personal mission to try and grow grass, but the rototiller and even the twenty-five horse-powered *Super Roto* I borrowed from maintenance didn't make a scratch in the packed earth so I gave up on that for awhile.

On a Tuesday we tried the concept of putting two pygmies together. If the experiment was successful, they could both be in the outdoor pool at the same time, and it would free up an indoor stall for something else, maybe even a rhino.

Mike Lamb, Mary Jane, and I were working that day so I explained what we were going to try.

"It just makes sense that two female pygmy hippos would coexist.

Unless they're solitary in the wild. I guess we'll find out."

"We need to let them outside," Don began, "but we need to keep open an escape route in case one is aggressive."

Our plan unfolded in stages. First, we let Mushka out to get her five hundred pound bulk settled into the clean pool. Next, we opened the path for Bomi to join her offspring. Don, Mike, Mary Jane, and I peered out over the heavy plate steel barricade as the older hippo stepped happily out onto the concrete apron just outside the door. She stopped as if taking in the day when suddenly the younger and more powerful Mushka exploded up out of the pool. She was on Bomi in a blink; her snarling jaws ripped into her mother, who fled away at lightening speed. Bomi was racing for her life and moved faster than any animal I'd ever seen.

They ran in a large circle with Mushka biting and slashing at the older hippo's back and legs. With a great leap, Bomi landed in the center of the large pool. I thought the slaughter would now continue in the water as Mushka followed with a similarly incredible leap.

"Put the barricade back," Don yelled as the four of us moved away opening a path for Bomi who raced out of the water and back into the building. To my surprise, Mushka did not follow. She stopped at the entrance, evidently content that she had cleared her territory of an unwelcome intruder.

I ran through the keeper room and out into the front of the exhibit area. Racing around the corner of the gold and pink wall, I saw Bomi hunched down and shaking in the center of the concrete floor. She was staggering with twenty long tears on her back, neck, sides, and hindquarters. Blood gushed into pools around her feet. Haltingly, she moved toward me with her usual trusting look. She thought that I might do something, but I was helpless. Kuenzer joined me a few seconds later.

"Fill this pool with warm water. It will help her to get in the water," he said.

As the water began to flow, Bomi moved gingerly down the ramp to the bottom of the nearly empty pool. She was inches away from me now. The hard bottom of the pool streamed with blood swirling in the clean water. Bomi collapsed to the bottom of the concrete surface and looked up at me. I leaned out over the concrete with the wall hard against my stomach. I petted her on the flat top of her head. She opened her mouth and chewed the air with her usual friendliness.

"That's good," said Don, "I'm going to go call the vet." He then hurried away.

I didn't see Mary Jane or Mike anywhere, but I could see Bomi partially submerged, but something was happening. The blood was not flowing as it had, but seemed to be forming droplets in the water. For the first time, I could see Bomi's wounds clearly. She looked as if she were cut open by a filleting knife, and I was looking into deep folds, a great gash of raw meat.

I petted the hard flat top of her head. I hoped it would provide some sense of comfort, and I wished I had some as well as I cried openly.

Suddenly, she was no longer bleeding. All the wounds sealed themselves before my eyes, the folds of the cuts were apparently zipped shut. White lines, like instant scars, outlined the places where the wounds had been just seconds before. The blubbery folds of her flesh had glued themselves back together. Bomi seemed completely healed.

I ran into the keeper room where Don was on hold with the vet.

"Don, you've got to see this, come here, quick."

He set down the phone and followed me back to the pool. I reached down into the water and ran my hands over the hippo's back.

He was as amazed as I was. "I think I'll tell the vets that we don't need them."

I wondered what had happened to Mary Jane and Mike, and finally found them by the Bull Room. Mary Jane was kneeling down on the concrete floor, her face red from crying.

"I'm sorry," she said, "I just really lost it. Seeing poor Bomi torn to pieces."

"I just stayed with her," said Mike. "I figured whatever needed to be done, you and Don would do it better than I could."

Other than a bewildering array of new scars, Bomi had no lasting effects from her terrifying ordeal. But, obviously, the pygmies would not cohabitate. We had put Bomi into Mushka's territory. Had we done the opposite, Bomi may have been the aggressor. It was all about territory.

Our efforts had been a dismal failure, but we could be confident that the two Niles would welcome consolidation. Red and Blackie had been together for many years, and there was no reason to think that the mated pair would balk at the chance to be together again.

Against all the warnings, however, I still was trying to make friends with Red. One afternoon later that summer, she actually took a clump of grass from my hand as I extended it through the doorway.

"That's a good girl," I praised her. "That's my sweet Red." That same day something else happened that was memorable. I was the last to leave and, as I was closing up the building, I saw the zoo's Chevy wagon gleaming in the late day sun. It was headed toward Monkey Island, and it was being driven by John Sich who was grinning broadly, probably on his way to shoot rats. He looked exactly as he did the first time I ever saw him. That was the last time I set eyes on him.

CHAPTER THIRTY-SIX

Vince Rimedio had become my mentor in all things related to the Nile hippopotamus. Like Ellen, Vince never said the first thing that I didn't find interesting, and I was a good audience for the talkative and highly opinionated fellow. He didn't know Latin names or anything that came out of a book. His knowledge was practical and based on experience.

"We're going to put Red and Blackie into the same exhibit today," I said, when he stopped by.

"It's about time, that'll be good. They were always together for years, but about five years ago they separated them. I think the zoo just didn't want any more babies."

"How many babies have they had?"

Without hesitation, Vince said, "Twelve. Having a baby Nile here was the usual circumstance in this building for a long time."

"Whatever happened to them?"

"Well, I don't know. I mean, I don't know where they all went. A few of them didn't make it. One or two died as infants or were born dead. But most of them were sold to other zoos or circuses. There's only two of them that I know for sure; one went to a zoo in Japan, and the other to the zoo in Philadelphia. They moved them out as soon as they were weaned.

"What time are you putting them back together? I want to be here." I told him that by the time everything was ready, it'd be later that morning, but after the incident with the pygmies, I was a bit worried.

"Oh, hell," said Vince interrupting. "They're like babies with each other, well, except during sex. I'll tell you right now, Red and Blackie have the greatest love for each other of any two animals on this planet. You won't have any problems there. They haven't been together for five years, and this will be the day they walk back into heaven through the front door."

In spite of Vince's reassurance, Mike, Donna, Mary Jane, and I still had misgivings, but by the end of the morning, when the big pool in the center of the building was nearly full, Vince returned. Blackie was patiently waiting in his stall. He knew it was *his day* and the outdoor area was his to occupy.

Red was in her stall as well, but wary as always. She had eaten her morning meal and was expecting to spend the next twenty-four hours standing on concrete. The zoo was empty of visitors when Mike and Mary Jane pulled the electric switches so that both huge metal doors slid open at the same time.

The two hippos walked to the edge of the pool from opposite sides and looked across toward each other. They stopped and stood unmoving for about ten seconds. Then, like images in a mirror, they stepped down the stairs at opposite ends of the pool and slipped into the water simultaneously. They swam toward each other, met, and gently touched noses. That was all. Turning, they took positions side by side, bobbing just beneath the surface, both facing toward the front.

Vince and I watched for a few minutes. Mary Jane and Mike came around to the front also. Red didn't even soil the pool; the water remained perfectly clear. We watched the two blubbery, bobbing Niles, who were suspended, weightless in their watery world.

"If you really wanted a big event," said Vince, "you'll put them together when Red's in heat." At this he chuckled. "But that's just beautiful." With that, he was gone.

A few days later, Vince returned and asked if the Niles had bred yet. "I don't know. How would I be able to tell?" I asked.

At this question, Vince roared and slapped his hands together. "You'll hear what sounds like a railroad train with two engines and a caboose going through here at a hundred miles an hour, snorting and wheezing, that's Blackie and Red doing the wild thing. Have you noticed anything like that? You would, if it happened."

I hadn't and his assessment was simple. "Well, then it didn't happen. They haven't bred yet. She hasn't been in heat since they've been back together, has she?"

It had been about three weeks since Red had been in heat, and Vince speculated that it'd be a week or so before I'd hear the sound of a locomotive flying off the tracks. "It'll shake the whole building up to the roof. There won't be any doubt about it. You'll know when it happens."

I wondered if it could take place at night when no one was around, but he didn't think that very likely.

Like clockwork, Mike and I were in the building a week later when the water in the outdoor pool began to churn and roll. Blackie rose like a sea-shouldering whale right up out of the water and right up onto Red's broad rump. He bellowed and snorted as he bit at Red's back. During the ordeal, Red was often completely underwater. At other times she turned her head back toward him and bared her tusks. When they turned face to face, they appeared to be fighting with vicious snarls and biting. The grating sound of ivory tusks crashing together filled the air. Their tusks colliding sounded like bones being crushed.

I was really afraid they were going to kill each other. Their struggle was so violent that the splashing overflow dropped the water level by a few feet. This went on for about fifteen minutes, and then it stopped, and they were calm again. I wrote the date on the calendar in the keeper's room and included a note in my daily report.

The next day, when I cleaned their pool, I found that an eight-inch length of one of Blackie's tusks had broken off. When Don came by, I showed him the tusk and said it might go to the Education Building for a display. He told me to keep it as a memento so I hung it around my neck on a piece of rawhide. I wore it for awhile and then put it on my bedpost. Years later I had a party at my house, and the next day I found that the tusk was gone along with my mother's high school ring that I kept in the nightstand.

When I told Vince the news, he told me that the calf would be born within a day or two of eight months, which put the delivery in March.

CHAPTER THIRTY-SEVEN

Simba made believers out of the people who had only known her in her reformed state. Jim Bivens had never been trained with the elephant, but during his time at Pachy, he had been in the cage while other keepers were working. On at least one occasion, he took a wild ride on Simba's tusks. From his point of view it was invigorating, and the elephant was equally enjoying the play. At one point, however, Jim lost his grip and was thrown to the floor. Simba stood over him when she realized that he might have been hurt. This was the Simba we knew, playful and, at times, contrite. Fortunately, Jim was a bit shaken, but not injured.

The animal was powerful, and playfulness sometimes pushed the limit. What haunted me more was what Tresise had said about gasoline engines. It had bothered Ellen, too, and she had a hard and fast rule, "When an engine is running nearby, no one can go into the cage with Simba, not even me."

Donnie tried to get away when he was attacked, but she cut off his escape. Only through cleverness and strength did he save himself by holding on to her tusks. I thought about that in case it ever happened to me. No matter how friendly she had become, I had to have a plan.

Around 5:00 one afternoon, I was finishing with the elephants as everyone else was getting ready to leave. I wasn't in a big hurry. I had a softball game that evening and thought I'd kill the pre-game time by unclogging a drain in the back hippo hall.

The elephants were still outside in the yard. We always left them outside as long as possible so I was saving that for last.

I used hose pressure to open the drain, and by the time I was done, it was around 6:15, and I was running a little behind. My game was fourteen miles away and would start in just over an hour. I had to get going.

I quickly prepared the elephants' fruits and vegetables and mixed them with their feed as usual. I set the buckets of food at the front of the cage and went out in the yard. I cut open fresh bales of hay and issued the appropriate command, "Move up. Tiani. Simba, move up."

Normally, they'd come racing for their food, but tonight, they didn't budge. The early evening was just so pleasant that they simply wanted to stay out.

Our protocol required rewards for obeying, and a scolding when a command was ignored. The *ankus*, or elephant hook, was leaning against the wall just outside the keeper's room. I took it, but did not expect to use it. I figured that as soon as they saw it, they'd think, *Uh-oh. He means business.* Usually, it was enough to just be seen with it.

"Simba. Tiani. Move up." They were upset that I was insisting. Tiani, in fact, was so defiant she bellowed and shook her head. Even Ellen had seen this as a punishable offense, so I gave her a wallop on her left rump before repeating, "Tiani. Move up."

With that I grabbed the top of her left ear and she said, "Uncle," and the two of us headed into the building and right into the elephant cage.

When she was in her place, I said, "Good girl. Good. Good."

Now it was simply, *one in, one to go.* I went back outside.

"Simba. Move up."

For the third time, the huge African female didn't obey the command, so I gave her big rear end a smack with the *ankus*. It didn't hurt her at all. She bristled a bit toward me, but it didn't seem serious. "Move up."

The big elephant swung her tusks around toward me and rumbled. She was getting more cantankerous so I talked to her softly.

"Simba, sweetheart. I'm sorry. I know you want to stay outside. But, be a good girl." Of course, there was no point to any of that chitchat. A little louder I said, "Move up. Move up."

Simba rumbled again. She was really out of character and I wondered what this was all about. Again, she threatened me with her tusks and her ears flared out, and she trumpeted like an elephant about to charge. I could understand why she wanted to stay out, but she also had to be hungry. What was going on?

"Simba. Move up. Move up." Then she swung her trunk at me to knock me away, hitting me with a glancing blow in the chest.

It was then that I noticed she was facing east with the sun behind her, and I was facing west. I turned around to see what she was seeing. Squinting into the fading sunlight, I saw something emerging from the direction of Refreshment Stand Number 1. The manager of the Greenhouse was approaching the edge of the yard. He was driving a large backhoe.

The engine was quite loud, and Simba had been hearing the noise for a long time. The sound was coming closer, and I was in trouble. Her big tusks swooped past me. I suspect that she missed me on purpose, but the message was clear: "Get away from me. I don't know what I'm going to do next. Get away before I get out of control."

Simba wanted to fight the madness, but she was losing. The towering pachyderm was very close, and her eyes opened wide like saucers, her ears standing straight out on her head. I was backed against the log wall, and then she charged right into me, driving toward me with her tusks lowered toward my chest. The same thing was happening to me that happened to Donnie. My instinct was to turn and run to my right, to flee past the front of the animal. But I didn't. Instead I ran toward her body, escaping past her hindquarters and to her right. Like a fleeing mouse, I sped into the narrow corridor between the huge gray body and the heavy log fence.

Simba spun around counterclockwise to cut me off. She wheeled and swung her tusks, driving them into the log wall right where I was headed, but by then, I wasn't there. I was running like Greg Pruitt; I took one step and reversed direction. Simba was completely turned around and goring the log wall.

Simba was quick, but not a speed demon (like a hippo). I could outrun her as long as I didn't trip or fall. I ran around to the other side of the pool and kept the water between us.

The backhoe roared away into the distance, heading down toward the flowerbeds around Monkey Island. Cautiously, I moved closer toward Simba. She was still tense so I kept my distance. Within about two minutes, she'd calmed down.

"SIMBA. NO. SIMBA. MOVE UP."

If I'd had more time, I would have let her settle for half an hour or so but I was still playing cat and mouse.

"MOVE UP."

The backhoe was long gone, and the animal in front of me was drained of her insanity. A look of guilt and sorrow came into her eyes. Her trunk lowered and her ears dropped. I stepped closer. Reaching out, I dared to touch her massive left ear at the bottom. I took hold of the bottom of her ear.

Softly, I said, "Simba. Move up."

As with Tiani, the two of us ran along together at top speed toward the back of the building. The run was wonderful. I let go of her ear, and Simba barreled in through the back door and into the elephant cage.

"Get in line."

Now totally normal, Simba hurried into line, and began rocking back and forth with great energy. I chained her as fast as I could. Sweat had beaded up on my face, and my heart was racing. My adrenalin was very high. I emptied the buckets of fruit and feed down in front of each elephant and said, "All right." That was the signal for the elephants to dig in, and they did.

Remembering Ellen's words, I went back and cut up more apples. She always said, "Whenever you quarrel with Simba, make up with her."

I stepped over in front of Simba. She plucked the pieces of apple out of my hands one at a time with the dexterous fingers of her trunk and put them into her mouth.

I said, "You're a good girl, Simba."

The rush to the game may have broken a few speeding laws, but, fortunately, none of the laws of physics. I changed into my uniform in the car and rushed to the field where my teammates were freaking out. It was still the top of the first, and we were at bat.

"Holy shit," said Carl, our cleanup hitter, "where have you been?"

"I had a little trouble with the elephants."

"We didn't have enough players," he explained. "We told them we had nine and we only had eight. (A full team is ten.) If you hadn't got here by the time we took the field, we would have had to forfeit. Okay, you're batting last. We put you there and hoped to hell you'd get here before this half-inning was over."

My adrenalin was still pulsing, and it was probably enhanced by the fact that we were batting through the entire lineup in the first inning. I was ninth and on deck. It was dark, and we were under the lights.

Carl came over to warn me about their third baseman. He explained that he had hit a homerun and, though there was no play on him, the guy on third stepped into the baseline and knocked him over. Since I was the only other guy on the team that was a power hitter, he thought I should be warned. "When you're running toward third, he'll try to knock you over."

I look down to third base at a guy who was about six-foot-two, and weighed around two hundred and forty pounds.

I must have laughed involuntarily. This guy was nowhere near Simba's size, but he had Simba's stare as he watched Carl talking to me.

"I just spent the last forty-five minutes fighting with a six-ton elephant who was mad at me." My laughter must have seemed inappropriate to Carl, and to the third baseman who was sharpening his tusks.

"That guy doesn't scare me at all."

I'm sure that Carl thought I was snorting catnip or something, but I was feeling very good as I stepped into the batter's box. I had been running with elephants and dodging ivory tusks. I wondered what would happen if I grabbed that third baseman's ear on my way around the base path. I was glad to be alive, and he looked so serious.

I had to step out of the batter's box so I could stop laughing. "Sorry. Sorry," I said to the catcher, "I can do this."

I hit the first pitch into the gap between center and left fields. It was gone into the night somewhere beyond the light poles.

I turned on the full jets and was heading past second base and looking back to see where the outfielder was. I knew, however, that a big third baseman would be getting ready to give me a love tap. I saw it looming ahead, and I was watching the guy near third.

Running at top speed, I approached third base, and saw the third baseman inching toward the baseline. He was getting readying to *accidentally* knock me over. I was bearing down on third as he stepped out in front of me.

It had worked on Simba; why not on an ape? I gave him one step to the right, and then a quick left. He was almost completely fooled by my stutter-step. Almost. Unfortunately for him, his reflexes sent him right back into my path. I planted my right foot, and my shoulder slammed right into the center of his chest. He was still on the ground when I crossed the plate. The throw to the plate never came, but my teammates were up on their feet. The third baseman was carried from the field and had to call it a night.

CHAPTER THIRTY-EIGHT

When an animal in the building was ill or out-of-sorts, our lives changed. Our focus had to be on figuring out what could be done to provide comfort and healing. Amelia the aardvark was rooming in the Pachyderm Building and was now bunking in a hippo pen that could no longer be used for its intended purpose due to leaks in the pool. Mostly, she slept all day. Her feed consisted of a big bowl of ground hamburger with a concoction of additives containing vitamins and minerals.

Amelia had only been there for a few weeks before she started to come down with something. Seems odd to say that an animal that we mostly saw sleeping appeared lifeless, but that's what we felt. Soon, her face swelled up, and her eyes flowed with creamy, yellow pus. Within a day, her eyes were swollen completely shut, and she started to wheeze. She was no longer eating, and barely conscious. Out of every pore of her body an odd odor oozed, like a putrid fungus.

As with humans, symptoms from a virus can come on suddenly and the best course of treatment, as you know, is plenty of liquids, eating, and bed rest. As keepers, our first job was to encourage her to take nutrition, but that was not going to happen. She didn't touch her food. Mary Jane and I spent a lot of time trying to take care of her by constantly cleaning her bowl and putting out fresh food. We held it up to her nostrils, but couldn't coax her to take even a nibble. I wiped her off with warm, wet cloths and dried her carefully. That made her smell a little better, but it was mostly done out of our feelings of hopelessness. Mary Jane built a wall of hay around her to cut down any drafts. When her wheezing increased, we began turning her every couple of hours, like moving an old person to prevent bed sores. Of course, we put this in our reports.

About the fourth day, the zoo's vet came in with his solution. He gave us a vitamin C powder to put in her food. I argued that she wasn't touching her food, but apparently he heard what I was saying as my questioning his authority.

For the next two days, we sprinkled vitamin C powder into Amelia's ground meat and worked it in with a spoon. This struck us as colossally moronic because we'd hold the food up to her face, and she wasn't even a little tempted. It seemed like we had been condemned to watch her die.

Of course, in those days I had my own strange ideas about animals and life. I knew that wolves and dogs sniff around the floor of the forest to find natural antibiotics. I knew that when I threw dirt to the zoo's wolves, they gobbled it down greedily. I knew that Simba and Tiani found special spots of soil out in the elephant yard and ate the dirt judiciously.

Amelia was an aardvark, and so it was impossible that when she stuck her tongue into a termite mound or ant hill that she did not also eat considerable quantities of dirt. Surely, that soil was teeming with life, with molds, bacteria, and indeed, natural antibiotics.

One day, after everyone was gone, I got a gray plastic bucket and took a long walk around the perimeter of the Pachyderm Building. I dug beneath the brown leaves and started collecting rich soil samples. I carried two pails back to her stall and mixed the contents into her bucket of food kneading it into a sort of meatloaf. When I offered this, she began to sniff the air excitedly. The next thing I knew, she was standing and eating my vitamin C-free blend of natural ingredients. When she was finished, it was back to the mat and sleep. I covered her with a blanket.

The next morning when I came into work, Amelia was a hundred percent better. She hungrily ate her morning meal. Her eyes were wide open and clear, and her nostrils were totally free of mucus. The lovable animal was lively and bouncy. What I've described is exactly what happened. At 10:00 a.m. the vet came in and examined her. Praising his remedy of vitamin C powder, he walked away. I said nothing. After all, I didn't want to be accused of challenging authority.

If Amelia had been raised from the dead, Sironen came with news that she would soon be in heaven. He came and told us that the zoo was going to attempt breeding aardvarks. He brought in a handsome aardvark stud. Amelia was now part of a breeding pair.

"We're going to put them in an outside yard," he said.

The tapirs had been moved to new digs, so Amelia and *Andy* went into the pen at the south end of the building. That was the last we ever saw of them. It wasn't that something untoward happened, it's just that they were in aardvark heaven. Once they were in the yard, they started digging. Within a few days, there was an enormous tunnel that disappeared into the ground. There was also a six-foot pile of dirt. This was incredible. This was the soil that had resisted rototiller and mattock, but it was nothing to two aardvarks in a committed relationship. I never saw Amelia and Andy again. But they were down in their huge burrow. They slept in the daytime, but obviously came out at night because the pile of dirt continued to grow.

CHAPTER THIRTY-NINE

Red's baby was due in March, and about a week before the date I had circled on the calendar, we separated her from Blackie. This had been done at Vince's suggestion.

"Blackie won't deliberately hurt the baby, but he could accidentally step on it. You'll have two big bodies moving around, and it's better to just let Red and the baby be alone until the baby gets to be three hundred pounds. It'll only be about sixty pounds when it's born, and Red'll like being alone with it. After a month, you can bring Blackie back in. But here's what you need to know for right now. Red has to have access to the big pool at all times. She gets the pool every night from now on. Clean the pool when she's up in the stall eating and make it available to her again as quickly as you can. Blackie will be all right. Red will give birth in the water, and the baby will nurse while completely submerged. That's how Nile babies feed, underwater.

"This will be a good experience for you. I've see you at the back door of Red's stall, feeding her out of your hand. You're the first person to ever do that, that's for sure. You'll do fine with that baby. Red trusts you."

Don Kuenzer started to come around frequently to see what Red looked like, but many were tentative about the whole thing. The big hippo hadn't changed a bit, at least not on the outside. Red looked the same as always.

One morning I was talking to Don in front of Red's stall where she was eating her morning meal.

"I didn't get to name the giraffe," I began, "what do you think about my naming the baby Nile? Both Red and Blackie have colors as their names, so I was thinking that a male could be called *Blue*, and a female, *Violet*."

"That would be fine. You can name the hippo."

Like everyone else, I suspect that Don was skeptical that there even was a pregnancy, so letting me give the name was a real longshot anyway. Luckily for me, none of the wives of the benefactors of the zoo knew anything about this since a pregnancy had not been announced.

Red's *pregnancy* became a great source of speculation around the time clock. If Vegas odds makers had been allowed, the wager would not have been on the sex of the offspring but on, *Was she or was she not in a family way?*

The vet announced that a visual inspection could not provide adequate evidence in the case of such a large animal, but he suspected that she was not pregnant. He was talking to Don when he said this, and though I was standing there, I was not considered present.

"Well, for the last few months we haven't seen her coming into heat," I offered, leaning on what Vince Rimedio had taught me to observe.

Apparently I hadn't said anything because the doctor turned back toward Don and said, "We'd have to have blood work to know for sure."

Don gave me a sympathetic glance and asked the vet, "If she is pregnant, would there be any way of knowing when the birth might be?"

"Well," said the vet, "even if it were certain that she is pregnant, and I'm not saying that she is or isn't... with an animal that large, it's completely impossible to predict the birth. She's just so large. Looking at her right now, I see absolutely nothing about this animal that makes me think she's expecting, but it's simply impossible to tell."

I looked toward Red who was now looking at us. There was a lot of loose, red skin hanging down from her enormous body. I understood what the vet had said. If there was a sixty pound fetus inside her uterus, who could tell?

About an hour later, I was dry mopping the floor in front of the hippos, when Vince came in. "How ya doin'?" he said.

"You know, the vet was here awhile ago, and he said there's no way to tell if Red's pregnant or when the baby will be..."

At this, Vince was riled. He was a man of action who said things with certainty. He wasn't interested in discussing what he considered an ignorant opinion.

"Horsefeathers," he scoffed pointing at Red. "You watch her. You just watch her like a hawk. When you see that milk sack drop," he slapped his hands. "The baby will come that night. That milk sack's going to drop any time now. Within thirty-six hours. You keep watching. That drops, and it's time."

At that moment, he seemed like the man of science. His theory was based on repeated observation and experience. He sealed his findings with a clap of his hands and was off toward the coffee pot.

The next day in the afternoon, I was hosing down the work area along the length of the hippo stalls. It was around 3:30 and I looked over at Red. I turned back to my work, and when I looked at Red again, something had changed. Her milk sack had dropped. There was an udder hanging down, like a fleshy bag between her back legs.

As the day ended, I was very excited. I went up to the Commissary Building to punch out, and turn in my report. I folded the green paper into a tiny square and slid it into the slot of the gray metal desk. I wondered what Don and Alan would think when they read it the next morning. There was no equivocation in my words: *Red's milk sack dropped today around 3:30 p.m. Birth is imminent. The baby Nile hippo will be born tonight, March 10-11. By the time you read this, the baby will have already arrived.*

CHAPTER FORTY

The next morning I arrived early, but Mike and Mary Jane were already there. Before I had taken off my coat, Mary Jane came running with the news, "It's here."

I never saw anyone so happy in my life as we ran down along the front of the hippo stalls toward the big pool. The water was crystal clear. Red hadn't soiled it. She'd left the water clean for her baby.

As I approached, Mike spoke in a soft, reverent whisper. "Look at this."

Down into the water, Red had come toward us to the front of the pool. She was calm and contently bobbing in the water like a tub of joy. Red was floating on her side, and I suspect she was proudly showing us her new treasure.

Three feet below the surface, swimming in and out near her hind quarters was a snub-nosed baby Nile. Tiny only by hippopotamus standards, the newborn was a little more than three feet long and chunky. Perfectly formed and robust, he swam with the ease of a champion.

As her baby moved his little nose along her belly, Red's entire body turned and she let him suckle. Red's movements were slow and steady, and when the baby found a nipple, it was as if they had become a single animal floating together. She was at peace, totally unbothered by the fact that we were there. We had her trust.

As she nursed, the newborn was suspended in the water, about two feet below the surface. After a few minutes, the corpulent youngster swam away from the mother, kicked his legs, and popped through the surface to take a breath. He was a rich, steel-blue color.

"Look. He's *Blue*," I said.

The three of us stood watching the mother and baby for a long time, and it was easily the most peaceful moment of my zoo career. We probably stood there for twenty minutes without speaking. All our thoughts and emotions were centered around the tender mother and her nursing baby suspended in the shimmering depths of the sparkling clean water.

CHAPTER FORTY-ONE

Red always fouled the water in her pool. I had often thought it was her natural way of concealing her presence. It was odd to see her sitting in a clean pond. That did not last long, however. Apparently, she held off her instincts only long enough to be sure her Blue knew how to find the nipple. Around 9:00 that first morning, she was evidently satisfied with his progress because she deliberately set to the task of pulling the shades over their privacy. In a matter of minutes, the pair became ninety-nine percent invisible.

For all our delight at watching, there was work to be done. I closed Red's stall and cleaned it. I put her morning meal down on the floor as usual. By 10:30 or so, Red's meal was waiting in a pile on the center of the concrete floor of her stall, and it was time to let her up to eat. The switch to open her gate was in the back hall so I threw it and ran back as quickly as I could to join Mary Jane and Mike. We were watching Red, and unsure how she would respond. Would she come up to eat? If she did, would the baby stay in the pool alone? If Blue tried to follow, how would it climb out or get back in the pool? Of course, there was also the possibility that Red simply would not eat until her baby was a little larger.

Our questions were answered when Red came up out of the water as she normally did when a meal was placed in her stall. She surged up out of the pool like a car-sized leather football. Behind her, short-legged little Blue followed. At forty inches long and a foot tall, he was adorable. The steel-blue, rubbery newborn struggled with each step as he began the imposing journey up the ramp of the pool. Each sloped concrete step was a huge obstacle. He climbed like a determined puppy, and he was plucky and surprisingly muscular. As he made it to the top of a step, he would sometimes stumble forward, hitting the concrete with his chest and chin. He took the rock-hard punches to the chin and just kept moving.

Red arrived in the stall, but suddenly turned and hurried back to the edge to watch and hover over him as he made it to the top of the climb. Blue arrived with a little speedy burst out onto the floor of the stall. Red touched her wide muzzle to his slippery, wet back, and the baby scooted between her stout legs. She walked to her meal slowly with the baby beneath her. As she began eating, Blue didn't hold still. He darted back and forth beneath her, hiding in the forest of his mother's limbs.

"It looks precarious, but she knows where that baby is at all times.

She'll never accidentally step on him. Never in a million years." It was Vince who was now speaking. He had come in unnoticed and was looking toward Red and Blue, his eyes moving thoughtfully over the entire scene.

"He's a beauty. That is a beautiful baby. It's her prettiest one yet," he said. We watched for a short while before Vince pinched some coffee and headed back to work.

The calf was taking in everything with a youthful curiosity. Everything in the world was new: the pool, people, concrete steps, a pile of hay, walls, bricks, hissing electric lamps, and the massive windows of the far wall. He processed the information, accepting it as the natural order.

That day, we didn't clean the pool after Red and Blue climbed out. Cleaning and filling the pool would have taken several hours, and Vince had said that we should make sure Red had access to the pool at all times. All during her meal, the gate remained open so that she could return to the water without notice.

When Red had finished eating, she went straight back. She paused at the edge to check on the baby and then launched herself down the sloped steps with a *whoosh* as she crashed into the water. Little Blue walked to the edge of the pool, still puppy-like and a bit confused.

His mother was swimming about twenty feet away. She swirled the water creating waves that hit the steps and sides of the pool like oncoming breakers. Blue moved closer to the edge of the ledge, and looked down at the steps trying to figure them out. At one point you could see he had made a decision and it was *Here I go*.

His first precarious step on his right foot became a slide down the slimy surface. Before the fall could become a disaster, Red rose out of the water stretching her wide muzzle toward her baby catching him with her soft upper lip. She caught him and held him perfectly still as he sat back on his haunches.

Surefooted, Red backed up very slowly over the *stepping stones* beneath her. Cushioned against his mother's nose, Blue stumbled down the precarious stairs, often sliding and being caught again. At every moment, his mother's big muzzle was against him, holding him and guiding him down into the water. At the bottom of the steps, Red released him and he slipped into the water, swimming like a speedy mink. Red glided gently to the center of the pool, and closed her large doe eyes. Blue disappeared beneath the choppy brown surface and dove out of sight to nurse.

It was time to get going on the rest of the morning work. Blackie, the pygmies, elephants, and giraffes needed our attention. That was the morning when we saw baby Blue for the first time. He'd been born in the night on the date Vince had predicted eight months earlier.

"Adam, why don't you work with Red and the baby every day for awhile?" Mike's offer was welcome. "We'll work the elephants. You stay down here with them."

"We don't mind," said Mary Jane.

I entered a period of time in which I worked with Red and the baby Nile every day as their keeper. Of course, Don and Alan visited often to see the youngster.

"How's Blue doing?" Don asked, and I realized he had accepted the name I gave the baby.

CHAPTER FORTY-TWO

Over the next several days, a few visitors came to see the new baby. We weren't into the real tourist season so I expect these were people who were on the zoo mailing list or something. A woman in her mid-fifties came all the time looking to see Blue. I explained that he was submerged in the pool, and if she wanted a good view she should come back at 3:00 which was Red's next feeding. She did. In fact, she appeared regularly for many days at 10:00 a.m. and 3:00 p.m., and I realized that Blue made keeping the exact schedule important for our patrons.

There was a professional photographer who also came. I don't know his name, but he was a *Friend of the Zoo*. He came every day for awhile, and we'd go out of our way to help him get the best photos. When he showed them, I was impressed. He used a large format camera and made black and white prints.

It was nearly April and getting warmer outside, but still too chilly for the hippos and giraffes. Only elephants ever went out that early. Blackie and Red were still separated, but in a few weeks, the outdoor temperatures would support a reunited hippo family. I figured that would become quite a public draw.

I told Kuenzer that if we kept them all in one exhibit, we'd have quite an attraction. In a roundabout way, I was asking Don if we could keep Blue, and he seemed to like the idea of a family group.

"It will be great for the visitors as Blue grows larger," he said.

My translation of this was, "Don says we can keep Blue." Mary Jane and Mike were as happy as I about this. Of course, my mind was also leaping to larger ideas. One idea involved the old public swimming pool that had been in Brookside Park since the 1920s. It was huge and unused. Why couldn't that become a hippopotamus pond?

"Imagine this," I said to Kuenzer, "the zoo could build a walkway that goes halfway through the center of the pool, with glass sides. Then people can walk right in, sort of under the water. We can fill the pool with Niles in the summer. It will be the greatest hippo exhibit in the world."

"How would you clean it? It would be enormous," he said.

"I'd build a big waterfall. There would be pump stations in two places in the pool. Water would be pumped up and flow down the big waterfall. As it flowed, it would run through big cages of activated charcoal, filter screens, and barricades of rocks. Then we would clean the screens and rinse out the charcoal. Kind of like a giant aquarium filter. In the fall, we'd walk all the hippos back into the building through a corridor. In the summer, up on the hillside, they would come up out of the water at night to graze. We could grow plants and rotate the grazing areas so the vegetation could thrive."

Don just smiled at that overly ambitious fantasy. Of course he knew that the zoo had other plans for that area. In fact, the construction of an amphitheater had already begun, and the old pool, which was nearby, would soon be torn out and the land reclaimed. The workers on the project had an open invitation to come and get coffee in our building, and the ones who didn't mind the smell actually did. The guy who planted the lawn came into the Pachy all the time. After seeding the new lawn, he had to keep it watered. For this, he used small sprinkler connected to a garden hose. He'd let it run in one spot for a half hour, then move it twenty feet. It was tedious and thankless since the entire area was hundreds of feet wide.

"You don't need to do that," I said one day, "I'll show you." I then went and dragged our long fire hose out to a rise on the edge of the newly seeded area. The spray shot about eighty feet into the air, and the water came down like a rain shower. With a simple redirection of the nozzle, I could reach the entire area, and the watering took only ten minutes.

After that, Lamb and I took turns keeping the area moist until the grass was well established.

The opening of the amphitheater was to be marked by a big hoopla. Some well connected event planner decided that it would be great if one of the elephants pulled a cloth off the sign that marked the new venue. (There are also people who believe that pigs should fly.) I don't know why she stopped there. What if we had some of the grizzly bears dancing on the stage while the California sea lions balanced beach balls on their noses? Then Simba could pull the silk cloth off the sign while bleeding heart pigeons flew out of her butt into the sky and exploded. That would have been my suggestion.

Since I was now the senior keeper in the Pachyderm Building, Don came around and explained the situation. He was a bit nervous about it since it was a stupid idea, and it didn't take an Einstein to know that we didn't want to walk Simba among all those people, and so the lot was cast. I needed to train Tiani to pull the veil off the sign. I told him that I had only the most rudimentary concept of how to train an elephant, but I'd try.

I worked with Tiani every day. I carried some bales of hay into the elephant cage and built them up to the same height and shape as the sign. That was a bit of failed thinking because I had to first discourage Tiani from eating it. I put a huge cloth over the stack of hay bales, the same one we'd use at the dedication. I just needed to teach her to pull the cloth off, and, if she did, I would reward her. *If she did* was a wild hypothetical. She never did.

I was getting desperate. This animal was curious about everything; why not the stupid cloth? I had apples and bananas in my pocket and decided I'd reward her if she just *touched* the cloth. Surely she would do that. After several days, I started to think that the dancing grizzly bears would be a better idea, and I was sure that I could get bleeding heart pigeons to explode.

The day before the dedication, Don asked how it was going, and I told him I was still trying

"I sure hope you guys can pull this off," he said.

I think he was worried, and for good reason.

Every time I tried to get Tiani to pay attention, she'd want to run away and play. When she did that, the first thing she did was run and pick up her car tire, which was her favorite toy. Simba and Tiani had old tires in their yard and cage. They would pick them up and kick them all over the place. Tiani couldn't walk past a tire without picking it up. (At this point, the illustrator draws a light bulb over Ziggy's round head.)

I got a piece of cord and tied one end around Tiani's smallest tire. I tied the other end around the corner of the cloth, which was draped over the hay bales. I made Tiani hold still as she stood right next to the tire. She was dying to pick it up.

"All right," I commanded. She grabbed the tire and carried it away. The cloth whisked off the bales of hay and trailed after her. I praised her to the heavens and poured treats down her throat. Then I put the cloth back on the bales and placed the tire out of view under a fold of the cloth.

"Steady." She held. "All right," and she was off running with the tire.

I phoned Don, "Don't worry. She's got it."

The next day, Tiani went on a wild rampage and killed six people. Just kidding. (But wouldn't that have been a powerful story?) Instead, it was torture for poor Tiani who had to stand at attention next to the cloth-covered sign *forever.* There were about forty-five people there, including the press, and people kept giving speeches. I don't remember who any of the people were, a bunch of big shots, I guess. Nobody said anything about how nice the lawn looked. In fact, they were walking all over it. Some people were drinking champagne, and it was only 10:00 in the morning. Meanwhile, Tiani's eyes were as big as saucers as she stared at that tire which was about ten inches from the flicking end of her trunk.

She was dying, and I had to keep whispering, "no... no..."

I had the gold *ankus* with me so I probably should have smacked each of the speech-givers on the ass and said, "C'mon. Speed it up a little." But I didn't. Kuenzer was also there, and I think he had a tie on. (I'd never seen that.) He wasn't listening to speeches, either. Don was just standing there wondering whether Tiani would pull the cloth off the new sign when the time was right. That was all we cared about.

Every time one big shot finished talking, a lot of people applauded vigorously. They were happy his speech was finished; so they clapped and smiled. That's how you knew that guy was done. Otherwise, you wouldn't be able to tell since there wasn't any content or sensible flow to the speechifying. As soon as one guy was done, another guy started.

Don, Tiani, and I were bored out of our minds, but also nervous. One speaker remarked that the amphitheater would be an asset for hundreds of years. Another one thanked everyone in the Cleveland phone book who was rich. It would have been interesting if someone had noted that the Cleveland Zoo Softball Team had clobbered the team from the downtown office because they were a bunch of candy-coated pencil-pushing geeks.

I had a banana in my front left pocket, and Tiani kept shifting her weight back and forth, staggering around in her spot. The tip of her trunk flicked about like a worm on a hook. She *really, really* wanted that tire.

Another speaker starting talking about how life sucked without an amphitheater. He read his speech off of a stack of papers, and I wondered if he had actually written all those *uhs* in his prepared text.

Tiani was falling asleep. I let her snooze through several speeches, then I reached over and petted the hairy head. She woke up and there was her tire, *waiting...waiting...waiting*. The truly remarkable thing, at least from a keeper's perspective, was that through the course of endless words, Tiani hadn't taken a dump.

The guy giving the next speech said, *without any further ado* nineteen times, and finally, twenty minutes later, a woman said, "And now, we'll have Tee-eye-ann-eye the elephant pull aside the cloth to officially unveil the new Metroparks Amphitheater."

Twenty men with flash cameras ran at Tiani, got down on one knee, and leaned forward into Tiani's face.

"All right," I said. Tiani grabbed the tire and dozens of camera flashes popped in her face. Wide-eyed and terrified, Tiani screamed with a shrill trumpeting that exploded out of her throat. She turned and ran two hundred and fifty feet straight toward the gaping garage door of the Pachyderm Building. Luckily, she held onto the tire for about twenty feet and the cloth was pulled off the sign amid polite clapping. I ran after Tiani as fast as I could, carrying the tire and the cloth, but she had a head start and I couldn't catch her.

Tiani was in her cage when I got there, and being comforted by Simba who had clearly been worried about what we were doing to her companion. At that moment, Tiani squatted and let it all out.

CHAPTER FORTY-THREE

It was nearly April, and Blue was still small, weighing, perhaps, a hundred pounds and still scurrying under Red's legs when she was up out of the pool eating. Blackie hadn't been in the pool for weeks, but it would not be long when they'd all be in a pool all the time.

The Egyptian Geese were back out in Bomi's old yard, and there were now about twenty-seven of them. Still, there was only one mating pair. Moms and Poppy were alone in that regard, and the other twenty-five were wallflowers.

"They'd breed if you made it possible for another pair to have their own territory," said Vince one day. "That mating pair is the royalty of the yard they're in now, but if you moved all those other geese to a new place, another pair would mate and nest." That made me think, and I decided to ask Don Kuenzer what he thought.

"Don, are Egyptian geese good?" I asked, "I mean, is that a species we'd want to breed? Because Vince told me how we can breed a lot more of them. Do you think if we had a lot of Egyptian geese that other zoos might even want them?"

"Well, yeah," said Don. "Or we could move them into other areas around the zoo. It would be okay if we had more."

Don had no idea how serious I was about *more*. I was intrigued to think that in the group of non-mating birds there might be others just waiting to be moved into their own territory. As long as they were trapped in Bomi's yard, they couldn't move toward another space.

I opened the outside door to Wolee's yard. Then went out into Bomi's yard and herded all twenty-five of the unpaired geese into the building, through the back hippo hall, and out into Wolee's yard. Within a day or two, a mating pair separated from the rest. (So, it was completely true that Vince knew about all kinds of *goosing*.)

Once I'd identified that pair, I opened the back door to the outdoor Nile yard. Then I herded the twenty-three remaining unpaired geese into that space. Once again, a mating pair emerged. So I herded the twenty-one single geese into Mushka's yard. When that was sorted out, I moved nineteen to the elephant yard. A pair of those found a safe spot just beyond the electric fence, and then, with only the giraffe yard still available, I drove seventeen into this final frontier. Two became the breeding pair there, and fifteen were out of luck.

Six mating pairs were now established, and pretty soon there were mating nests and eggs everywhere. We should have sold the eggs. After a few days, I was busy building shelters for the nests. The Cleveland Zoo was going to have a real butt-load of Egyptian geese as well as a grand cacophony of honking. In a month we had eighty or ninety geese running around.

We had a lot of big thunderstorms that spring. Heavy rainstorms always meant the lower levels of the zoo would flood. One night, during a thunderstorm, I woke up wondering if our building was flooding. There was a valve in the basement. If the valve was closed during a bad storm, the basement of the Pachyderm Building would fill up with water. I should have gotten in my car right then, but I waited until morning. I thought that the valve was probably open and everything would be okay. It wasn't.

At 7:30 that next morning, I arrived to a flood scene. Brown water around four feet deep was in the basement, and the water was halfway up the stairway.

Intrepid as always, I waded down into the chilly, chest-high water, which smelled like fuel oil and sewage. I walked through it for about thirty feet as I headed toward the northeast corner. The valve was somewhere down under several feet of water. As I bent over and felt around for the round, iron wheel under the water, my head went down right to the surface. I found the gate valve and gave it several turns counterclockwise. Then I stood back up.

Overhead, I heard echoing footsteps on the steel staircase. Matyas came partly down the stairs, but stayed clear of the water. He sat down on the stairs.

"Thanks for opening that valve for me. I've spent a long time wondering how a sane person could do that. I couldn't come up with a solution."

It hadn't seemed like that big a deal to me. All I'd done was wade out into the water and open the valve.

"If I were you, I'd try to walk out the same way you went in," he added. "I am certain that in that water, there are several currents of 220-volt AC power. All along that back wall are the 220 outlets. I'd say the juice is going off every which way toward anything grounded. It's probably flowing all around you, right through the water. Personally, I would have turned off the power before wading out there where you are." He was grinning as he spoke.

I turned around and walked out along the same *L-shaped* route, now terrified that at any second I'd get electrocuted. Obviously, that didn't happen, but I carried a lot of water with me as I mounted the stairs.

"Let's get coffee while we wait for that to drain some," he said, and I began that day soaking wet from head to toe. It wasn't too unusual for me on that job.

Joe made a call to the top of the zoo about the condition of the Pachy, and before long other guys from Maintenance came to the building. They worked in the basement all morning after it drained. They had hair dryers and were drying electrical components. They also sprayed some units with *Wire Dryer*, which was some magical demoisturizing aerosol spray.

Mary Jane, Mike, and I did our usual morning work with the animals. Mary Jane worked elephants. Simba and Tiani went outside and loved the fact that stray leaves and branches were strewn around their yard. Mike and I teamed up to work the hippo side of the building.

In the afternoon the work started again. I put Red's food in her stall and brought Red and Blue out of the pool. Since Blue was much more comfortable with the zoo routines by that time, we cleaned the big indoor pool every day. While Mike and I cleaned it, mother and son were isolated in Red's stall. We hauled wheelbarrows full of waste out of the big pool through Blackie's stall; he didn't care. Finally, we started the big pool filling.

After about ten minutes Jim Bivens, the Monkey Island keeper, came into the building.

"Monkey Island is a mess today. I mean there were trees down in the moat this morning, and I've spent the whole morning cleaning out the debris. I haven't even hosed the island yet today. Now that you guys are filling the hippo pool, there's no water pressure."

"I'll shut it down, and go with you to give a hand." I offered. "The Nile pool is about half full, but if I turn it off now, the water in the boilers will have some time to heat up. I'll finish filling the pool when we're done at your place, and Red and Blue will have warm water."

With my filling postponed, the water pressure in the zoo returned to normal. Jim and I walked over to Monkey Island. By that time in the day, the rain had totally stopped. Once at the Island, we dropped down into the empty moat and walked across as the rhesus macaques ran away from us in great waves, fleeing to the other side of the concrete mountain. I don't remember much about what we did next, but I do remember the monkeys scurrying to get past us as we entered a small concrete room on the island.

Jim started preparing food so I reverted to my normal scrubbing and opened the nozzle of the hose to blast the monkey doo-doo down the drains at the outer edge of the moat. Eventually, I was at the top of the mountain and seeing a completely different view than the one I had pointed out from the tour train so many years before. Nothing unusual happened that day; it was just that I had actually been on Monkey Island and even went inside. For me, it was like being inside the scoreboard at Fenway Park or something. It was then that I realized my life had circled back to a particular moment. As a young boy in 1960, I first experienced the wonder of the animals. Later, as a train driver, I passed Monkey Island day after day and first heard the story of Brutus and the complexities of an animal society. In both cases, I had been an outsider looking in, but now I was an insider looking out over a place that I loved. This is the way I want to remember those days and recall *My Life in the Cleveland Zoo.*

EPILOGUE by Rob Smith

Besides being my brother, Adam was one of the most imaginative people I have ever known. That particular talent, however, comes with its own set of liabilities. He had a strong vision of the world as it *should be* and was often not swayed by such mundane things as reality. By 1983, shortly after the events in this book, Adam had relocated to Knoxville, Tennessee and was beginning a new career in advertising and video production.

In his early years in Knoxville, he continued with his cartooning and honed his skills creating offbeat ads for automobile dealerships. My niece, Lisa, was at a business seminar once when one of her colleagues made the connection between her and her creative uncle. His comment was, "In advertising, people are encouraged to *think outside the box.* Adam hasn't yet discovered that there is a box."

In time, he married, had a family, and his son, Jay, inherited some of his father's love of visual arts and is on the way to becoming an accomplished video editor like his Dad. The question that should bring closure to *My Life in the Cleveland Zoo,* is why did he ever leave the zoo? The answer to that is not easy to unravel.

Adam first sent me a draft of his book in 2008. By then, a couple of my novels had been published, and he wanted to know about his prospects for getting this book in print. If a stranger had asked this, the answer would have been easier to give, but this was my brother and I knew that this *intellectual property* was sacred to his inner core. He viewed his zoo experiences as the golden era of his transition into the adult world. On the other hand, the draft I was reading was a narrative of repetition.

In real life, Adam could entertain a crowd with his antics and as I read, I could see him waving his arms and gauging his listeners to see if they wanted to see that scene again. His book was really a movie with pages and pages of thousand word pictures complete with moving parts called *engines, brooms,* and *elephant tusks.* The draft had more than eighteen hundred pages and well over half-a-million words.

I told him that the book could not be printed in its current form. In typical Adam style, he challenged that until I explained that the binding that would be most likely be used was limited to twelve hundred pages. A few days later, he explained that it could be done as a three volume boxed-set.

I showed him a few formatting tips that reduced the page count by several hundred pages, but still it was not within any practical limits. When we got together, he would say that he was still working on it.

Adam had turned his back on the medical community. As a result, when he first developed symptoms, he tried to cure himself through diet and strength of will. Eventually, his condition worsened to the point where he *had* to do something to fight his growing discomfort. In February 2014, we learned that he had advanced colon cancer. Throughout March and the first part of April, my sister Leslie (yes, the one who took blurry pictures of elephants), her daughter Lisa, his son Jay, and I literally moved into his house. My wife, Nancy, was there part of the time, and people graciously sent in food. Caris Hospice provided medical support, and Adam initially took charge as I would have expected. As time went on, his indomitable spirit gave way to his persistent question, *When is this movie going to be over?*

During those days, he extracted promises and had Jay burn DVDs of his books and plays so that we could do something with them. He asked us specifically to edit *My Life in the Cleveland Zoo.* We assured him that we would at least try.

As I am typing this, I have an edited draft of a book that stands just under five hundred pages. To arrive at this point I eliminated rodents, beautifully unattainable women, and innings of baseball. I attempted to keep the narrative within the boundaries of the zoo itself. Still, I cannot say with certainty why Adam left the zoo.

The story itself says that the issue was with the fact that the zoo was moving toward replacing full-time union keepers with part-time lower wage workers. I don't doubt that that may have bothered him, but it was not high among the various accounts he gave to us over the years. In *another* version, he missed being near family. He used to say that he was the only one who hadn't left the Cleveland area, but no longer had any family around. That was true. My father, step-mother, and youngest brother had moved to northern Georgia. My sister, after living in Sydney,

Nova Scotia, moved to Knoxville and I had lived in New Jersey, western Pennsylvania, and Dayton, Ohio. His response was to move to Knoxville where he had family support.

But there was another reason, the one, I suspect, that really haunted him. He had thought Red, Blackie, and Blue would somehow live together happily ever after. The fact was that the administrators and keepers had different priorities which conflicted with his vision. Adam had become emotionally attached in a situation that had to be informed by a more realistic view of possibilities. Blue was sold, and Adam was enlisted to help separate him from his mother. The outcome was not pretty. In desperate rage following the separation, Red rammed the steel doors until she was totally concussed. She died a few days later. Adam felt guilty for his complicity in this, and, though the zoo reached out to help, he broke with and abandoned that important part of his life.

What the zoo, and even his closest friends, did not see or know was his emotional vulnerability. Adam was two years old when our mother died in childbirth. After her death, my sister was scheduled to be adopted by an aunt and uncle, and Adam and I were to be adopted by another. We loved our extended family, but our father did a fine thing when he pulled us back and we made our way into the future, the three of us together. Leslie was older, and our rock. Adam and I were the *Smith Brothers*, and loved the cough drops that bore our adopted names, *Trade* and *Mark*.

Psychologists call it *transference*, when the attitudes toward the present are unconsciously overwhelmed by events from the past. I am not trying to make a diagnosis; I just know what has affected the three of us for a lifetime. By the end, we were once again in our childhood roles. Leslie was fixing everything in the adult world of personal responsibility, and I was being the older brother who could be relied on to tell the truth. We were being a family, and I would not have changed a thing. Especially rewarding was to see the caring maturity of a niece and nephew. Lisa loved her Uncle Adam, and Jay was a son to make a father proud, even to the end.

As I started my editing, I went on the Internet to see if there were any online stories about Cleveland's hippos and elephants. I found one that I have to include. In January of 2014, Blackie, the oldest Nile hippo in captivity, died at the age of fifty-nine. Three months later, Adam, his keeper also passed away. Jay was by his side, and proved the truth of John Sich's admonition: *to be an old man some day and not have someone calling you Poppa, is not good.*

Adam's life was good.

Acknowledgements

My Life in the Cleveland Zoo took shape as Adam reflected on the years he worked there and on the people he came to love and respect. It was his vision to honor those men and women by recounting the stories which occupied a lasting place in his memory. By the time this book came to me, it was massive. Additionally, he had scoured the Internet and online sites to purchase photos and documents that related to the history of the zoo. His goal was to create an archive which would perpetuate the memory of the park and its past.

When he was diagnosed and enrolled in hospice, he became anxious to see that his work would last and not be an orphaned file lost on his hard drive. In a relatively short time, he was unable to sit at his desk and his son Jay became the one who found the files and burned the CDs that represented Adam's creative mind. We found that he had written biographies, modern stage adaptations of Shakespeare, and, of course, this book. My sister Leslie is an author in her own right, and I am as well so he extracted promises that we would do something with *My Life in the Cleveland Zoo*. I knew how large it was and dreaded the prospect of editing what had now become three books. We both found ourselves, however, saying *Yes* to our brother. I tried to limit the project by saying that we would at least deal with the first section, the *Tour Driver Years*. He accepted that and knew we would keep our word. Leslie, Jay, and I became the first acknowledged compatriots in this adventure.

After I created the draft of the first book, I realized that, by itself, the story was incomplete. Adam had won his argument. The three books needed to be inside one cover. By this time, the circle had expanded. Now we were my sister Leslie Howe, my brother Jeff Smith, nephew Jay, and Nancy Brady Smith, who has been my proofreader and editor since my novels first came into print.

Our goal was to drop more than three hundred and eighty thousand words, hopefully without losing Adam's voice. I was the hatchet man, but the others read along to be sure that this was still his story.

Finally, two of our Cleveland friends, Jackie and Chuck Duffy became our neutral parties who could say whether the stories we loved from our brother and father were stories that readers would want to share.

Rob Smith, August, 2014

About the Author

Adam Smith (1949-2014) was born and raised in northeast Ohio where he had a varied career that ranged from cartoonist to elephant keeper at the Cleveland Zoo. After relocating to Knoxville, TN, he gained a reputation as a free-lance advertiser who wrote and produced radio and television ads.. He also wrote and edited a number of documentaries for cable television networks. Adam's creativity has been well-documented in magazines, TV scripts, and stage plays.

He graduated from Westminster College with a Bachelor's degree in English, and was an avid baseball player and fan.

Rob Smith is the author of nine novels. In 2006, he received the Robert Frost Poetry Award from the Frost Foundation in Lawrence, Massachusetts. For information about his fiction and poetry, visit www. SmithWrite.net.

CPSIA information can be obtained at www.ICGtesting.com
Printed in the USA
BVOW05s1245030914

364597BV00002B/8/P